SPORT AND AMERICAN SOCIETY: SELECTED READINGS

SPORT AND AMERICAN SOCIETY: SELECTED READINGS

Third Edition

GEORGE H. SAGE
University of Northern Colorado

ADDISON-WESLEY PUBLISHING COMPANY
Reading, Massachusetts • Menlo Park, California
London • Amsterdam • Don Mills, Ontario • Sydney

This book is in the
ADDISON-WESLEY SERIES IN PHYSICAL EDUCATION

Library of Congress Cataloging in Publication Data

Sage, George Harvey, comp.
    Sport and American society.

    Bibliography: p.
    1. Sports—Social aspects—United States—
Addresses, essays, lectures. 2. Sports—Social
aspects—Addresses, essays, lectures. I. Title.
GV706.5.S23 1980   796   79-25573
ISBN 0-201-06717-X

ISBN 0-201-06717-X
ABCDEFGHIJ-AL-89876543210

PREFACE

At the time the first edition of the book was published in 1970 there were only one or two books available dealing with the social aspects of sport in America, despite the fact that there was some research and considerable writing on the subject scattered throughout a variety of publications, from popular magazines to quite scholarly journals. During the past decade this subject has gained enormous appeal. A number of sociology of sport and psychology of sport conferences have been held at the national and international levels; several anthologies on this subject have been published; and textbooks which attempt to treat the subject more or less systematically are now available.

As with the first two editions, this volume is intended as a selective survey of the interdisciplinary literature on the general subject of the social aspects of sport in American society. I make no claim to have "covered the field." Like any reader, the present book has had to omit what some will think should have been included. Any single volume can only hope to have a sampling of the studies and writing on this topic. My aim has been to present readings which illuminate the very broad social science parameters of American sport.

The organization of topics in this edition is essentially the same as in the second edition, but about two-thirds of the readings are new to the book. The rationale for making so many changes is based upon the recommendations of my students and professional colleagues and to the rapidly expanding literature in this field of study. I have added a brief set of additional readings at the end of each chapter, which I think will be helpful to both students and instructors who wish to pursue the topic in more depth.

Approximately one-third of the readings in this edition are my own work and consist of research studies and conference presentations completed in the past few years. Other authors of the selected articles are sociologists, historians, journalists, and physical educators. Although they are scholars in their own particular field, they share one common interest—sport. They have studied sport from various points of view and they write about it with expertise in their own areas of specialization.

The readings in this volume are not restricted to the realm of theoretical concerns. In selecting readings I was guided by a belief that a book of this type might be used by instructors and students with widely diverse interests and should therefore not be limited to a narrow scope of the literature on sport. Certainly the theoretical and so-called "scientific" sources have important information to offer, but so do speculative and interpretive writings. Many times the questions and problems posed in speculative and interpretative writing serve to stimulate research into a particular area. I have also purposely included materials on widely different levels of writing. I had two basic reasons for such a procedure. First, I felt that any single writing style of format would be too narrow. While academic scholars may be able to describe sports phenomena that are significant at the .05 level of confidence, they frequently cannot provide us with as comprehensive an overview as can the essayists. My second reason for incorporating stylistic variety was for the sake of readability. I felt that a variety of materials would be much more exciting for readers of this book.

The study of sport is a puzzling paradox. While sports, games, and other play forms have been a prominent part of almost every culture, scholars have shown little inclination to undertake theoretical and scholarly studies of these phenomena. Historians have been curious about every conceivable part of societies of the past, but have virtually ignored the role of sport in the growth, development, and decline of civilizations. Except for several cursory efforts, few systematic histories of sport have been attempted. Psychologists have exhaustively studied the behavior of man and lower animals, but have displayed a blissful unconcern with the psychosocial parameters of sport. Recently, one psychologist admitted that few psychologists care much about sports qua sports. Such an attitude is rather bewildering in view of the enormous amount of human behavior that is devoted to sports and games. Sociologists have shown even greater disdain for studying sports. It is true that this discipline has only recently established itself as truly a distinct subject; nevertheless the systematic study of sports has not appeared as a prominent topic for sociological investigation. Although sports take place in social settings, and sports have a profound influence on the social life of great numbers of people, sociologists apparently find other social phenomena more interesting to study.

American physical educators have, by contrast, shown an inordinate amount of interest in sport and its social-psychological dimensions. Indeed, the basic curricular structure of American physical education since 1900 has been firmly based on the belief that physical education and sports experiences provide a rich environment for the socialization of the individual and the modification of behavior. Unfortunately, very few physical educators have verified these beliefs with good solid social or psychological research. Instead, physical education researchers have traditionally been more concerned with the physiology of exercise and biomechanics of sports movements.

It is encouraging to observe, however, that the academic fashions of the past are changing and contemporary scholars are discovering sports as a legitimate field of study. Scholars from various disciplines are beginning to undertake serious investigations of the subject. For example, the field of physical education is giving emphasis to history, psychology, and sociology of sport as special academic sub-fields within the study of human movement, and these new academic specialties now appear in undergraduate and graduate curricula. Whether the marriage between these specialties and professional physical education will endure or whether the disciplines from which the basic subject matter is derived will expand to include these specialties is still to be ascertained. In any case, the upsurge of interest is beginning to produce some significant research.

What is emerging from all of these studies is a body of knowledge emphasizing the significance of sport as a social phenomenon. However, it is difficult for the interested person to gain a comprehensive view of the literature because many of the relevant writings are widely scattered in books and journals. The purpose of this book is therefore to bring together in one volume some of the pertinent literature on the social aspects of American sport.

In selecting and organizing the material, I had in mind several groups of potential readers. First, the book should be particularly appropriate for physical education courses in sociology of sport, psychology of sport, introduction to physical education, and foundations of physical education. Second, this volume might be used as a supplemental text for certain courses in departments of sociology and psychology.

Undoubtedly, the greatest appeal will be directly to physical educators and sociologists, for it is within these fields that the most concentrated study and investigations of sport are taking place. Physical educators from ancient Greece to modern America have affirmed psychological and social values for sports and games participation. The Greek paidotribe (the teacher of physical exercise) believed that the character development of the body was as important as his athletic skill. The Battle of Waterloo was supposed to have been "won on the fields of Eton." The "new physical education" of Thomas Wood and Clark Hetherington in the early 20th century provided an eminent place in its objectives for psychosocial development. American physical education programs have been the nursery for sports in this society. It would seem, then, that the content of the book is particularly pertinent for physical educators and aspiring physical educators. Sociologists are showing an increasing interest in sport, and courses in sociology of sport have more than doubled in the past five years. Thus, this book would seem appropriate for this course.

The readings are grouped under eight major headings. The topical headings may seem arbitrary and without purpose, but any attempt to organize this subject into neat packages is arbitrary and reflects more on the orientation of the organizer than any other single factor. There is no single organizing concept or theoretical frame of reference which could be used to select and arrange the readings in a way that would satisfy all instructors and categories such as sport as a social institution, sport as a social process, etc., might have been used, but in many ways these organizational frameworks are no less arbitrary than the ones I have chosen.

The readings are not mutually exclusive, and certain ones clearly overlap my classifications. Each chapter of readings is preceded by an introduction. In each introduction I have attempted to describe and clarify the importance of that particular dimension of sport and its social significance; I have also written a brief explanatory note on the contents of each reading. As noted above, each chapter ends with a list of additional readings appropriate to the topic of that chapter.

I would like to express appreciation to my colleagues at the University of Northern Colorado for providing interest and constructive criticism while the book was taking form. Also I am indebted to students and colleagues throughout the United States who used the second edition and contributed helpful suggestions for this third edition.

I would be remiss if I did not extend a grateful "thanks" to my able and dependable secretary, Gertrude Fillinger, for the many ways she helped in preparing the manuscript for publication.

One's family invariably shares in the burden of preparing a book for publication. To my wife Liz and my sons Mike and Larry, I express my sincere appreciation for the support, encouragement, and inspiration which they provide.

Finally, I wish to thank the many editors and authors who gave permission to use their published materials in this book.

Greeley, Colorado   G.H.S.
January, 1980

CONTENTS

Chapter 1 STUDY OF THE SOCIAL ASPECTS OF SPORT   1

Sport in American Society: Its Pervasiveness and Its Study
George H. Sage   4

Sociology of Sport: An Overview *Eldon Snyder and Elmer
Spreitzer*   15

A Critical Look at the Sociology of Sport *Merrill J.
Melnick*   38

Chapter 2 SOCIOL-CULTURAL ASPECTS OF AMERICAN SPORT   55

The Technological Revolution and the Rise of Sport, 1850-1900
John Rickards Betts   58

Mass Culture and School Sports *Joel H. Spring*   58

Social Change and the Commercialization of Professional Sport
R. Terry Furst   97

Sport and American Society: The Quest for Success *George
H. Sage*   112

Chapter 3 SOCIALIZATION AND SPORT   123

Aspects of Socialization in Sports and Physical Education
Eldon E. Snyder   126

Socialization and Sport *George H. Sage*   133

Socialization Effects of Participation in Sport: A Critical View
of the Research *Christopher L. Stevenson*   143

Socialization of Coaches: Antecedents to Coaches' Beliefs and
Behaviors   *George H. Sage*   160

Chapter 4   SPORT AND AMERICAN EDUCATION   171

Athletics in the Status System of Male Adolescents: A
Replication of Coleman's *The Adolescent Society*
D. Stanley Eitzen   174

Consequences of Participation in Interscholastic Sports:
A Review and Prospectus   *John C. Phillips and Walter
E. Schafer*   182

High School Athletes and Their Coaches: Educational Plans and
Advice   *Eldon E. Snyder*   191

The Collegiate Dilemma of Sport and Leisure: A Sociological
Perspective—A Reaction   *George H. Sage*   203

Beating Their Brains Out   *John Underwood*   210

Chapter 5   SOCIAL STRATIFICATION AND SPORT   225

The Sports People Play   *Walter A. Zelman*   230

Levels of Occupational Prestige and Leisure Activity   *Rabel J.
Burge*   236

College Football and Social Mobility: A Case Study of Notre
Dame Football Players   *Allen L. Sack and Robert
Thiel*   250

Chapter 6   WOMEN AND SPORT   261

The Androgynous Advantage   *Mary E. Duquin*   263

Sex Differences in the Complexity of Children's Play and
Games   *Janet Lever*   281

The Female Athlete and Role Conflict   *George H. Sage and
Sheryl Loudermilk*   291

Women in Sport: Cooptation or Liberation?   *George H.
Sage*   309

Chapter 7   RACE AND SPORT   313

The Myth of the Racially Superior Athlete   *Harry
Edwards*   317

Immune from Racism?   *D. Stanley Eitzen and Norman R.
Yetman*   322

The Segregation by Playing Position Hypothesis in Sport: An
Alternative Explanation   *Barry D. McPherson*   339

Chapter 8   SPORT AND SOCIAL CHANGE AND CONFLICT   349

Humanism and Sport   *George H. Sage*   353

Social Discontent and the Growth of Wilderness Sport   *Wayne Wilson*   369

Change and Crisis in Modern Sport   *Harry Edwards*   376

Modernization and Sport   *Vern Dickinson*   383

CHAPTER 1

STUDY OF THE SOCIAL ASPECTS OF SPORT

Several years ago sociologist, James S. Coleman (1961), observed that a stranger to an American high school "might well suppose that more attention is paid to sports by teenagers, both as athletes and as spectators, than to scholastic matters" [p. 34]. A comparable statement might be made with regard to American society; thus, a stranger to this country might well suppose that more attention is paid to sport than to almost any other activity. Indeed, some foreign observers have claimed that the United States is "sports crazy" —that we are obsessed with sport.

While there are claims that Americans overdo sports, we are periodically criticized, by both foreign and domestic observers, as being "soft Americans." Thus, we are frequently characterized as "unfit" and we are accused of having a dread disease called "spectatoritis." Although periodic reports do indicate that the average American, youth and adult, lacks the kind of physical fitness that physical educators and physicians consider reasonable for proper health maintenance, Americans of all ages do participate in a wide variety of sports activities. Community sponsored programs of sports are offered to persons of all ages, from Little League baseball for elementary school age youth to shuffleboard for senior citizens. Schools devote enormous resources to inter-school sports programs. Professional sports, which collectively constitute a major form of entertainment in American society, employ a great many athletes. At the informal level, millions of Americans participate in skiing, boating, tennis, golf, and a great many other sports for recreation. Indeed, facilities for most of these recreational activities cannot meet the needs of the participants.

Most sport involvement takes place within a social context; that is, typically sports participants (athletes) and sports consumers (spectators) engage in sport in the company of other persons. Sports which are organized on a team basis require that the participants band together and coordinate their efforts to overcome the opponent. Sports which are considered "individual," such as golf or tennis, do not require teammates but they do require an opponent and they are frequently played before spectators, so they may correctly be considered "social" in nature. Attendance by spectators at sports contests is a major form of entertainment in the United States. Support for the high school sports teams is considered a public duty in many communities. In collegiate sports, the practice of student support for the institution's teams is carried over from high school, and the only connection which most college graduates have with their alma mater is through attendance at its athletic events. Finally, professional sports depend upon spectators for their very livelihood, and sports fans all over the nation identify with the professional team nearest their residence. "Spectating," whether it be for the hometown high school or the New York Mets, is a social event, and anyone who has ever attended a sports event between two rivals was probably aware of the interesting social dynamics of the situation as fans booed the opponents, cheered the home team, and heckled the referee for what was considered a "bad" call.

The prominent position which sport has attained in American society in recent decades has not only affected the lifestyle of many persons, as broader and more diverse sports involvement impinges upon their daily experiences, but it has ushered in a scholarly interest on the part of social scientists. New courses in sport sociology, sport psychology, and sport history have been introduced in colleges throughout the country within the last decade, and there are signs that theoretical and empirical work on the social aspects of sport will become quite popular in the coming years.

In the first reading, Sage emphasizes that sports permeate American society and that, from infancy throughout adulthood, Americans find sport involvement a dominant activity in their lives. This involvement ranges from active participation to viewing sports via television. It is noted that sport is visible within all the major cultural institutions. However, despite the pervasiveness of sport, Sage points out that only recently have social scientists begun to bring sport into the mainstream of social analysis and research.

Within the past ten years several excellent programmatic essays have outlined and described the potential theoretical and empirical focus for the sociology of sport. Bowling Green State University sociologists, Eldon Snyder and Elmer Spreitzer, have written what many consider the best of these essays, and their's is the second reading.

They begin their article with the suggestion that although sport sociology has not yet become a "mainline specialty" within sociology it has as much claim to legitimacy as such traditional sociology topics as family, religion, politics, etc. Snyder and Spreitzer argue that sport is an excellent environment for generating and testing social theories. The authors synthesize and interpret the research on the social aspects of sport from the perspectives of social institutional relationships, social stratification, small groups, and social psychology. Most of the sport sociology research completed since Snyder and Spreitzer's article was published could comfortably fit into one of their units of analysis. The article concludes with a prediction that the sociology of sport will grow in theoretical and empirical sophistication. Events of the past five years indicate that this prediction is accurate.

For over a century sociologists have debated the issue of whether sociology should be restricted to a value-neural scientific orientation or whether attempts to structure social policy and nurture social change were also appropriate roles for sociologists. In the last reading Merrill Melnick discusses the emergence of this issue within the sub-field of sport sociology.

Melnick argues that the value-free approach to sport sociology has been advanced by several noted sport sociologists over the past decade and that the stature and influence of these scholars may be establishing the model that will be accepted as the only appropriate one in the sociology of sport. While agreeing that the canons of scientific objectivity need to be observed in research, Melnick is concerned that the value-free doctrine of inquiry may lead to "moral indifference." Melnick emphasizes that there is room within sport sociology for the social critic, and he proposes that sport sociology research that attempts to ferret out and expose illegal activities, social inequality, gaps between values and actual practices, etc. are quite appropriate, indeed, even necessary.

Melnick also notes that the sociological paradigm that is most closely linked with the value-free perspective is functionalism, and that a functionalist approach to sport sociology is also advanced by those who advocate the value-free doctrine. Melnick proposes that there are other equally appropriate paradigms, such as muckraking or "dirty" sociology of sport as well as humanistic-existential sport sociology.

REFERENCES

Coleman, J. S. "Athletics in High School," *Annals of the American Academy of Political and Social Science,* **338**: 33-43, 1961.

SPORT IN AMERICAN SOCIETY: ITS PERVASIVENESS AND ITS STUDY

George H. Sage

THE PERVASIVENESS OF SPORT IN THE UNITED STATES

Sport is such a pervasive activity in contemporary America that to ignore it is to overlook one of the most significant aspects of this society. It is a social phenomenon which extends into education, politics, economics, art, the mass media, and even international diplomatic relations. Involvement in sport, either as a participant or in more indirect ways, is almost considered a public duty by many Americans.

A stranger to America would soon realize that sport involvement is ubiquitous in our culture. Primary involvement in sport begins for most boys while they are still in elementary school. The Little League baseball program initiates boys to the world of organized sport at seven or eight years of age, and if a boy shows a little interest and aptitude for the sport, he will likely pass through the Pony League, Babe Ruth League, and American Legion baseball programs on his way to adulthood. Pop Warner football programs capture the efforts of young boys who are inclined toward rough, contact activity. Bitty basketball, Pee Wee Hockey, age group swimming, soccer, gymnastics, track and other sports are available in most communities to youngsters who wish to participate. Within the past decade similar programs have emerged for girls, and youth sports programs for girls are growing rapidly. An estimated 20 million boys and girls participate in youth sports programs.

The programs mentioned above are sponsored by community, club, or service groups, but American schools also provide abundant opportunities for sports involvement. Most states have legislation requiring the teaching of physical education through high school, and sports activities form the basic curriculum of the physical education programs. In addition to the required physical classes, most schools throughout the country sponsor inter-school athletic programs beginning in the junior high school and continuing through college. According to recent (1978) statistics compiled by the National Federation of State High School Associations, more than 6.4 million boys and girls participate on interscholastic athletic teams each year. The significance of these programs in the life of high school students is best exemplified in Coleman's statement that a visitor to a typical American high school "might well suppose that more attention is paid to athletics by teen-agers, both as athletes and as spectators, than to scholastic matters. He might even conclude . . . that the school was essentially organized around athletic contests and that scholastic matters were of lesser importance to all involved" [Coleman, 1961, p. 34]. Although his comments were made some 20 years ago, they are as appropriate today as when they were written.

4

Professional sports are responsible for an enormous amount of sports involvement in American society. During the past 20 years professional sports teams have multiplied at a bewildering rate, thus providing job opportunities for an increasing number of professional athletes. The growth of professional sports may be exemplified by noting that the National Hockey League began the 1960's with six teams and the 1970's with 14. Also during the 1960's professional basketball proliferated from one league to two and from 12 teams to a total of 22 teams, when the leagues merged in the mid-1970's; major league baseball broke the longstanding 16-team tradition and went to 24 teams; professional football witnessed the birth of a new league, the merger of that league with the NFL, and a new 28-team league, thus more than doubling the teams which existed in 1960. The growth of other professional sports could be described but the pattern is the same.

The major form of involvement with professional sport, however, is through watching the contests, either by actually attending the contests or by viewing them on television. Professional football attracts some 16 million spectators each year, and major league baseball 32 million, but horse racing and auto racing attract the most sports fans with some 50 million paid admissions to each sport each year. Television viewing is probably the single way in which most adults are involved in sport, especially professional sport. Up to 25 hours of professional sports are beamed into home television sets per week and it is not unusual for six to eight hours of professional sports to be aired on a single Sunday.

The economic impact of sport in the United States is awesome; sport is big business. It is a commercial interest with a commanding position in the entertainment industry. Professional sports are one of the most successful and expanding industries in the United States. As has already been noted, in the past ten years the numbers of professional football, baseball, and hockey teams have more than doubled. Horse racing, golf, and bowling have moved into the big business arena and sundry other sports give evidence of capturing more sports dollars in the future. Professional athletes' salaries reflect the value placed on sports. A minimum salary of over $20,000 is guaranteed in several sports and annual salaries of over $100,000 are not uncommon. A few of the so-called "super stars" receive salaries in excess of $300,000. The average salary in the National Football League in 1979 was over $45,000, while professional golfers compete for over 8 million dollars in prize money each year. Professional sports franchises are worth anywhere from 5 million to 20 million dollars. But few professional sports franchises could exist without television revenue. Television contracts with professional sports is a billion dollar-a-year business. Professional sports virtually is television.

Big business is not just confined to professional sports. In the process of fostering wholesome recreation, high school and college sports have unwittingly entered the field of professional entertainment. Over 170,000 student-athletes participate in NCAA-sponsored competitions in 35 different sports each year at a dollar investment of 5 billion dollars. Sport, in the form of participant recreation, is promoted by companies for their employees to the extent that industry buys more sports goods and equipment than United States schools and colleges combined, and it schedules more entertainment than the nation's night clubs. Americans spend about 60 billion dollars on recreation annually. This money is spent primarily in the purchase of equipment, supplies, and memberships, in the payment of dues, and in other necessities of active engagement in sports. Even gambling on sports is a major economic activity; estimates of the amount of money that Americans wager on sports range from 15 billion to 50 billion dollars per year. Between 12 and 15 million Americans bet on pro-football games on any given weekend.

Sport is a prominant feature of American politics. In their own way, of course, politicians realize the pervasiveness of sport and make every effort to use it for political gain. Presidents are well aware of the political potential of big-time sports, and this is why they seldom miss an opportunity to publically associate themselves with sports. Nixon's telephone calls to the locker rooms of sports victors garnered publicity for him as well as for sport. Gerald Ford capitalized on his background as a football player at the University of Michigan. But the President is only the most visible politician to be linked with sport, Politicians from the local level to the national level capitalize as much as possible on sport for political self-promotion.

The linking of politics and sport extends beyond the local, state, and national levels and into international affairs. Today, most countries of the world use sport to some extent as an instrument of international policy. Communist countries make quite clear their motive for supporting and promoting national and international sports: sport is used as a visible example of the success of the ideological political system. As Morton (1963) says: "The Soviets have made serious business out of sport competition. . . . They have forged a direct propaganda link between sport triumphs on one hand and the viability of a social system on the other." [p. 82] Perhaps the most visible example of blatant sport diplomacy is in the German Democratic Republic (Kirshenbaum, 1976; Chapman, 1978). The Communist countries are not, of course, the only countries who practice sports diplomacy. Canada has undertaken a federally financed program of support to amateur athletics designed to enhance the caliber of athletes and thus bring prestige and respect to the nation (Report of Task Force, 1969). The United States supports international level competitors and teams largely through the U.S. State Department and the military services. Although the federal government does not directly support American participation in the Olympic Games, untold millions of dollars are spent to indirectly assist the Olympic team so that the United States may field teams to impress other nations throughout the world. The Final Report of the President's Commission on Olympic Sport issued in 1977 recommends governmental intrusion into amateur sports in America and calls for an enormous expenditure of taxpayer money to support elite athletes.

While there may seem to be little in common between sport and religion, each institution is actually making inroads into the traditional activities and prerogatives of the other. Churches have had to alter their weekend services to accommodate the growing involvement in sport. Frank Deford (1976), in a three-part series for *Sports Illustrated,* noted that "the churches have ceded Sunday to sports.... Sport owns Sunday now, and religion is content to lease a few minutes before the big games." Contemporary religion uses sport by sponsoring sports events under religious auspices and/or proselytizing athletes to religion and then using them as missionaries to spread the Word and recruit new members.

Sport is even making a considerable impact on the literary and art fields. Although sport has occupied a prominent place in the newspapers for the past 70 years, serious writers have tended not to use sport to any extent, although the most powerful passages in Hemingway deal with blood sports and Fitzgerald captures an atmosphere and perception of an American in Paris with the term "football weather." But sport themes were tangential to the writings of noted novelists, but with the rise of mass sport interest, there is a trend toward serious writing about sport, and in the past decade American novelists have increasingly employed sport themes in their writing (Higgs and Isaacs, 1977; Chapin, 1976); indeed, over 30 novels since 1960 have either referred to football or used it as a central theme (Burt, 1975). Perhaps the greatest impact of sport in the literary field, however, is coming from former athletes and sports journalists. Within the past decade there has been a virtual deluge of books by professional athletes (most are actually ghost written) who describe their experiences in sports. A number of former athletes have written "kiss and tell" books which have either mocked their sports experiences or have been highly critical of them. The underpaid, unheralded sport journalist has also gotten into the publishing windfall of sports books in recent years, and several have written what might be called exposé or muckraking type of books.

Sport has even invaded Broadway and shows evidence of making a happy marriage with drama. Several years ago, the story of Jack Johnson, the first Black heavyweight boxing champion, came to life in the play *The Great White Hope* and became an immediate success. This was followed up with several other dramas about sport. Jason Miller's grimly funny account of a high school basketball team's 20th reunion, *The Championship Season,* was voted the best play of 1972 by the Drama Critics Circle. In 1972, *The Jockey Club Stakes,* and *The Changing Room* became two of the most popular plays in New York. Sports themes are increasingly used in motion pictures. Movies such as *Rollerball, Slap Shot, Rocky,* and *Black Sunday* are only a few of the movies of the past few years that involved sports themes.

Even everyday language reflects the influence of sport. One who goes beyond normative behavior is said to be "off side" or "out-of-bounds." A person who begins an activity before the agreed-upon time is said to have "jumped the gun" or engaged in "foul play." Politicians and businessmen frequently sprinkle such euphemisms as "taking a cheap shot," "laying the ground rules," "game plan," and "fumbled the ball" into their professional conversations. The swain can gain nods of appreciation among his friends by saying he "scored" or gestures of sympathy if he admits he "struck out."

James Reston wrote in *The New York Times*:

> Sport in America plays a part of our national life that is probably more important than even the social scientists believe. Sports are now more popular than politics in America, increasingly so since the spread of television. The great corporations are now much more interested in paying millions for sports broadcasts than they are for all political events except for the nominations and inaugurations of Presidents, because the general public is watching and listening.

He appears to be a very insightful observer of American society.

STUDY OF THE SOCIAL ASPECTS OF SPORT

Since sports involvement consumes so much of the daily activity of American people, it seems logical that it should be of major importance to our understanding of their behavior. It would seem that social scientists would probably have devoted a great deal of their scholarly energy to it. In this regard, sport sociologist, John Loy (1972), said:

> One would think that the sheer magnitude of the public's commitment to sport would attract the attention of a number of social observers of human conduct. Moreover, sport seems to be an ideal proving ground for the testing of many social theories, and it also appears to offer several suitable settings for the development of formal theories of social behavior [p. 229].

Unfortunately, the serious study of sport has been virtually non-existent in the social sciences until the past decade. Thus a body of knowledge, from a social science perspective, is in its infancy.

In surveys conducted by the American Sociological Association in 1950 and 1959 (Riley, 1969) each member of this association was asked to list three sociological fields in which he felt qualified to teach or to do research. The sociologists were free to describe their competencies in their own terms, thus the categories which emerged were not predetermined. Sport as a topic for teaching or research did not appear in enough cases to be classified as a topic.

By 1970 the American Sociological Association classified its membership into 33 areas of competence, and area #14 was entitled "Leisure, Sports, Recreation, and the Arts" and, according to a survey of its membership

(Stehr and Larson, 1972), 60 sociologists out of 8,350 who returned the questionnaires marked this area as an area of personal competence. This represents 0.7 percent of the total group and places this area as the 30th out of 33 categories, in terms of rank position. Loy (1972) reports that the actual specialization of sociologists within this "grab bag" area divides up something like this: ". . . approximately one-third identify the arts as their special area of competence, another one-third leisure, while a final one-third cite sport as their specific domain of interest and expertise [p. 50]." According to Loy (1978), more recent analyses of ASA membership lists indicate that the number of sociologists with a special area of competence in sport is not increasing appreciably. He says: "In sum, at the time of this writing, only two dozen members (excluding students) of the American Sociological Association are identified with the sociology of sport and less than half of this number can be considered productive researchers (i.e., at least one paper per year)" [p. 41].

Comparable conditions exist in the other social sciences. In psychology, for example, the American Psychological Association does not have a separate section on sport psychology, although it has a multitude of sections for the various specialties within the field of psychology. Historians, anthropologists, economists, etc. have not given much recognition to sport as a special topic for study either.[1]

There are undoubtedly several reasons why the study of sport has not been in the mainstream of any of the social sciences. American philosopher, Paul Weiss (1969) and French philosopher Rene Maheu (1962) both suggest that the relative neglect of sport by scholars is largely due to the prevailing tradition in Western Civilization which views sport as a lower form of culture and not worthy of serious study. Second, even though sport may be considered a socially significant aspect of society, it is often seen as frivolous and ephemeral and thus not easily incorporated into the prevailing theoretical frameworks of the social sciences. Third, the study of sport, since it has not been in the mainstream of the social sciences, has not provided the scholar with opportunities to earn prestige with colleagues. The "proper" scholar in a given field is expected to study topics that scholars in that field are studying because it is by following this path that one gains recognition, rewards, and prestige in a field of study. Although there are certainly exceptions to this pattern in every discipline, it is easy to find a few topics that are well mined by the majority of scholars in that field. The social science scholar who chose to study sport was not only isolating himself from the "proper" topics for study in his field but he was also laying himself open to ridicule for studhing "a frivolous children's pastime." The limitations on publishing outlets for sport research may be a fourth reason for the reluctance to study sport. Prior to 1966, there were no journals specifically concerned with sport social science. Sociologist Gregory Stone (1972) humorously describes the difficulty a scholar has had in getting a piece of research on this topic published in the sociology journals. He says: "When sociologists speak of play, those ghosts who control and patrol the journals strike terror into their hearts! . . . it is very difficult to find a resting place for an article on play in the graveyards staked out by major journals of sociology. Consult the gravestones—I mean, of course, the table of contents" [pp. 3-4]. A fifth reason for the unwillingness to study sport may be related to the same reluctance in studying the sociology of education which Gross (1959) identified, namely the quality of the literature is poor, consisting mainly of essays, and the scant research has little or no relevance to existing social science theory and research.

A final reason that sport has not been seriously studied until recently may be related to its recent rise to omnipresence. Until the last generation or so, sports participation was primarily a recreation of the upperclasses, when it was engaged in by adults. Long working hours, physically exhausting labor, and limited income made sports prohibitive for the working class. Except for major league baseball, professional sports were not prominent until after World War I. Even in baseball, since only 16 major league teams existed throughout the United States and transportation was rather cumbersome, very few persons actually got to see the games. It was not until the 1920's that radio began reporting live-action baseball games, and while this was an improvement over newspaper accounts of games, it could not compare with the impact that television had on the development of professional sports. College football has been popular since the late 19th century with the college students and alumni, but mainstream America was not really a part of the college scene until after World War II, and even here TV had the greatest impact on popularizing college sports. So, although sports interests certainly existed prior to television, this particular mass media has had the most dramatic effect on the sports mania of today, and television is a phenomenon of the past thirty years.

Although the study of the social aspects of sport is in its infancy, recent trends indicate that progress in developing a cogent body of knowledge is increasing at an accelerating rate. Physical education departments throughout the United States are now offering courses in sport sociology, sport history, sport psychology, and other courses with a social science perspective, and this general field has become a favorite area for specialization among graduate students in physical education. A few sociology departments now have professors within the department who are making sport their primary interest. Several sociology departments are cooperating with physical education departments by employing a sport sociologist on a dual appointment basis; that is, the faculty member is assigned to both physical education and sociology departments. Another evidence that interest in the study of sport is growing is that in their conventions national and regional professional social science associations are including sessions devoted to research papers and seminars on sport.

Development of a Sociology of Sport

Although it is always difficult, as well as risky, to identify a given incident or piece of writing as being the first of its kind, Steinitzer's book, *Sport and Kultur,* published in Germany in 1910, may be identified as one of the pioneer works in the sociology of sport because it was concerned with the relationship of sports and culture. A better known book entitled *Soziologie des Sports* written by Risse in 1921 and published in Germany is often referred to as the first treatise on the sociology of sport. Both of these books lacked systematic and empirical research data for the ideas which were discussed. They were, Wohl (1966) says, "reflections on social phenomena and social consequences of sports, inspired by the fact that this subject was particularly thrown into relief at this time. Thus . . . we can safely consider both belonging to the type of publicistic works, based only on one's own suggestions, that are the outcome of generally accepted opinions and prejudices about sports" [p. 5]. However, Risse did discuss various social issues related to sports and recommended that these phenomena be given systematic scientific study.

These books did not stimulate any immediate substantive study of sport but they did trigger a number of publications, especially in Europe, concerned with the relationship between sport and various social issues. Although most of these publications were not empirically based, the social sources and consequences of sport were thoroughly analyzed.

Few physical educators have devoted their careers to a study of the social aspects of sport. While the early 20th century leaders of the so-called "new physical education" such as Thomas Wood, Clark Hetherington, Jesse Feiring Williams, and Rosalind Cassidy gave a privileged position to "social development," the term went largely undefined and the social outcomes of physical education and inter-school sports programs went unmeasured. These physical educators were not researchers; they did not document the claims they made with regard to the social outcomes of physical education. Actually, they were more interested in justifying programs of physical education than they were of studying the broad scope of social behavior in sport contexts, and they did not attempt to develop a basic subject matter on the social science of sport. Charles Cowell (1937, 1959), a physical educator at Purdue, published a few empirical studies between 1935 and 1960 and a book entitled *Sports in American Life* (1953) by two physical educators, Frederick Cozens and Florence Stumpf, was a pioneering effort to discuss the social role of sport in American society. However, it was not until the publication of an article entitled "Toward a Sociology of Sport" in the *Journal of Health, Physical Education, and Recreation* in 1965 by Gerald Kenyon and John W. Loy that physical educators began to seriously pursue this subject.

The first generation of American sociologists gave passing attention to sport. For example, W. I. Thomas (1901) published an article in the *American*

Journal of Sociology entitled "The Gaming Instinct," and in his book, *Folkways* (1906), William G. Sumner wrote a chapter on "Popular Sports, Exhibitions, and Drama." But it was not until post-World War II that empirical interest in sport began to accelerate. In the 1950's studies such as Weinberg and Arond's (1952) report on the sub-culture of the boxer and Riesman and Denney's (1951) presentation of football as an avenue of cultural diffusion provided pioneer work in the sociology of sport in the United States. Subsequently Stone (1957) and Grusky (1963) offered interesting studies related to sport involvement and its relation to socio-economic status and the application of social organizational theory to sport teams.

Two books published in England in the post-World War II period have had a marked impact on the development of the study of the social aspects of sport in America. These books, *Sport in Society* (McIntosh, 1963) and *Sport and Society* (Natan, 1958), were basically descriptive accounts of the social dimensions of sport, but they were well-written and illuminated the potential for the study of sport.

Sports journalists have provided the most extensive literature on sports during the 20th century. Their contribution to sport has been considerable; although most have done reportorial work primarily, some have written on the sociological, historical, economic, and political aspects of sport. One professional sociologist said that "sports writers are among my favorite list of sociologists" [Page, 1969, p. 196]. While those who work in the social science of sport might agree with Professor Page, they would undoubtedly emphasize that there is need for exhaustive empirical research to support or refute the essay-type writing of the journalist.

One of the most significant events for the promotion and development of a sociology of sport occurred in the mid-1960's. In 1964, the International Committee for Sport Sociology was founded as an affiliate of two UNESCO organizations, the International Council of Sport and Physical Education and the International Sociological Association. This Committee sponsored its first conference in Cologne, Germany in 1966, with an invited group of around 50 participants. The second conference sponsored by this Committee was held in 1968 in Vienna, Austria, and several subsequent conferences have been held in the past decade. An outgrowth of the first conference held in Cologne was the establishment of the *International Review of Sport Sociology* which is published in Poland and which carries essays and research articles. One issue per year was published from 1966 to 1973, then it became a quarterly journal.

The future is promising. Undoubtedly physical educators and social scientists who are currently concentrating their efforts on the social dimensions of sport will attract others. Indeed events of the past few years in graduate schools of physical education give evidence that a "bandwagon" effect is occurring toward this subject, as students are electing to specialize in the sociology, or psychology, or history of sport instead of the old standbys of physiology and bio-mechanics. Sociology, psychology, history, and anthropology departments have already begun turning out Ph.D's with sport as their area of specialty. The prospects for the future are very exciting.

NOTE

1. Since the parent social science associations have not given much recognition to the study of sport, separate associations have been formed. The International Society of Sports Psychology was formed in 1965, the North American Society for the Psychology of Sport and Physical Activity, 1967, North American Society for Sport History, 1974, Association for the Anthropological Study of Play, 1974, North American Society for the Sociology of Sport, 1978.

REFERENCES

Burt, D. "A Helmeted Hero: The Football Player in Recent American Fiction," presented at the Convention of the Popular Culture Association, 1975.

Chapin, H. B., *Sports in Literature*, New York: David McKay, 1976.

Chapman, Brian, "East of the Wall," *Runner's World* (March 1978) pp. 60–67.

Coleman, J. S., "Athletics in High School," *Annals of the American Academy of Political Science*, **338** (November): 33–45, 1961.

Cowell, C. C. "Physical Education as Applied Social Science," *Educational Research Bulletin*. (Ohio State University), **1**: 147–155, 1937.

Cowell, C. C., "Validating an Index of Social Adjustment for High School Use," *Research Quarterly*, **29**: 7–18, 1958.

Cozens, F., and Stumpf, F., *Sports in American Life*, Chicago: University of Chicago Press, 1953.

Deford, Frank, "Religion in Sport," *Sports Illustrated*, **44** (April 19, 26, May 3) 1976.

Gross, N., "The Sociology of Education," in R. K. Merton, *et al.* (eds.), *Sociology Today*, New York: Basic Books, 1959, pp. 128–152.

Grusky, O., "Managerial Succession and Organizational Effectiveness," *American Journal of Sociology*, **69** (July): 21–31, 1963.

Higgs, R. J., and Isaacs, N., (eds.) *The Sporting Spirit: Athletics in Literature and Life*, New York: Harcourt Brace Jovanovich, 1977.

Kenyon, G. S., and Loy, J. W., "Toward A Sociology of Sport," *Journal of Health, Physical Education, and Recreation*, **36** (May): 24–25, 68–69, 1965.

Kirshenbaum, Jerry, "Assembly Line of Champions," *Sports Illustrated*, **45** (July 12, 1976), pp. 56–65.

Loy, J. W., "Toward a Sociology of Sport," in R. N. Singer, *et al., Physical Education: An Interdisciplinary Approach,* New York: The Macmillan Company, 1972, pp. 229–236.

Loy, J. W., "A Case for the Sociology of Sport," *Journal of Health, Physical Education, and Recreation,* **43** (June): 50–53, 1972.

Loy, John W., McPherson, B. D., and Kenyon, Gerald S., *The Sociology of Sport as an Academic Speciality: An Episodic Essay on the Development and Emergence of Hybrid Subfield in North America,* Canadian Association for Health, Physical Education, and Recreation, 1978.

McIntosh, P. C., *Sport in Society,* London: C. A. Watts Company, 1963.

Maheu, René, "Sport and Culture," *International Journal of Adult and Youth Education,* **14**: 169–178, 1962.

Morton, H. W., *Soviet Sport,* New York: Collier Books, 1963.

Natan, A., *Sport and Society,* London: Bowes & Bowes Publishers, 1958.

National Federation of State High School Associations, "Sports Participation Survey," 1978.

Page, C. H., "Symposium Summary, With Reflections Upon the Sociology of Sport as a Research Field," in G. S. Kenyon (ed.), *Aspects of Contemporary Sport Sociology,* Chicago: The Athletic Institute, 1969, pp. 189–209.

Palmer, M. D. "The Sports Novel: Mythic Heroes and Natural Men," *Quest,* Monograph XIX, January, 1973, pp. 49–58.

President's Commission on Olympic Sport, *Final Report,* Washington, D.C.: U.S. Government Printing Office, 1977.

Riley, M. W., "Membership in the ASA, 1950–1959," *American Sociological Review,* **25**: 914–926, 1960.

Riesman, D., and Denney, R., "Football in America: A Study of Cultural Diffusion," *American Quarterly,* **3**: 309–319, 1951.

Risse, H., *Soziologie des Sports,* Berlin, 1921.

Roberts, J. M., Arth, M. J., and Bush, R. R., "Games in Culture."

Roberts, J. M., and Sutton-Smith, B., "Child Training and Game Involvement," *Ethnology,* **1**: 166–185, 1962.

Stehr, N., and Larson, L. E., "The Rise and Decline of Areas of Specialization," *The American Sociologist,* **7** (No. 7); **3**, 5–6, 1972.

Steinitzer, H., *Sport and Kultur.* München: 1910.

Stone, G., "Some Meanings of American Sport," *60th Proceedings of the College Physical Education Association,* Washington, D.C.: American Association for Health, Physical Education, and Recreation, 1957, pp. 6–29.

Sumner, William G., *Folkways,* Boston: Ginn, 1906.

Thomas, W. I., "The Gaming Instinct," *American Journal of Sociology*, **6**: 750–763, 1901.

Weinberg, S. K., and Arond, H., "The Occupational Culture of the Boxer," *American Journal of Sociology*, **57** (March): 460–469, 1962.

Weiss, P., *Sport: A Philosophical Inquiry*, Carbondale, Ill.: Southern Illinois University Press, 1969.

SOCIOLOGY OF SPORT: AN OVERVIEW

Eldon E. Snyder and Elmer Spreitzer

The sociology of sport has yet to become a mainline specialty within the discipline, and some might question whether it should ever become one. Given the proliferation of specializations within sociology, we might ask to what end is such elaboration of descriptive content directed? In other words, does a discipline grow by spinning off more and more content areas, or does it develop through the creation of paradigms that are generic in nature. The "hard" sciences did not develop by continually carving out new content areas; rather, they developed through the creation of theoretical frameworks that transcended specific content. Why, then, should we legitimate an area such as the sociology of sport by instituting journals and convention sessions on that topic, textbooks and courses, and state-of-the-field articles?

We suggest that sport as a substantive topic has as much claim on the sociologist's attention as the more conventional specialties of family, religion, political, and industrial sociology. Sports and games are cultural universals and basic institutions in societies, and are some of the most pervasive aspects of culture in industrialized societies. Moreover, all of the traditional content areas are, in principal, equal—unless we impose a value judgment of some type to assert that some institutional spheres are more important. Empirically, we could impose a hierarchy on the content areas in terms of their lineage (religion via Weber would be high here) or in terms of their explanatory power (economic sociology would be high here).

Basically, we argue that a sociologist studies sport for the same reasons as any other topic—for intrinsic interest and to impose sociological frameworks as a means for constructing and refining concepts, propositions, and theories from the larger discipline.[1] A scholar's claim, however, on institu-

Eldon E. Snyder and Elmer Spreitzer, "Sociology of Sport: an Overview," from *The Sociological Quarterly*, Volume 15 (Autumn 1974), pp. 467–487. Reprinted by permission.

tional and societal resources to pursue one's intrinsic interests does not carry much weight these days. We suggest that the sociology of sport is of value to the larger discipline primarily in terms of its capacity to serve as a fertile testing ground for the generating and testing of theoretical frameworks. Sociology will not grow by filling in dots on the canvas of social life; rather, it grows by imposing order on clusters of dots. Substantive specialties such as the sociology of sport can feed back to the larger discipline in terms of concept formation, theory construction, and theory verification. Glaser and Straus (1967) recommend the inductive approach to theory building through wrestling with empirical content and ultimately deriving generic frameworks that are applicable to a variety of subject areas. From a theory verification perspective, substantive areas such as the sociology of sport represent a testing ground to explore the generality and explanatory power of theories in a variety of social settings.

One might suggest that the sociology of sport is a species of the sociology of leisure. Clearly, sport could be subsumed under leisure studies as simply another way in which people spend their discretionary time. Since both the sociology of leisure and sport focus on the noninstrumental facets of social life, they probably will merge into a more generic specialization such as the sociology of expressive behavior. Presently, however, the two content specialties are very distinct in the sense of having their own associations, conventions, professional registers, journals, and sessions within the conventions of general sociology. Given the separate evolution of the two specialties of leisure and sports, the present analysis focuses solely on sports.[2]

The phenomenon of sport represents one of the most pervasive social institutions in the United States. Sports permeate all levels of social reality from the societal down to the social psychological levels. The salience of sports can be documented in terms of news coverage, financial expenditures, number of participants and spectators, hours consumed, and time samplings of conversations. Given the salience of sports as a social institution, a sociology of sport has emerged that attempts to go beyond the descriptive level by providing theoretically informed analyses and explanations of sports activity.

One might speculate as to why sport is a recent entry to the substantive specialties within sociology. If, in fact, sociology is a residual field that assimilates topics unclaimed by more established fields, why is it that sports (also, leisure and recreation) were not an early part of the sociological package? Perhaps one answer to this question lies in the increased salience of these spheres as concomitants of economic development and affluence. Another explanation may be that sports previously were viewed as primarily physical, rather than social interaction, and thus devoid of sociological significance. Still another explanation may be that the world of sports is often perceived as illusionary, fantasy, and a sphere apart from the "real" world (Huizinga, 1955). Perhaps Americans are uneasy with play and this ambivalence may explain the relative lack of interest in sports on the part of sociologists (Stone, 1971:48). In a similar vein, Dunning (1967) argues that sociologists who have defined play and sport in terms of fantasy, and who are thus ambivalent about seriously studying the topic, may be reflecting a Protestant Ethic orientation toward work and leisure. In fact, an element of snobbery is probably involved: "The serious analysis of popular sport is construed to be beneath the dignity of many academics" (Stone, 1971:62). In response to such sentiments, Dunning (1971:37) emphasizes that "sports and games are 'real' in the sense they are observable, whether directly through overt behavior of people or indirectly through the reports which players and spectators give of what they think and feel while playing and 'spectating'." There is increasing realization that sport as an institution permeates and articulates with other institutions. Consequently, a substantial literature is developing in the sociology of sport, some of which is cumulative, and much of which goes beyond description toward explanation.[3] Disciplines other than sociology contribute to this literature; physical educators are particularly visible in this specialty. Moreover, some prominent physical educators researching in this area are, in effect, sociologists, either through formal or informal training.

DEFINITION OF SPORT

The meaning of sport, like time, is self-evident until one is asked to define it. There is little disagreement in classifying physical activities such as basketball, football, handball, tennis, and track as sports. Hunting, fishing, and camping are often considered sports, but do they contain the same elements as, say, football and basketball? Can mountain climbing, bridge, and poker be classified as sports? Edwards (1973) presents a typology to clarify the concepts of play, recreation, contest, game, and sport. He arrays these activities on a continuum in the above order with play and sport as the polar activities. As one moves from play toward sport the following occurs (Edwards, 1973:59):

Activity becomes less subject to individual prerogative, with spontaneity severely diminished.

Formal rules and structural role and position relationships and responsibilities within the activity assume predominance.

Separation from the rigors and pressures of daily life become less prevalent.

Individual liability and responsibility for the quality and character of his behavior during the course of the activity is heightened.

The relevance of the outcome of the activity and the individual's role in it extends to groups and collectivities that do not participate directly in the act.

Goals become diverse, complex, and more related to values emanating from outside of the context of the activity.

The activity consumes a greater proportion of the individual's time and attention due to the need for preparation and the degree of seriousness involved in the act.

In summary, Edwards (1973:57–58) defines sport as "involving activities having formally recorded histories and traditions, stressing physical exertion through competition within limits set in explicit and formal rules governing role and position relationships, and carried out by actors who represent or who are part of formally organized associations having the goal of achieving valued tangibles or intangibles through defeating opposing groups." Lüschen (1967:127; 1970:6; 1972:119) defines sport as an institutionalized type of competitive physical activity located on a continuum between play and work. Sport contains intrinsic and extrinsic rewards; but the more it is rewarded extrinsically (including socially), the more it tends to become work in the sense of being instrumental rather than consummatory (also see Loy, 1968). These attempts to define sport are admittedly imprecise. Sport may be defined in terms of the participants' motivation or by the nature of the activity itself. Sport is a playful activity for some participants, while others participate in the context of work or an occupation. Moreover, the boundaries of sport as an activity blend into the more general sphere of recreation or leisure. In the present paper, we shall not attempt to carve out boundaries for the topic; rather, we delineate the specialty in operational terms of what sociologists actually do with the content of sport. We attempt to synthesize and interpret the work done in this area while organizing the literature in terms of the unit of analysis. We begin by analyzing sociological research concerning sport at the macro level.

SOCIETAL PERSPECTIVES

One research tradition within the sociology of sport focuses on the relationship between sports and the larger society. The analysis involves the following basic questions (Lüschen, 1978:8): What is the nature of sport as a social institution, and how does it relate to other institutions? What is the structure and function of sport, and what social values does it promote?

This macro level of analysis is probably the most well-developed area in the sociology of sport. Sport as a microcosm of society is a *leitmotiv* that permeates much of the literature. Particular emphasis involves the social values, beliefs, and ideologies that are expressed and transmitted through the institutional configuration of sport. This theme is discussed by Boyle (1963) in *Sport: Mirror of American Life;* he analyzes sport as a mirror of society involving elements of social life such as stratification, race relations, commerce, automotive design, clothing style, concepts of law, language, and ethical values. In this context, a recent study by Snyder (1972a) classifies slogans placed in dressing rooms by high school coaches into motifs that are

used to transmit beliefs, values, and norms to athletes. These slogans emphasize the development of qualities such as mental and physical fitness, aggressiveness, competitiveness, perseverence, self-discipline, and subordination of
self to the group. Many of these characteristics are supported by values
inherent in the Protestant Ethic. In this sense, sport is a "value receptacle" for
the dominant social values (Edwards, 1973:355). Furthermore, cross-cultural
data concerning sports and games show that they tend to be representative of
a particular society's values and norms (Roberts and Sutton-Smith, 1962).

Numerous researchers have documented the interrelationship between
sport and society by analyzing specific sports. Riesman and Denny (1954)
describe how rugby changed to become the game of football that was
congruent with the American ethos. Similarly, cultural themes in major league
baseball reflect American values of specialization, division of labor, individual
success and the importance of teamwork (Voigt, 1971; Haerle, 1973).

The prevalence of writings on the social functions of sport are supported
from several disciplines—sociology, history, philosophy, and physical education. Methodologically, this literature relies on historical accounts, autobiographies, content analysis, and other qualitative techniques. These studies
explicitly or implicitly embrace the theoretical posture of functionalism. In
this regard the study of sports provides ample evidence of pattern maintenance,
tension management, integration, and systemic linkages with other social
institutions.

Many observers have pointed to the safety value function that sport
serves for society. On a structural level of analysis, a vulgar Marxism is sometimes invoked in viewing sports as an opiate and as producing unreality,
mystification, and false consciousness. Similarly, many scholars have commented on the psychodynamic function of sports. Gerth and Mills (1954:63),
for example, suggest that "Many mass audience situations with their 'vicarious' enjoyments, serve psychologically the unintended function of channeling
and releasing otherwise unplaceable emotions. Thus, great values of aggression
are 'cathartically' released by crowds of spectators cheering their favorite
stars of sport—and jeering the umpire."

In related context, several empirical studies have attempted to document
political concomitants of participation in sports. For instance, several surveys
found that athletes tend to be more conservative, conventional, and conformist than their nonathletic counterparts (Phillips and Schafer, 1970; Rehberg,
1971; Schafer, 1971; and Scott, 1971). According to these observers, sport
has a "conservatizing" effect on youth through its emphasis on hard work,
persistence, diligence, and individual control over social mobility. Clearly, the
transmission of societal values is an important function of schools anywhere.
Schafer (1971) suggests, however, that the value mystique surrounding high
school sports might be dangerous in the sense of producing conformist,
authoritarian, cheerful robots who lack the autonomy and inner direction to

accept innovation, contrasting value systems, and alternative life-styles. This provocative hypothesis is worthy of testing with a longitudinal design.

Although the above observations are intuitively persuasive, Petrie (1973), reports no significant political differences between athletes and nonathletes among Canadian college students in Ontario. Perhaps there are subcultural differences between the intercollegiate athletic programs in Canada and the United States that would account for his findings. Many questions in this area await further research. If sport promotes a conservative ideology, how pervasive is its influence, and what is the *process* by which it has this effect? Furthermore, how much transfer effect is there into adult life? And, if sport induces this type of politicoeconomic mentality, are the consequences primarily for athletes, or are other segments of the population likewise affected?

The economic, commercial, and occupational facets of sport also have been analyzed. Furst (1971:165) attributes the rise of commercialism in sport to the increasing number of people "with time, money, and energy to engage in and embrace the world of sports." Kenyon (1972) cites the change in American society toward mass consumption and professionalism as having ramifications within sport. The economic aspects of sport are evident in conflicts in several cities over the securing of professional sports franchises, the location of new stadia and arenas because of the multiplier effect on restaurants, hotels, parking lots, theatres, bars, etc. The fact that general scheduling of television programs is partly determined by the timing of prominent sports events bespeaks the economic salience of sports in the United States. We will discuss occupational and career aspects of sports later.

The articulation of sport with the religious institution is also of interest. As the ancient Olympic games were grand festivals with much religious and political significance, contemporary sports events can be seen as America's "civil religion" (Rogers, 1972:393). Athletic events often open with prayer as well as the national anthem, teams frequently have a chaplain, and many teams have prayer sessions prior to the contest. In a survey of high school basketball coaches and players, Snyder (1972a:91) reports that the majority of the teams sampled invoke prayer before or during games. Football coaches generally welcome reinforcement from the religious sector. "Louisiana State University's coach . . . credits a Graham campus crusade in the Fall of 1970 with helping his football team win a victory over Auburn University. Dallas Cowboy's head football coach . . . presided over a Billy Graham Crusade For Christ held on the Cowboy's home field, the Cotton Bowl, in 1971" (Edwards, 1973:124). Rogers (1972:394) suggests that "sports are rapidly becoming the dominant ritualistic expression of the reification of established religion in America." In this context, a number of writers have suggested that religion and sport interact to reinforce the status quo and to reaffirm the conventional wisdom.

Similarly, the linkage between sport and the educational institution has been explored by sociologists. The United States differs from most nations in that amateur athletes are almost totally dominated by high schools and colleges; very little is carried on under the aegis of clubs or the government. The incorporation of amateur athletics into educational institutions has important consequences. As early as 1929 the Lynds noted the position of honor attributed to athletics and the low esteem accorded to academic pursuits in the high school status hierarchy of *Middletown*. Waller (1932) viewed the high school as a social organism and suggested that interscholastic athletics are justified because they promote the competitive spirit, act as a means of social control and system integration, and prepare students for adult life. The various sports themselves constitute a status hierarchy in schools and colleges; generally there is more interest in football and basketball than all the other sports and extra-curricular activities combined (Hollingshead, 1949:193; Gordon, 1957; Coleman, 1961). These studies provide quantitative and qualitative documentation of the value orientations among youth and the relative importance of sports in the spectrum of high school activities.

A cumulative research tradition in the sociology of sport focuses on the relationship between participation in sport and academic performance and aspirations. Coleman's (1961) study of students in ten midwestern high schools suggests that the nature of interscholastic athletic competition focuses an inordinate amount of attention on sport which results in a depreciation of academic pursuits. His data, however, do not consistently support his hypothesis. For example, in six of the ten high schools, the grade averages of the top athletes were higher than their nonathletic peers. Additional studies generally show that, with qualifications, athletes tend to have as high or higher educational achievement and expectations than their nonathletic counterparts (Bend, 1968; Rehberg and Schafer, 1968; Schafer and Armer, 1968; Schafer and Rehberg, 1970; Spreitzer and Pugh, 1973). Additional analysis of the psychological and social concomitants of participation in interscholastic athletics is presented below in the section on social psychological aspects.

It is interesting to note that although conflict has long been defined as an essential element of most sports, nevertheless a functional model is inherent in most social scientific research on sport. In other words, the ways in which sport facilitates social integration and equilibrium have been of more interest than social conflict over scarce resources in the world of sport. The paradox of viewing explicit, structured conflict in the world of sport through the lens of an equilibrium framework is indicative of a root orientation toward harmony that spilled over from the larger discipline. It is curious that contemporary research on sport almost completely neglects current structural conflicts in the world of sport—exemption from anti-trust laws, inter-league raiding of players, player drafts, the reserve clause, league expansions and mergers, strikes, and working conditions. The players themselves have not been unaware of economic antagonism in sport as evidenced by the players' ready reception of competing leagues, strikes, formation of players' associations (unions), exposé books, and use of the judicial system for redress of economic grievances.

It is only in the last five years that the back regions and infrastructure of organized sports have been brought to light, and most of this writing appears in semi-popular outlets such as the *Intellectual Digest, Psychology Today,* and the *New York Times Sunday Magazine.* Serious observers in this tradition (Edwards, 1969, 1973; and Scott, 1971) show how the youth movement of the late 1960s had reverberations in the world of sport. Perceived injustices in the sports establishment came under blistering attack. One segment of this "revolution" involved the black athlete and traces its roots to the civil rights movement. The threatened boycott of the XIX Olympiad and the clenched fist demonstration by black sprinters on the victory stand exemplify this reaction. Another facet of the conflict trend centers around the objections by athletes to imposition of a monolithic life-style (short hair, clean shaven, etc.). More recently, women's liberation appeared in the world of sport to seek more equitable distribution of the resources and rewards as well as to emancipate women from arbitrary sex role definitions regarding appropriate physical activities.

In sum, we argue that sport contains many of the sources of conflict inherent in the larger society. The contours of conflict in the world of sport are evident in bold relief as compared to the veiled manipulation of power in society at large. Therefore, the arena of sport represents a potentially rich area for the testing of generic theoretic frameworks concerning conflict:

> It seems not unreasonable to suggest that football and other similar sports can serve as a kind of "natural laboratory" for studying the dynamics of group conflicts in a more detached manner than has often proved possible in the past with respect, for example, to the study of union-management conflict, class, international and other types of group conflicts where the strength of the involvements on one side or the other has acted as a hindrance to the achievement of full objectivity (Dunning, 1971:43).

STRATIFICATION ASPECTS

When one considers the pervasiveness of social stratification, it is not surprising that processes of social differentiation operate within the world of sport. As early as Veblen (1899), social scientists have noted the patterning of leisure behavior along social class lines. Veblen suggested that a new era was emerging in which leisure for the few was yielding to leisure for the masses. Sport as a species of leisure is no exception to the pattern of differential participation across class lines. Lüschen (1969), for example, reports a positive relationship between socioeconomic status and sports involvement in Germany. Differences by class also have been reported in the preference, meaning, and salience of sports (Stone, 1969; Lüschen, 1972). Kenyon (1966) studied patterns of indirect and direct involvement in sports among adults in Wisconsin; he found no consistent relationship between social status and the degree of sports participation. Burdge (1966) analyzed involvement in sport according to level of occupation; he found that both active participation and spectatorship were more common at the higher occupational levels. Although the above research documents the expected variations in sports activities by social class, recent research indicates additional complexity. For example, recent data collected in the Midwest using a refined measure of sports involvement found a positive relationship between socioeconomic status and *cognitive* involvement (knowledge about sports), but no consistent relationship was observed on the *behavioral* and *affective* dimensions of involvement (Snyder and Spreitzer, 1973a). This study suggests that sports involvement tends to cut across social categories. Sport is so much a part of the cultural air through mass media and conversation that one cannot be totally insulated from its influence.

Within the sociology of sport, athletic achievement is frequently cited as an avenue for social mobility, particularly for minority groups, and there are a sufficient number of superstar celebrities to sustain this perception. Clearly, such cases are a tiny fraction of professional athletes; however, there are other ways in which sport can facilitate social mobility. Loy (1969) suggests that participation in athletics can stimulate higher levels of educational aspirations in order to extend one's athletic career, and thus indirectly result in higher educational achievement and the acquisition of secular skills that are functional in the nonathletic sphere. Youth who excell in athletics frequently receive educational and occupational sponsorship by influential persons which gives them leverage in the secular world. In this connection, a recent study shows that high school athletes rank their coach second only to parents in terms of influencing their educational and occupational plans (Snyder, 1972b). Moreover, coaches often gratuitously advise their players on educational and occupational matters. In addition, ever since the English gentleman proclaimed that the Battle of Waterloo was won on the playing fields of Eton, it has been argued that participation in sport generates character traits that transfer to other areas of life. There is limited evidence for this contention; we shall analyze the pertinent studies below in the section on social psychological aspects of sport.

Contrasting research findings suggest, however, that sport may also have a negative effect on the social mobility of participants. Spady (1970) interprets his findings as showing that athletic involvement is sometimes counterproductive in the sense of raising educational aspirations without providing the necessary cognitive skills for educational achievement. With respect to blacks, sports may function as a magnet attracting youth to one specialized channel of mobility which tends to cut down the number of mobility options perceived as available for minority youth. Edwards (1973:201-202) argues that the success of black athletes tends to have a boomerang effect of attracting black youth away from higher level occupations as an avenue for mobility. Of course, the actual number of individuals of any race who achieve eminence in sports is very small.[4]

Most of the literature concerning sports and social mobility is conjectural, anecdotal, or at best descriptive. Most studies are based on cross-sectional data, and thus the inferences drawn are tentative and exploratory. One study, however, provides a follow-up analysis of former high school and collegiate athletes (Bend, 1968). This research indicates that athletic participation is associated with postgraduate occupational mobility. This is an area ripe for systematic research particularly with longitudinal designs. Recently some interesting research has emerged concerning the career patterns and mobility processes of athletic coaches (Loy and Sage, 1972; Snyder, 1972c). This line of research contributes to the literature on the sociology of occupations.

Sociologists have also focused considerable attention on race as a dimension of stratification within sport. Since coaches are likely to recruit and play the most capable athletes regardless of race in order to enhance their own reputation as successful (winning) coaches, sport is often seen as a sphere of pure achievement and racial integration. Several research efforts challenge this assumption. Rosenblatt (1967) analyzes the batting averages of baseball players from 1953 to 1965 and concludes the discrimination is not directed at the superior black players; rather, he sees discrimination being directed at black players of the journeymen level. Rascal and Rapping (1970) extend this line of research and conclude that black pitchers must be superior to white pitchers in order to play in the big leagues. Yetman and Eitzen (1971, 1972) reach a similar conclusion from their findings that black players are disproportionately distributed in starting (star) roles. Johnson and Marple (1973) provide evidence to suggest that journeymen black players are dropped from professional basketball faster than comparable whites, a fact that would have dire economic consequences because pension plans are based on the number of years played.

There are several explanations for the apparent discrimination against medium-grade black players. One interpretation is that some coaches are prejudiced against blacks, but they must recruit the best minority players to remain competitive; yet they informally use a quota system to limit the number of blacks on the team. Thus, black players are more likely to be on the starting team (Yetman and Eitzen, 1972). Brower (1973:27) reports two reasons cited by owners of professional football teams for preferring white players: ". . . white players are desirable because white fans identify with them more readily than blacks, and most paying customers are white;" and "there are fewer problems with whites since blacks today have chips on their shoulders."

Another form of apparent discrimination in sports involves the practice of "stacking" wherein black athletes are allegedly assigned only to certain positions on the team (Edwards, 1973:205). In an interesting, theoretically informed study based on propositions derived from Grusky's (1963a:346) theory of the structure of formal organizations and Blalock's (1962) theory of occupational discrimination, Loy and McElvogue (1970:7) hypothesized that "There will be less discrimination where performance of independent tasks are largely involved, because such do not have to be coordinated with the activities of other persons, and therefore do not hinder the performance of others, nor require a great deal of skill in interpersonal relations." Loy and McElvogue found support in the data for their hypothesis that blacks are less likely to occupy central positions on professional baseball and football teams.

These studies are interesting contributions to the sociology of minority group relations. The work by Loy and McElvogue (1970) in this area is noteworthy since it synthesizes two theoretical frameworks from the larger discipline—Grusky's propositions on the formal structure of organizations and Blalock's (1962) propositions on racial discrimination. Such research efforts illustrate fruitful reciprocity between the sociology of sport and the larger discipline.

Recent research also focuses on discrimination in sport with respect to females. A girl actively involved in sport is likely to have her "femininity" called into question (Harris, 1973:15). Traditional sex role definitions either do not legitimate athletic pursuits for females or they narrowly define the range of appropriate physical activities (Griffin, 1973; Harris, 1971, 1973; Hart, 1972). In this regard, women are clearly at a disadvantage in terms of opportunities and resources available for physical expression of the self in the form of sport. Metheny (1965) traces the historical antecedents of the feminine image and the degree of acceptance for females in competitive sports. It is generally considered inappropriate for women to engage in sports where there is bodily contact, throwing of heavy objects, aggressive face-to-face competition, and long distance running or jumping. A recent survey by the authors of this article asked the respondents: "In your opinion, would participation in any of the following sports enhance a woman's feminine qualities?" The frequency distribution of affirmative responses was as follows: swimming 67 percent, tennis 57 percent, gymnastics 54 percent, softball 14 percent, basketball 14 percent, and track and field 13 percent.[5] The impact of the women's liberation movement on female involvement in sport represents a topic for additional research, and it is a research area that can feed back to the larger discipline in areas such as socialization, sex roles, and social movements.

SMALL GROUP PERSPECTIVES

The sociology of sport is a natural testing ground for theoretical frameworks in areas such as small group processes, collective behavior, personal influence, leadership, morale, and socialization. In sport the roles are clearly defined; performance measures are comparatively straightforward; and the contamination involved with artificiality and obtrusiveness of the investigator is less problematic than most areas of sociological research. Nevertheless, the sociology of sport includes relatively little experimental or even field studies. Sport teams represent an *in vivo* laboratory for the study of communication networks, cooperation, competition, conflict, division of labor, leadership, prestige, cohesion, and other structural properties of small groups. Several small group studies have focused on the effect of interpersonal relations among team members on team performance. One of the first studies (Fiedler, 1954) in this area analyzed the relationship between team effectiveness and the personal perceptions that team members have of one another. His findings suggest that winning teams are characterized by players who prefer to relate to one another in a task-oriented manner as contrasted with affective relations. Klein and Christiansen (1969), on the other hand, report a positive relationship between cohesiveness (interpersonal attractiveness) and performance of basketball teams. Their study also suggests that focused leadership (consensus concerning the peer leader) is conducive to team success. Heinicke and Bales (1953) likewise find an association between focused leadership and achieving task-oriented group goals. In a recent study, Eitzen (1973) shows that homogeneity in background characteristics of team members is related to team success. The relationship is interpreted in terms of heterogeneity increasing the likelihood of cliques within the team, which reduce cohesion and ultimately cause poor team performance.

Other studies, however, fail to replicate the finding of a relationship between cohesion and team success (Fielder, 1960; Lenk, 1969; Martens and Peterson, 1971). Nevertheless, these studies indicate the fruitfulness of research on sport teams using small group theoretical frameworks. The ambiguity of the findings shows the need for additional research to clarify our understanding of team structural characteristics, cohesiveness, and conflict according to the type of sport. For example, the role relations among a rowing crew require a synchronization of effort with each member performing a similar task, whereas most team sports involve individualization, specialization, and division of labor. Clearly, the dependent variable of team success is an applied perspective and approaches a market research orientation; however, we suggest that theoretically informed propositions that are derived from this type of research ultimately can be generalized to intergroup relations in general.

The utility of the sport context to test sociological propositions is illustrated in a further extension of Grusky's (1963a) concept of organizational *centrality* to the study of professional baseball team managers. Grusky analyzed differential recruitment of baseball players into managerial positions in terms of the centrality of the player's position. He found support for the hypothesis that centrality of position (e.g., infielders, catcher) is associated with higher rates of recruitment into managerial positions. Loy and Sage (1968) extend the centrality framework to explain the emergence of informal leaders on baseball teams. They found support for Grusky's hypothesis; infielders and catchers were more likely to be chosen as team captains, best liked, and perceived as highly valuable members of the team.

Grusky (1963b) also studied managerial succession (firing the manager) and team performance in major league baseball. He found that changing managers was negatively associated with team performance; however, he rejected the intuitive notion that managers are fired because of the team's poor performance. Rather, he suggested that causal direction is two-way since managerial succession can also produce poor team performance. In a stimulating exchange, Gamson and Scotch (1964:70) argue that "the effect of the field manager on team performance is relatively unimportant." They suggest that Grusky's findings should be interpreted in terms of ritual scapegoating. Grusky's (1964) response included a specification of the relationship in terms of "inside" successors to the managerial position being less disruptive than "outside" successors (cf., Gouldner, 1954). Eitzen and Yetman (1971) also used Grusky's propositions concerning managerial succession in their study of coaching changes and performance of college basketball teams. They found support for Grusky's hypothesis, but basically they concluded that teams with poor performance records are likely to improve their records with or without a coaching change. Thus, the critical variable is the degree of team success before the arrival of the new coach—not the performance of the new coach.

SOCIAL PSYCHOLOGICAL ASPECTS

When viewed from the standpoint of the collectivity, socialization refers to the process of transmitting social values and norms to the individual members. Viewed from the perspective of the individual, socialization refers to the resulting changes that occur within the individual. Numerous observers have pointed to the potential of sport as an agency for socialization.[6] The theoretical rationale for examining socialization within the world of sport is implicit in the classic works of symbolic interaction (Cooley, 1922; Mead, 1934), where play and games are analyzed as part of the socialization process. More recently, psychologists have analyzed games and sport in the context of socialization (Piaget, 1962; Erickson, 1965; and Sutton-Smith, 1971). Ingham et al. (1973:243) observe that "the processes involved in the social construction of life-worlds are also in evidence in the social construction of play worlds. Similarly, the processes by which we come to know the life-world are the processes by which we come to know the play-world."

Basically, it is suggested that the athlete undergoes a socialization process when interacting with coaches and fellow athletes in the subculture of sport (Phillips and Schafer, 1970). If this line of reasoning is extended, we would expect the potency of the socialization process to vary according to the individual's degree of involvement in sport. Kenyon (1969) provided a theoretical discussion of this process, and Snyder (1927b) offers empirical support for this hypothesis of differential consequences according to degree of sport involvement. In the latter study, interestingly, the interaction patterns between the coach and outstanding athletes were markedly different from the coach's relations with marginal players.

Kenyon (1969:81) proposes that the socialization consequences of sports involvement be considered from a temporal perspective—particularly in terms of the stages of becoming involved, being involved, and becoming uninvolved. He suggests that research from this perspective could be informed by role theory and reference group frameworks. An intriguing study would be to trace the social psychological dynamics that trigger changes in the individual's progression from one stage of involvement to another.[7] In a similar vein, Page (1969:20) suggests the possibility of an identity crisis emerging after a successful athlete has completed his/her active playing days. A study of prominent soccer players in Yugoslavia reveals some negative psychological concomitants of the players' disengagement from athletic careers (Mihovilovic, 1968). The study indicates the importance of gradual withdrawal from the active role, especially when the athletic role is the individual's sole identity anchor. Taking on the role of coach, referee, or similar official has been one way in which the transition process is softened for former athletes (Snyder, 1972d).

Perhaps the topic that has received the most cumulative, quantitative research in the sociology of sport concerns the social psychological consequences of active participation in athletics by youth. A series of studies focus on the question of whether athletes differ from nonathletes on personality dimensions such as extraversion, conformism, conventionality, aspirations, conservatism, and rigidity (Schendel, 1965; Schafer and Armer, 1968; Phillips and Schafer, 1970). Earlier in this paper we discussed the positive relationship between participation in athletics and academic performance and aspirations among high school boys. Rehberg and Schafer (1968) report that participation in sport has the most effect on boys least disposed to attend college by raising their educational expectations to attend college. We alluded above to the possible two-edged sword effect of sport serving as a channel for mobility while also raising levels of aspiration without providing the corresponding instrumental skills (Spady, 1970). Similar studies on college level athletes yield inconsistent findings (Pilapil et al., 1970; Sage, 1967; and Spady, 1970). Additional research at the college level is needed.

A relatively underdeveloped area in this subfield is the social psychology of consciousness states, intrinsic satisfaction, body perceptions, and affective concomitants of sport. Some journalistic reports argue that commercialized sports desensitize, exploit, and manipulate players to achieve the ultimate goal of winning and profits (Meggyesy, 1971; Hoch, 1972; Shaw, 1972). On the other hand, several studies point to positive affective consequences of sport involvement (Layman, 1968, 1972). There is empirical evidence to suggest, for example, that sports participation is associated with life satisfaction (Washburne, 1941; Snyder and Spreitzer, 1973b). This finding is consistent with many studies documenting a positive relationship between social participation and psychological well-being (Wilson, 1967). Further explanation may rest with the intrinsic satisfaction that flows from involvement in sport. Dunning (1967:148) reasons that sport participation generates a "tension-excitement" that forms a pleasurable contrast to routinized aspects of everyday life.

A pertinent study by Snyder and Kivlin (1974) studied the self-perceptions of outstanding female athletes with the expectation that female athletes would evidence low scores on measures of psychological well-being and body image on the basis of role conflict reasoning. The findings did not support the hypothesis, and the authors concluded that the intrinsic satisfaction flowing from sports participation tended to counteract any negative impact from sex role stereotyping. Additional research is needed on this topic.

The "athletic revolution" described above involves protests against authoritarian practices within sport, particularly among coaches (Scott, 1971). A popular explanation is that the coaching profession either attracts persons with an authoritarian personality or, alternatively, coaches are socialized into this personality type. This explanation ignores the structural interpretation of authoritarian behavior developed in recent years.[8] In the latter context, Edwards (1973) reasons that the coach is *fully responsible* for the team's victories and defeats; yet he has *limited control* in determining the outcomes. Under these circumstances, then, Edwards (1973:139) points out that coaches insist upon running a tight ship and, consequently, a democratic leadership style would not enable the coach to maintain compliance under the tense conditions of a match where unquestioning obedience is required. The analysis of the coach's role shows that the authoritarian aspects of coaching behavior are structurally induced. Although the behavior of athletic coaches is not a particularly significant problem, it is a context in which the interpenetration of social structure and the personality is readily apparent.

CONCLUSION

Basically we have argued that sport is a social institution that interfaces with, and reflects, many dimensions of social life. Despite the pervasiveness of sport in society, the sociological study of sport is still not completely legitimated within the larger discipline. We suggest that research in this area will enter the mainstream when it reaches the level of theoretical and methodological self-consciousness characteristic of the better works in the larger discipline. In other words, it is vain to argue in the abstract that the world of sport is worthy of social scientific study. A more fruitful approach to legitimacy for a new specialty is simply for the practitioners in that area to produce research that will be interesting to social scientists at large. Research that is of interest only to persons who are already intrinsically interested in sports will necessarily be of dubious value from a social scientific perspective.

It is clear that most researchers in the sociology of sport have a strong intrinsic interest and existential involvement in the subject matter of the sub-field that is not characteristic of most other specialities within sociology. We suggest that this intrinsic interest needs to be tempered by a generalizing orientation if the sociology of sport is to contribute to the large discipline. A basically content-oriented strategy will not result in a body of systematic knowledge about social life. In other words, when content from the world of sport is analyzed by the sociologist, it should be selected because it is informative about the nature, antecedents, and consequences of basic social processes, and not simply because of intrinsic interest on the part of the investigator. The content of the world of sport must at times be viewed in instrumental terms if the subfield is to be truly in a reciprocal relationship with the larger discipline. General sociologists are likely to be interested in contributions from the sociology of sport only if some generalizing thrust is contained therein: "The purpose of a generalizing investigation is to test, reformulate, refine, or extend an abstract, general theory. A large number of concretely quite different settings serve equally well as instances of the process, for no particular one of them has any special importance for the investigation" (Berger et al., 1972:*xi*).

In analyzing the sociology of sport, we were struck by the "loyalty" of the scholars in this area. That is, many of the researchers in the specialty have published regularly in the area over the years. This is apparent because of the fact that most of the literature in this specialty is contained in comparatively few outlets. Moreover, judging from the congregation of the scholars in the sociology of sport at conventions, there is a strong affinity among social scientists in this specialty. There is always a danger that a given specialty will become too insulated from the larger discipline; this is particularly a problem with the sociology of sport because of the multidisciplinary composition of the specialty.

This argument is based on the assumption that a strong identification with, and immersion in, the larger discipline is necessary to keep the taproot of the sociological imagination alive. If this assumption is valid, the most enduring contributions to the sociology of sport are likely to come from research efforts informed by intellectual concerns derived from the larger discipline.

In this context, it is interesting to note that more developed specialties such as medical sociology involve more practitioners who are just passing through and happen to touch down for an episodic research effort on the content of a given specialty. For example, prominent general sociologists have contributed important studies to medical sociology (e.g., Parsons, Merton, Srole, Becker, Hollingshead). This is not to suggest, however, that individual scholars should be only occasional or episodic contributors to an academic specialty. Rather, we argue that from an aggregate or macro level, it is desirable that a circulation of practitioners occur within a specialty. The circulation of practitioners assures a steady flow of theoretical and methodological nutrition from the larger discipline and, most importantly, will function to keep the resident practitioners sensitive to significant research questions of generic sociological interest.

We predict that the field will continue to be strengthened by increased theoretical and methodological sophistication. The present state of development reveals less barefooted empiricism and more theoretically informed hypothesis testing. The research designs and interpretations of data show increasing sensitivity to alternative explanations and spurious relationships.[9] We observe a greater use of multivariate statistical techniques, but most importantly, the sociological imagination is increasingly evident by research that is going beyond the surface manifestations of sports to pose generic theoretical questions stemming from the larger discipline. Consequently, we conclude that the sociology of sport is shedding its *lumpen* heritage and is gaining respectability. Sociologists in general can look forward to some interesting contributions from this fledgling subfield in the years to come.

REFERENCES

Bend, Emil, *The Impact of Athletic Participation on Academic and Career Aspiration and Achievement.* Pittsburgh: American Institutes for Research 1968.

Berger, Joseph, Zelditch, Morris, and Anderson, Bo, *Sociological Theories in Progress,* New York: Houghton Mifflin 1972.

Blalock, H. M., "Occupational discrimination: some theoretical propositions," *Social Problems,* **9** (Winter) :247-249 1962.

Boyles, Robert H., *Sport: Mirror of American Life,* Boston: Little, Brown 1963.

Brower, J. J., "Whitey's sport," *Human Behavior,* 2 (November) :22–27 1973.

Burdge, R. J., "Levels of occupational prestige and leisure activity," *Journal of Leisure Research,* 1 (Summer) :262–274 1966.

Coleman, James S., *The Adolescent Society,* New York: Free Press 1961.

Cooley, Charles H., *Human Nature and the Social Order,* New York: Scribner's 1922.

Dunning, E., "Some conceptual dilemmas in the sociology of sport," Pp. 34–37 in *Magglinger Symposium, Sociology of Sport.,* Basel, Switzerland: Birkhauser Verlag 1971.

Dunning, E., "Notes on some conceptual and theoretical problems in the sociology of sports," *International Review of Sport Sociology* 2:143–153 1967.

Edwards, Harry, *Sociology of Sport,* Homewood, Illinois: Dorsey Press 1973.
Edwards, Harry, *The Revolt of the Black Athlete,* New York: The Free Press 1969.

Eitzen, D. S., "The effect of group structure on the success of athletic teams," *International Review of Sport Sociology* 8:7–17 1973.
Eitzen, D. Stanley, and Yetman, Norman R., "Managerial change and organizational effectiveness," presented at the Ohio Valley Sociological Society, Cleveland, Ohio 1971.

Erickson, Erik H., *Childhood and Society.* New York: W. W. Norton Company 1965.

Fiedler, F. E., "The leader's psychological distance and group effectiveness," in Dorwin Cartwright and Alvin Zander (eds.), Group Dynamics. Evanston: Northwestern, pp. 526–606 1960.

Fiedler, F. E., "Assumed similarity measures as predictors of team effectiveness," *Journal of Abnormal Social Psychology,* 49 (July) :381–388 1954.

Furst, R. T., "Social change and the commercialization of professional sports," *International Review of Sport Sociology,* 6:153–173 1971.

Gamson, W. A., and Scotch, N. A., "Scapegoating in baseball," *American Journal of Sociology,* 70 (July) :69–72 1964.

Gerth, Hans H., and Mills, C. Wright, *Character and Social Structure.* New York: Harcourt, Brace and World 1954.

Glaser, Barney G., and Strauss, Anselm L., *The Discovery of Grounded Theory,* Chicago: Aldine Publishing Company 1967.

Gordon, C. Wayne, *The Social System of the High School,* New York: The Free Press 1957.

Gouldner, Alvin W., *Patterns of Industrial Bureaucracy*, Glencoe, Illinois: The Free Press 1954.

Griffin, P. S., "What's a nice girl like you doing in a profession like this?" *Quest*, **19** (January) :96-101 1973.

Grusky, O., "Reply to Gamson and Scotch," *American Journal of Sociology* **70** (July :72-76 1964.

Grusky, O., "The effects of formal structure on managerial recruitment: a study of baseball organization," *Sociometry* **26** (September) :345-353 1963a.

Grusky, O., "Managerial succession and organizational effectiveness," *American Journal of Sociology*, **69** (July) :21-23 1963b.

Haerle, Rudolf K., Jr., "Heroes, success themes, and basic cultural values in baseball autobiographies: 1900-1970," paper presented at the Third National Meeting of the Popular Culture Association, Indianapolis, Indiana 1973.

Harris, D. V., "Dimensions of physical activity," pp. 3-15 in Dorothy V. Harris (ed.), *Women and Sport: A National Research Conference*, University Park: The Pennsylvania State University 1973.

Harris, D. V. "The sportswoman in our society," pp. 1-4 in Dorothy V. Harris (ed.), *Women in Sports*, Washington, D.C.: American Association for Health and Physical Education, and Recreation 1971.

Hart, M. M., "On being female in sport," pp. 291-302 in M. Marie Hart (ed.), *Sport in the Socio-Cultural Process*, Dubuque, Iowa: Wm. C. Brown, Company 1972.

Heinicke, C. and Bales, R. F., "Developmental trends in the structure of groups," *Sociometry*, **16** (February) :7-38 1953.

Hoch, Paul, *Rip Off the Big Game*, Garden City, New York: Doubleday and Company 1972.

Hollingshead, August B., *Elmtown's Youth*, New York: John Wiley and Sons 1949.

Huizinga, Jan, *Homo Ludens: A Study of the Play Element in Culture*, Boston: Beacon Press 1955.

Ingham, A. G., Loy, J. W., and Berryman, J. W., "Socialization, dialects, and sport," pp. 235-276 in Dorothy V. Harris (ed.), *Women and Sport: A National Research Conference*. University Park: The Pennsylvania State University 1973.

Johnson, N. R. and Marple, D. F., "Racial discrimination in professional basketball: an empirical test," paper presented at the North Central Sociological Association Meetings, Cincinnati, Ohio 1973.

Kenyon, G. S., "Sport and society: at odds or in concert," pp. 33-41 in Arnold Flath, *Athletics in America*, Corvallis, Oregon: Oregon State University Press 1972.

Kenyon, G. S., "Sport involvement: a conceptual go and some consequences thereof," pp. 77-87 in Gerald S. Kenyon (ed.), *Aspects of Contemporary Sport Sociology.* Chicago: The Athletic Institute 1969.

Kenyon, G. S., "The significance of physical activity as a function of age, sex, education, and socio-economic status of northern United States adults," *International Review of Sport Sociology* 1:41-57 1966.

Killian, L. M., "The effects of southern white workers on race relations in northern plants." *American Sociological Review* 17 (June) :327-331 1952.

Klein, M. and Christiansen, G., "Group composition, group structure, and group effectiveness of basketball teams," pp. 397-408 in John W. Loy, Jr. and Gerald S. Kenyon (eds.), *Sport, Culture and Society,* London: Macmillan Company 1969.

Kohn, M. L. and Williams, R. M., Jr., "Situational patterning in intergroup relations," *American Sociological Review,* 21 (April) :164-174 1956.

Layman, E. M., "The contribution of play and sports to emotional health." pp. 163-185 in John E. Kane (ed.), *Psychological Aspects of Physical Education and Sport,* London: Routledge and Kegan Paul 1972.

Layman, E. M., "The role of play and sport in healthy emotional development: a reappraisal," pp. 249-257 in Gerald S. Kenyon and Tom M. Grogg (eds.), *Contemporary Psychology of Sport:* Proceedings of the Second International Congress of Sport Psychology, Chicago: The Athletic Institute 1968.

Lenk, H., "Top performance despite internal conflict: an antithesis to a functional proposition," pp. 392-397 in John W. Loy, Jr. and Gerald S. Kenyon (eds.), *Sport, Culture and Society,* London: Macmillan Company 1969.

Lohman, J. and Reitzes, D., "Note on race relations in mass society," *The American Journal of Sociology,* 53 (November) :240-246 1953.

Loy, J. W., Jr., "The study of sport and social mobility," pp. 101-119 in Gerald S. Kenyon (ed.), *Aspects of Contemporary Sport Sociology,* Chicago: The Athletic Institute 1969.

Loy, J. W., "The nature of sport: a definitional effort," *Quest,* 10 (May) :1-15 1968.

Loy, J. W., and McElvogue, J. F., "Racial segregation in American sport," *International Review of Sport Sociology,* 5:5-24 1970.

Loy, J. W., Jr. and Sage, G. H., "Social origins, academic achievement, and career mobility patterns of college coaches." Paper presented at the American Sociological Association, New Orleans, Louisiana 1972.

Loy, J. W., Jr. and Sage, J. N., "The effects of formal structure on organizational leadership: an investigation of inter-scholastic baseball teams," paper presented at Second International Congress of Sport Psychology, Washington, D.C. 1968.

Luschen, Gunther, "On sociology of sport—general orientation and its trends in the literature," pp. 119–154 in Ommo Grupe et al. (eds.), *The Scientific View of Sport*, Heidelberg: Springer-Verlag Berlin 1972.

Luschen, Gunther, "Sociology of sport and the cross-cultural analysis of sport and games," pp. 6–13 in Gunther Luschen (ed.), *The Cross-Cultural Analysis of Sport and Games*, Champaign, Illinois: Stripes Publishing Company 1970.

Luschen, Gunther, "Social stratification and social mobility among young sportsmen," pp. 258–276 in John W. Loy, Jr. and Gerald S. Kenyon (eds.), *Sport, Culture and Society*. London: Macmillan Company 1969.

Luschen, Gunther, *The Sociology of Sport*, Paris: Mouton and Company 1968.

Luschen, Gunther, "The interdependence of sport and culture," *International Review of Sport Sociology*, 2:127–141 1967.

Lynd, Robert S. and Lynd, Helen M., *Middletown*, New York: Harcourt, Brace and Company 1929.

Martens, R. and Peterson, J. A., "Group cohesiveness as a determinant of success and member satisfaction in team performance," *International Review of Sport Sociology*, 6:49–61 1971.

Mead, George H., *Mind, Self, and Society*, Chicago: University of Chicago Press 1934.

Meggyesy, Dave, *Out of Their League*, New York: Paperback Library 1971.

Metheny, E., "Symbolic forms of movement: the female image in sports," pp. 43–56 in E. Metheny (ed.), *Connotations of Movement in Sport and Dance*, Dubuque, Iowa: Wm. C. Brown Company 1965.

Meyersohn, R., "The sociology of leisure in the United States: introduction and bibliography, 1945–1965," *Journal of Leisure Research*, 1 (Winter) :53–68 1969.

Mihovilovic, M. A., "The status of former sportsmen," *International Review of Sport Sociology*, 3:73–96 1968.

Miller, Arthur, *Death of a Salesman*, New York: Viking Press 1958.

Page, C. H., "Symposium summary, with reflections upon the sociology of sport as a research field," pp. 189–202 in Gerald S. Kenyon (ed.), *Aspects of Contemporary Sport Sociology*. Chicago: The Athletic Institute 1969.

Pascal, Anthony H. and Rapping, Leonard A., *Racial Discrimination in Organized Baseball*, Santa Monica, California: Rand Corporation 1970.

Petrie, Brian M., "The political attitudes of Canadian university students: a comparison between athletes and nonathletes," paper presented at the National Convention of the American Association of Health, Physical Education, and Recreation, Minneapolis, Minnesota 1973.

Phillips, John C. and Schafer, Walter E., "The athletic subculture: a preliminary study," paper presented at the American Sociological Association 1970.

Piaget, Jean, *Play, Dreams and Imitation in Childhood,* New York: W. W. Norton Company 1962.

Pilapil, Bonifacio, Stecklein, John E., and Liu, Han C., *Intercollegiate Athletics and Academic Progress: A Comparison of Academic Characteristics of Athletes and Nonathletes at the University of Minnesota,* Minneapolis: Bureau of Institutional Research 1970.

Rehberg, Richard A., "Sport and political activism," paper presented at the Conference on Sport and Social Deviancy, SUNY, Brockport, New York 1971.

Rehberg, R. A. and Schafer, W. E., "Participation in interscholastic athletics and college expectations," *American Journal of Sociology,* **73** (May) :732–740 1968.

Reitzes, D. C., "Institutional structure and race relations," *Phylon,* (Spring) :48–66 1959.

Riesman, D. and Denny, R., "Football in America," pp. 242–257 in David Riesman (ed.), *Individualism Reconsidered,* Glencoe, Ill.: The Free Press 1954.

Roberts, J. M. and Sutton-Smith, B., "Child training and game involvement," *Ethnology,* **1** (April) :166–185 1962.

Rogers, C., "Sports, religion and politics: the renewal of an alliance," *The Christian Century,* **89** (April 5) :392–394 1972.

Rosenblatt, A., "Negroes in baseball: the failure of success," *Trans-action,* **4** (September) :51–53 1967.

Sage, John N., "Adolescent values and the non-participating college athlete," paper presented at the Southern Section California Health, Physical Education and Recreation Conference, San Fernando Valley State College 1967.

Schafer, Walter E., "Sport, socialization and the school: toward maturity or enculturation?" paper presented at the Third International Symposium on the Sociology of Sport, Waterloo, Ontario 1971.

Schafer, W. E. and Armer, J. M., "Athletes are not inferior students," *Trans-action,* **5** (November) :21–26, 61–62 1968.

Schafer, W. and Rehberg, R., "Athletic participation, college aspirations and college encouragement," *Pacific Sociological Review,* **13** (Summer) :182–186 1970.

Schendel, J. S., "Psychological differences between athletes and non-participants at three educational levels," *Research Quarterly,* **36** (March) :52–67 1965.

Scott, Jack, *The Athletic Revolution,* New York: The Free Press 1971.

Shaw, Gary, *Meat On the Hoof,* New York: Dell Publishing Company 1972.

Snyder, E. E., "Athletic dressingroom slogans as folklore: a means of socialization," *International Review of Sport Sociology,* 7:89–102 1972a.

Snyder, Eldon E., "Athletes' careers: the role of the coach in the athletes' future educational attainment," paper presented at the Scientific Congress in conjunction with the XXth Olympic Games, Munich 1972b.

Snyder, E. E., "High school athletes and their coaches: educational plans and advice," *Sociology of Education,* **45** (Summer) :313–325 1972c.

Snyder, E. E., "Social characteristics and motivations of basketball officials and aspects of sports involvement," *The Ohio High School Athlete,* **32** (November) :66–67, 83 1972d.

Snyder, E. E. and Kivlin, J. E., "Women athletes and aspects of psychological well-being and body image," paper read at the Popular Culture Association, Milwaukee 1974.

Snyder, E. E. and Spreitzer, E. A., "Family influence and involvement in sports," *Research Quarterly,* **44** (October) :249–255 1973a.

Snyder, E. E. and Spreitzer, E. A., "Involvement in sports and psychological well-being," *International Journal of Sport Psychology,* **5** (1) :28–39 1973b.

Spady, W. G., "Lament for the letterman: effects of peer status and extracurricular activities on goals and achievement," *American Journal of Sociology,* **75** (January) :680–702 1970.

Spreitzer, E. A. and Pugh, M. D., "Interscholastic athletics and educational expectations," *Sociology of Education,* **46** (Spring) :171–182 1973.

Stone, G. P., "Some meanings of American sport: an extended view," pp. 5–16 in G. S. Kenyon (ed.), *Aspects of Contemporary Sport Sociology.* Chicago: The Athletic Institute 1969.

Stone, G. P., "American sports: play and display," pp. 47–65 in Eric Dunning (ed.), *Sport: Readings from a Sociological Perspective,* London: Frank Cass and Company 1971.

Sutton-Smith, Brian, "A developmental approach to play, games and sport," paper presented at the Second World Symposium on the History of Sport and Physical Education, Bannf, Alberta, Canada 1971.

U.S. Department of Labor, Bureau of Labor Statistics, "Careers in professional sports," *Occupational Outlook Quarterly,* **17** (Summer) :2–5 1973.

Veblen, Thorstein, *Theory of the Leisure Class,* New York: Random House 1899.

Voigt, David Q., *America's Leisure Revolution,* Reading, Pennsylvania: Albright College Book Store 1971.

Waller, Willard, *The Sociology of Teaching,* New York: John Wiley and Sons 1932.

Washburne, J. N., "Factors related to the social adjustment of college girls," *Journal of Social Psychology*, **13** (May) :281–289 1941.

Wilson, W., "Correlates of avowed happiness," *Psychological Bulletin*, **67** (April) :294–306 1967.

Yetman, N. R. and Eitzen, D. S., "Black Americans in sports: unequal for equal ability," *Civil Rights Digest*, **5** (August) :21–34 1972.

Yetman, N. R. and Eitzen, D. S., "Black athletes on intercollegiate basketball teams: an empirical test of discrimination," paper presented at the American Sociological Association, Denver, Colorado 1971.

Yinger, J. Milton, *Toward a Field Theory of Behavior*, New York: McGraw-Hill Co. 1965.

A CRITICAL LOOK AT THE SOCIOLOGY OF SPORT

Merrill J. Melnick

SPORT SOCIOLOGY AS A DISCIPLINE

The growth and development of American sociology of sport since 1965, when Kenyon and Loy first identified for the readers of the *Journal of Health, Physical Education and Recreation* the nature of the discipline, has been impressive. The past ten years have witnessed a virtual explosion in the publication of empirical investigations and some promising attempts at theory generation and model building. Important strides have been taken with respect to the description, explanation, and prediction of sport.

Changes in Sport Sociology

The establishment of a cumulative and systematic body of knowledge is well under way, and consequently it seems important, at this juncture in its history, for sociology of sport to do some stock-taking in order to see where it has been and where it is headed. This introspection is all the more important, given the ferment and change presently taking place in its parent discipline, sociology. Gary Marx (1972) has noted:

Merrill J. Melnick, "A Critical Look at Sociology of Sport," *Quest*, Monograph 24 (Summer), 1975, pp. 34–47. Reprinted by permission of the publishers and author.

A sociology at once more critical, and more concerned with studying immediate human problems, reaching a wide audience and granting legitimacy to a wider range of methods, has come to partly displace the concern with technique and broad theory which has characterized American sociology in recent decades [pp. 1–2].

Even the very role of the sociologist is undergoing redefinition. Gouldner (1971a) speaks of deepening ". . . the sociologist's awareness of who and what he is as a member of a specific society at a given time, and of how his social roles and his personal life affect his professional work" [p. 57]. If, as Marx believes, traditional perspectives, methodologies, styles, assumptions, and masters in the social sciences and especially sociology, are being questioned, this would have important implications for sociology of sport, since it has endeavored to mold itself in the image of sociology. It is for these reasons that sport sociologists Loy and Segrave (1974) are to be commended for raising some important questions about sociology of sport that must and should be answered. Their questions include:

1. What is (or should be) the primary focus of the sport sociologist?

2. What constitutes significant research problems within the context of the sociology of sport?

This paper attempts to answer these questions while posing others for the discipline's consideration. First, the dominant value orientation current within sociology of sport will be discussed. The sport sociologist as a person will then be discussed and some alternative work roles suggested. Lastly, the investigative paradigms most frequently used by sport sociologists will be looked at and an argument made for the development of new paradigms. Two such paradigms, "muckraking sociology of sport" and "humanist-existential sociology of sport," will then be defined.

Value-Free Sociology of Sport

That American sociology of sport must and should be "value-free" has been argued throughout the brief but exciting ten-year history of this academic discipline. Beginning with Kenyon and Loy's eloquent appeal for the study of physical activity as a sociological and social psychological phenomenon, the call has gone out that if sociology of sport is to gain acceptance within the academic community, its perspective or value-orientation must be a "value-free," "value-neutral," "non-normative," or "nonethical" one. To quote Kenyon and Loy (1965):

Sport sociology, as we view it, is a value-free social science. It is not an effort to influence public opinion or behavior, nor is it an attempt to find support for the "social development" objective of physical education. . . . The sport sociologist is neither a spreader of gospel nor an evangelist for exercise. His function is not to shape attitudes and values but rather to describe and explain them [p. 25].

British sport sociologists Kane and Murray (1966) echoed similar sentiments when they wrote ". . . any serious sociological study should not concern itself with value judgments. 'Must' and 'ought' questions, cannot intrude on the presentation of material . . ." [p. 112]. More recently, Loy (1972) observed:

> By nonethical is meant that sociologists as scientists are concerned with "what is" rather than "what ought to be." They are interested in social analysis, not social amelioration—in explanation not evaluation [p. 191].

Kenyon (1969) has argued that the sport sociologist ". . . who allows his personal values or social philosophy to influence his observation . . . or color his interpretations is simply engaging in bad science, by definition" [p. 172]. Further Kenyon is fearful that the sport sociologist who is "value-committed" will confine his research to the study of current social problems and by so doing, forestall the development of the very knowledge upon which social action often depends. Finally, he points out that the sport sociologist who allows his research activities to be guided by a single philosophy ". . . could prevent the discovery of new and often more elegant explantory systems" [p. 172].

None of these sport sociologists means to imply that the research process is totally devoid of value judgments. On the contrary, value judgments are implicit in the selection of research problems, research methodologies, and statistical procedures. Moreover, the very choice of the scientific method of inquiry, such as phenomenological analysis, reflects a value bias. However, once these choices have been made, scientific objectivity, according to these sport sociologists, takes over and becomes of paramount concern if new and valid explanatory principles are to be discovered. The role that objectivity plays, according to the psychologist Clark (1967) is ". . . not in the refusal to to make hypotheses, but in the rigorous assessment of the evidence accumulated for that hypothesis, so as to guard, as far as possible, against any distortion of these facts" [p. 511].

The fact that American sociology regards itself as a value-free social science should not be surprising. Western sociology has steadfastly maintained, with few exceptions, a similar stance. As Gouldner (1963) has noted:

> Today, all the powers of sociology, from Parsons to Lundberg, have entered into a tacit alliance to bind us to the dogma that "Thou shalt not commit a value judgment," especially as sociologists [p. 35].

According to Friedrichs (1970), ". . . Jeremy Bentham observed that the word 'ought' ought never to be used except in saying it ought never to be used . . ." [p. 99]. The strict adherence to a value-free doctrine both in sociology and sociology of sport can be explained historically. The value-free conception of social science emerged during the period 1875-1900, when classical sociology was gaining acceptance in institutions of higher learning in Germany and France. The doctrine performed the important *latent* function of bringing peace within the German university by reducing intra-faculty competition for students. The possibility of a charismatic professor spouting provocative value judgments about man and society and thereby attracting a disproportionate number of students to his fold was eliminated. In addition, Weber for one ". . . feared that the expression of political value judgments in the University would provoke the state into censoring the University and would imperil its autonomy" [Gouldner, 1963, p. 40]. It is apparent that, apart from any scientific consideration, the value-free doctrine served academic or professional sociology well by allowing it to maintain a low profile and gain a measure of autonomy. The well-publicized conflict between Mills and the academic sociology establishment in the 1940's and 1950's could be partially accounted for by his total disdain for value-free sociology. According to Bennett Berger (1963), Mills' "sin" consisted of being

> . . . a political activist and a polemicist in a period when professional sociologists were more concerned with establishing their discipline as an objective science and institutionalizing it in the universities than they were with saying something important about the world and making what they said effective in the arenas of political combat [p. 3].

Thus, the value-free approach of sociology of sport can be understood by recognizing the fact that the discipline has and still is struggling to establish itself as an accredited member of the scientific fraternity. As Willhelm (1970) pointed out:

> This inclination to reject social involvement by injecting the notion of value-free inquiry is . . . typical of the scientific elite; it is characteristic for a social group that finally arrives, especially following what it considers to have been a hard-fought engagement to come onto the scene, to immediately sanctify its elevated status [p. 115].

There can be no argument with a value-free approach to sociology of sport, as posited by Loy, Kenyon, and others, when it refers to the norms of scientific objectivity. Scott (1972), a frequent critic of the sports establishment and "physical educators-sport sociologists," has never condemned the scientific method of inquiry in his writings. According to Scott, ". . . the nature of sports in American society can best be examined and elucidated by a scientific approach. However . . . it should be understood that science is our means, not our end" [p. xvii]. What concerns Scott—and this author—most is our need to distinguish between the indispensable canons of scientific inquiry and *moral indifference*. It is when the value-free ideology, motivated principally by a concern for professional respectability, becomes a cloak for moral indifference or is used to rationalize scientific nonaccountability, that sport sociologists must stand up and take notice of their discipline's future. Gouldner (1963) has argued that where "value-free" means moral indifference, it becomes useful to those who want to neglect their public responsibilities and escape from the world. He characterizes these sociologists as ". . . living huddled behind self-barricaded intellectual ghettos" [p. 43]. No one is suggesting that sport sociologists have or are planning to construct such "barricades;" however, we must guard against this happening, lest the value-free perspective make sterile our moral sensibilities and discourage us from engaging in constructive criticism. The label "social scientist" or "sport sociologist" certainly does not require us to surrender our critical impulses.

Finally, it has been suggested by a growing number of sociologists that those who hold to a value-free approach may be engaging in an exercise of self-delusion. Gouldner (1971a) has written:

> When they confine work to the demanding, misleading and unfulfillable paradigm of a value-free, high-science model, sociologists are wasting, indeed sacrificing, a part of themselves . . . the notion of contaminated research presupposes the existence of uncontaminated research, and this is pure folly. All research is contaminated, for all research entails relationships that may influence both sociologist and subject [p. 96].

THE SPORT SOCIOLOGIST

There is the tacit suggestion with the value-free approach that the social scientist should set aside his personal feelings, affective states, and sentiments when engaged in scientific work. This schizoid-like characterization of the scientist was suggested by Bierstedt (1953) when he wrote:

> Science and citizenship are two different things. While a given individual may play two different roles, that of scientist and that of citizen, it is of vital importance that he not try to play them both at once. . . . To adopt another course is to prostitute the prestige of science and of a scientific reputation [p. 6].

The Sport Sociologist as a Person

I would like to suggest that what Bierstedt is calling for and what the value-free approach seems to demand is wellnigh impossible to achieve. The non-feeling, robot-like social scientist suggested by this approach is an artificial stereotype at best. The sport sociologist is, first and foremost, a person; he has feelings, ethical and cultural preferences, some stereotypical beliefs, and probably a prejudice or two. As Willhelm (1970) pointed out:

> We must realize, however, that explicit declarations concerning a value-free activity do not in fact make activities value-free. . . . In short, it is not at all possible for the socialized person . . . to escape values; it is only a matter of holding to one set of values rather than another [p. 119].

It would be well for the sport sociologist to study *himself* in addition to the social systems that strike his fancy. As Gouldner (1971b) has observed, the work of the sociologist is influenced at every turn by his "domain assumptions," such as "dispositions to believe that men are rational or irrational; that society is precarious or fundamentally stable; that social problems will correct themselves without planned intervention; that human behavior is unpredictable . . ." [p. 31]. According to Gouldner, these domain assumptions are derived from more general "background assumptions" which he defines as ". . . affectively-laden cognitive tools that are developed early in the course of our socialization into a particular culture and are built deeply into our character structure" [p. 32]. In short, background and domain assumptions are related in a significant way to the work of the sociologist and provide him with his conception of the "real" social world.

Especially interesting is Gouldner's (1971b) observation that domain assumptions are even built into scientific methodology itself. For example, he suggests that ". . . the conventional methodologies of social research often premise and foster a deep-going authoritarianism, a readiness to lie to and manipulate people: they betray a bureaucratic numbness" [p. 50]. Gouldner has summarized his argument in the following way:

> When viewed from one standpoint, "methodology" seems a purely technical concern devoid of ideology; presumably it deals only with methods of extracting reliable information from the world, collecting data, constructing questionnaires, sampling, and analyzing returns. Yet it it is always a good deal more than that, for it is commonly infused with ideologically resonant assumptions about what the social world is, who the sociologist is, and what the nature of the relation between them is [pp. 50–51].

Some sociologists make a specious argument when they declare that ". . . *they* [other people] are bound by society; *I* am free of it." [Gouldner, 1971b, p. 54]. Strictly speaking, it is doubtful whether any social scientist can be "value-free." We are all creatures molded by social structure and culture and respond accordingly, even when engaged in the scientific enterprise. As Gouldner (1963) pointed out:

> . . . there is and can be no value-free sociology. The only choice is between an expression of one's values, as open and honest as it can be . . . and a vain ritual of moral neutrality which . . . leaves it at the mercy of irrationality [p. 51].

While there are obvious dangers in being "value-bound," it is better, according to Gouldner (1971a) to ". . . accept the dangers of a value commitment, because the risk of ending in distortion is better than beginning there, and a dogmatic and arid value-free sociology cannot be other than a myth" [p. 91].

The Sport Sociologist as Sport Critic

Friedrichs (1970), author of *A Sociology of Sociology,* described the traditional role of the sociologist when he wrote, "His is *not* the reformer's role
but rather a dedication to the chaste pursuit of what *is*" [p. 78]. He further
stated that the task of students entering sociology during the 1950's and
1960's ". . . was to discover empirical uniformities that can be used to predict
and control other empirical phenomena" [p. 81]. Taking this cue, sport
sociologists have gone about their work careful ". . . not to shape attitudes
and values but rather to describe and explain them" [Kenyon & Loy, 1965, p.
25]. Social amelioration and social evaluation are not the concern of today's
sport sociologist. The acquisition and establishment of a cumulative body of
knowledge *is.* While little fault can be found with the sport sociologist who
chooses to follow this particular professional role, the question remains as to
whether or not this is the *only* role for the sport sociologist to play. I think
not. The sport sociologist as sport critic is a new professional role that has
been left largely unexplored. Such a role would be consistent with traditional
scholarship a͵ '. . . the legacy of the intellectual, namely, the right to be
critical of tradition" [Gouldner, 1963, p. 45]. Mills (1967) offered an important observation about the role of the intellectual in society when he
wrote:

> The independent artist and intellectual are among the few remaining
> personalities equipped to resist and to fight the stereotyping and conse-
> quent death of genuinely lively things. Fresh perception now involves the
> capacity continually to unmask and to smash the stereotypes of vision
> and intellect with which modern communications swamp us [p. 299].

He was especially critical of social scientists who ". . . censor themselves
either by carefully selecting safe problems in the name of pure science, or by
selling such prestige as their scholarship may have for ends other than their
own" [p. 302]. The net result is the acceptance of the status quo or a fantasy
look into the future.

The fact that an increasing number of sociologists are calling for a review
of the traditional role of the sociologist has extremely important implications
for the sport sociologist. As Gouldner (1963) sees it, we are witnessing today
a clash ". . . between the older heritage of the critical intellectual and the
modern claims of the value-free professional" [p. 45]. On the methodological
front, the fact that more and more sociologists are showing a preference for
". . . the offbeat to the familiar, the vivid ethnographic detail to the dull
taxonomy, the sensuously expressive to dry analysis, and naturalistic observation to formal questionnaires . . ." [Gouldner, 1963, p. 47], also has important implications for research methodology in sociology of sport. Marx (1972)
raises a fundamental question when he asks:

> Should sociology be a disinterested calling pursued for purely intellectual
> and esthetic reasons, or should it be committed to, and involved in

solving current problems [p. 4] ?

While the question implies that a choice must be made between two distinctly different approaches, probably no choice need be made. There is certainly enough room within sociology of sport to accommodate both. The point is that there *are* choices for the sport sociologist and the "intellectual and esthetic" approach that seeks out "knowledge for knowledge's sake" or the discovery of "elegant explanatory systems" is only one approach to the study of sport. The sport sociologist who chooses instead to seek out gaps between values and actual practices, who questions established orthodoxies and through his social criticism, hopes to initiate social change, would add a new and exciting dimension to the discipline.

THE DOMINANT PARADIGM IN SOCIOLOGY OF SPORT

According to Loy and Kenyon (1969):

> . . . the social significance of sport might be profitably analyzed in terms of its contribution to the functional problems of society, especially to the problem of pattern-maintenance and tension management [p. 86].

More recently, Loy and Segrave (1974) reiterated the same point of view when they advised that "the best of all possible methodological worlds is of course, to utilize a complete social system model of data collection and analysis" [p. 291]. Generally speaking, the investigative paradigm which has served sociology of sport most often has been one which has focused on ". . . how well sport serves the existing social system when confronted with its 'functional problems' of adaptation, attaining collective goals . . . assuring continuity of beliefs and orientations, training, integrating, and coordinating" [Hoch, 1972, p. 15]. This paradigm, developed in the United States by Talcott Parsons and Robert Mertons among others, assumes an equilibrating social order and the "social system" as its basic conception of society. The task of the sport sociologist, given this paradigm, becomes one of describing, explaining, and predicting the ways in which sport contributes to society. Lee (1973) refers to it as the "managerial-bureaucratic" or "functional-systemic" paradigm in his discussion of the different ideologies present within contemporary American sociology. He describes the paradigm in the following way:

> This systemic structure, with congeries of subsystems nested within it, is usually subjected to what is called functional analysis, a concern with how the system's parts satisfy the system's and its members' needs and maintain an adequate degree of integration and balance. This usually implies the indispensability of certain functions in the maintenance of the system as an ongoing enterprise. . . . If "the system" is to persist, these needs "must" be satisfied [p. 124].

While the application of this paradigm to the study of sport groups and the interrelationships among sport, culture, and society has contributed in some important ways to the body of knowledge of sociology of sport, it remains nevertheless an ideology vulnerable to the weaknesses inherent in all paradigms. Hoch (1972) has criticized the "functional-systemic" paradigm and its followers because

> In their characteristic eagerness to manage the tensions of this society, our academic sociologists . . . completely lose sight of what kind of society this is: Does a small power elite dominate? Are the masses of poor and black people oppressed? Do the existing patterns of this society *deserve* to be managed and maintained [p. 15]?

Questions such as these raise serious doubts as to the utility of this paradigm and, at the least, encourage the sport sociologist to seek out alternatives. For the sociologist concerned with the dignity and possible autonomy of "mass man," a paradigm which places primary emphasis (Lee, 1973) on ". . . how he can be managed, led to preconceived goals, and with how the bureaucratized 'system' can be maintained and flourish" [pp. 125–126] would seem to fall short of the mark. Given this perspective of man and society, it is understandable why its adherents contend so strongly that they must be "value-free"in their scientific work. To do otherwise would reveal the paradigm's glaring insensitivity to the plight of "mass man."

Functional-Systemic Sociology of Sport as "Normal Science"

Another way of looking at "functional-systemic sociology of sport" is to see it for what it is, namely, a paradigm, or theoretical achievement that, as Kuhn (1970) stated:

> . . . was sufficiently unprecedented to attract an enduring group of adherents away from competing modes of theoretical activity. Simultaneously, it was sufficiently open-ended to leave all sorts of problems for the redefined group of practitioners to resolve [p. 10].

According to Kuhn, whenever a scientific or theoretical achievement shares these two essential characteristics we have a paradigm, ". . . a term that relates closely to 'normal science' " [p. 10]. We have a normal science wherever researchers share a similar paradigm and are ". . . commited to the same rules and standards for scientific practice. That commitment and the apparent consensus it produces are prerequisites for normal science, i.e., for the genesis and continuation of a particular research tradition" [Kuhn, 1970, p. 11].

While sociology of sport's adoption of the functional-systemic paradigm and the esoteric research it engenders can be rightfully construed as a sign of the discipline's maturity, it remains, nevertheless, a paradigm incapable of explaining all the facts with which it is confronted. It is understandable, however, why sociology of sport selected this paradigm over others, such as a conflict paradigm. Besides having descriptive value, its Parsonian character is in keeping with the theoretical proclivities of professional sociology, thus ensuring for itself a hospitable reception within the sociological community. The danger of this or any other paradigm occurs when the sport sociologist takes it for granted and feels that ". . . he need no longer, in his major works, attempt to build his field anew . . ." [Kuhn, 1970, p. 19]. It is this type of laxity that sport sociologists can ill afford. Such "mopping-up" operations (Kuhn, 1970) as ". . . extending the knowledge of those facts that the paradigm displays as particularly revealing . . . increasing the extent of the match between those facts and the paradigm's predictions, and . . . further articulation of the paradigm itself" [p. 24] can seriously retard the growth and development of the discipline if pursued to the exclusion of all else. Sociology of sport is too young a discipline to become strapped to one particular theoretical orientation; a "normalized" sociology of sport would not seem in the best interests of the discipline at this point in its history. As a final thought Kuhn's discussion of "normal science as puzzle solving" is particularly relevant to sociology of sport. The fascination of the "normal" research problem for the social scientist lies in his achieving the expected in an unexpected way. The solution, Kuhn says of ". . . all sorts of complex instrumental, conceptual, and mathematical puzzles" [p. 36] becomes the scientist's major interest. If this be true, then it would seem imperative for sociology of sport not to engage exclusively in the exercise of puzzle-solving (Kuhn, 1970) lest it blind itself to looking at ". . . those socially important problems that are not reducible to the puzzle form, because they cannot be stated in terms of the conceptual and instrumental tools the paradigm supplies" [p. 37].

NEW PARADIGMS FOR SOCIOLOGY OF SPORT

Brown and Gilmartin (1969) after reviewing a total of 402 articles and papers that appeared in the *American Sociological Review* and the *American Journal of Sociology* during the periods 1940–41 and 1965–66, concluded that ". . . rarely encountered in our sample were intensive investigations of specific concrete social situations" [pp. 289–290]. They further noted that the ". . . construction and testing of predictive hypotheses concerning the interrelations of abstract variables" [p. 290] has become the dominant sociological orientation among researchers. And finally, the authors cautioned, "If sociology is the scientific study of human social behavior, then behavior other than verbal statements of opinions and feelings warrants intensive investigation" [p. 290]. Similar charges can be made with some justification against sport-related sociological research. It too is characterized by a lack of "concreteness," a concern for the abstract over the practical, and a preference for the recordings of verbal statements rather than the observation of social behavior. As Loy and Segrave (1974) recently noted in an excellent review of research methodology in sociology of sport:

Nevertheless, our survey of research subsumed under the rubric of sport sociology indicates that there is a notable lack of "strictly" sociological investigations into the nature of sport [p. 290].

Given the somewhat mythical notion of a "value-free" sociology of sport, the inherent biases of the functional-systemic paradigm, the constraints imposed by a "normalized" discipline, and the research returns yielded so far, it would behoove sport sociologists to seriously consider the initiation and development of alternative value orientations and investigative paradigms. Loy and Segrave (1974) have identified three such alternatives for sport sociology. First, they see a *sociology through sport,* in which the basic emphasis is placed on testing general sociological propositions and developing sociological models and theories. Second, they identify an *action-oriented sport sociology,* devoted to the solving of practical problems and achieving a more humanistic understanding of sport. And third, they envision a *sociology of sport,* ". . . emphasizing the generation and verification of substantive theories about the significant social phenomenon of sport" [p. 292]. It is in this spirit of identifying "alternatives" for the sport sociologist that the following suggestions are made.

Muckraking or "Dirty" Sociology of Sport

For those sport sociologists who believe that critical research is a necessary prerequisite for social change, muckraking or "dirty" sociology of sport may be an alternative worth considering. According to Marx (1972), muckraking sociology is a particular style of social science research which ". . . documents conditions that clash with basic values, fixes responsibility for them and is capable of generating moral outrage" [p. 2]. The sport sociologist who engages in muckraking research would be primarily interested in searching out and publicly exposing misconduct on the part of prominent individuals as well as discovering scandal and incriminating evidence. For example, social issues such as drug usage in sports, illegal recruiting in intercollegiate athletics, the bureaucratic power of the National Collegiate Athletic Association, racial discrimination in professional baseball, sexism in American sports, and the effects of adult-sponsored athletic programs on preadolescent value systems, would be of particular interest to the muckraking sport sociologist. For obvious reasons, such a perspective would neither be especially popular among establishment-oriented sport sociologists nor among college and university officials who have traditionally encouraged, either explicitly or implicitly, a conservative "don't rock the boat" attitude from their faculties. It remains to be seen whether muckraking sport sociology with its ". . . exposé, sacred cow-smashing, anti-establishment, counter-intuitive, even subversive quality . . ." [Marx, 1972, p. 3] could be practiced in an institutional setting. It would be extremely unfortunate if it could not be, because there would seem to be great value in a perspective which points out discrepancies between the abstract values of the sports establishment, such as character building, and its actual practices. By discovering and raising various social issues as a result of its probing and critical analysis of the sport institution, the sport sociologist would be performing an important educative role for the public at large.

A distinction should here be made between muckraking sociology of sport and the suggestion by Loy and Segrave (1974) of action-oriented sport sociology, mentioned earlier. For the muckraking sport sociologist, the "problems" of racism, sexism, militarism, and elitism in American sport would not be viewed as "disorders" or evidence of the breakdown of the sport institution, but rather as ". . . the products of *organized* efforts—the reality of deliberate intent . . . outgrowths of an ongoing value system which emphasizes the merits of economic gain at the expense of human dignity" [Willhelm, 1970, p. 120].

From a methodological point of view, Marx (1972) has written:

> To be credible, muckraking research must respect the traditional canons of science and be judged by them, although it may not be inspired by the esthetic contemplation of ideas for their own sake or the desire to advance an abstract body of knowledge [p. 7].

One could envision the muckraking sport sociologist making much greater use of such research methodologies as participant observation, ethnography, case study, role and institutional analysis.

Muckraking sociology of sport would be no less an ideology than functional-systemic sociology of sport and would carry with it its own set of biases and domain assumptions about man and society. According to Marx, the potential pitfalls of "committed" research include:

1. The conflict in the researcher between maintaining scientific objectivity in the face of his own strong value positions.

2. The inability of descriptive documentation to add measurably to a cumulative body of knowledge.

3. The failure to solve social problems, thereby making muckraking research little more than shocking exposé.

In any case, for the sport sociologist who believes that expediency and social change take priority over the building of a theoretically based social science, muckraking sociology may be the answer. If, as Marx (1972) believes, the immediate value of critical research lies in its contribution ". . . to greater public awareness and more sophisticated and humane theories about social issues" [p. 29], then the sport sociologist who ventures forth into the world of "dirty" sport may have a profound effect on the future course of sport in American society.

Humanist-Existential Sociology of Sport

Closely related to muckraking sociology of sport is the humanist-existential paradigm, one of the newest and most roughly defined paradigms presently vying for consideration within academic sociology. Consequently, its biases, domain assumptions, and research methodologies, as they relate specifically to the study of sport, are still to be defined. For the present, only a brief discussion of the flavor and spirit of this unique and promising paradigm will be attempted. Lee (1973) suggests that the humanist-existential paradigm ". . . calls for a man-centered sociology in the service of human needs and goals as they are popularly defined" [p. 128]. He defines an "existential humanist" as someone who deals with sociology and social science only insofar as they shed light on ". . . the current problems that impinge upon people's lives" [p. xi]. Lee's ". . . intellectual focus is upon what exists and upon what is most relevant to man" [p. xiii]. Sociologists who assume this intellectual orientation believe (Lee, 1973) that

> . . . first causes (or origins) and ultimate consequences, as well as absolutes and infinites, are irrelevant except as human artifacts to be considered as such. Methods and tenets useful in other sciences are to be treated as possible helpful suggestions. Techniques of research and theories must serve human understanding of man's lot [p. xii].

Sport sociologists should be wary of paradigms bearing this label, for, as Lee points out:

> Just calling some methodological mumbo jumbo *humanist* does not make it relevant to human concerns. Just labeling some philosophical gamesmanship *existential* does not make it an acceptable interpretation of events [p. 129].

Whereas muckraking sociology of sport is primarily interested in searching out sport-related social issues and exposing them to an analytical process (Marx, 1972) which moves ". . . from documentation, to causal analysis, to policy suggestions, to actual policy implementation of a given piece of research" [p. 23], a humanist-existential sociology of sport would deal in a more philosophical way (Lee, 1973) with the relevant implications of ". . . social control, conflict, and exploitation, of degradation, degeneracy, creativity, and nobility and of individual, group and societal multivalence" [p. 129] as they relate to individuals involved in sport.

Besides expressing concern about those institutional problems which impinge on the athlete's life, such as loss of freedom, the sport sociologist with a humanist-existential orientation would also be interested in discovering the self-actualizing potential of the sport experience. In order to do so, he might find useful the methods of logical and phenomenological description which some sport philosophers have used (Kleinman, 1968, 1972) in order to reveal the essence of the sport experience.

Peter Berger (1963), a sociologist whose work has been instrumental in the development of a humanistically based paradigm, explains his perspective in the following way:

> ... if there is something like a sociological anthropology, there may also be something like a sociological humanism ... sociological understanding can be an important part of a certain sense of life that is peculiarly modern, that has its own genius of compassion and that can be the foundation of a genuine humanism [pp. 161-162].

Berger hints that he may also be a muckraker at heart when he observes:

> Before the tribunals that condemn some men to indignity because of their race or sexuality, or that condemn any man to death, this humanism becomes protest, resistance and rebellion ... compassion can become the starting point of revolution against systems of inhumanity sustained by myth [p. 162].

To summarize, while the specific details of the humanist-existential paradigm are still to be determined, the sport sociologist whose consuming interest is in the world of men, and specifically in the social and emotional well-being of individuals involved in sport situations, should find this perspective an especially rewarding one.

THE FUTURE OF SPORT SOCIOLOGY

American sociology of sport has traveled a somewhat uneven but nevertheless exciting path over the last decade. This fledgling discipline has made rapid strides in developing a theoretical and scholarly cumulative body of knowledge. Research methodologies appropriate to the study of sport have been developed and sophisticated statistical techniques devised for data analysis. Propositions, models, and theories, some borrowed from sociology, others developed specifically for sport, are appearing with increasing frequency. As a result, certain trends have emerged which, when taken together, give sociology of sports a distinctive character at this juncture in its history. An attempt has been made to set forth some of these characteristics and to identify what might be called a "modal sport sociologist." We find that he is someone who subscribes most passionately to a "value-free" orientation; he draws a distinction between himself as a working social scientist and as a private citizen; his bias leans toward the functional-systemic investigative paradigm; he views his professional task as helping to build a cumulative body of knowledge; and lastly, he is someone who is very much concerned with gaining professional respectability within the academic community.

While there can be no quarrel with the discipline's progress to date, there is an uneasy feeling which suggests that sociology of sport has become "locked into" a single paradigm that may eventually inhibit its future growth and development, its general acceptance by the public, and ultimately its value to man and society. Gouldner (1963) has observed:

> Social science can never be fully accepted in a society, or by a part of it, without paying its way; this means it must manifest both its relevance and concern for the contemporary human predicament. Unless the value relevances of sociological inquiry are made plainly evident . . . it must inevitably be scorned by laymen as pretentious word-mongering [p. 43].

In order to guard against sociology of sport becoming "pretentious word-mongering," alternative value orientations have been discussed and new investigative paradigms presented. It is hoped that these ideas will prove stimulating and provide sociology of sport with the challenge it needs if it is to mature as a discipline and realize its fullest potential for mankind.

REFERENCES

Berger, B. M. Review of *Power, politics and people: The collected essays of C. Wright Mills,* edited by I. L. Horowitz, *New York Times Book Review,* April 28, 1963, pp. 3, 50.

Berger, P. L. *Invitation to sociology: A humanistic perspective.* New York: Anchor, 1963.

Bierstedt, R. Social science and social values. In S. Koenig, R. D. Hopper, and F. Gross (Eds.), *Sociology—A book of readings.* Englewood Cliffs, N.J.: Prentice-Hall, 1953.

Brown, J. S., & Gilmartin, B. G. Sociology today: Lacunae, emphases and surfeits. *American Sociologist,* 1969, **4**, 283–291.

Clark, K. B. The psychology of the ghetto. In P. I. Rose (Ed.), *The study of society.* New York: Random House, 1967.

Friedrichs, R. W. *A sociology of sociology.* New York: Free Press, 1970.

Gouldner, A. W. Anti-minotaur: The myth of a value-free sociology. In M. Stein and A. Vidich (Eds.), *Sociology on trial.* Englewood Cliffs, N.J.: Prentice-Hall, 1963.

Gouldner, A. W. Sociology today does not need a Karl Marx or an Isaac Newton: It needs a V. I. Lenin, *Psychology Today,* 1971, **5**, 53–57 and 96–97. (a)

Gouldner, A. W. *The coming crisis of western sociology.* New York: Equinox, 1971. (b)

Hoch, P. *Rip off the big game.* New York: Anchor, 1972.

Kane, J. E., & Murray, C. Suggestions for the sociological study of sport. In J. E. Kane (Ed.), *Readings in physical education.* London: Physical Education Association, 1966.

Kenyon, G. S. A sociology of sport: On becoming a sub-discipline. In R. C. Brown, Jr., and B. J. Cratty (Eds.), *New perspectives of man in action.* Englewood Cliffs, N.J.: Prentice-Hall, 1969.

Kenyon, G. S., & Loy, J. W. Toward a sociology of sport—A plea for the study of physical activity as a sociological and social psychological phenomenon. *Journal of Health, Physical Education and Recreation,* 1965, **36**, 24-25 and 68-69.

Kleinman, S. Toward a non-theory of sport. *Quest,* 1968, **10**, 29-34.

Kleinman, S. The significance of human movement: A phenomenological approach. In E. W. Gerber (Ed.), *Sport and the body: A philosophical symposium.* Philadelphia: Lea and Febiger, 1972.

Kuhn, T. S. *The structure of scientific revolutions.* Chicago: University of Chicago Press, 1970.

Lee, A. M. *Toward humanist sociology.* Englewood Cliffs, N.J.: Prentice-Hall, 1973.

Loy, J. W. Sociology and physical education. In R. N. Singer et al. (Eds.), *Physical education: An interdisciplinary approach.* New York: Macmillan, 1972.

Loy, J. W., & Kenyon, G. S. (Eds.) *Sport, culture, and society: A reader on the sociology of sport.* New York: Macmillan, 1969.

Loy, J. W., & Segrave, J. O. Research methodology in the sociology of sport. In J. H. Wilmore (Ed.), *Exercise and sport sciences reviews.* Vol. 2. New York: Academic Press, 1974.

Marx, G. T. (Ed.) *Muckraking sociology: Research as social criticism.* New Brunswick, N.J.: Transaction Books, 1972.

Mills, C. W. The social role of the intellectual. In I. L. Horowitz (Ed.), Power politics and people: *The collected essays of C. Wright Mills.* London: Oxford University Press, 1967.

Scott, J. Introduction. In P. Hoch, *Rip off the big game.* New York: Anchor, 1972.

Willhelm, S. M. Elites, scholars, and sociologists. In L. T. Reynolds and J. M. Reynolds (Eds.), *The sociology of sociology.* New York: David McKay, 1970.

FOR FURTHER READING

1. Greendorfer, S. L., "The Social Science of Sport: A Need for Further Knowledge," *78th Proceedings of the National College Physical Education Association for Men,* 1975, pp. 25-33.

2. Gruneau, R. S., "Conflicting Standards and Problems of Personal Action in the Sociology of Sport," *Quest* **30** (Summer): 89-90, 1978.

3. Loy, J. W., "Sociological Analysis of Sport." In *Physical Education: An Interdisciplinary Approach,* eds. Robert N. Singer, et al, New York: Macmillan, 1972, pp. 207–228.

4. Lüschen, G., "The Development and Scope of a Sociology of Sport," *American Corr. Ther. J.* **29** (March-April): 1975.

5. McPherson, B. G., "Past, Present, and Future Perspectives for Research in Sport Sociology," *International Review of Sport Sociology* **10** (1): 55-72, 1975.

6. McPherson, B. G., "Avoiding Chaos in the Sociology of Sport Brickyard," *Quest* **30** (Summer): 72-79, 1978.

7. Sage, G. H., "The Current Status and Trends of Sport Sociology," In *The Dimensions of Sport Sociology* ed. March L. Krotee. West Point, New York: Leisure Press, 1978.

8. Snyder, E. E. and Spreitzer, E., "Basic Assumptions in the World of Sport," *Quest* **24** (Summer): 3-9, 1975.

CHAPTER 2

SOCIOL — CULTURAL ASPECTS OF AMERICAN SPORT

A review of the past helps to explain current conditions and may even provide a basis for the prediction of future events; it enables us to understand why things are as they now are and to predict what might reasonably be expected in the future. The study of any social phenomena which is based entirely upon the present is bound to reveal a very incomplete picture of reality. Current social circumstances are related to events of the past. Social institutions, organizations, and processes of the past have, after all, produced the present.

Contemporary sport in the United States owes its structure and functions to the past. The major historical forces which have molded American sport are the religious influence of the colonial Puritans, industrialization and urbanization in the nineteenth century, the growth and development of universal public education, and the emergence of mass media during this century.

In the past 200 years the United States has grown from a small number of widely scattered and disunited settlements located along the eastern seaboard of North America into the most modern and industrially powerful nation in the world. It has also become the most advanced nation in sports. Americans are sports enthusiasts, and their natural love for sports, fostered by a variety of historical, social, and economic institutions, has generated sports into a tremendous national pastime. From a nation of farmers who had little time for games and sports, except for special occasions, the United States has developed into a nation of urbanites who watch ten to twenty hours of sports on television each weekend and almost consider it a duty to participate in some form of sport for recreation. Social, religious, economic, and geographic factors have all contributed to this development. Therefore, to understand the character of sport in contemporary society, we must examine the factors responsible for molding American sport from a historical perspective.

Colonial America was divided into three distinct geographic regions. The New England colonies were settled by religious dissenters who were, ironically, often intolerant of the views of others. Religion dominated the lives of these people, and the prevailing attitude toward games and sports was one of condemnation. The reward for toil and hard work was salvation; games and sports were a temptation that was the handiwork of Satan. In the Middle Atlantic colonies there was no religious uniformity. A variety of religions—Catholicism, Lutheranism, and Quakerism—were prominent. Strong religious prohibition of games and sports, while not absent in this region, was not as dominant as it was further north. In the early Southern colonies subsistence living left little time for leisure activities, but the plantation system which emerged changed lifestyles. With their one-crop economy and social structure of aristocrats at one extreme and slaves at the other, the Southern colonists exhibited a very heterogeneous sport pattern. Since many of the plantation owners were members of the liberal Anglican Church or other tolerant groups, games and sports were enjoyed by these Southerners without church disapproval.

Sports retained the form of informal games up to the late 1880's, when there was a virtual explosion of organized sports. Sports clubs, college and professional sports, and sports fads all combined to plunge Americans into an obsession with sports. In the first reading, John R. Betts, the late social historian, describes the various factors that were responsible for the growth and development of sport in the half century from 1850 to 1900.

According to Betts, industrialization and urbanization were the two fundamental factors responsible for the developments in sport during this era. Betts shows how social conditions were altered by technological, industrial, and urbanization trends and how these in turn influenced sports. Betts' article is an excellent work of social history, and is considered by many to be a classic study on American sport, since it so eloquently accentuates the reciprocal relations between sport and society.

The second reading, authored by Joel Spring, extends Betts' examination of the development of organized sport by bringing the analysis into the twentieth century, but narrowing the focus more directly on school sports. It was during the first thirty years of this century that interscholastic and intercollegiate athletics gained a firm foothold in secondary schools and colleges, and Spring describes how the formal gymnastic exercises which characterized physical education in the latter nineteenth and early twentieth century were supplanted by athletics. Indeed by the 1920's physical education had become subordinated to athletics.

According to Spring, one of the major ideological foundations on which mass sport and school sport was promoted in this era was that sport and leisure were to serve as antidotes for urbanization and industrialization, that these activities would serve as correctives for the ills of an urban-industrial society.

In the process of fostering sports participation, school and college sports became big business, and instead of achieving the goal of mass participation the result was mass spectatorship. Moreover, the dream that athletics would reduce the monotony and boredom of work, reduce crime and violence, provide wise use of leisure time, and promote democratic citizenship traits has not been achieved. Spring pessimistically concludes that much of what passes today as use of leisure time through sport is merely passive television viewing of events.

The social factors that underlie the commercialization of modern professional sport in America is the primary focus of the third reading by R. Terry Furst. The author shows how professional sports have grown at an incredible rate in the past twenty years. Furst uses a play-work analysis to illustrate how the major professional sports have been transformed from basically play activities to work forms. The transformation of play to work is described for baseball, football, hockey, and basketball; in each case the progression from inception to codification to professionalization is recounted.

The author then discusses the factors that have influenced the change from play to work. He concludes with examples of how rules changes, spectator accouterments, and publicity stunts have been employed to attract spectators and suggests that these innovations have altered the games to support the entertainment function of sports.

The final reading in this chapter, by George H. Sage, takes the theme that sport is a microcosm of society—that societal values tend to be reinforced in sport and that values learned in sport are probably internalized and promoted in social relations outside sport.

The "success" value is singled out for analysis since it is the most salient value in American society. Sage argues that the achievement of success is one of the most dominating motives in American life, and that the drive for success overrides moral and ethical considerations for many people. He then illustrates the elective affinity between the success value in society and in sport. He describes some of the more dysfunctional consequences of this obsessive success orientation in both American society and American sport. The essay concludes with a plea for social change in the form of values that emphasize cooperation, self worth based on human dignity, and humane concern for others rather than the achievement of material and psychic success at any cost.

THE TECHNOLOGICAL REVOLU-
TION AND THE RISE OF SPORT,
1850-1900

John Rickards Betts

The roots of our sporting heritage lie in the horse racing and fox hunting of the colonial era, but the main features of modern sport appeared only in the middle years of the nineteenth century.[1] Organization, journalistic exploitation, commercialization, intercommunity competition, and sundry other developments increased rapidly after 1850 as the agrarian nature of sport gave way gradually to the influences of urbanization and industrialization. Just as the Industrial Revolution was to alter the interests, habits, and pursuits of all classes of society, it was to leave a distinct impress on the development of sport.

Many other factors were responsible for the directions taken by sport in the half century from 1850 to 1900. Continuing rural influences, the decline of Puritan orthodoxy, the English athletic movement, the immigrant, frontier traditions of manliness and strength, and the contributions of energetic sportsmen were to have a significant effect on the sporting scene. Industrialization and urbanization, however, were more fundamentally responsible for the changes and developments in sport during the next generation than any other cause. Manufacturers, seeking cheap labor, encouraged immigration; factories were most efficiently run in larger towns and cities; urban masses, missing the rustic pleasures of hunting and fishing, were won to the support of commercialized entertainment and spectator sports; the emergence of a commercial aristocracy and a laboring class resulted in distinctions every bit as strong in sport as in other social matters; and the urgency of physical exercise as life became more sedentary was readily recognized.

The revolution in manufacturing methods, which had such profound social consequences for the American way of life, derived from a powerful inventive spirit which flourished throughout the nineteenth century. From England and western Europe we borrowed many mechanical innovations and most of our scientific theory, but Americans demonstrated a native ability soon recognized everywhere as "Yankee ingenuity." These inventions were to revolutionize transportation, communication, manufacturing, finance, and all the many facets of economic life. Although the tendency in narrating the history of sport has been to emphasize the role of individuals, the changing

John Rickards Betts, "The Technological Revolution and the Rise of Sport, 1850–1900." *Mississippi Valley Historical Review,* XL (September, 1953), pp. 231–256. Copyright © 1953 by the Organization of American Historians. Reprinted by permission.

social scene was of equal importance in directing sport into the channels it eventually took in modern society. The impact of invention had a decisive influence on the rise of sport in the latter half of the century. By 1900 sport had attained an unprecedented prominence in the daily lives of millions of Americans, and this remarkable development had been achieved in great part through the steamboat, the railroad, the telegraph, the penny press, the electric light, the streetcar, the camera, the bicycle, the automobile, and the mass production of sporting goods.

The transformation of the United States from a rural-agrarian to an urban-industrial society, of course, affected the development of sport in other ways. Urbanization brought forth the need for commercialized spectator sports, while industrialization gradually provided the standard of living and leisure time so vital to the support of all forms of recreation. But it is the relationship of invention to sport, and that alone, which constitutes the theme of this study.

Early American interest in outdoor exercise was largely confined to hunting, fishing, horse racing, field sports, and the informal games of the local schoolyard. As the nation became more commercially minded in the decades after the War of 1812, many of those who lived in rapidly growing cities became concerned over the sedentary habits of clerks, office workers, and businessmen. In the years before 1850 there emerged a limited interest in rowing, running, prize fighting, cricket, fencing, and similar activities, but the only organized sport which excited the minds of most Americans was the turf. A more general interest in horse racing appeared in the 1820s and 1830s, and many jockey clubs held meetings attended by throngs of spectators in their carriages and barouches.[2]

From the early years of the century steamboat captains engaged in racing on the Hudson, Ohio, Mississippi, and other rivers, and the steamboat served as a common carrier of sports crowds. By the 1850s it became an indispensable means of transport to the races along the eastern seaboard and in the Mississippi Valley. As one of the first products of the age of steam it played a significant role in the rise of the turf and outdoor games.[3]

In the years preceding the Civil War the turf was also encouraged by the development of a railroad network. As early as 1838 Wade Hampton was transporting race horses to Charleston by rail;[4] in 1839 the Nashville Railroad was carrying New Orleans crowds to the Metairie Course;[5] in 1842 the Long Island Railroad was already suffering the abuse of irate passengers swarming to the races; and three years later it carried some 30,000 passengers to the Fashion-Peytona race at more than fifty cents each.[6] Kentucky became the leading breeding center for thoroughbreds and Louisville could announce in 1851: "Lexington, Georgetown, Frankfort, Paris and other towns in this State, are now but a short ride from our city by railroad conveyance. Horses can come from Lexington here in five hours."[7] The famous trotter Flora Temple began barnstorming tours; racing and trotting benefited from the cooperation of railroad lines; and "speed trials" at agricultural fairs during the 1850s were attended by excursionists.[8] Other outdoor sports also profited from the interest shown by certain lines. When excitement over rowing began to catch on in the late 1830s the first boat shipped west of the Appalachians went by way of the Erie Canal.[9] It was a railroad, however, which encouraged the holding of the first intercollegiate rowing race between Harvard and Yale in 1852.[10] Baseball clubs were organized throughout the East and Midwest during the decade and the National Association of Base Ball Players was formed in 1857, soon after both sections had been connected by rail. Chicago had its first baseball team in 1856, two years after it was linked by rail to Baltimore, Maryland, and Portland, Maine. In 1860 the Excelsior Club of Brooklyn made a tour of upper New York state. Most of the early prize fights were held along the rivers served by steamboats; the Harlem Railroad carried fight crowds in the early 1850s to the Awful Gardiner-William Hastings (*alias* Dublin Tricks) match sixty miles north of New York City and to a highly publicized championship fight at Boston Four Corners, New York,[11] and the John Morrissey-John Heanan match on the Canadian shore near Niagara Falls in 1858 was advertised by the Erie Railroad.[12]

The Civil War failed to halt turf meetings and outdoor recreation in the North. It was, however, only with the return of peace that the nation felt a new sporting impulse and began to give enthusiastic support to the turf, the diamond, the ring, and other outdoor activities. The game of baseball, spreading from cities to towns and villages, became a national fad, and matches were scheduled with distant communities. A tournament at Rockford, Illinois, in 1866 was attended by teams from Detroit, Milwaukee, Dubuque, and Chicago.[13] In 1869 Harry Wright's Cincinnati Red Stockings were able to make a memorable transcontinental tour from Maine to California; a New Orleans club visited Memphis, St. Louis, and Cincinnati; and eastern teams condescended to travel as far west as the Queen City. The Erie line offered to convey a New Orleans club, then visiting Cincinnati, to New York and return at half-fare rates. When the Cincinnati Red Stockings made their tour by boat, local lines, and the Union Pacific in 1869 it was reported: "The boys have received every attention from the officers of the different roads. . . . At all the stations groups stare us almost out of countenance, having heard of the successful exploits of the Club through telegrams of the Western Associated Press."[14]

Baseball clubs made use of the rapidly expanding networks of the 1870s, and the organization of the National League in 1876 was only possible with the continued development of connecting lines. In the 1886 edition of *Spalding's Official Base Ball Guide* the Michigan Central advertised: "The cities that have representative clubs contesting for the championship pennant this year are—Chicago, Boston, New York, Washington, Kansas City, Detroit, St. Louis and Philadelphia. All of these cities are joined together by the Michigan Central Railroad. This road has enjoyed almost a monopoly of

Base Ball travel in former years." Throughout the 1870s and 1880s the expanding railroad network played an indispensable role in the popularization of the "national game."[15]

A widespread interest in thoroughbred and trotting races also was in great part sustained by railroad expansion. In 1866 the Harlem, Rensselaer and Saratoga Railroad Company, realizing the advantage of encouraging the racing public, arranged to convey race horses at cost by express train from New York to Saratoga. *Turf, Field and Farm* pointed to the need for better transportation arrangements and predicted, "The completion of the Pacific Railroad will not be without effect upon the blood stock interests of the great West."[16] Jerome Park, Long Branch, and Gravesend catered to New York crowds, Baltimore attracted huge throngs of sportsmen, and in California racing was encouraged by the building of lines into the interior of the state. In the 1870s western turfmen began sending their horses by rail to eastern tracks, the Grand Circuit linked Hartford, Springfield, Poughkeepsie, and Utica with Rochester, Buffalo, and Cleveland, and racing associations formed in virtually every section. When Mollie McCarthy and Ten Broeck raced at Louisville in 1877, "Masses of strangers arrived by train, extra trains and steamboats." People from "all over the land" attended the Kentucky Derby in 1885, the City Council declared a holiday, and sixteen carloads of horses were sent from Nashville to Louisville.[17] Agricultural fairs, with the cooperation of numerous companies, drew thousands to their fairground tracks, and the railroads encouraged intersectional meetings by introducing special horse cars in the middle eighties.[18]

In the decades after the Civil War an apologetic but curious public acquired a "deplorable" interest in prize fighting, and railroad officials were not slow to capitalize on the crowd appeal of pugilism despite its illegality. When Mike McCoole met Aaron Jones in 1867 at Busenbark Station, Ohio, "Tickets were openly sold for excursion trains to the bout" and sporting men from the East were in attendance, while another McCoole fight in 1869 encouraged the lines to run specials from Cincinnati and other nearby cities.[19] After 1881 John L. Sullivan, the notorious "Boston Strong Boy," went on grand tours of the athletic clubs, opera houses, and theaters of the country, his fights in the New Orleans area with Paddy Ryan, Jake Kilrain, James J. Corbett luring fans who jammed the passenger coaches. When the Great John L. met Kilrain near Richburg, Mississippi, in 1889, the Northeastern Railroad carried a tumultuous crowd from New Orleans to the site, even though Governor Robert Lowry of Mississippi issued a proclamation against the affair and called out armed guards to prevent any invasion of the state. After the brawl the Governor requested the attorney general "to begin proceedings to forfeit the charter of the Northeastern railroad."[20] Railroad companies expressed only a minor concern for such sporadic events, it is true, but the prize ring was greatly aided by their cooperation.[21]

Poor connections, uncomfortable cars, and the absence of lines in rural sections remained a problem for some years.[22] Many of the difficulties and inconveniences of travel remained throughout these expansive years of rail-roading, but all sports were encouraged by the improved transportation of the post-bellum era. Immediately after the war a New York crew visited Pittsburgh to participate in a regatta held on the Monongahela River.[23] The first inter-collegiate football game between Rutgers and Princeton was attended by a group of students riding the train pulled by "the jerky little engine that steamed out of Princeton on the memorable morning of November 6, 1869."[24] Intercollegiate athletics depended on railroad service for carrying teams and supporters to football, baseball, and rowing, as well as track and field contests.

Harvard's crack baseball team made the first grand tour in 1870, "the most brilliant in the history of college baseball," according to Henry Chad-wick almost two decades later. Playing both amateur and professional clubs, Harvard won a majority of the games played in New Haven, Troy, Utica, Syracuse, Oswego (Canada), Buffalo, Cleveland, Cincinnati, Louisville, Chi-cago, Milwaukee, Indianapolis, Washington, Baltimore, Philadelphia, New York, and Brooklyn.[25] Amateur and professional cycling races were held throughout the country,[26] while rod and gun enthusiasts relied on branch lines into rural preserves.[27] By the closing years of the century virtually every realm of sport had shared in the powerful impact of the railroad on American life.

Almost contemporaneous with the development of a continental railroad system came the diffusion of telegraph lines throughout the nation. From its invention in 1844 the electric telegraph rapidly assumed a significant role in the dissemination of news.[28] When the Magnetic Telegraph Company's line reached New York, James Gordon Bennett's *Herald* and Horace Greeley's *Tribune* installed apparatus in 1846. Direct contact was made between the East and New Orleans two years later, largely to meet the urgent demand for quicker news from the Mexican War front. By 1861 San Francisco was connected by wire with the Atlantic coast, and throughout the war years use of the telegraph was extended in military operations.

During the pioneer years telegraphic messages were both costly and brief, and sports events were reported on a limited scale. One of the first reports by wire was that of the Tom Hyer-Yankee Sullivan brawl at Rock Point, Maryland, in 1849. A New York dispatch read, "We hope never to have to record a similar case of brutality in this country," and even Greeley, an inveterate foe of the prize ring, permitted the printing of dispatches of this brutal encounter. Interest was not confined to Baltimore, Philadelphia, and New York, for some newspapers in the West noticed it. In the next decade several fights were widely reported by telegraph. When Morrissey and Heanan fought for the American championship in Canada in 1858, anxious crowds waited at Western Union offices for the news; when Heanan met Tom Sayers In England two years later the news was spread by wire after it was brought to America by the *Vanderbilt*.[29] Horse racing and yachting news was less novel and less sensational, but Lady Suffolk's appearance on the course at the Rochester, New York, fair in 1851, the victory of Commodore John Cox Stevens' yacht *America* at Cowes in the same year, and the exciting trotting races of the decade were given extensive wire coverage.[30] When Lexington met Lecomte at New Orleans in 1855, however, there seems to have been little reporting of the race in the North. Newspapers of that section were primarily concerned in that year with the trouble in Kansas, the rise of the Republican party, the heat of the abolitionist crusade, and the public furor over the murder of pugilist William Poole.

The expansion of sporting news in ensuing years was directly related to the more general usage of telegraphy, which made possible instantaneous reporting of ball games, horse races, prize fights, yachting regattas, and other events. Box scores, betting odds, and all kinds of messages were relayed from one city to another, and by 1870 daily reports were published in many metropolitan papers. In that year the steamboat race of the *Natchez* and the *Robert E. Lee* was reported throughout the country in one of the most extensive telegraphic accounts of any nonpolitical event prior to that time.[31] Not only did the newspapers make a practice of publishing daily messages from all corners of the sporting world, but crowds formed around Western Union offices during any important contest.[32] When the Associated Press sent its representatives in 1889 to the Sullivan-Kilrain fight in New Orleans, reporters appeared from "every prominent journal in the Union," and Western Union was said to have employed 50 operators to handle 208,000 words of specials following the fight. Poolrooms and saloons were often equipped with receiving sets to keep customers and bettors posted on baseball scores and track results, while newspapers set up bulletin boards for the crowds to linger around.[33] And the business transactions of sporting clubs and associations were often carried on by wire.

Sport had emerged into such a popular topic of conversation that newspapers rapidly expanded their coverage in the 1880s and 1890s, relying in great part on messages sent over the lines from distant points. Among the leaders in this field during these formative years of "yellow journalism" were such New York papers as Bennett's *Herald*, Charles Dana's *Sun*, and Joseph Pulitzer's *World*. The sports page was not solely the result of improvements in telegraphy, however, for popular interest had encouraged the employment of specialists who were extremely quick, as were the publishers, to capitalize on the news value of sporting events. Chicago produced the pioneers in baseball writing in such masters of breezy slang and grotesque humor as Leonard Washburne, Charles Seymour, and Finley Peter Dunne. Cincinnati newspapers, staffed by experts like Harry Weldon, O. P. Caylor, and Byron (Ban) Johnson, were among the most authoritative journals in the diamond world. In 1895, when William Randolph Hearst invaded the New York field and bought the *Journal*, he immediately brought in western writers and, within a few years, developed the first sports section.[34] The telegraph retained its functional importance in recording daily box scores and racing statistics, but it was no longer the one indispensable factor it had been in earlier decades.

The Atlantic cable, successfully laid in 1866 by Cyrus Field, had overcome the mid-century handicap of reporting two- or three-weeks-old English sporting news. At the end of that year James Gordon Bennett, Jr., with the aid of the Associated Press, featured cable dispatches of the great ocean race. When the Harvard crew rowed against Oxford in a highly publicized race in 1869, "the result was flashed through the Atlantic cable as to reach New York about a quarter past one, while the news reached the Pacific Coast about nine o'clock, enabling many of the San Franciscans to discuss the subject at their breakfast-tables, and swallow the defeat with their coffee!"[35] The combination of cable and telegraph aroused a deeper interest in international sport. Nor must we ignore that forerunner of the modern radio, the wireless which was demonstrated publicly in America for the first time in the yacht races of 1899. From Samuel F. B. Morse to Guglielmo Marconi the revolution in communication had encouraged the rise of sport.

Public interest in sport was also aroused by the enlarged format and greater circulation achieved by numerous inventions which revolutionized the printing process. By 1830 the Napier double-cylinder press was imported from England and developed by R. Hoe and Company, printing those cheap and sensational papers which were the first to feature horse races, prize fights, and foot races—the *New York Sun,* the New York *Transcript,* and the Philadelphia *Public Ledger.*[36] James Gordon Bennett, Sr., recognized the value of catering to the whims of the masses and occasionally featured turf reporting in the *Herald* of the 1840s.[37] In 1846 the Hoe type-revolving cylinder press was introduced by the *Public Ledger,* enabling newspaper publishers, after improvements were made in the machine, to print 20,000 sheets an hour.[38] Other inventions facilitated the mass publication of the daily paper, making possible the sensationalized editions of Bennett, Pulitzer, and Hearst.[39] With the arrival of the new journalism of the 1880s, sporting news rapidly became a featured part of the metropolitan press.[40]

Publishers also aided in the popularization of outdoor sport throughout this whole era. From the 1830s onward sporting books appeared, the most famous of prewar authors being Henry William Herbert, whose illustrious psuedonym was Frank Forester. After the Civil War cheap methods of publication gave a great stimulus to the dime novel and the athletic almanac. While the vast majority of the thrillers and shockers concerned the Wild West or city crime, athletic stories and manuals were put out by Beadle & Adams, the leading publisher of the paper-backed dime novel.[41] After the establishment of A. G. Spalding & Brothers the *Spalding Guide* developed into the leading authority on rules of play, and all sorts of handbooks were included in the *Spalding Library of Athletic Sports.* The *New York Clipper* began publishing a theatrical and sporting *Clipper Almanac* in the 1870s, and newspapers like the New York *World,* the New York *Tribune,* the Chicago *Daily News,* the Washington *Post,* and the Brooklyn *Daily Eagle* issued almanacs listing athletic and racing records and sporting news. Richard Kyle Fox of the *National Police Gazette* published *Fox's Athletic Library* and sporting annuals. By the end of the century book publication had grown to astronomic proportions when compared to the Civil War era, and the Outing Publishing Company issued more than a hundred titles on angling, canoeing, yachting, mountain climbing, hunting, shooting, trapping, camping, cycling, and athletics.

A few dime novels had taken up the athletic theme in the 1870s, but more mature stories like Mark Sibley Severance's *Hammersmith: His Harvard Days* (1878), Noah Brooks's *Our Baseball Club* (1884), and, of course, Thomas Hughes's English classics, *Tom Brown at Rugby* and *Tom Brown at Oxford,* were responsible for the rising desire for sports fiction. By the 1890s a demand for boys' athletic stories was met in the voluminous outpouring of the heroic sporting achievements of Gilbert Patten's "Frank Merriwell."[42] Along with the newspaper and the sporting journal the field of publishing, with its improved techniques and expanded output, did much to attract attention to athletics at the turn of the century.

Much of the angling and hunting equipment and horseman's supplies came from England in the colonial era, but in the years before and after the American Revolution several dealers in sporting wares appeared in Philadelphia, New York, and Boston. From the early years of the nineteenth century merchants and gunsmiths in Kentucky supplied the settlers west of the Appalachian range.[43] Field sports were still enjoyed mainly by schoolboys and sportsmen with their simple rods in the 1840s and 1850s, but from the 1830s onward fishing and hunting purely for recreation developed into a sporting fad, the end of which is not in sight. Charles Hallock, noted sportsman, conservationist, and journalist of the post-Civil War era recalled how the rural folk of Hampshire County, Massachusetts, responded to a visiting sportsman of the 1840s who brought with him a set of highly finished rods, reels, and fly-fishing equipment.

> Ah! those were halcyon days. No railroads disturbed the quiet seclusion of that mountain nook. . . . Twice a week an oldfashioned coach dragged heavily up the hill into the hamlet and halted in front of the house which was at once post-office, tavern, and miscellaneous store. . . . One day it brought a passenger. . . . He carried a leather hand-bag and a handful of rods in a case. The village *quidnuncs* said he was a surveyor. He allowed he was from Troy and had "come to go a-fishing." From that stranger I took my first lesson in fly-fishing.[44]

By the 1850s the manufacture of cricket bats and stumps, billiard tables, archery equipment, guns, fishing tackle, and other sporting accessories was carried on by a host of individual craftsmen and by such concerns as J. W.

Brunswick & Brothers of Cincinnati, Bassler of Boston, Conroy's of New York, and John Krider's "Sportsmen's Depot" in Philadelphia.

Mass-production methods of manufacture were still in their infancy in post-Civil War decades, but the factory system became ever more deeply entrenched. While the sporting goods business never attained any great economic importance in the nineteenth century,[45] much of the popularity for athletic games and outdoor recreation was due to standardized manufacturing of baseball equipment, bicycles, billiard tables, sporting rifles, fishing rods, and various other items.[46] Although most American youths played with restitched balls and a minimum of paraphernalia, college athletes, cycling enthusiasts, and professional ballplayers popularized the products of George B. Ellard of Cincinnati, Peck & Snyder of New York, and other concerns.[47]

By the end of the century A. G. Spalding & Brothers was the nationally recognized leader in this field. As a renowned pitcher for the Boston and Chicago clubs and then as the promoter of the latter, Albert Spalding had turned to the merchandising of athletic goods in 1876.[48] One of the most avid sponsors of the national game, he branched out into varied sports in the 1880s, and acquired a virtual monopoly over athletic goods by absorbing A. J. Reach Company in 1885, Wright & Ditson in 1892, as well as Peck & Snyder and other firms. By 1887 the Spalding "Official League" baseball had been adopted by, the National League, the Western League, the New England League, the International League, and various college conferences, and balls were offered to the public ranging in price from 5 cents to $1.50. To gain an even greater ascendancy over his rivals A. G. Spalding published a wide range of guides in *Spalding's Library of Athletic Sports,* in which his wares were not only advertised but those of rivals were derided as inferior.

The sewing machine was one of many inventions which made possible the more uniform equipment of the last decades of the century when local leagues and national associations took shape throughout the United States. Canoeing and camping were other diversions which gave rise to the manufacture of sporting goods on an ever larger scale. In the latter years of the century the mail-order house and the department store began to feature sporting goods. Macy's of New York began with ice skates, velocipedes, bathing suits, and beach equipment in 1872, although all sporting goods were sold by the toy department. By 1902, with the addition of numerous other items, a separate department was established. Sears, Roebuck and Company, meanwhile, devoted more than eighty pages of its 1895 catalog to weapons and fishing equipment, and within a decade not only hunting and fishing equipment but also bicycles, boxing gloves, baseball paraphernalia, and sleds were featured.[49]

When Thomas A. Edison developed the incandescent bulb in 1879 he inaugurated a new era in the social life of our cities. Although the first dynamo was built within two years, gas lighting did not give way immediately, and the crowds which jammed the old Madison Square Garden in New York in 1883 to see John L. Sullivan fight Herbert Slade still had to cope not only with the smoke-filled air but also with the blue gas fumes. The Garden had already installed some electric lights, however. At a six-day professional walking match in 1882 the cloud of tobacco smoke was so thick that "even the electric lights" had "a hard struggle to assert their superior brilliancy" over the gas jets. Even "the noisy yell of programme, candy, fruit and peanut venders who filled the air with the vilest discord" failed to discourage the crowd, according to a philosophically minded reporter who wondered what Herbert Spencer would think of "the peculiar phase of idiocy in the American character" which drew thousands of men and women to midnight pedestrian contests.[50]

Within a few years electric lighting and more comfortable accommodations helped lure players and spectators alike to Y.M.C.A.'s, athletic clubs, regimental armories, school and college gymnasiums, as well as sports arenas. In 1885, at the third annual Horse Show in Madison Square Garden, handsomely dressed sportswomen reveled in the arena, "gaudy with festoons of racing flags and brilliant streamers, lighted at night by hundreds of electric lights," while visitors to the brilliantly lighted New York Athletic Club agreed that "fine surroundings will not do an athlete any harm."[51] The indoor prize fight, walking contest, wrestling match, and horse show were a far cry from the crude atmosphere of early indoor sport. In 1890 carnivals were held at the Massachusetts Mechanics' Association by the Boston Athletic Association and at the new Madison Square Garden in New York by the Staten Island Athletic Club; the horse show attracted fashionable New Yorkers to the Garden; and indoor baseball, already popular in Chciago, was taken up in New York's regimental armories.[52] A decade of electrification, paralleling improvements in transportration and communications, had elevated and purified the atmosphere of sport. The saloon brawls of pugilists in the 1850s and 1860s were gradually abandoned for the organized matches of the 1880s and 1890s. At the time of the Sullivan-Corbett fight in the New Orleans Olympic Club in 1892, an observer wrote in the Chicago *Daily Tribune,* September 8, 1892: "Now men travel to great boxing contests in vestibule limited trains; they sleep at the best hotels . . . and when the time for the contest arrives they find themselves in a grand, brilliantly lighted arena."

Basketball and volleyball, originating in the Y.M.C.A. in 1892 and 1895, were both developed to meet the need for indoor sport on winter evenings. The rapid construction of college gymnasiums and the building of more luxurious clubhouses after the middle eighties stemmed in great part from the superior appointments and more brilliant lighting available for athletic games, and much of the urban appeal of indoor sport was directly attributable to the revolution which electric lighting made in the night life of the metropolis.

Electrification, which transformed everything from home gadgets and domestic lighting to power machinery and launches, exerted an influence on the course of sport through the development of rapid transit systems in cities from coast to coast. Horse-drawn cars had carried the burden of traffic since the 1850s, but the electric streetcar assumed an entirely new role in opening up suburban areas and the countryside to the pent-up city populace. Soon after the Richmond, Virginia, experiment of 1888, the streetcar began to acquaint large numbers of city dwellers with the race track and the ball diamond.[53] Experimental lines had been laid even earlier in the decade, and Chicago crowds going to the races at Washington Park in 1887 were jammed on "the grip," one reporter noting the "perpetual stream of track slang," the prodding and pushing, and the annoying delay when it was announced that "the cable has busted."[54] Trolley parks, many of which included baseball diamonds, were promoted by the transit companies; ball teams were encouraged by these same concerns through gifts of land or grandstands; and the crowds flocked to week-end games on the cars.[55] At the turn of the century the popular interest in athletic games in thousands of towns and cities was stimulated to a high degree by the extension of rapid transit systems, a development which may possibly have been as significant in the growth of local sport as the automobile was to be in the development of intercommunity rivalries.

Numerous inventions and improvements applied to sport were of varying importance: the stop watch, the percussion cap, the streamlined sulky, barbed wire, the safety cycle, ball bearings, and artificial ice for skating rinks, among others. Improved implements often popularized and revolutionized the style of a sport, as in the invention of the sliding seat of the rowing shell, the introduction of the rubber-wound gutta-percha ball which necessitated the lengthening of golf courses, and the universal acceptance of the catcher's mask.

Vulcanization of rubber by Charles Goodyear in the 1830s led to the development of elastic and resilient rubber balls in the following decade, and eventually influenced the development of golf and tennis balls as well as other sporting apparel and equipment. The pneumatic tire, developed by Dr. John Boyd Dunlop of Belfast, Ireland, in 1888, revolutionized cycling and harness racing in the next decade. Equipped with pneumatic tires, the sulky abandoned its old highwheeler style, and the trotter and pacer found it made for smoother movement on the track. Sulky drivers reduced the mile record of 2:08¾ by Maud S. with an old highwheeler to 1:58½ by Lou Dillon in 1903 with a "bicycle sulky." According to W. H. Gocher, a racing authority, the innovation of pneumatic tires and the streamlining of the sulky cut five to seven seconds from former records, which was "more than the breeding had done in a dozen years."[56] The pneumatic tire, introduced by racing cyclists and sulky drivers, went on to play a much more vital role in the rise of the automobile industry and the spectacular appeal of auto racing.

The camera also came to the aid of sport in the decades following the Civil War. Professional photography had developed rapidly in the middle period of the century, but nature lovers became devotees of the camera only when its bulkiness and weight were eliminated in the closing years of the century. Development of the Eastman Kodak after 1888 found a mass market as thousands of Americans put it to personal and commercial use. Pictorial and sporting magazines which had been printing woodcuts since the prewar era began to introduce many pictures taken from photographs, and in the late 1880s and early 1890s actual photographic prints of athletes and outdoor sportsmen came into common usage. *Harper's Weekly, Leslie's Illustrated Weekly, Illustrated American,* and the *National Police Gazette* featured photography, and by the end of the century the vast majority of their pictures were camera studies.[57] Newspapers recognized the circulation value of half-tone prints, but because of paper and technical problems they were used sparsely until the New York *Times* published an illustrated Sunday supplement in 1896, soon to be imitated by the New York *Tribune* and the Chicago *Tribune.* The year 1897 saw the half-tone illustration become a regular feature of metropolitan newspapers, rapidly eliminating the age-old reliance on woodcuts. At the turn of the century sport was available in visual form to millions who heretofore had little knowledge of athletics and outdoor games.[58]

It was in 1872 that Eadweard Muybridge made the first successful attempt "to secure an illusion of motion by photography." With the help of Leland Stanford, already a noted turfman, he set out to prove whether "a trotting horse at one point in its gait left the ground entirely."[59] By establishing a battery of cameras the movements of the horse were successively photographed, and Muybridge later turned his technique to "the gallop of dogs, the flight of birds, and the performances of athletes." In his monumental study entitled *Animal Locomotion* (1887) he included thousands of pictures of horses, athletes, and other living subjects, demonstrating "the work and play of men, women, and children of all ages; how pitchers throw the baseball, how batters hit it, and how athletes move their bodies in record-breaking contests."[60] Muybridge is considered only one among a number of the pioneers of the motion picture, but his pictures had presented possibly the best illusion of motion prior to the development of flexible celluloid film. A host of experimenters gradually evolved principles and techniques in the late 1880s which gave birth to the true motion picture. Woodville Latham and his two sons made a four-minute film of the prize fight between Young Griffo and Battling Barnett in 1895, showing it on a large screen for an audience, an event which has been called "the first flickering, commercial motion picture."[61] When Bob Fitzsimmons won the heavyweight championship from James J. Corbett at Carson City, Nevada, in 1897, the fight was photographed for public distribution. With the increasing popularity in succeeding years of the newsreel, the short subject, and an occasional feature film, the motion picture came to rival the photograph in spreading the gospel of sport.[62]

When sport began to mature into a business of some importance and thousands of organizations throughout the country joined leagues, associations, racing circuits, and national administrative bodies, it became necessary to utilize on a large scale the telephone, the typewriter, and all the other instruments so vital to the commercial world. Even the phonograph, at first considered a business device but soon devoted to popular music, came to have an indirect influence, recording for public entertainment such songs as "Daisy Bell," "Casey at the Bat," "Slide, Kelly, Slide," and, early in the present century, the theme song of the national pastime, "Take Me Out to the Ball Game." All of these instruments created a great revolution in communication, and they contributed significantly to the expansion of sport on a national scale.

The bicycle, still an important means of transport in Europe but something of a casualty of the machine age in the United States, also had an important role. After its demonstration at the Philadelphia Centennial, an interest was ignited which grew rapidly in the 1880s and flamed into an obsession in the 1890s.[63] Clubs, cycling associations, and racing meets were sponsored everywhere in these years, and the League of American Wheelmen served as a spearhead for many of the reforms in fashions, good roads, and outdoor exercise. Albert H. Pope was merely the foremost among many manufacturers of the "velocipede" which became so popular among women's clubs, temperance groups, professional men, and, at the turn of the century, in the business world and among the trades. Contemporary observers speculated on the social benefits to be derived from the cycle, especially in enticing women to the pleasures of outdoor exercise. Bicycling was discussed by ministers and physicians, it was considered as a weapon in future wars, police squads in some cities were mounted on wheels, mail carriers utilized it, and many thought it would revolutionize society.[64]

As a branch of American industry the bicycle was reputed to have developed into a $100,000,000 business in the 1890s. Mass-production techniques were introduced, Iver Johnson's Arms and Cycle Works advertising "Every part interchangeable and exact." The Indiana Bicycle Company, home of the Waverley cycle, maintained a huge factory in Indianapolis and claimed to be the most perfect and complete plant in the world: "We employ the highest mechanical skill and the best labor-saving machinery that ample capital can provide. Our methods of construction are along the latest and most approved lines of mechanical work."[65]

Much of the publicity given to competing manufacturers centered around the mechanical improvements and the speed records of their products. Between 1878 and 1896 the mile record was lowered from 3:57 to 1:55-1/5. While recognizing the effect of better riding styles, methodical training, improved tracks, and the art of pacemaking, one critic contended, "The prime factor . . . is the improvement in the vehicle itself. The racing machine of 1878 was a heavy, crude, cumbersome affair, while the modern bicycle, less than one-sixth its weight, equipped with scientifically calculated gearing,

pneumatic tires, and friction annihilators, represents much of the difference."[66] Roger Burlingame has pointed out the impact of the bicycle on the
health, recreation, business, and the social life of the American people, and on
the manufacture of the cycle he claimed that "it introduced certain technical
principles which were carried on into the motor car, notably ball bearings,
hub-breaking and the tangential spoke."[67] Little did cycling enthusiasts
realize that in these same years a much more revolutionary vehicle, destined
to transform our way of life, was about to make its dramatic appearance on
the national scene.

One of the last inventions which the nineteenth century brought forth
for the conquest of time and distance was the automobile. During the 1890s
the Haynes, Duryea, Ford, Stanley Steamer, Packard, and Locomobile came
out in quick succession, and the Pierce Arrow, Cadillac, and Buick were to
follow in the next several years.[68] Manufacturers of bicycles had already
turned to the construction of the motor car in a number of instances. As early
as 1895 Herman H. Kohlsaat, publisher of the Chicago *Times-Herald,* sponsored the first automobile race on American soil. One of the features of this
contest, run through a snowstorm and won by Charles Duryea, was the
enhanced reputation achieved for the gasoline motor, which had not yet been
recognized as the proper source of motor power. A number of European races
inspired American drivers to take to the racecourse, and the experimental
value of endurance or speed contests was immediately recognized by pioneer
manufacturers. Nor were they slow to see the publicity value of races featured
by the newspapers.[69]

Henry Ford "was bewitched by Duryea's feat," and he "devoured reports
on the subject which appeared in the newspapers and magazines of the day."
When other leading carbuilders sought financial backing for their racers, Ford
determined to win supremacy on the track. After defeating Alexander Winton
in a race at Detroit in 1902, "Ford's prowess as a 'speed demon' began to
appear in the columns of the widely circulated trade journal *Horseless Age.*"[70]
In later years he was to contend, "I never thought anything of racing, but the
public refused to consider the automobile in any light other than as a fast
toy. Therefore later we had to race. The industry was held back by this
initial racing slant, for the attention of the makers was diverted to making
fast rather than good cars." The victory over Winton was his first race, "and
it brought advertising of the only kind that people cared to read." Bowing to
public opinion, he was determined "to make an automobile that would be
known wherever speed was known," and he set to work installing four cylin-
ders in his famous "999." Developing 80 horse power, this machine was so
frightening, even to its builders, that the fearless Barney Oldfield was hired
for the race. Oldfield had only a tiller with which to drive, since there were
no steering wheels, but this professional cyclist who had never driven a car
established a new record and helped put Ford back on his feet. The financial

support of Alex Y. Malcomson, an admirer of "999," gave him a new start: "A week after the race I formed the Ford Motor Company."[71]

The next few years witnessed the establishment of Automobile Club of America races, sport clubs in the American Automobile Association, the Vanderbilt Cup, and the Glidden Tour. Reporting on the third annual Glidden Tour in 1906, *Scientific American* defended American cars, heretofore considered inferior to European models: "Above all else, the tour has demonstrated that American machines will stand fast driving on rough forest roads without serious damage to the cars or their mechanism. Engine and gear troubles have practically disappeared, and the only things that are to be feared are the breakage of springs and axles and the giving out of tires. Numerous shock-absorbers were tried out and found wanting in this test; and were it not for the pneumatic tires, which have been greatly improved during the past two years, such a tour would be impossible of accomplishment."[72]

The Newport social season featured racing, Daytona Beach soon became a center for speed trials, and tracks were built in various parts of the nation, the first of which may have been at Narragansett Park in 1896.[73] Not until the years just prior to World War I did auto racing attain a truly national popularity with the establishment of the Indianapolis Speedway, but the emphasis on speed and endurance in these early years spurred manufacturers to build ever faster models and advertisers to feature the record performances of each car. Henry Ford had long since lost interest, while the Buick racing team was discontinued in 1915. By then mass production had turned the emphasis toward design, comfort, and economy. Racing was not abandoned and manufacturers still featured endurance tests in later years, but the heated rivalry between pioneer builders had become a thing of the past.[74]

Technological developments in the latter half of the nineteenth century transformed the social habits of the Western World, and sport was but one of many institutions which felt their full impact. Fashions, foods, journalism, home appliances, commercialized entertainment, architecture, and city planning were only a few of the facets of life which underwent rapid change as transportation and communication were revolutionized and as new materials were made available. There are those who stress the thesis that sport is a direct reaction against the mechanization, the division of labor, and the standardization of life in a machine civilization,[75] and this may in part be true, but sport in nineteenth-century America was as much a product of industrialization as it was an antidote to it. While athletics and outdoor recreation were sought as a release from the confinements of city life, industrialization and the urban movement were the basic causes for the rise of organized sport. And the urban movement was, of course, greatly enhanced by the revolutionary transformation in communication, transportation, agriculture, and industrialization.[76]

The first symptoms of the impact of invention on nineteenth-century sports are to be found in the steamboat of the ante-bellum era. An intensification of interest in horse racing during the 1820s and 1830s was only a prelude to the sporting excitement over yachting, prize fighting, rowing, running, cricket, and baseball of the 1840s and 1850s. By this time the railroad was opening up new opportunities for hunters, anglers, and athletic teams, and it was the railroad, of all the inventions of the century, which gave the greatest impetus to the intercommunity rivalries in sport. The telegraph and the penny press opened the gates to a rising tide of sporting journalism; the sewing machine and the factory system revolutionized the manufacturing of sporting goods; the electric light and rapid transit further demonstrated the impact of electrification; inventions like the Kodak camera, the motion picture, and the pneumatic tire stimulated various fields of sport; and the bicycle and automobile gave additional evidence to the effect of the transportation revolution on the sporting impulse of the latter half of the century. Toward the end of the century the rapidity with which one invention followed another demonstrated the increasingly close relationship of technology and social change. No one can deny the significance of sportsmen, athletes, journalists, and pioneers in many organizations, and no one can disregard the multiple forces transforming the social scene. The technological revolution is not the sole determining factor in the rise of sport, but to ignore its influence would result only in a more or less superficial understanding of the history of one of the prominent social institutions of modern America.

NOTES

1. Among the most useful works to be consulted on early American sport are John A. Krout, *Annals of American Sport* (New Haven, 1929); Jennie Holliman, *American Sports, 1785-1835* (Durham, 1931); Foster R. Dulles, *America Learns To Play: A History of Popular Recreation, 1607-1940* (New York, 1940); Robert B. Weaver, *Amusements and Sports in American Life* (Chicago, 1939); and Herbert Manchester, *Four Centuries of Sport in America, 1490-1890* (New York, 1931). For certain aspects of ante-bellum sport, see Arthur M. Schlesinger and Dixon R. Fox (eds.), *A History of American Life*, 13 vols. (New York, 1927-1948).

2. See the New York *American*, May 27, 1823; New Orleans *Daily Picayune*, March 27, 1839; New York *Weekly Herald*, May 17, 1845, July 11, 1849; and accounts of many races in the *Spirit of the Times* (New York) for prewar years. In an era when bridges were more the exception than the rule the ferry was an indispensable means of transportation. See, for example, Kenneth Roberts and Anna M. Roberts (eds.), *Moreau de St. Méry's American Journey, 1793-1798* (Garden City, 1947), 173; New York *American*, May 27, 1823.

3. For examples of the steamboat in early sport, see the New York *Herald*, June 17, 1849; *Wilkes' Spirit of the Times* (New York), XII (August 5, 1865), 380; New Orleans *Daily Picayune*, December 1, 1855, December 10, 1859; *Spirit of the Times*, XX (June 19, 1869), 276; New York *World*, June 19, 1869. When the passenger lines began converting to steam in the Civil War era, the development of international sport was

facilitated to a considerable degree. In the latter decades of the century the steam yacht became the vogue among American millionaires.

4. John Hervey, *Racing in America, 1665-1865,* 2 vols. (New York, 1944), II, 101.

5. New Orleans *Daily Picayune,* March 27, 1839.

6. *American Turf Register and Sporting Magazine* (Baltimore), XIII (July, 1843), 367; New York *Daily Tribune,* May 14, 1845.

7. *Spirit of the Times,* XXI (July 12, 1851), 246.

8. Albert L. Demaree, *The American Agricultural Press, 1819-1860* (New York, 1941), 203-204. Specific instances of such aid can be found in the *Cultivator* (Albany), IX (March, 1842), 50; *American Agriculturist* (New York), II (October 16, 1843), 258; New York *Daily Tribune,* September 18, 1851; *Transactions of the Illinois State Agricultural Society* (Springfield), I, 1853-54 (1855, 6; II, 1856-57 (1857), 24-32; *Report and Proceedings of the Iowa State Agricultural Society . . . October, 1855* (Fairfield, 1856), 24; *Fifth Report of the Indiana State Board of Agriculture . . . For the Year 1856* (Indianapolis, 1858), 34, 482-83; *Kentucky Farmer* (Frankfort), I, (July, 1858), 12: *Wisconsin Farmer and North-Western Cultivator* (Madison), IX (October, 1857), 873; XI (October, 1859), 386-87; Springfield *Weekly Illinois State Journal,* September 5, 19, 1860. The "ploughing matches" of the ante-bellum era attracted large crowds seeking both entertainment and the latest improvements in agricultural implements.

9. Samuel Crowther and Arthur Ruhl, *Rowing and Track Athletics* (New York, 1905), 11.

10. James N. Elkins, superintendent of the Boston, Concord and Montreal Railroad, agreed to pay all transportation costs for the crews and their equipment to the New Hampshire lake where the race was to be held. Robert F. Kelley, *American Rowing: Its Background and Traditions* (New York, 1932), 100-101.

11. New York *Daily Times,* October 13, 1853; Boston *Advertiser,* October 14, 1853.

12. New York *Herald,* October 23, 1858.

13. Wilkes' *Spirit of the Times,* XIV (July 7, 1866), 294. More rural areas felt the impact somewhat later, Warrenton, Mississippi, holding a tourney in 1885 to which special trains were sent. New Orleans *Daily Picayune,* July 19, 1885.

14. New York *World,* August 21, 1869; Cincinnati *Commercial,* September 22, 1869; San Francisco *Evening Bulletin,* October 5, 1869. Their use of Pullman cars set a precedent in sports circles. Advertising by local lines for an approaching game appeared in the Cincinnati *Commercial,* August 24, 1869.

15. See *Spalding's Official Base Ball Guide* (New York, 1886), appendix. The Memphis Reds Base Ball Association sent a printed circular to Harry Wright of the Boston team in 1877 in which it stressed the reduced rates to any club visiting St. Louis or Louisville. Harry Wright Correspondence, 7 vols., I (1865-1877), 40, Spalding Baseball Collection (New York Public Library). In the 1880s enthusiastic crowds turned out to the railroad station to welcome home the victorious nines. *Frank Leslie's Boys' and*

Girls' Weekly (New York), XXXV (October 6, 1883), 174; New York *Sun*, September 7, 1886.

16. *Turf, Field and Farm* (New York), I (September 2, 1865), 69; VIII (May 28, 1869), 344.

17. *Wilkes' Spirit of the Times*, XIV (May 19, 1866), 185; San Francisco *Evening Bulletin*, October 15, 1869; Baltimore *American and Commercial Advertiser*, October 25, 1877; New Orleans *Daily Picayune*, April 20, 1884, May 9, 15, 1885; Charles E. Trevathan, *The American Thoroughbred* (New York, 1905), 371.

18. New York *World*, April 29, 1884.

19. Alexander Johnston, *Ten—And Out! The Complete Story of the Prize Ring in America* (New York, 1947), 42–43.

20. Dunbar Rowland (ed.), *Encyclopedia of Mississippi History*, 2 vols. (Madison, 1907), II, 142; St. Paul and Minneapolis *Pioneer Press*, February 8, 1882; New Orleans *Daily Picayune*, August 6, 1885; New York *Sun*, May 12, 1886.

21. Railroad interest in sport was illustrated by the *New York Railroad Gazette:* "Horse-racing tracks of the violest [*sic*] character are encouraged (indirectly, it may be) in more than one case by railroads normally law-abiding. Sunday excursions patronized chiefly by roughs who conduct baseball games of a character condemned by all decent people are morally the same as prize fights in kind though not in degree." Quoted in the New Orleans *Daily Picayune*, August 6, 1885.

22. For illustrations of the difficulties of railroad travel, see the Walter Camp Correspondence, Box 64 (Yale University Library, New Haven).

23. *Wilkes' Spirit of the Times*, XIII (October 14, 1865), 102.

24. Parke H. Davis, *Football, The American Intercollegiate Game* (New York, 1911), 45.

25. *Outing* (New York), XII (August, 1888), 407–408.

26. By the 1890s many railroads carried bicycles as free freight and professional cyclists could tour their National Circuit in luxury cars. New York *Journal*, September 18, 1897.

27. Scores of railroads in every section of the country served those seeking to hunt or fish in the rustic countryside. See, particularly, Charles Hallock (ed.), *The Sportsman's Gazetteer and General Guide* (New York, 1877), Pt. II, 1–182. See also the Chicago and Northwestern Railway advertisement in the *Spirit of the Times*, SCII (August 19, 1876), 53.

28. For the early development of the telegraph, see James D. Reid, *The Telegraph in America and Morse Memorial* (New York, 1887); Waldemar Kaempffert (ed.), *A Popular History of American Invention*, 2 vols. (New York, 1924); and Robert L. Thompson, *Wiring a Continent: The History of the Telegraph Industry in the United States, 1832–1866* (Princeton, 1947).

29. Boston *Daily Journal*, February 7, 8, 9, 1849; New York *Daily Tribune*, February 8, 9, 1849; Milwaukee *Sentinel and Gazette*, February 10, 1849; Boston *Daily Courier*, October 21, 1858; New York *Times*, October 21, 1858; New Orleans *Daily Picayune*, May 6, 7, June 29, 1860; Nashville *Daily News*, April 29, 1860.

30. New York *Daily Tribune,* September 19, 1851; Natchez *Courier,* September 19, 1851.

31. New Orleans *Daily Picayune,* July 6, 1870.

32. *Ibid.* See also New York *Times,* October 21, 1858; *Harper's Weekly* (New York), XXVII (October 13, 1883), 654.

33. Oliver Gramling, *AP; The Story of News* (New York, 1940), 232; New Orleans *Daily Picayune,* July 10, 1889. For poolrooms, saloons and bulletin boards, see the New York *Sun,* October 6, 1878; New York *Herald,* February 7, 1882; New Orleans *Daily Picayune,* May 17, 1884, July 6, 1885; New York *World,* September 8, 1892. Also see *Harper's Weekly,* XXVII (October 13, 1883), 654; XXXVI (April 2, December 17, 1892), 319, 324, 1210. Henry L. Mencken, in *Happy Days, 1880–1892* (New York, 1940), 225, nostalgically recalled how, since there were few sporting "extras" in Baltimore in the 1880s, "the high-toned saloons of the town catered to the [baseball] fans by putting in telegraph operators who wrote the scores on blackboards."

34. The New York *Transcript* and the *Sun* sensationalized the news as early as the 1830s and began reporting prize fights. James Gordon Bennett's *Herald* exploited sporting interests in pre-Civil War years and his son continued to do so in the period following the war. Magazines which capitalized on sport included the *American Turf Register and Sporting Magazine,* the *Spirit of the Times,* the *New York Clipper,* and the *National Police Gazette* (New York), as well as a host of fishing and hunting journals. Through the 1880s and 1890s the New York *Sun* and the *World* competed for the sporting public, only to be outdone by the *Journal* at the end of the century. Among the prominent writers of the era were Henry Chadwick, Timothy Murnane, Harry Weldon, Harry C. Palmer, Al Spink, Sam Crane, Walter Camp, Caspar Whitney, and Charles Dryden. See William H. Nugent, "The Sports Section," *American Mercury* (New York), XVI (February, 1929), 329–38; and Hugh Fullerton, "The Fellows Who Made the Game," *Saturday Evening Post* (Philadelphia), CC (April 21, 1928), 18 ff.

35. New York *Herald,* December 30, 31, 1866; Cincinnati *Commercial,* August 24, 28, 1869; *Frank Leslie's Illustrated Newspaper* (New York), XXIX (September 28, 1869), 2.

36. The origins of the penny press are ably discussed in Willard G. Bleyer, *Main Currents in the History of American Journalism* (Boston, 1927), 154–84; and in Frank L. Mott, *American Journalism, A History* (New York, 1941), 228–52.

37. Bleyer, *History of American Journalism,* 197, 209; Alfred M. Lee, *The Daily Newspaper in America* (New York, 1937), 611; New York *Weekly Herald,* May 15, 17, 1845, and *Herald* files for the 1840s.

38. Bleyer, *History of American Journalism,* 394.

39. *Ibid.,* 394–98.

40. Joseph Pulitzer's New York *World* began an intensive exploitation of sport as a front-page attraction almost immediately after its purchase in 1883, and by the following year first-page accounts of pedestrian matches, dog shows, and similar topics became regular features.

41. Albert Johannsen, *The House of Beadle and Adams and its Dime and*

Nickel Novel: The Story of a Vanished Literature, 2 vols. (Norman, 1950), I, 260, 377–79.

42. John L. Cutler, *Gilbert Patten and His Frank Merriwell Saga,* University of Main *Studies* (Orono), Ser. II, No. 31 (1934).

43. Charles E. Godspeed, *Angling in America: Its Early History and Literature* (Boston, 1939), 285 ff.

44. Charles Hallock, *The Fishing Tourist: Angler's Guide and Reference Book* (New York, 1873), 18.

45. In 1900 the value of sporting goods manufactured was only $3,628,496. United States Bureau of the Census, *Statistical Abstract of the United States* (Washington, 1909), 188.

46. See the *Spirit of the Times,* XX (May 4, 1850), 130; Natchez *Courier,* November 26, 1850; Madison *Daily State Journal,* March 26, 1855; New Orleans *Daily Picayune,* April 4, 1856. As midwestern merchants began to purchase large stocks from the East, John Krider advertised widely. Madison *Daily State Journal,* April 13, 1855. Michael Phelan, who in 1854 developed an indiarubber cushion permitting sharp edges on billiard tables, joined with Hugh W. Collender in forming Phelan and Collender, the leading billiards manufacturer until the organization of the Brunswick-Balke-Collender Company in 1884. Gymnastic apparatus, created by Dudley A. Sargent and other physical educators, was featured by many dealers, while the readers of *American Angler* (New York), *Forest and Stream* (New York), and other sporting journals were kept informed of the latest models of rifles, shotguns, and fishing rods and reels.

47. George B. Ellard, who sponsored the Red Stockings, advertised his store as "Base Ball Headquarters" and "Base Ball Depot," with the "Best Stock in the West." Cincinnati *Commercial,* August 24, 1869. Other merchandisers included Horsman's Base Ball and Croquet Emporium in New York and John H. Mann of the same city. Peck & Snyder began dealing in baseball equipment in 1865 and by the 1880s claimed to be the largest seller of sporting goods.

48. Moses King (ed.), *King's Handbook of the United States* (Buffalo, 1891), 232; Arthur Bartlett, *Baseball and Mr. Spalding: The History and Romance of Baseball* (New York, 1951), *passim; Fortune* (New York), II (August, 1930), 62 ff.; Arthur Bartlett, "They're Just Wild About Sports," *Saturday Evening Post,* CCXXII (December 24, 1949), 31 ff.; *Spalding's Official Base Ball Guide for 1887* (New York and Chicago, 1887), *passim.*

49. It was on mass manufacture of baseballs and uniforms that Spalding gained such a leading position in the sporting goods field. Since the business was restricted in these early years certain difficulties had to be overcome. To make the most out of manufacturing bats Spalding bought his own lumber mill in Michigan, while Albert Pope received little sympathy from the rolling mills in his first years of manufacturing bicycles. *Wheelman* (Boston), I (October, 1882), 71. For department and mail-order stores, see Ralph M. Hower, *History of Macy's of New York, 1858–1919* (Cambridge, 1946), 103, 162, 234–35, 239; Boris Emmet and John C. Jeuck, *Catalogues and Counters: A History of Sears, Roebuck*

and Company (Chicago, 1950), 38; David L. Cohn, *The Good Old Days* (New York, 1940), 443–60.

50. New York *Herald,* October 23, 1882; New York *Sun,* August 7, 1883. The introduction of electric lighting in theaters was discussed, while the opposition of gas companies was recognized. *Scientific American,* Supplement (New York), XVI (November 10, 1883), 6535–36.

51. *Harper's Weekly,* XXIX (February 14, November 14, 1885), 109, 743.

52. See *ibid.,* XXXIV (March 1, 8, 1890), 169, 171, 179. A new Madison Square Garden with the most modern facilities was built in the years 1887–1890; the California Athletic Club in San Francisco featured a "powerful electric arc light" over its ring; and electric lights in the Manhattan Athletic Club's new gymnasium in 1890 "shed a dazzling whiteness." *Ibid.,* XXXIV (April 5, 1890), 263–64; New York *Daily Tribune,* November 2, 30, 1890.

53. After the completion of the Richmond line rapid transit spread throughout the country. Although in 1890 there were only 144 electric railways in a national total of 789 street lines, by 1899 there were 50,600 electric cars in operation as compared to only 1,500 horse cars. Gilson Willets *et al., Workers of the Nation,* 2 vols. (New York, 1903), I, 498. For the suburban influence, see the *Street Railway Journal* (New York), XVIII (November 23, 1901), 760–61.

54. Chicago *Tribune,* July 5, 1887.

55. *Street Railway Journal,* XI (April, 1895), 232; XII (May, November, 1896), 317, 319, 708; *Cosmopolitan* (New York), XXXIII (July, 1902), 266; *Collier's (New York), CXXV (May, 1950), 85; Oscar Handlin,* This *Was America* (Cambridge, 1949), 374; New Orleans *Daily Picayune,* February 27, 1899.

56. W. H. Gocher, *Trotalong* (Hartford, 1928), 190.

57. Robert Taft, *Photography and the American Scene: A Social History, 1839–1889* (New York, 1910), II, 534–35.

58. Photography developed throughout the nineteenth century as an adjunct of the science of chemistry. Chemical and mechanical innovations were also responsible for the improvements of prints and all kinds of reproductions. Woodcuts were featured in the press, engravings were sold widely, and lithographs were found in the most rural home. Nathaniel Currier (later Currier & Ives) published hunting, fishing, pugilistic, baseball, rowing, yachting, sleighing, skating, trotting, and racing scenes for more than half a century. Cheap prints, calendars, and varied reproductions of sporting scenes did much to popularize the famous turf champions and sporting heroes of the era. See Harry T. Peters, *Currier & Ives: Printmakers to the American People* (Garden City, 1942).

59. Frank L. Dyer and Thomas C. Martin, *Edison: His Life and Inventions,* 2 vols. (New York, 1910), II, 534–35.

60. Kaempffert, *Popular History of American Inventions,* I, 425.

61. Lloyd Morris, *Not So Long Ago* (New York, 1949), 24.

62. The pioneer years of the motion picture industry are described by numerous other works, among them Deems Taylor, *A Pictorial History of the Movies* (New York, 1943), 1–6; Leslie Wood, *The Miracle of the Movies* (London, 1947), 66 ff.; George S. Bryan, *Edison: The Man and His Work*

(Garden City, 1926), 184–94; Josef M. Eder, *History of Photography,* trans. by Edward Epstean (New York, 1945), 495 ff.; Taft, *Photography and the American Scene,* 405–12; Morris, *Not So Long Ago,* 1–35.

63. There was a brief craze in 1869, during which year, according to Albert H. Pope, "more than a thousand inventions were patented for the perfection and improvement of the velocipede." *Wheelman,* I (October, 1882), 70. Interest declined, however, until the Philadelphia celebration of 1876. Although race meetings and cycling clubs were widely reported in the 1880s, there were only 83 repair establishments in 1890 and the value of products in bicycle and tricycle repairs was only about $300,000. By 1900 there were 6,378 repair shops and the value in repairs exceeded $13,000,000. United States Bureau of the Census, *Statistical Abstract of the United States* (Washington, 1904), 516.

64. For summaries of the impact of the bicycle, see E. Benjamin Andrews, *History of the Last Quarter-Century in the United States, 1870-1895,* 2 vols. (New York, 1896), II, 289–90; Arthur M. Schlesinger, *The Rise of the City 1878-1898* (New York, 1933), 312–14; Roger Burlingame, *Engines of Democracy: Inventions and Society in Mature America* (New York, 1940), 369–74.

65. *Harper's Weekly,* XL (April 11, 1896), 365. It is interesting that the "father of scientific management," Frederick W. Taylor, a tennis champion and golf devotee, was said to have learned through sport "the value of the minute analysis of motions, the importance of methodical selection and training, the worth of time study and of standards based on rigorously exact observation." Charles De Fréminville, "How Taylor Introduced the Scientific Method Into Management of the Shop," *Critical Essays on Scientific Management,* Taylor Society *Bulletin* (New York), X (February, 1925), Pt. II, 32. Mass-production techniques, however, were only partially responsible for the outpouring of athletic goods which began to win wider markets at the turn of the century. The manufacture of baseball bats remained a highly specialized trade, while Scotch artisans who came to the United States maintained the personalized nature of their craft as makers of golf clubs. Despite the great improvements in gun manufacture, Elisha J. Lewis asserted in 1871 that there were thousands of miserable guns on the market: "The reason of this is that our mechanics have so many tastes and fancies to please, owing principally to the ignorance of those who order fowling-pieces, that they have adopted no generally-acknowledged standard of style to guide them in the getting up of guns suitable for certain kinds of sport." Elisha J. Lewis, *The American Sportsman* (Philadelphia, 1871), 435. Although numerous industries had taken up the principle of interchangeable parts, mass-production techniques were to come to the fore only with the assembly lines of Henry Ford and the automobile industry in the years before World War I.

66. *Harper's Weekly,* XL (April 11, 1896), 366.

67. Burlingame, *Engines of Democracy: Inventions and Society in Mature America,* 3.

68. Herbert O. Duncan, *World on Wheels,* 2 vols. (Paris, 1927), II, 919 ff.

69. Lawrence H. Seltzer, *A Financial History of the American Automobile Industry* (Boston, 1928), 91; Pierre Sauvestre, *Histoire de L'Automobile*

(Paris, 1907), *passim;* Ralph C. Epstein, *The Automobile Industry, Its Economic and Commercial Development* (Chicago, 1928), 154; Reginald M. Cleveland and S. T. Williamson, *The Road Is Yours* (New York, 1951), 175–76, 194–97.

70. Keith Sward, *The Legend of Henry Ford* (New York, 1948), 14.

71. Henry Ford and Samuel Crowther, *My Life and Work* (Garden City, 1927), 36–37, 50–51.

72. *Scientific American,* XCV (August 11, 1906), 95.

73. G. F. Baright, "Automobiles and Automobile Races at Newport," *Independent* (New York), LIV (June 5, 1902), 1368.

74. In these years the motorcycle and the motorboat also created interest, Sir Alfred Harmsworth (later Lord Northcliffe) establishing the Harmsworth Trophy for international competition in 1903. Air races also won widespread publicity in the press from 1910 onward. Glenn H. Curtiss achieved an enviable reputation as an aviator, newspapers sponsored air meets, and considerable attention was given to the "new sport of the air." *Ibid.*, LXIX (November 3, 1910), 999.

75. Lewis Mumford, *Technics and Civilization* (New York, 1934), 303–305; Arnold J. Toynbee, *A Study of History*, 6 vols. (London, 1934–1939), IV, 242–43.

76. Technological developments throughout the business world transformed the pattern of city life. The electric elevator and improvements in the manufacture of steel made possible the skyscrapers of Chicago and New York in the late 1880s. Concentration of the business community in the central part of the city was increased also by the telephone switchboard and other instruments of communication. Less and less open land remained for the youth living in the heart of the metropolis, and it was to meet this challenge that the Y.M.C.A., the settlement house, the institutional church, the boys' club, and other agencies expanded their athletic facilities. The playground movement and the public park grew out of the necessity for recreational areas for city dwellers, and public authorities early in the twentieth century began to rope off streets for children at play. The subway, the streetcar, and the automobile made possible the accelerated trend toward suburban development, where the open lot or planned play area offered better opportunities to participate in sport. The more general implications of the impact of the technological revolution on society, already considered by several outstanding scholars, are not discussed here, the principal aim of this study being to describe the interrelationship of sport and invention in the latter half of the nineteenth century. Although the account of the auto slightly transgressed the limits of this study, it was felt necessary to give it an abbreviated treatment. The twentieth century, and the role of improved sporting equipment, racing and training devices, the radio, television, improved highways, and bus and air transport, would require an equally extensive study.

MASS CULTURE AND SCHOOL SPORTS

Joel H. Spring

One could easily construct an argument that modern professional sports, played within the capitalist atmosphere of competitive salaries and managerial techniques, provides the mass spectator with a sense of relief and adventure from the dull monotony and drudgery of our modern technological and urban environment. An extension of this argument would be that spectator sports by occupying the leisure time of the mass man dilutes his political consciousness and diffuses his feelings of rebellion. Within this framework sports could be considered one of the controlling instruments of our technological culture.

What is important to realize about the above argument is that these goals were implied in the intentions of those who provided the ideological arguments for support of modern recreation movements and the development of athletics in the public schools and universities in the United States. While the goal was mass participation, the result was mass spectatorship.

Before turning to a detailed study of the arguments surrounding the development of athletics in the United States in the latter part of the nineteenth and early twentieth century let us first consider one example of a rather polished statement given in the 1930's about the necessity for athletics and recreation. This particular argument summarized many of the views of those who had given support to the rapid expansion of recreation centers and athletics in the schools and parks in the United States. This example is taken from a college textbook published in 1935 titled *The Theory of Play*. The authors were Elmer D. Mitchell, Director of the Department of Intramural Sports and Associate Professor of Physical Education at the University of Michigan and author of a book titled *Intramural Athletics,* and Bernard S. Mason, a member of the Department of Sociology at Ohio State University and author of *Camping and Education.* This particular textbook had been written as a replacement for a 1923 text, *The Theory of Organized Play,* co-authored by Mitchell.

Mitchell and Mason argued that modern society had replaced the all-around physical activities of the past with specialization and industrial activity which was monotonous, artificial and weakening to the body and mind of the worker. The one benefit of modern society which allowed correction of these inherent evils was leisure time. The authors wrote, "It is during the leisure time that the body must be trained in the wholesome activity that

Joel H. Spring, "Mass Culture and School Sports," *History of Education Quarterly,* Vol. 14 (Winter, 1974). pp. 483–498. Reprinted by permission.

one's occupation denies." The picture painted by Mitchell and Mason of the life of the modern worker was not very pleasant. The modern factory worker merely existed while he worked. "He comes as the slave to the galley," they wrote, "and he leaves with the gladness of the convict who is pardoned." They found the same drab meaninglessness as part of schooling and argued that when the rank and file in large cities escape the school for industry they find it as meaningless as the school. For the authors of this textbook a great deal of labor unrest could be explained in terms of rebellion against repetition and a search for adventure and new experience. Labor existed in a continual state of unrest where even shorter hours and higher wages, earned through strikes, provided little increase in satisfaction. "The laborer," the authors stated, "is like the horse pawing in a stall or a wolf in a cage—he longs for a freedom he does not know how to obtain."

One solution to this rather grim picture of modern man was a search for a new social and economic order that would make life and work more meaningful. This was never a solution promoted by the modern recreation movements and by those advocating the extension of athletics. Their hope was essentially conservative. It was to maintain the existing social order by compensating for its defects through proper utilization of leisure time. The modern worker was told that one of the great benefits of modern labor saving industry was less work and more leisure. At the same time the worker was told that what he did was so meaningless that he had to find compensation during his leisure time. This conservative strain in the modern recreation and athletics movement was clearly and bluntly stated by Mason and Mitchell. "There are two alternatives in solution," they wrote, "strike at the industrial system and change it to something more satisfying to human wishes, or make life possible in its fullest extent to all men in the margin outside of work. It is to the cultivation of life in this margin that modern recreational movement is dedicated." [1]

In detailing the original goals and theoretical base for the development of mass sport in the United States the crucial period is from the 1890's to the latter part of the 1920's. It is during this period that athletics gains a firm foothold in the public schools, interscholastic sports is brought under the control of the schools and universities, a national campaign for parks and recreation centers is launched, basketball is invented, college football becomes a mass spectator sport and professional baseball is hailed as the national pastime.

In considering the development of athletics one must recognize several important distinctions. The first is the difference between athletics and what had been traditionally called physical education. Physical education was primarily thought of in terms of gymnastics and the teaching of health. It was geared towards the training of the body and physical hygiene. The idea of gymnastic training was borrowed from Germany and received its first formal introduction into the schools in 1821 and 1825 when German gymnastic equipment was added to the Salem Latin School and the Round Hill School at Northampton, Massachusetts.[2] Competitive team games were not a part of nineteenth century physical education.[3] Now this requires a second distinction between inclusion and non-inclusion in the educational program. Games and competitive team sports were played throughout the nineteenth century. They were played because people enjoyed them. Their inclusion in the educational programs of colleges and public schools in the latter part of the nineteenth century and early twentieth century was in part because they were believed to fulfill certain functions in the social training of the student. Under the control and promotion of the schools, athletics were given greater organization and importance in the cultural life of the United States and in the fulfillment of social objectives.

By the 1920's the social objectives of athletics and their promotion by the schools had overwhelmed the traditional physical training objectives of the gymnasium. One of the most extensive studies of athletics was conducted by The Carnegie Foundation for the Advancement of Teaching which issued a series of reports in 1929 and 1931. The study was launched in early 1926 and included in its survey 148 colleges and secondary schools in the United States and Canada. The report of the Carnegie Foundation defined the period from 1886 to 1906 as the crucial period for the development of modern school athletics. Prior to this time intramural and extramural games were conducted between school clubs under the control of students. Students managed the teams and the players paid all of the expenses out of their own pockets. Between 1887 and 1906 within the institutions surveyed by the foundation these conditions rapidly changed. Coaching became a technical profession, and paid coaches were hired to manage the teams. Management and control was taken from students and given to faculty, administration and alumni. Fees began to be charged for admission to athletic events, particularly football, and national athletic associations were formed. The most important ones were the Southern Intercollegiate Athletic Conference in 1894, the Intercollegiate Conference or "Big Ten" in 1895 and the National Collegiate Athletic Association in 1910. After 1906, the Foundation survey stated that coaches began to receive faculty appointments, gymnastics declined in importance and athletics expanded under the "rallying-cry that athletics are 'educational'."[4]

The Carnegie survey also found that in the secondary school physical education had tended to become subordinate to athletics. While forty-seven states had interscholastic athletic associations, only seventeen states had directors or departments of physical education. The survey stated: "If public recognition be a criterion of judgment, physical education is considered to be far less important than inter-school athletics; the part is emphasized at the expense of the whole." This subordination of physical education to athletics had occurred in the context of a changing view of schooling. This view saw physical training and athletics as part of physical education which, in turn, was a component of a larger field of school hygiene. Within this expanded idea of school hygiene and physical education athletics assumed the dominant role.[5]

The important point for this essay is the assumption which supported the idea that athletics was educational and gave credence to its rapid expansion in secondary schools, college and American life. These assumptions appeared as a series of interwoven arguments which gave play and athletics a major role in curing the ills of an urban, technological democracy. These arguments included a concern with juvenile delinquency, adolescent sexuality, the social problems or urbanization, leisure time, social unrest, industrialization and economic individualism. None of these themes can be easily separated from each other. They all flowed together to make a larger argument that placed organized sports at the center of the life of modern mass man.

If one looks at America's response to the process of urbanization, one can see how these themes become interwoven. Americans have always had the tendency to favor the rural over the urban. The countryside has tended to be pictured as the home of moral virtues while the urban center has been painted as a college of vice.[6] One of the great fears has been the development of a restless, disorganized urban poor. At the beginning of the nineteenth century the institution which was directed toward the control and rescue of the urban poor was the public school. In fact, a substantial argument is developing among historians that one of the primary causes for the expansion of schooling in the United States was the desire to control a growing urban proletariat.[7]

By the end of the nineteenth century this concern was extended to a belief that fresh air and athletics would provide moral rescue and control of the urban masses. This movement began to flourish in the 1890's when parks and recreation centers were established in major urban centers around the country. It became a well organized movement in 1906 when the Playground and Recreation Association was organized in Washington D.C. with Theodore Roosevelt and Jacob Riis as honorary President and Vice-President. This group held its first national meeting in 1907 in Chicago to honor Chicago's newly developed park and recreation system.[8]

In 1917 a book titled *The Play Movement and Its Significance* written by one of the leaders of the recreation movement was published. It was written to give the reader a detailed understanding of the various elements of the playground and recreation movement in the United States and the reasons for its development. The book covered not only municipal playgrounds and recreation within the schools but also organizations such as the Boy Scouts and the Camp Fire girls. The author wrote from the perspective of one who had dedicated his life to the recreation movement. Curtis had been a secretary of the Playground and Recreation Association of America and Supervisor of the playgrounds of the District of Columbia. His other writings included two books titled *Education Through Play* and *The Practical Conduct of Play*.

Curtis argued that the development and support of the recreation movement reflected the attitude that playgrounds and recreation centers would
be a corrective measure for the ills of an urban industrial society. The need
for physical exercise, Curtis argued, was a result of children and adults being
confined to the monotonous work of assembly lines without the opportunity
to exercise their bodies. Added to this was the increased nervous strain of
urban living. Curtis wrote that people in urban areas needed fresh air and
exercise to avoid "the rapid increase of insanity and the growing instability of
the nervous system. . . ." While Curtis viewed the above as important reasons,
they were not from his perspective the major motive. He gave as the major
concern and dominant motive of the leaders of the play movement a belief
that there was "little for the children to do in the cities, and that in this time
of idleness the devil has found much for idle hands to do. . . . The home seems
to be disappearing, and crime despite an increasingly effective police and
probation system, is increasing everywhere."[9] This point of view had been
more briefly stated several years before in a report of the Committee on
Small Parks in New York City which claimed, "Crime in our large cities is
to a great extent simply a question of athletics."[10]

Many of Curtis's ideas reflected the thinking of one of his friends and key
figures in the development of recreation and athletics in the United States,
Luther Halsey Gulick. Gulick's importance to the development of athletics
and recreation in the United States cannot be overemphasized. Gulick was
the principal founder and first President of the Playground and Recreation
Association while Curtis was its secretary. In 1906 as leader of physical training in New York City he introduced class athletics into the public schools
and organized the Public School Athletic League. He was also one of the
founding organizers of the Boy Scouts of America. In 1912 he and his wife
organized the Camp Fire Girls, and Gulick became their first president.[11]
He was also active in the development of physical training programs for the
Y.M.C.A. It was in the 1890's at a Y.M.C.A. Training School that Luther
Gulick asked James Naismith to invent a new game that could be played
inside during the winter. From this request was invented the game of basketball.[12]

Luther Gulick believed that play and athletics would provide the means
by which a democracy would adjust to the demands of a modern urban
industrial society. Gulick wrote, "Through the loyalty and self-sacrifice
developed in team games by the mutual-consent control, we are laying the
foundations for wider loyalty and a more discerning self-devotion to the
great national ideals on which democracy rests." Gulick shared with many
of his contemporaries a belief that a world of the past which centered around
the home, community and small shop was rapidly giving way to a society
where the family was losing its importance, specialization was occurring in
the industrial structure and the individual was experiencing alienation at
work and in the city. If a democracy were to continue, it required a replace-

ment of the economic individualism of the past with a new corporate conscience which led the individual to self-sacrifice for the good of the social
whole. Within this context society was viewed as interdependent and required a person who would not only be free of evil doings in his personal
activities but also engage in social self-sacrifice. As Gulick wrote, "His corporate life must not only be free from evil, but must have in it positive
social good." [13]

Gulick believed that the two great evils of modern society were exploitation and uncontrolled behavior. Gulick did not argue that exploitation would
be solved through changing the nature of economic relationships. He felt that
exploitation was a product of the development of an interdependent society
which allowed a few to exploit the many. "This exploitation," he wrote, "is
in itself neither good nor evil." Without giving consideration to economic and
social power Gulick firmly believed that economic and social exploitation
could be ended in modern society by creating a new corporate conscience on
the playing fields of America. Out of this corporate conscience would be built
a concept of freedom that was not based on exploitation but upon the good of
the corporate whole. This type of freedom found in play would be "Conditioned by the rules of the game . . . It is for this freedom and this control that
play gives preparation and training." [14]

Gulick also linked the problem of uncontrolled behavior to the realities
of social interdependence. Control was necessary because of the mutual
effect that people had on each other. Underlying this was a fear of the
uncontrolled behavior of urban masses. Gulick expressed a concern that
national celebrations held in urban areas were accompanied by confusion and
mass surges of aimless wanderings: "We have no social forms in which to
express our common emotion." The correction and control of this behavior
could be through play and recreation. "These folk-dances and games," he
wrote, "in which many individuals can participate afford one of the few
avenues that exist for the expression of mass feeling." [15]

Gulick, as one of the national advocates of play and athletics, summarized
his view of play as the mainstay of the modern corporate state:

> The sand pile for the small child, the playground for the middle-sized
> child, the athletic field for the boy, folk dancing and social ceremonial
> life for the boy and the girl in the teens, wholesome means of social
> relationships during adult life—these are fundamental conditions without
> which democracy cannot continue, because upon them rests the develop-
> ment of that self-control which is related to an appreciation of the needs
> of the rest of the groups and of the corporate conscience that is rendered
> necessary by the complex interdependence of modern life. [16]

The ideas of Luther Gulick and Henry Curtis were supported by current
psychological theories which argued that maintenance of order in modern
society depended on the proper channeling of adolescent sexuality. Organized

team games were viewed as one important means of controlling sexuality and utilizing it for the good of society. This idea was given its theoretical statement by G. Stanley Hall, one of America's leading psychologists. Hall argued in his classic work, *Adolescence,* published in 1904, that each stage of a child's development recapitulated a stage of development of the race. He related childhood between the years of four and eight to the cultural epoch when hunting and fishing were the main activities of man. From eight to twelve the child recapitulated the humdrum life of savagery. The developing sexual passions of puberty began the development of the social man and in cultural terms the development of civilization.[17]

Part of Hall's concern, shared by others during his time, was that urban, industrial life did not allow for the free development of these stages of growth. Gang life in cities was attributed to genetic development in children.[18] Juvenile delinquency was attributed to a lack of athletics. Hall became a leading advocate of social organizations that would utilize these stages of human development. One example of how this thinking became a part of the rhetoric used to support social organizations for children and youth is Henry Curtis's discussion of Gulick's development of the Boy Scouts of America. Curtis wrote, "the order of the Boy Scouts is almost exactly what the genetic psychologists like G. Stanley Hall have been preaching for years as the great need of boys. The boy should repeat the racial history." Languishing in the city the boy's quest for adventure became directed toward a life of crime. Within the scouts the instinctual life found an opportunity to return to nature and live a life of chivalry. Curtis wrote, "Nearly all of the active games, which in various forms are played by the children . . . are derived from the hunt and the chase, which have been the occupations of our ancestors. . . . The scout's life is the life itself of which games are single expressions."[19]

The idea that athletics provided release for primitive instinctual drives received widespread currency in the literature of the day. One influential book on play theory, *The Play of Man,* written by Karl Groos, a professor of philosophy at the University of Basel and published in the United States in 1901, argued that certain natural or hereditary impulses that are present, especially in youth, produce activity that would be called play. For instance, games such as football or baseball were activities which expressed the fighting impulse in humanity. The attempt to cross the opponents' goal line in football Groos described as "a specialized form of reciprocal mass contest, since the enemy is not attacked in person, but the effort is made to wrest from him a symbolic stronghold. . . ." Groos's description of baseball and cricket noted that "when the ball which is thrown becomes the goal as well . . . the same instrument is at once weapon and symbol of the enemy."[20]

Very often the primitive impulses associated with youth were linked to sexual drives. Jane Addams argued that most of the problems for youth in urban areas were a result of their sexual "susceptibility" being seduced by the flashing lights and cheap entertainment of the city. She believed these sexual energies could be harnessed for the reform of society if they were channeled through parks, playgrounds, parades, education and national ceremonies.[21] Rhetoric of this type can easily be found in the educational literature of the period. For instance a report of the National Education Association in 1911 on a system of teaching morals in the public schools argued that high school social training had to be different than grammar school because the high school age was a "time of life when passion is born which must be restrained and guided aright or it consumes soul and body. It is the time when social interests are dominant and when social ideals are formed."[22]

A major concern was that modern civilization did not allow for the expression of these adventurous primitive impulses and that they found release in immoral and destructive activities. Playgrounds, athletics, Boy Scouts and similar organizations provided a socially controlled outlet. Jane Addams, writing in 1907 on "Public Recreation and Social Morality" in the *Proceedings of the First Annual Playground Congress* of the Playground Association of America, described the plight of the modern worker as finding himself forced to submit to the environment rather than conquer it. "The appeal to his eye is complicated and trivial, the use of his muscles is fussy and monotonous, the relation between cause and effect is obscure." The worker, Addams argued, found release in cheap drama because it "succeeds in putting a man back into ancestral and primitive emotions. . . ." Public recreation was of more value because it provided for individual participation and greater release of primitive instincts. She wrote, "There is no doubt that while men almost universally enjoy a renewal of the primitive processes of food getting, as the wide-spread pleasure in fishing and hunting can testify, they are also able in constructing their games upon the reminiscent basis to draw upon a varied ·and inexhaustable store of other human experiences."[23]

One of the most famous statements of this attempt to channel the seemingly primitive impulses of humanity was William James's essay "The Moral Equivalent of War" written in 1910. James claimed that "modern man inherits all the innate pugnacity and all the love of glory of his ancestors." He believed that some of the useful results of proper channeling were patriotism, heroism, romance and hardihood. The problem was to find an equivalent that utilized man's innate pugnacity and reproduced the heroics and romance of war. The solution offered by James was a conscription of the youthful population to war against nature by being forced to work in coal and iron mines, road building, fishing fleets, construction and railroads.[24]

G. Stanley Hall's work and emphasis on primitive social drives had a profound effect on the development of the high school in the United States and its emphasis on extra-curricular activities and athletics. Hall firmly believed that the crucial ingredient in the development of any civilization was how it captured and utilized the sexual drives of youth. It was these sexual drives that developed the social man. Hall wrote, "The whole future of life depends on how the new powers of adolescence now given suddenly and profusion are husbanded and directed." Hall believed that the key to husbanding these social-sexual drives were well organized social institutions for youth. The primary organization, of course, was the high school.[25]

It was precisely during this period that the American high school began to undergo a rapid transformation. The objectives of the high school began to shift from that of just teaching academic subjects to that of being an institution whicn encompassed the social life of youth. It was during this period that athletics and extra-curricular activities were brought under the umbrella of the school. The document which exemplifies these changes was the 1918 report of the National Education Association titled *Cardinal Principles of Secondary Education*. This document is widely recognized as being the classic statement of the modern comprehensive high school.[26]

One of the major goals of the high school, the Cardinal Principles Report stated, was giving men "common ideas, common ideals, and common modes of thought, feeling, and action that made for cooperation, social cohesion, and social solidarity." The creation of this corporate being could be accomplished through the "social mingling of pupils through the organization and administration of the school." The report called for the "participation of pupils in common activities. . . , such as athletic games, social activities and the government of the school."[27] The cardinal principles report not only legitimized the inclusion of athletics in the total program of the high school but also placed it in the framework of developing the social instincts of youth and creating the type of corporate conscience that had been slated by Luther Gulick.[28]

One of the other goals given the high school by the *Cardinal Principles* was worthy use of leisure time. This was an issue which permeated discussions of the development of athletics and recreation centers. For instance, Mitchell and Mason in their 1930's text, noted that one of the major factors contributing to the expansion of athletics was the development of intra-mural programs which could be carried over to the leisure hours of adult life. They wrote, "This emphasis was greatly encouraged by schoolmen because of the inclusion of this objective in the Seven Cardinal Principles of Education. Since the increasing hours of leisure will comprise the great social problem for the coming generation, it is imperative that the schools anticipate this need." Their argument extended beyond leisure time being used through individual participation and included the role of spectator as worthy use of leisure time. They wrote, "There is leisure-time value in reading accounts of important sporting events in their season, such as the National Open Golf Tournament, the International Tennis match, and the big football game."[29]

The important thing to realize about the argument that leisure time should be used in participation or spectatorship at athletic events or at parks and recreation centers was that this contradicted the goals of those union groups in the United States which had fought for a shorter working day and more leisure time for the American worker. Their goal was to provide leisure for the American workers so that he could gain a greater understanding of the political and economic system and bring about some fundamental changes in that system. For instance, the campaign for the eight-hour day was launched by the National Labor Union in 1866 as a means for labor to acquire enough knowledge and capital to establish a cooperative commonwealth and abolish the wage system. Ira Steward, the prophet of the eight-hour day, saw the eight hour day as a means of forcing an increase in technological productiveness through the leisure time spending of the worker. This would increase the capital available to labor and make possible the purchase of cooperative enterprises.[30] George Gunton, one of Steward's disciples, argued that the eight-hour day allowed for leisure that could profitably be used in attending half time schools and participation in informal modes of education.[31]

Nowhere in the labor literature can one find a union or union spokesman arguing that a worker could best use the leisure time gained through the shorter working day by participating in or watching an athletic event. For the labor movement this would hardly be considered a "worthy use of leisure time." From the Knights of Labor in the nineteenth century to the AFL in the twentieth century there has been a steady advocacy of labor lyceums, night schools, study groups, colleges, summer camps, chautauquas and libraries.[32]

To say that labor thought of worthy use of leisure as studying and preparing for social change is not to say that those who thought of it in terms of athletics were reacting to labor's philosophy. In fact, those who advocated athletics and recreation tended to view social unrest and social problems as things that could be solved through institutional manipulation and the proper molding of character. Athletics and recreation would channel the instinctual unrest and create the proper democratic character. They did not see the problem in the same terms as labor nor speak the same language.

In this connection it is also useful to ask whether sports did in fact begin to occupy a majority of leisure time activities and if this led the American workingman to shift his attention from political and economic concerns to athletic events. There is no definite way to answer this question but there are some suggestive materials available in the form of studies of the changing content of newspapers. One study was conducted by the Carnegie Foundation for their survey on *American College Athletics*. This survey looked at the extension of the sports page in relationship to the growth of space assigned to other departments of six representative newspapers for the years 1913, 1920, and 1927. They found that in the three New York newspapers studied sports news increased 167 percent between the years of 1913 and 1927. In the three other newspapers which were located in Boston, Salt Lake City and San Francisco the increase was about equal to the growth of other news space. There was no significant increase in the proportion of news space devoted to athletics. The most interesting and important discovery was the effect of the rise of school athletics on the expansion of the sports page. In the three New York newspapers the space given to school and college athletics increased 245 percent while the space given to professional sports advanced 110 percent. In the other three newspapers it was found that by 1927 school athletics occupied three times the space of professional athletics. Clearly one of the major elements in the expansion of the sports page was the development of school and college athletics.[33]

Another survey conducted by the President's Research Committee on Social Trends appointed by President Herbert Hoover in 1929 concluded that the "increased emphasis upon sport news has gone along with the expansion of other departments of the newspaper but in general the space given to sports had tended to show the most rapid growth." This survey used not only the findings of the Carnegie Foundation but also those of other studies. One study was a close comparison of news space in the *Chicago Daily* and *Sunday Tribune* for the years 1920 and 1930. This study found that while total news space increased by 76 percent, sports increased by 79 percent. The major reason for the increase in the sports page was football which at this time was primarily a high school and college sport. Space devoted to football increased by 145 percent while that devoted to baseball increased by 23 percent. Another study used in the report was Robert and Helen Lynd's famous social analysis of Middletown. This study of the content of newspapers is significant because it extended back to 1890 when athletics were beginning to be promoted and organized on a mass basis. They found that organized sports showed a greater increase since 1890 in the relative amount of news space than any other department of news. In Middletown the increase was from 4 percent of the total news content in 1890 to 16 percent in 1923. In another study of rural Minnesota weekly newspapers it was found that the average column inches increased from 3.23 in 1900 to 14.23 in 1929.[34]

One cannot arrive at a firm conclusion from the surveys of the Carnegie Foundation or the President's Research Committee on Social Trends that there was a shift in concern and study of social and economic problems to an interest in athletics by the general American public. There are a host of unanswered questions related to these surveys dealing with who read what in newspapers and how much that reflected interest and concern in any particular area. But if one were to assume that newspaper content represented some form of political map of the mind of the general public the studies do suggest a shifting concern toward organized athletics. The studies also suggest that within the limitations of the number of newspapers surveyed the cause of that shift was primarily the rise of organized athletics in the public schools and colleges.

Another way of looking at the issue of leisure time is in terms of spectatorship versus participation. Certainly one of the goals of those who saw athletics as one of the cures for the ills of modern society was mass participation. Basketball was not invented as a spectator sport but as a game to replace traditional gymnastic activities during winter months. The emphasis in basketball was on participation not spectatorship. The development of intramural athletics was in terms of extending athletic participation as was the park and recreation movement. Athletic leaders did not deny the importance of spectatorship but considered it secondary to participation.

One major concern about athletics by the 1920's was its growing commercialism and the rise of spectatorship over participation. While athletics was promoted as a cure to technological society, that very society turned it into a commercial enterprise. Athletics became big business. The naivete that led to the belief that athletics could cure society's problems overlooked the fact that without any fundamental change in the social and economic structure athletics would be turned into a business enterprise. This occurred in public school and college athletics as well as professional sports.

In colleges and public schools commercialization not only meant profit but also became a form of public relations in which athletics was used to sell the school to the community. For instance, in terms of attendance and gate receipts college football underwent a phenomenal rise in the 1920's. The President's Research Committee on Social Trends reported that attendance at football games at 49 major colleges around the country increased from 1,504,319 in 1921 to 3,617,421 in 1929. Gate receipts increased at a more rapid rate from 2,696,345 dollars to 9,032,160 dollars during the same period.[35] It seems clear that more startling increases could be shown if figures were available from the beginning of the century. A survey of land grant colleges undertaken by the Office of Education in the late 1920's revealed a tremendous investment in athletic plants. At many schools this investment exceeded 10 percent of the total capital investment of the entire school. For example, at the University of Illinois the capital invested in the athletic plant was 13 percent of the total capital investment, at the University of Wyoming it was 16 percent, at Ohio State University it was 12 percent and at the University of Nebraska it was 12 percent.[36]

It was often argued that interscholastic athletics was justified because the gate receipts covered the expenses of the athletic plants and intramural athletics. The figures presented by the Office of Education fail to support this conclusion and in fact suggested that intramural athletics was sacrificed to interscholastic athletics. Most of the athletic plants were financed by a combination of large loans, state appropriations, gifts and athletic receipts. Ohio State University borrowed $555,000 for its athletic plant, the University of Minnesota borrowed $450,000, and the University of Illinois borrowed $358,800. It was found that in most colleges athletic receipts were not even enough to cover the expenses of interscholastic athletics let alone intramural sports. The study stated, "The reports show that only 8 of the land-grant institutions defray the operating costs of intercollegiate [athletics] from earnings alone, while 27 institutions assess a special athletic fee against the students. . . ." In the remaining schools the deficit from intercollegiate athletics was covered by State subsidies. Only two institutions reported paying for intramural athletics from athletic receipts alone.[37]

The emphasis in intercollegiate athletics was not on participation but spectatorship. While huge crowds flowed in and out of the stadiums only a minority of students participated on the teams. Only 3 percent of the total student population at land grant colleges earned athletic letters in 1928. And, of course, student control of athletics had been lost in most colleges. The study stated, "In only seven of the colleges giving students representation on this board of control does student membership outvote the faculty membership."[38]

Now why did interscholastic athletics continue up to the present even though the emphasis was on spectatorship and was very often conducted at a financial loss to the educational institution and at a loss to the educational goals of athletics? One answer is the public relations factor and the belief that the pride engendered in the local community ultimately leads to its financial growth. Athletics became a form of boosterism, a symbolic representation of the dynamics of the community. As the Carnegie Foundation stated, "a series of fast, hard games at basketball or football, forming a season that culminates in a championship match, whether lost or won, leads to much excitement, town pride, and ultimate profits in sales of goods by local merchants."[39] In 1927 the National Collegiate Athletic Association recommended as one of the primary objectives of intercollegiate athletics, "To reflect through representation the spirit of the institution."[40] Even today in professional sports this boosterism is rampant in buying teams for areas and building stadiums. When O. J. Simpson of the Buffalo Bills broke the professional football rushing record in 1973, Erie County, New York proclaimed O. J. Simpson Month. A proclamation issued by the County extolled the team for "the prestige and honor they have brought to our area." The proclamation stated that O. J. Simpson's selection by the Bills was a "wise one not only for the Buffalo Bills but also for Erie County, which is also reaping national acclaim, fame, prestige and honor."[41]

The Carnegie Foundation found the emphasis on boosterism led to the buying and selling of players, funds to support players in school and other corrupt activities in college and public school athletics. Their report stated that "we must condemn utterly the activities of those older persons, be they alumni, townsmen, or college officers, who recruit and subsidize athletes, corrupt young habits under the guise of charity, and imperil private morals to the detriment of society. They stand among the secret enemies of the social order." But even though sports was open to the secret enemies of society it was still praised by the Carnegie Foundation report as a guide in "the wise use of leisure time." "If there is good reason to believe," the report stated, "that schoolboy athletics tend to decrease such crimes as larceny, burglary, embezzlement, assault, manslaughter, and murder, there is no less reason to believe in similar powers for college sports."[42]

While college and public schools athletics tended toward an emphasis on spectatorship the general public turned in that direction. Increased attendance at college and high school football games was matched by increased attendance at professional baseball games. There was noted an increased involvement of adults in games like tennis and golf.[43] But in these two cases the involvement tended to be from the middle and upper middle classes of society. The popular game of bowling became a truly commercial venture requiring the paying for lanes in privately owned bowling alleys. The rise of basketball and football continued the direction toward mass spectatorship rather than mass participation.

The ideology which supported the rise of athletics in American life argued that it would relieve the monotony and tedium of work in an industrial society, end social unrest and crime, provide worthy use of leisure time and build a corporate democracy. Today many parks and recreation centers in large cities stand vacant because people fear urban crime. Crime and social unrest does not appear to have played itself out on the athletic fields of America. The goal of use of leisure might have been fulfilled through spectatorship. The dream of labor leaders of the worker devoting himself to study and social change does not appear to have been achieved. Instead, we can think of many American workers escaping the monotony and tedium of work in front of the hypnotic glow of the television, watching endless series of athletic events that have been planned in terms of market research and are periodically interrupted by commercials. Maybe organized athletics now provides an escape from our corporate world by portraying a lost American dream that the poor can rise on the basis of merit and that winning the game is done by playing by the rules. But even here that dream is tainted as teams are shifted from city to city in search of a good market, players are drugged and traded in the marketplace, and competition is maintained through the monopolistic hiring practices of the college draft.

NOTES

1. Elmer D. Mitchell and Bernard S. Mason, *The Theory of Play* (New York, 1935), pp. 171–194.

2. Clarence E. Rainwater, *The Play Movement in the United States* (Chicago, 1922), pp. 13–14.

3. Howard J. Savage, Harold W. Bentley, John T. McGovern and Dean F. Smiley, *American College Athletics* (New York, 1929).

4. Ibid., pp. 3–33.

5. Ibid., pp. 52–76.

6. See Charles N. Glaab and A. Theodore Brown, *A History of Urban America* (New York, 1967), pp. 53–83.

7. See Carl Kaestle, *The Evolution of an Urban School System* (Cambridge, 1973); and Stanley K. Schultz, *The Culture Factory* (New York, 1973).

8. Henry S. Curtis, *The Play Movement and Its Significance* (New York, 1917), pp. 15–18.

9. Ibid., pp. 1–11.

10. Sadie American, "The Movement for Small Playgrounds," *American Journal of Sociology* (September, 1898): 167.

11. Curtis, *Play Movement,* pp. 15, 17, 39, 130, 246, and 247.

12. James Naismith, "How Basketball Started and Why It Grew," in *Aims and Methods in School Athletics,* edited by E. Dana Caulkins (New York, 1932), pp. 221–236.

13. Luther Gulick, "Play and Democracy," *Proceedings of the First Annual Playground Congress* (New York, 1907): 11–16; and *A Philosophy of Play* (New York, 1920).

14. Gulick, *A Philosophy of Play,* pp. 254–261.

15. Ibid., pp. 236 and 263.

16. Ibid., p. 265.

17. G. Stanley Hall, *Adolescence: Its Psychology and Its Relations to Physiology, Anthropology, Sociology, Sex, Crime, Religion, and Education* (New York, 1945).

18. See J. Adams Puffer, *The Boy and His Gang* (Boston, 1912).

19. Curtis, *Play Movement,* pp. 251–252.

20. Karl Groos, *The Play of Man* (New York, 1901), p. 182.

21. Jane Addams, *The Spirit of Youth and the City Streets* (New York, 1909).

22. "Tentative Report of the Committee on A System of Teaching Morals in the Public Schools," *National Education Association Proceedings* (1911): 360.

23. Jane Addams, "Public Recreation and Social Morality," *Proceedings of the First Annual Playground Congress* (New York, 1907): 22–24.

24. William James, "The Moral Equivalent of War." A copy of this essay can be found in *American Issues,* ed. by Merle Curti, Willard Thorp and Carlos Baker (Chicago, 1960), pp. 916–923.

25. Hall, *Adolescence,* Vol. I, p. xv.

26. See Edward A. Krug, *The Shaping of the American High School* (New York, 1964) and Joel Spring, *Education and the Rise of the Corporate State* (Boston, 1972), pp. 108–125.

27. *Cardinal Principles of Secondary Education* (Bureau of Education, 1918).

28. For a study of the relationship between concepts of sexuality and instinct and the development of the high school, see Joel Spring, "The American High School and the Development of Social Character" to be published in *Work, Technology and Education* (Urbana: The University of Illinois Press, 1974).

29. Mitchell and Mason, *Theory of Play,* pp. 438–439.

30. Gerald N. Grob, *Workers and Utopia* (Evanston, Illinois, 1961), pp. 18–19.

31. Philip R. V. Curoe, *Educational Attitudes and Policies of Organized Labor in the United States* (New York, 1926), pp. 100–101.

32. Ibid., pp. 66–193.

33. Savage, *American College Athletics*, pp. 266–290.

34. Jesse Fredrick Steiner, *Americans at Play: Recent Trends in Recreation and Leisure Time Activities* (New York, 1933), pp. 97–100.

35. Ibid., pp. 86–94.

36. *Survey of Land-Grant Colleges and Universities*, directed by Arthur J. Klien, Bulletin 1930, No. 9, Office of Education (Washington D.C., 1930), p. 230.

37. Ibid., pp. 229–236.

38. Ibid., pp. 457–466.

39. Savage, *American College Athletics*, p. 61.

40. *Survey of Land-Grant Colleges*, p. 457.

41. "O. J. is Big in Buffalo," *Plain Dealer* (Cleveland, December 17, 1973), Section D, p. 1.

42. Savage, *American College Athletics*, pp. 296–300.

43. Steiner, *Americans at Play*, pp. 100–102.

SOCIAL CHANGE AND THE COMMERCIALIZATION OF PROFESSIONAL SPORT

R. Terry Furst

The identification and understanding of the social factors that underlie the burgeoning commercialization of modern professional sport in the United States is the primary objective of this paper. Within this framework the transformation of baseball, football, basketball and hockey from play to professionalization is explored. By presenting sociological patterns in present sports, the immediate past and the distant past, light will be shed on the historical antecedents that engender changes in professional sports.

Specifically, we would like to know what are the effect of increasing commercialization on the intrinsic nature of sports? What are the indicants that set today's sports apart from other periods? To answer these questions and to raise others, let us start by scanning the present situation and then examine the relationship between play and work.

Present versus Past

Professional spectator sports in the United States in the last twenty years have grown at an unprecedented rate. The following quotation characterizes this upward movement in professional sports:

> In a time of booming population, inflation and television, everything is coming up dollar signs, from Super Bowl Commercials at $135,000 a minute to new stadiums at $50 million apiece. . . It is a time when Braulio Baeza makes a quarter of a million dollars a year riding horses, when a college senior Lew Alcindor may make a million dollars playing pro-basketball—and when Joe Namath makes a fortune playing football and treads on a white llama rug in the splendor of his East Side pad (Durso, 1969:1).

The fact that historically the quest for money through sports has been present at all times does not mean that today's zealous pursuit of pecuniary reward is just an extension of the past. Professional sports, in their present mercantilistic forms, evince an aura which is ubiquitous in the history of sports. Moreover, the ambience that surrounds athletics today conceals a fundamental transformation which is qualitatively and quantitatively distinct. The historical uniqueness and validity of this proposition can be demonstrated

R. Terry Furst, "Social Change and the *Commercialization of Professional Sports,*" *International Review of Sport Sociology,* Vol. 6 (1971), pp. 153–173. Reprinted by permission.

in part by identifying historical trends and relating them to contemporary manifestations in sports. To facilitate the identification of the uniqueness of modern sports, an examination of the historical relationship between play and work will be helpful.

Play and Work

Caillois (1961:1–10) defines play as a "free" activity that is not obligatory, and is unproductive; it does not create new goods. There is the same amount of wealth at the beginning and end. Play is also "make-believe" in the sense that the reality of play is separate from the reality of everyday life. Later in this social process, play emerges as a game. Games are the product of rules. Organized games have their modern origin in the first quarter of the nineteenth century in England (Huizinga, 1964:197). At that time the sporadic, spontaneous play of individuals was superseded by the initiation of permanent teams and organizations devoted to the playing of "ballgames." The systematic approach to play was a reflection of increasing regimentation and organization in British society. Until the twentieth century, hunting and fishing, for the most part, denoted work in the U.S. But through a composite of social conditions, the most important being industrialism, these subsistence occupations were gradually transformed into play (hunting and fishing for pleasure). Still later in this process, play reverts back to work. Through organization and professionalization, men emerge who act as hunting and fishing guides thereby assuming a work role.

The lumberjack profession has had a parallel development. Initially it fulfilled a work role. Later lumberjacks competed in contests (play) to demonstrate their skills. With encroaching commercial pressures, many of them competed as professionals, thereby reverting to a work form. This cyclical process is not restricted to primary industries; it can be evidenced in modern business where play and work overlap.

When the play-work model is applied to sports, the evident difference is that the four major American professional sports started out as play instead of work. With this exception, the tripartite transmutation identified in fishing, hunting and lumbering, correspond to present-day professional athletics. Brief outlines of the four major sports will show the transformation of play into work. Emphasis will be on three points: first appearance of the sport in which it resembles its present forms: when the play element in sport was superseded by codification of the rules and became a game; and when the players first engaged in the sport for money (work).

Baseball first appeared in Boston in 1831 as a verisimilitude of its present form and was called "town ball." In 1845 the first regular ball club was organized in New York City. The popularity of the game increased in 1869 in the Cincinnati Red Stockings became the "first salaried team in the game's history." (Menke, 1969:47, 64).

Football, in its early stages, emanated from rugby and soccer. A combination of rugby and soccer with variations was played as early as 1860 in the U.S., and had a slight resemblance to the contemporary game. But it was not until 1874, in a game between Harvard and McGill universities, that a format similar to present-day football appeared. For the first time players were able to "pick up the ball at any time and also were permitted to run with it if pursued." In 1882 rules of "downs" and "yards" were introduced, thus establishing rules which definitely differentiated the game from the earlier rugby-soccer game. Twenty-one years later in Latrobe, Pennsylvania, the first professional game was played. (Menke, 1969:367,427)

Hockey was imported from Canada. It originated in Kingston, Canada, in 1855; some reports suggest hockey was played in that city in the 1830's. In 1875 students at McGill University in Canada laid down a set of rules. Hockey made its first appearance in the U.S. in 1893 at Yale University in Connecticut and Johns Hopkins University in Maryland. The first professional team was organized in 1903 and was ". . . known as (the) Portage Lakers from the small Michigan mining town of Houghton." (Menke, 1969:628,630)

As far as it is known, basketball did not have a period of unrestrained play, where rules guiding play were customary rather than codified. Instead of the usual progression from traditional play forms, the game of basketball was invented in 1891 by James A. Naismith. The game was introduced by fastening two peach baskets to a gymnasium balcony and stipulating a set of thirteen rules. Seven years later, the National Basketball League, the game's first professional organization was founded (Menke, 1969:150-152).

The Table on page 100 summarizes these four major spectator sports and three other popular professional sports in the U.S.; the statistics are vertically ordered according to the temporal progression of each sport from inception to codification, and finally professionalization. A perusal of this Table indicates that each sport endured for varying lengths of time as play, as a game and then as work (professionalization).

HISTORICAL ANTECEDENTS OF MODERN SPORTS

The immediate task will be to locate the determinants that affected the change from play to work in sports. To accomplish this the essential factors will be historically ordered from the early nineteenth century to the first quarter of the twentieth century. This period, which will be called contemporary, constitutes an infrastructure—a primal era—that has evoked, in part, the immediate influences affecting modern sports; that is, a time from the end of the contemporary era to the present. The primary factors in the modern epoch will also be set forth in their temporal sequence.

Within contemporary sports, the following factors will be discussed: 1) industrialization; 2) decline of the work week; 3) immigration and internal migration; 4) community spirit; 5) mass education; 6) religion. The factors in modern sports to be discussed will include: 1) large scale organization; 2) growth of the community; 3) rationalization of sport; 4) television; and 5) emerging new middle class.

Industrialization and the Decline of the Work Week

Without increased leisure,[1] the development of sports would have been seriously hampered. From 1850 to 1960, free time increased from 2.18 hours per day to 7.48 hours per day. (Kaplan, 1960:38) A steadily increasing gross national product over the last 120 years, with the exception of periodic declines, and rapidly rising output per worker, a response to technological innovation, has markedly raised the standard of living—thus increasing free time, the time left after eating, sleeping and other necessities. (Kaplan, 1960:38) More specifically, the impetus for this growth can be attributed to an array of industrial and social concurrences. The introduction and initial operation of a national railway system, along with a growing population, stand out as primary stimuli to engendering economic progress in the last half of the nineteenth century.

One of the most important consequences of increased free time was the facilitation of the transition of sport from play to a game form. But the transformation has a unique element that needs to be briefly explored. Looking at the Table, it can be seen that the majority of sports listed have a longer period as a game when compared with the time they existed as play. This difference is a result of the disproportionate increase in free time in the last half of the nineteenth century and the beginning of the twentieth century. Most[2] of the sports listed were games in the last quarter of the nineteenth century, a time when the work week was decreasing and free time was very rapidly increasing.

Glancing at the Table under the horizontal column marked work, it is interesting to note that five of the sports turned professional at approximately the same time—the period from 1895 to 1903. The general organizational tenor that pervaded this period in American history might account for this trend toward professionalization.

In the late 1880's and 1890's the century was industrializing. Rational calculations of operating costs and increments of production became administrative policies. Furthermore, expanding firms required coordination between larger departments, and accounting procedures became increasingly important as the web of affiliations became more complex. In light of these developments seeking to maximize profit, it is not difficult to understand how this organizational ethos influenced sports. Within eight years (1895-1903), five sports had reorganized on a professional basis.

Table 1

	Baseball	Football	Hockey	Basketball	Golf	Tennis	Bowling
Play	1831–1845 (14 yrs.)	1874–1882 (8 yrs.)	1855–1875 (20 yrs.)	—	1779–1786 (7 yrs.)	1874–1881 (7 yrs.)	1825–1875 (50 yrs.)
Game	1845–1869 (24 yrs.)	1882–1895 (24 yrs.)	1875–1903 (28 yrs.)	1891–1898 (7 yrs.)	1786–1894 (108 yrs.)	1881–1926 (45 yrs.)	1875–1895 (20 yrs.)
Work	1869–1970 (101 yrs.)	1895–1970 (75 yrs.)	1903–1970 (67 yrs.)	1898–1970 (72 yrs.)	1894–1970 (76 yrs.)	1926–1970 (44 yrs.)	1895–1970 (75 yrs.)

Immigration, Migration and Community Spirit

By the turn of the century, the population had swelled to seventy-six million, three times larger than it was in 1850. In 1900, forty percent of the population lived in urban centers. (Petersen, 1963:33) The effects of increased population and internal migration upon sports are interwoven. The myriad movement of immigrants and pioneers had an important effect upon the development of sports vis-a-vis the emergence and decline of community life.

Frohlich (1952:5) addressed himself to the relationship between the intense interest in sports evinced by some communities and their historical development. He studied the community of Athens, Ohio and found that football and basketball aroused the residents' passionate interest because of several factors.

The predominant factor was designated as the "Community Service System" which was at its peak between 1910 and 1930. Athletes and members of the community, explicitly and implicitly, mutually supported each other. By intensive participation by way of consistent attendance at the games, and through frequent laudatory comments about the team, the spectators demonstrated loyalty, if not devotion, to the home team. In turn, the team enhanced community pride: when the athletes were victorious, the whole town shared in the glory. Frohlich (1952:64) speculates that emphasis on victory or defeat works directly upon the self-attitudes of the individual. If there is a win, the self is vindicated. The idea of the winning team expands to include other selves into a "we feeling." If a loss is sustained, the spectator's self is damaged. He may withdraw with an elimination of the "we" feeling, depending upon the closeness of the score and the quality of play. Using this notion as a conceptual framework, Frohlich's thesis suggest that at a time (1910-1920) when the community was losing its collective solidarity, sports were a means to re-introduce the spirit of togetherness into the community. "Thus the week-end football or basketball game is not just a few hours' diversion for players and fans; it is a symbol and a ritual, a reaffirmation of unity and collective pride." (Frohlich, 1952:274)

Three ideas pertinent to the historical development of sports can be abstracted from this study:

1. Immigration and internal migration in the last half of the nineteenth century affected social solidarity in many communities during a time when sports were either in a play or game form. Frohlich (1952:197) makes a similar point when he observes that "the influx of over 3000 strangers into the community in ten years (1900-1910) certainly could not occur without same loosening in the interlocking patterns of social interaction."
2. There is an interdependent relationship between a community and the progression of a sport. The Athens, Ohio, community study reports that football and baseball had been well established before the community used the spectacle of sport as a source of cohesion in response to a decline in social

solidarity between 1910 and 1920. On the other hand, an influx and migration of residents into a community would seriously affect social integration, thereby inhibiting the growth of sport in an embryonic stage.

3. Inter-community sports rivalries were weak in the last half of the nineteenth century due to the recurrent waves of immigration and migration that had an unsettling effect upon the community. Opposition between community teams in the twentieth century has been a powerful reason for the rise and popularity of sports. The inter-town basketball rivalries currently observable in the Midwest attest to the importance of community pride in the development of sports.

Mass Education

Another aspect that relates to the understanding of the growth of contemporary sports in the U.S. is the introduction of mass education in the 1880's. Education became more important as a reaction to a waning agrarian society. Attendance, at all levels of education, increased. Consequently, primary and secondary schools, along with colleges and universities, were built. The migration of college students to small communities enhanced the development of sports. Football, hockey and basketball were dependent upon students to develop and popularize them. The perpetuation of amateur sports was a direct outgrowth of school athletics, albeit amateurism flourished in the school system. It has paradoxically acted as a recruiting agent for today's market of professional athletes.

Religion

Recreation was recognized as a basic need by the Puritans. But diversionary pastimes that did not include productivity were thought to be sinful. The Christian church interpreted sport in its play and game forms as an activity that did not reflect religious piety but instead connoted a reckless abandon signifying improper public behavior—a sin in the eyes of the church. The Christian church cannot be entirely blamed for inhibiting the development of sports. The church in the U.S. generally advocated that "one day in seven shall be a day of rest." Originally this day was to be one devoted to religious worship and abstention from physical labor. In the nineteenth century, the six-day work week was prevalent, Sunday was usually the only day on which sports activities could be engaged in. But moral, religious and legal sanctions were a strong deterrent to engaging in sports on Sunday. The New England colonies, under the influence of Puritanism, passed "Blue Laws" which curtailed activities on the Sabbath. (Lee, 1964:175) Many other states passed laws which either prohibited work or limited the kinds of activities permitted on Sunday.

Assuming that the Puritan revulsion against sports was omnipresent but declining in the nineteenth century, it can be advanced that sports introduced at a later time in the century went through a transition from play to work more rapidly than sports introduced at an early period because of religious restraints. Partial evidence exists for this proposition. By tracing the development of football, hockey, basketball and tennis, and comparing the progression of these sports to that of baseball and bowling, it becomes apparent that sports introduced at an earlier time had a slower transition than those initiated at a later date. Football, which was introduced at a later time than baseball, had a thirty-two year span from play to professionalism. Baseball took thirty-eight years to reach the same point. Hockey, introduced in this country in 1893, took ten years to become professionalized. Basketball took only seven years to start being played for money. Bowling, which was introduced in a premodern form in 1825, required seventy years to make the transformation to professional status. This evidence, although not conclusive, does indicate a trend sufficient for positing that religion, particularly the Christian ethic, acted as a barrier to the growth of sports.[3]

Upsurging industrialism, spiraling immigration, extensive population movements, mass education, religion and the application of prebureaucratic organizational forms in business combined to exert varying pressures on the accretion and unfolding spectacle of sports in the nineteenth century and the first quarter of the twentieth century. This delineation does not mean these influences were restricted to this period; it suggests that they exerted their maximum effect during the contemporary era, and shaped the forces that were to have a direct effect upon modern sports.

MODERN SPORTS

No single event or momentous occurrence heralded the beginning of what has been designated as the era of modern sports. The roaring twenties acted as a bridge connecting contemporary sports with modern sports. The influence that characterizes modern sports was forming although not fully operative in the twenties. The beginning of modern sports coincides with the beginning of the recovery of the economy in the 1930's. During this time the "organizational society" became firmly entrenched and replaced the prebureaucratic enterprises (Presthus, 1962:59). It is difficult to cite an exact time when this mode of planning affected the operations within sport administration. A general indication would be the emergence of the public relations expert who usually accompanies the rise of large-scale organizations. (Presthus, 1962:70) When the entrepreneur, as a large-scale business operator, comes in conflict with society, the expert is called upon to ameliorate these differences and to promote the desired effect. By supplying specific information that facilitates the quelling of obstacles, the publicist fulfills a vital service. (Wilensky, 1967:10)[4]

Large-Scale Organization

From the aforementioned rationale an approximate date can be ascertained for the emergence of large-scale organization and planning in professional sports. By 1950 sport entrepreneurs were beset with decreasing attendance and the spectre of television. Their reaction to television was ambivalent: they wanted the revenues to supplant losses from declining attendance but feared the spectator would abandon the stadium permanently for the comfort of viewing the sport spectacle in his living room. It was a time when major changes were needed to confront or to embrace the unknown effects of television on the professional sports. It was a time when organizational approaches were being implemented by a new breed of sports entrepreneurs. Formerly sport franchise owners were men who generally approached the administration of teams with a mixture of deep emotional commitment to the sport and the belief that financial operations were a necessary adjunct to a successful season. Imbued with the organizational ethos, the new owner thinks primarily of maximizing profit through calculated business procedures. This new type of sports entrepreneur still appreciates the spectacle of sport but only as a secondary consideration. Consistently increasing revenues are the primary consideration.

Growth of the Community

From 1950 to 1960, the population increased by 29.4 million in what the U.S. Bureau of the Budget calls standard metropolitan statistical areas, meaning: "One or more contiguous non-agricultural counties containing at least one city of 50,000 or more, and having a generally metropolitan character based on the counties' social and economic integration with the central city." (Petersen, 1963:186) This increase in metropolitan areas did not go unnoticed by the more judicious sports owners. When the Braves baseball team decided to move from Milwaukee to Atlanta in 1966, the ostensible reason was declining attendance. But of equal importance was the potential increase in revenues from a larger telecast and radio market in the Southeast. The Braves estimated they would receive $750,000 in Atlanta compared with $525,000 in Wisconsin (*Newsweek,* 1965:67) because of the increased media market in this area providing high return per dollar invested in sports. The importance of television and radio markets has been unquestionably predominant in the expansion plans of many professional baseball, football, hockey and basketball teams.

The Effect of Technology on the Rationalization of Sport

The emergence of superior athletic performance is related to technological innovations. Discoveries in science and changes in industry are reflected in aids and techniques eagerly applied in the environs of the sport spectacle. The exigencies of the growing demands of excellence by both spectator and participant rapidly absorb all technical assistance.

Technological advances have been implemented directly and indirectly in sports. Changes in protective gear in football and the introduction of safety helmets in baseball are examples of direct application. Indirect effects are innovations that do not pertain to the equipment actually used in playing the game. One example of how technology indirectly affects the game is the introduction of night baseball into the major leagues in 1946. This might have been apocryphal of the renascent entertainment aura in sports.

In football, possibly because of its game format, rational techniques have been implemented for a longer period than in any other sport. In 1905 Knute Rockne and Gus Dorais teamed up to introduce the forward pass in football. This marked, as Denney (1957:116) suggests, the application of scientific principles to sports: utilizing the passing potential of the spiral-shaped ball. The "ethos of brawn" had given way to "inventiveness." The cerebral approach to sports engendered the two platoon system in college football in 1941. Soon afterwards, in 1943, professional teams adopted the same idea: free substitution of players.

In 1968, in Baltimore, baseball attempted to apply scientific principles to the game and conducted a time and motion study. One conclusion was that one-fifth of the game needed more lively, entertaining activity to eliminate what may be called dead time.

Perhaps the scarcity of outstanding boxing matches has evoked mass media's most notable effort to influence sport. The elimination of dead time would appear to be the idea behind simulated championship boxing matches between former champions vis-a-vis the lucubrations of a computer, e.g., programming the computer with strategic information such as the "punching power . . . general normal physical condition, stamina, power behind a left hook, power behind a straight right. . ." (Daniel, 1968:18). The computer then spews out a blow-by-blow account of champions of the past paired against each other. For example, "Cassius Clay outpointed Max Schmeling in 15 rounds with the score 10-3-2 . . . Rocky Marciano defeated Max Baer in the thirteenth round, TKO" (Daniel, 1968:19).

Television

Television has been an integral factor in the bourgeoning sports industry. More perplexing and in need of discussion is the degree to which historical circumstances have influenced television—facilitating the hegemony it present-ly maintains over professional spectator sports. Three conditions greatly aided the rise and importance of television in sports: 1) lagging attendance at major sports events in the early 1950's; 2) federal legislation; and 3) an emerging new middle class with increasing leisure time.

Since the attitudes of major sporting franchises in the U.S. were ambiva-lent in response to the introduction of television in the early fifties, the question the owners faced was: would the drain on their coffers be assuaged by potential revenues from television or would the possibility of a greater decline in attendance by TV negatively offset any gains from television? The question, amidst debate, is still unresolved (see Bogart, 1958:17; Wylie, 1955:29; Jordan, 1950:74). Whether the opinion of baseball entrepreneurs in general concurred with the notion that television would eventually establish a new audience or whether they thought it would be harmful is beside the historical fact. Baseball warily greeted television in the late forties, hesitantly accepted it in the early fifties and warmly embraced it in the latter part of the decade.

The action of the Justice Department was to have broad implication for professional sports. In 1951 it warned baseball and football officials that designating geographic areas where games could be televised was a restraint of trade. Baseball complied with the suggestion and stopped blacking out areas. However, Bert Bell of the National Football League resisted and eventually in 1953 defeated the Justice Department decision by obtaining a favourable ruling from Federal Court Justice, Alan K. Grim, who said in part: "The purpose of the Sherman (antitrust) Act certainly will not be served by prohibiting the defendant clubs . . . from protecting their home gate receipts from the disastrous effects of invading telecasts. . . ." (King, 1965:32)

Two important facts can be deduced from the manner in which football and baseball confronted the threat of federal intervention. Baseball was greatly intimidated by the specter of the Justice Department. It succumbed reluctantly, permitting networks to telecast games wherever they wished. This capitulation created a precedent for unlimited telecasting of baseball; a condition that, at times, undermined attendance.[5] Whereas, football took an aggressive posture in defeating the action of the Justice Department, thereby lessening the possibility of overexposure.

The disparate actions of baseball and football characterize their respective predisposition as commercial entities. When the football leagues' commissioners negotiate with television, they proceed with the knowledge of a league unified. Substantial financial benefits accrue from their unanimity. Obversely, baseball has bargained from a fragmented position. Individual teams dicker with television networks, inevitably weakening the collective position and rewards therein for baseball.

Television, while having a considerable effect upon sports as a dispenser of mass entertainment, only increased the tempo of change in sports from play to work rather than acting as a prime determinant in the evolution of sports. Needless to say, television presently enjoys a dominant position in the control of sports. Although the conjecture might be made that the direction of sports would not have been greatly impeded if television were not present, the factors previously elaborated upon strongly suggest that sports would have evolved in a similar manner, culminating in rampant commercialization. However, this is a moot argument.

The New Middle Class

The emergence of a new middle class has provided financial and spiritual support for the rapid expansion of sports. After the Second World War, approximately three million veterans received a college education under the sponsorship of the federal government, thus providing the educational basis for the rise of this class. Many of these undergraduates participated in or were exposed to sports which they may not have come in contact with previously. As these students graduated and began to develop careers, the world of sports was provided with a new audience, predisposed to seek an array of spectator sports. With increasing affluence, this audience could afford to support the growth of sports. However, for many of the new middle class, the price of affluence is the contravention of their individuality by large-scale business organization. Thus, sports spectatorship affords the possibility for reclaiming or maintaining one's autonomy.

Discussion

In addition to changing the fundamental nature of sports from play to work, the foregoing factors have also evoked a unique development that has been visible since the early 1950's. From this time, increasing numbers of people have invested time, money and energy to engage in, and to embrace the world of sports. In this frenetic quest, sport entrepreneurs have attempted to differentiate their product from their competitors through imaginative publicity and spectacular innovations. Whenever a sport does not seem able to sustain previous levels of interest, the creative sport entrepreneurs will endeavor to implement changes in the rules or the format of the game. The recent changes in the strike zone and the lowering of the mound in baseball would attest to this idea. Rule changes in the last twenty years in hockey, basketball and football would also support this notion. In brief, this development in sports includes: innovative promotion; rule changes; alterations in the playing environment and attire in participants (Oakland Athletics); spectacular accoutrements (scoreboard in Houston Astrodome). These components constitute what might be labeled as *sports as entertainment*. The following examples illustrate the presence and the diversity of this phenomenon.

On an October evening in 1968, if you were in the vicinity of midtown Manhattan, you would have witnessed a "boxing motorcade" traveling down Broadway. The object of this spectacular presentation was to promote the forthcoming match between Dick Tiger and Frankie DePaula at Madison Square Garden.

The New York Times reported in May of 1969 that Monticello Raceway, during the opening night ceremonies, would present a race that would be sensational in its import: a contest between a pacer and a man (former Olympic champion sprinter, Henry Carr). The race would be run on an eighth of a mile course with the man being allowed a handicap of ten yards. It is interesting to note the statement of Leon Greenberg, president and general manager of the raceway. In response to the idea that the contest was in reality a promotion device, he commented: "For opening night gimmicks, we will have a marching band, a choral group, acrobats, aerialists, and a musical comedy act. But a man racing a horse is not a gimmick, it's a contest." (*N.Y. Times,* 1969)

Another aspect of sport as entertainment is the gravitation of star professional athletes into the entertainment business. From the days of Jim Corbett's lead in "Sports McAllister" in 1892 to Archie Moore's attempt to establish a movie career in the 1950's, prominent athletes have tried to expand their careers in this direction. Today there are more star professional athletes in the entertainment business than fifteen years ago. But not only is there a quantitative difference, there is also a qualitative distinction.

Professional sports have reached a stage wherein a prominent athlete, at a particular point in his career, can envisage his current livelihood as merely a stepping stone: a means to other income domains which incorporate and utilize to financial advantage the public image he has attained previously as a star athlete.

In the past, a professional athlete, equivalent in popularity to a star athlete of today, generally did not seriously consider another career until his "playing days" were almost over. Today, the pecuniary-oriented athlete starts planning extra-athletic pursuits as soon as his popularity as an athlete warrants it. The exulted position associated with a batting championship or a most valuable player award catapults a well-respected player into national prominence and the concomitant increased monetary potential. The examples cited to illustrate sports as entertainment are analogous to occurrences at earlier periods in the history of sports. What distinguishes present sports from the past is the pattern of events (and the unique conjuncture of factors) which has succeeded in generating a new era in sports. The locus of this change suggests that the serious structure of games is being supplanted by the introduction of non-serious elements into games within the world of sports.

The huge sums of money devoted to sports have undoubtedly enhanced the idea of an immanent connection between spectator sports and entertainment. Most people think of sports as being synonymous with entertainment. And from an experiential construction this is essentially true. But upon reflection, sport and entertainment—a seeming synergism—are separate spheres of reality. Sport seeks to gratify the individual through his direct participation in the game. Entertainment endeavors to divert the individual through inactive acquisition of the salient features of the game. Fundamentally the format of games originated for the purpose of satisfying the competitive needs of participants. Only at a later time, when spectators started attending sport contests, did the distinction become blurred between sport as a game in and for itself and as entertainment.

In spite of the influence of spectators, what has occurred historically is that sports have changed within the context of the game rather than within the context of the spectators' predispositions. That is, games have maintained their basic format. Innovations have been made within this framework (e.g., rule changes) rather than completely dismantling the design of a game and starting anew with the entertainment inclination of the spectators as a guide.

As sports have progressed, this implicit disparity between the intrinsic notion of sport as a game and the divertissement orientation of the spectators has been reduced in proportion to the growing numbers of spectators attending sport events. The reason for this reduction has been the renascent awareness of this gap by sport promoters. In the last twenty years, more than ever before, they have taken the initiative to redress this imbalance. However, they are constrained by traditional formats and have been restricted to implement with these limiting configurations. Much of the value laden criticism directed toward innovation in sports emerges from this rudimentary conflict: the subversion and attempts to subvert the original purpose of the design of the game.

Paralleling this antagonism is the change of values in sports which also reflects changes in the structure of modern sports. Many sets of values inhere in sports, but *aesthetic assessment,*[6] *the heroic ethos, and sincerity of effort* are values paramount amongst players, spectators and other members of the sporting fraternity. These values are not equally represented in all individuals, but vary according to the person's experience and position in athletics. In other words, the professional baseball player possesses the same set of values as the baseball spectator but the order and significance of each value may be different. The interpretation of these values[7] is presented as a pure formulation and usually does not exist in sports in this ideal state.

Aesthetic assessment embodies the idea that playing the game is a creation which exists in and for itself. The game is not important because it is entertaining or because one team emerges victorious. Its importance is derived from the degree of skill attached to plays, individual effort, and the player's general excellence. In a pure formulation the game is an end in itself. Adherence to rules and sportsmanlike conduct are secondary aspects of aesthetic assessment.

Heroic ethos as a value emanates from historical periods during which feats of courage and endurance were highly esteemed. Today heroism suggests courage: the player demonstrates daring and bold imagination in his performance. Endurance implies high performance that is consistent and untiring. This value emphasizes the participant rather than the game and stems from aesthetic assessment but is not subordinate to it. Daring and imaginative acts by an individual stand out as spectacular feats and by their very nature tend to overshadow elements of aesthetic assessment. In addition, valorous conduct on and off the playing field are part of the heroic value.

Sincerity of effort suggests the player's undiluted desire to participate at peak performance and implies honesty and the absence of deceit. This value, common to both player and spectator, is more easily understood from the perspective of the latter—the spectator affects a psychic transference of trust and vicarious heroic emulation in the belief that the player is performing at his maximum ability and not perpetrating a fraud.

These values have been present in sports at all times, but have proportionately changed in their position of importance. In the past, hard physical training was a value espoused as a builder of character. Vigorous exercise was good in itself. Today this value is generally present in society but the focus has shifted. Physical training is now undertaken with a specific goal in mind: the ends achieved are more important than the intrinsic value of the training. Likewise, physical condition is important in sports today but more important is the ability to perform in order to obtain specific ends. Hits in baseball are acclaimed, but homeruns are more highly acclaimed. Offensive linework in football is appreciated but takes a subordinate position in comparison to touchdown-runs or passes caught for touchdowns.

In modern sports, the aesthetic value in a game has given way to the desire for heroism or, put differently, the game in its traditional, undiluted game-form has been supplanted by the spectacular, commercial game-form. The contemporary professional athlete drew a distinction between work and play. Imbued with the remnants of Puritan attitudes toward work, he approached his chosen field as a total means of expression. The modern athlete does not delineate work and play in this manner. This does not mean today's professional athlete does not think of his participation in sports as work. It suggests that high esteem and public notoriety do not lend themselves to a separation of work and play: this extension of heroic image provides opportunities to earn money in self-enhancing activities containing elements of play. Appearing as a guest on TV programs, personal appearances as part of promotional ventures, and modeling are extracurricular activities which help blur the line between work and play.

Although the professional athlete of today is cooperation-oriented, he remains economically independent. The professional athlete in the contemporary period was part of the collective insecurity pervading the time. The player in professional sports today—because of sports' overwhelming success and a higher level of education than his predecessors'—has many alternatives open to him. In conjunction with his independent status is the change of attitude toward authority. The players of today are more likely to challenge the established officials or owners the leagues. The players of the past tended to be less oriented toward confrontation with authority than the aggressive professionals of today. This attitude is exemplified by the recent threat of a baseball strike and the reluctance of first draft professional football players to sign contracts until they felt their negotiating position had improved.

SUMMARY

An attempt has been made to identify and explain the unique changes in professional sports in the U.S. A number of factors in both the nineteenth and twentieth centuries that have contributed to a transformation of play into work have been traced. This transition has evoked a fundamental conflict between the original format of "the game" and the predilection of audiences to seek the spectacular. The outcome of this strain is that professional sports have attempted to enliven the game by introducing rule changes, spectacular accoutrements, and innovative publicity promotions, concomitantly, values within professional sports have also changed, thus tending to support the entertainment value of sports rather than the idea of the intrinsic value of the game in and for itself. The emphasis upon entertainment has ushered in a new epoch that can be called the ascendant entertainment aura in professional sports.

NOTES

1. The concept of leisure is difficult to define. It can be thought of as a state of mind or it can be envisioned as an objective state clearly identifiable. Rather than pursue the logical extensions of the subjective or the objective arguments of leisure—and being fully aware of the danger of over simplification—leisure will be understood to be the antithesis of work and a state wherein a non-economic entity is pursued (Kaplan, 1960:22).

2. Golf, tennis and baseball are exceptions. Golf and tennis were upper class sports not seriously influenced by the decreasing work week. Baseball was affected by disproportionate increase in free time, whereby free time was accelerating faster from 1854 to 1869 (baseball as a game) as compared with 1831 to 1845 (baseball as play). While increasing free time is one of the significant factors that contributed to the transformation of play into a game, it is not a total explanation for this transition.

3. The slow development of golf could be argued along the same lines. However, this would require an extensive class analysis which is beyond the scope of this paper.

4. Public relations acumen existed from 1915 when the Univ. of Pittsburgh "". . . introduced numbers for players in order to spur the sale of programs . . ." (Denney, 1957:115).

5. Since the defeat of the antitrust action by football in 1953, baseball has reverted to limited telecasting of games.

6. The value of aesthetic assessment was suggested by Frohlich's (1952:88) formulation of an "aesthetic appreciation system."

7. Values in the above usage connote a deep-rooted belief akin to Sumner's (1968) use of mores.

REFERENCES

Bogart L., *The Age of Television,* New York 1958, Frederick Ungor Pub. Co.

Caillois R., *Man, Play, and Games,* New York 1961, The Free Press of Glencoe Inc.

Daniel D., *The Ring Computer Series Gets Top Rating With Few Booboos,* "The Ring", XLVII No. 1 (Feb.), 1968.

Denney R., *The Astonished Muse,* Chicago 1957, The University of Chicago Press.

Durso J., *Big Money and Professional Sports: Vexing Problems Go With Affluence,* "New York Times" 9 (Feb.):4, 1969.

Frohlich P. E., *Sports and the Community: a Study in Social Change in Athens,* Ohio 1952, unpublished Ph.D. dissertation, University of Wisconsin.

Huizinga J., *Homo Ludens,* Boston 1964, Beacon Press.

Jordan J., "Newsweek" 31 (Aug.):74, 1950.

Kaplan M., *Leisure in America,* New York 1960, John Wiley and Sons.

King J., *Baseball's No. 1 Job: Tame the TV Bully,* "New York World-Telegram" 20 (Dec.):18, 1965.

Lee R., *Religion and Leisure in America,* New York 1964, Abingdon Press

Marx K., *Das Kapital,* Vol I, tr. Samuel Moore and Edward Ovelting, Chicago 1921, Carles H. Kerr and Co.

Menke F. G., *The Encyclopedia of Sports,* New York 1969, A. S. Barnes and Co.

"Newsweek", "Newsweek" 31 (Aug.):74, 1950.

"New York Times", *Carr and Pacer Split Test Runs,* "New York Times" 13 (May), 1969.

Petersen W., *Population,* New York 1963, The Macmillan Co.

Presthus R., *The Organizational Society,* New York 1962, Vintage Books.

Sumner W. G., *Folkways,* New York 1968, Mentor Books.

Wilensky H., *Organizational Intelligence,* New York 1967, Basic Books Inc.

Wylie M., *Clear Channels,* New York 1955, Funk and Wagnalls Co.

SPORT AND AMERICAN SOCIETY: THE QUEST FOR SUCCESS *

George H. Sage

A recurrent theme of sport sociology is that sport is a microcosm of society. The types of sports played, the way in which sport is organized, who partici-pates, and who does not, all provide clues about the nature of a society. In this paper I shall examine the reciprocal relationship between sport and

*The author wishes to acknowledge his indebtedness to D. Stanley Eitzen for a number of ideas that are expressed in this paper.

American values. I say reciprocal because sport promotes and reinforces the American value system as well as reflects it. Very simply, the process occurs in this way: Adult members of the population who have internalized the value system socialize the younger generation by the way they organize, coach, and administer youth sports programs. Those who are socialized to the value system in this way reach adulthood and enter occupations carrying an internalized version of the value system. And they in turn transmit these values on to the next generation.

Humans are valuing creatures. That is, some things are preferred over others: some objects, people, or ideas are considered wrong, bad, or immoral while others are believed correct, good, or moral. Some goals are deemed worthy while others are not. Values are the bases for making decisions; they are the culturally prescribed criteria by which individuals evaluate persons, behavior, objects, and ideas as to their relative morality, desirability, merit, or correctness. The term "culturally prescribed" is an important qualifier in this definition because it implies that human beings are taught (socialized) the criteria by which to make such judgments. Children learn from their parents, peers, and the media what is right or wrong, moral or immoral, correct or incorrect.[1]

Each culture has a distinct value system. Functionally, a value system is a set of principles whereby conduct is directed and regulated and a guide for individuals and the social group. Common values may be viewed as the glue that holds a society together, as the controlling regulator that keeps the activities in a society in orderly relationship, and as the force that preserves stability in a society. A cultural value system does not describe the values of any individual. It is a summary construct in which the diverse value sets of individuals and groups are related as complementary elements of a single system.[2]

Although individuals may have their own idiosyncratic criteria for evaluation, our concern is with those values that most prominantly make up the American value system. Several vignettes are necessary, however, before we proceed. First the cultural pluralism of the United States precludes any universal holding of specific values. Very different values are represented by the various racial, ethnic, and religious groups, and there are differences in dominant value orientations by region, social class, age, and size of the community. Second, American values have not always been consistent. For example, Americans have always claimed to value equality of opportunity but the injustices perpetrated by Americans on members of minority groups throughout American history are inconsistent with this value.[3] Sociologist, Robin Williams, in his book *American Society*, concluded that:

> We do not find a neatly unified 'ethos' or an irresistible 'strain toward consistency.' Rather, the total society is characterized by diversity and

change in values. Complex diversion of labor, regional variations, ethnic heterogeneity, and the proliferation of specialized institutions and organizations all tend to insulate differing values from one another.[4]

Finally, no attempt will be made to identify and discuss a comprehensive list of American values in this paper. Instead, I shall focus on only the most dominant of American values: the emphasis on success striving.

THE SUCCESS VALUE IN AMERICA

The most salient and striking value permeating American culture is a central stress upon success through personal achievement. The success story and the respect accorded the self-made person are distinctly American, if anything is. Anthropologist Clyde Kluckhohn has stated that "the worship of success in the United States has gone farther than in any known culture."[5] Emphasis upon achievement must be distinguished from the broader valuation of personal excellence, however. Robin Williams noted:

> All societies have standards of character and proficiency, and accord rewards to those best meeting whatever standards are most highly appraised, whether of military prowess, ritual knowledge, asceticism, or whatnot. The comparatively striking feature of American culture is its tendency to identify standards of personal excellence with competitive occupational achievement. In the pure type, the value attached to achievement does not comprehend the person as a whole but only his accomplishments, emphasizing the objective results of his activity. Because of the preoccupation with business the most conspicuous achievements have been those centered in business enterprise.[6]

The primary social process by which success in America is to be achieved is through competition. Competition is so highly valued in American society that it is believed by many Americans to be the one quality that has made America great. Competition provides almost all aspects of American society; all of the major social institutions—economy, education, polity, religion— thrive on competition.

The highly esteemed individual in American society is the self-made person—i.e., one who has achieved money and status through his or her own efforts in a highly competitive system. "Our cultural heroes are persons like Abe Lincoln, John D. Rockefeller, and Joe Namath, each of whom rose from humble origins to the top of his profession."[6a] To be called a Horatio Alger hero in America is a badge of distinction. The Horatio Alger hero symbolizes the respect for the self-made man and faith in equality of opportunity. As a symbol it stands for a poor boy of lower-class origins, with no ascribed advantages except his own indominable character, who rises to the top by his own efforts and abilities. However, one does not have to have risen from poverty to be considered successful, indeed, most "successful" businessmen and political leaders did not follow this path at all. The label of "successful" can be conferred on anyone who has been able to outdo others, regardless of his or her original station in life. Economic success (one's income, personal wealth, and type of possessions) is the most commonly used criterion to measure success. Thus, in America success means making money and translating it into status, or becoming famous. Success is not simply *being* rich or famous. It means *attaining* riches or *achieving* fame.[7] Economic success, moreover, is often used to measure personal worth.

Having said this, I think that it is important to note that, despite the assumptions of many Americans, the idea of success in this country has not always been equated with unbridled competitive success striving in the pursuit of great wealth. Indeed, as Rex Burns succinctly points out in his recent book *Success in America:*

> . . . it was not until the mid-nineteenth century that such a definition became a sanctioned code. Before that . . . success was most often associated with a figure of middling income who worked his own fee-simple farm. This kind of success . . . may be defined as wealth somewhat beyond one's basic needs, freedom from economic or statutory sub-servience, and the respect of the society for fruitful, honest industry.[8]

It was not until the last third of the nineteenth century that the concept of success became one of opulent materialism and social prestige won and justified by the competitive aggression of Social Darwinism. Success, then, became equated with winning—winning money, contracts, land, social status or whatever one was competing for—in the quest for success.

SUCCESS VALUE IN SPORT

Sport is a vehicle by which the American value system is transmitted to the younger generation. This is one of the explicit reasons given for the existence of community youth sports programs and the tremendous emphasis on sports in American schools. As in the larger society, there is a tremendous emphasis in American sport on success in competition; indeed the goal that is most universally espoused in American sports competition is to succeed (to win). Thus coaches do all they can to instill in their athletes the character traits they believe will bring team success (e.g., loyalty, enthusiasm, initiative, self-control, confidence, poise, and ambition). And they use a variety of techniques to socialize their athletes with the value of winning, reinforcing winners with praise, honor, and status while ridiculing losers.[9] Harry Edwards says: "The overriding value orientation salient throughout the institution of sport and the dominant sports creed is that of . . . 'individual achievement through competition'."[10] As the former athletic director at the University of Southern California put it, "Athletics develop dedication and a desire to

excell in competition, and a realization that success requires hard work
. . . ." [11]

Winning is glorified by all who participate. The legendary professional
coach, Vince Lombardi, popularized the slogan: "Winning is not everything.
It is the only thing." Former University of Texas football coach, Darrell
Royal, said: "The only way I know of to keep football fun is to win. That's
the only answer. There is no laughter in losing." And Miami Dolphin coach,
Don Shula said: "No one ever learns anything by losing."

Coaches frequently place slogans on the dressing room walls to exhort
players to value winning. Slogans that coaches use to instill the winner spirit
are:

"A quitter never wins, a winner never quits."

"When the going gets tough, the tough get going."

"Never be willing to be second best."

"The greatest aim in life is to succeed." [12]

Americans want winners, whether it be in school, business, politics, or
sports. Indeed, in sports we *demand* winners. A coach, according to all
accepted standards, must win in order to have coached well. Coaches are fired
if they are not successful.[13] If this blind commitment to victory were found
only at the professional and college levels, it would be cause enough for alarm,
but the demand for winners is found at all levels of sport. Even among
youngsters "winning is everything" as evidenced by the pressures in Little
League Baseball, Pop Warner Football, and the Junior Olympics.

Young athletes soon learn that organized sport is not for the playing;
instead it is for winning. Listen to Mark Spitz's dad quizzing Mark at age nine,
as reported in a national publication: "Mark, how many lanes in a pool? Six.
And how many lanes win? One, only one." His father says: "Swimming isn't
everything, winning is . . . I told him [Mark] I don't care about winning age
groups, I care for world records." [14] This attitude is shared by many parents
and coaches of young boys and girls.

CONSEQUENCES OF SUCCESS STRIVING IN AMERICA

"Well," one may say, "what is wrong with success striving and achievement
through competition?" The answer is, of course, nothing—at a superficial
level. There is no doubt that success striving has been responsible for remarkable progress in American society but there is no need to document these
accomplishments. Americans are bombarded with testimonials to America's
competitive achievements every day via TV commercials paid for by Standard
Oil, Texaco, Phillips Petroleum and by weekly ads in *Newsweek* and *Time* by
ITT, General Motors, etc. What is proposed here is that among the healthy
cells in the American social organism there are many cancerous cells whose

growth is a product of the obsessive compulsion for success by some persons, and unless Americans recognize the existence of these diseased cells and do something about them this society may go the way of many previous ones.

The important consequence of this obsessive emphasis on success striving is that some persons take advantage of others in order to compete "successfully." America's success ethos has developed an amorality component to it, resulting in an attitude that the end justifies the means" "Success isn't everything, it's the only thing." One of the most obvious recent examples of this orientation was the abuses by governmental officials under the Nixon administration (the Watergate break-in, "laundering of money," taking of illegal contributions from individuals and corporations, use of the Internal Revenue Service to punish enemies, and "dirty tricks" against political opponents). All were done to assist Richard Nixon to win a second term as President. The "success at any cost" is aptly captured in this statement of Egil Krogh, former Nixon White House aide: "Anyone who opposes us we'll destroy. As a matter of fact, anyone who doesn't support us we'll destroy." Sociologist Amitai Etzioni has illustrated the pervasiveness of the "ends justify the means" mentality in this statement.

> Truth to be told, the Watergate gang is but an extreme manifestation of a much deeper and more encompassing American malaise, the emphasis on success and frequent disregard for the nature of the means it takes to achieve it. Not only high level administration officials, but many Americans as well, seem to have accepted the late football coach Vince Lombardi's motto, "Winning is not the most important thing, it's the only thing." Thus, the executives of ITT who sought to overthrow the government of Chile to protect their goodies, the Mafia chieftans who push heroin, the recording company executives who bribe their records onto the top-40 list, and the citizens who shrug off corruption in the local town hall as "that's the way the cookie crumbles," all share the same unwholesome attitude. True, the Watergate boys have broken all known American precedents in their violation of fair play, but they are unique chiefly in the magnitude of their crime—not in the basic orientation that underlies it. John Mitchell captured the perverted spirit of Watergate best when he stated that "in view of what the opposition had to offer" (i.e., McGovern), we felt justified in doing anything necessary to secure Nixon's re-election.[15]

Of course, the Nixon administration is not the only governmental agency involved in illegal activities. Everywhere you look you see the negative consequences of success at any cost. In Baltimore, Governor Marvin Mandel was accused of mail fraud and racketeering; Louisiana's recently resigned Rep. Richard Tonry is doing time for campaign financing violations; the former speaker of Missouri's House got seven years for extortion and mail fraud, and on Capital Hill an investigation has occurred about illegal Korean influence buying and other assorted hanky-panky.

In the business world theft, fraud, interlocking directorships, and price-fixing are techniques commonly used by businesses to "get ahead," to be successful. Abroad, American companies like United Brands and Gulf Oil have engaged in widespread bribery of governmental officials. At home, it's hard to keep up with the number of major corporations that have negotiated guilty pleas for illegal campaign contributions, price-fixing, and production of inferior and dangerous products. In a joint letter to the then Attorney General Edward Levi on August 24, 1975, Ralph Nader and four congressmen charged that the United States was "in the midst of a corporate crime wave." A related problem is the abuse of nature for corporate profit. To a large extent, the current ecology crisis has been caused by individuals, corporations, and communities, who find solutions to environmental problems too expensive, and in looking out for themselves, they ignore the short and long range effects on social and biological life.[16] Finally, in a poll of managerial ethics young managers in business today say they would have done just what the junior members of Nixon's reelection committee did—go along with their bosses to show their loyalty. Sixty percent of the managers supported their decisions.[17]

But the amorality in quest of success is not confined to government and large corporations. In one of his last public speeches, President Ford estimated that white collar crime now costs the public $40 million a year. Recent cheating scandals at the military academies merely highlight what is apparently going on throughout American education. Ninety-three percent of American high school seniors polled recently said they had cheated.[18]

CONSEQUENCES OF SUCCESS STRIVING IN SPORTS

As noted in the first paragraph of this paper, the underlying theme here is that there is a close and reciprocal relationship between American sports and the American value system. Powerful role models in the form of coaches are significant agents in the process of transmitting the cultural values. It is to them, then, that we must turn to learn how the value system is transmitted. Al McGuire, former basketball coach at Marquette University, said at a recent public dinner that he had learned three things in life he always tried to pass along to his players: "The first is to make as much money as you can. I forget the other two." McGuire's quip drew a big laugh, but it also got a big hand. He apparently was saying something that a lot of people believe. It didn't seem to make too much difference to McGuire what road people take to get rich and be a success, the important thing is to get there.[19]

On Watergate, Woody Hayes, formerly one of America's most exhalted coaches, said: "The way I see it, Nixon had to cover up to win the election. Hell, I'd have done the same thing if any of my coaches had done something and I found out about it. My first reaction would have been: "Well, shoot, we've done something wrong, but we can't make it right by letting the whole goddamned world know about it."[20]

Sully Krouse, wrestling coach at the University of Maryland, summed up this coaching philosophy: "Everybody talks about the gentlemen and scholars. I'd rather have bad guys who can win." Asked to what lengths he would go to win, he said: "I'd lie, cheat, and steal."[21] Another coach said "I'd give anything but my wife and family—to get it [an undefeated season]."[22]

Sports, as played in America, are expressions of Social Darwinism. It is a "survival of the fittest" approach where everyone competes to be at the top. Former professional football player, George Sauer notes:

I think football as it is now played reflects a segment of thought, a particular kind of thought, that is prevalent in our society. The way to get ahead is to compete against somebody, work your way up the ladder, and in so doing you have to judge yourself and be judged in relation to somebody else.[23]

George Atkinson, defensive back for the Oakland Raiders, has put it more succinctly: "It's [football] the law of the jungle. You know it's exactly like nature, the survival of the fittest."[24]

Scandals similar to those found in government, business, and education are also found in the sports world. The most blatant example of illegal and unethical behavior in sports is illegal recruiting of athletes by colleges and universities. Eitzen and Sage say: "In the quest to succeed (i.e., win), some college coaches have felt it necessary to violate NCAA regulations by altering transcripts to insure an athlete's eligibility, allowing substitutes to take admissions tests for athletes of marginal educational ability, paying athletes for non-existent jobs, illegally using government work studies moneys for athletes, and offering money, cars, and clothing to entice athletes to their school."[25] But coaches are not immoral, at least not in the American conventional sense of morality; they merely adapt personal morality to the social norm in order to be "successful." Forced with the "system" coaches acquiesce because the evaluation they receive will be important to their careers and their futures.

When IBM was recently accused of violating federal laws, the chairman of the board said, in defense of the illegal activities: "We don't train losers." Presumably they train executives to win at any cost, and the hell with federal laws—winning is everything, you know. But perhaps they didn't have to train them at all. They might have already possessed this ethical norm—learned from youth and school sports programs in which they had participated.

SPORT AND SOCIAL CHANGE

You may not like the summary of the consequences of the American success ethos that has just been made, but like it or not, basically it is accurate. The simplistic generalization that "Winning isn't everything, it's the only thing" has been canonized at every level of American society. The notion that the most important thing in life is to get a lot of money and it doesn't make any difference how you get it so long as you succeed carries with it a genuine peril for the individual who believes it and for the society that encourages it. The pressure to succeed, to win, in politics, business, and in sports is absolutely destructive to both the individual and the nation. There is nothing wrong with the pursuit of excellence as long as it is not harmful to others. Likewise, team spirit is to be admired when it comes from a sense of oneness with teammates. The time has come in this nation when we must look to some higher values other than material success and victory in games. As Richard Huber in his book *The American Idea of Success* has eloquently said:

> Success is not a harbor but a voyage with its own perils to the spirit. The game of life is to come up a winner, to be a success or to achieve what we set out to do. Yet there is always the danger of failing as a human being. The lesson that most of us on this voyage never learn, but can never quite forget, is that to win is sometimes to lose.[24]

Sociologist Harry Edwards has claimed that "America would gain far more than she would lose through the initiation of . . . an alternative sport structure . . . in which the younger generation can be socialized with values stressing cooperation rather than antagonism, participation and self-actualization rather than confrontation and domination."[27] But how incongruous can the actual institution of sport become in relation to the dominant social norms and values? No doubt, sport cannot alter its structure and functioning and still survive without change in the value prescriptions of American society as a whole. However, given the reciprocal relationships between sport and society it seems that those who direct sports programs could, if they wished, redirect the programs so as to stress the values that Edwards has suggested. The young persons who were exposed to these values would carry them into their adult lives, influencing all with whom they came in contact, including the succeeding generation. Thus, the cycle would have been completed—now with a new value system.

NOTES

1. D. Stanley Eitzen and George H. Sage, *Sociology of American Sport* (Dubuque, Iowa: Wm. C. Brown, 1978), p. 59.
2. Florence R. Kluckhohn and Fred L. Strodtbeck, *Variations in Value Orientations* (Evanston, Ill.: Row, Peterson, 1961).

3. Eitzen and Sage, *Sociology of American Sport*, pp. 59–60.

4. Robin Williams, *American Society* (3rd ed.), (New York: Alfred A. Knopf, 1970), p. 451.

5. Clyde Kluckhohn, *Mirror for Man* (New York: 1949), p. 235.

6. Robin Williams, *American Society*, pp. 454–455.

6a. Eitzen and Sage, *Sociology of American Sport*, p. 60.

7. Richard M. Huber, *The American Idea of Success*, p. 1.

8. Rex Burns, *Success in America* (Amherst, Mass.: University of Massachusetts Press, 1976), p. 1.

9. See for example Eldon Snyder, "Athletic Dressing Room Slogans as Folklore: A Means of Socialization," *International Review of Sport Sociology*, 7 (1972), pp. 89–102.

10. Harry Edwards, *Sociology of Sport* (Homewood, Ill.: Dorsey Press, 1973), p. 334.

11. Quoted in Harry Edwards, *Sociology of Sport*, p. 71

12. Eldon Snyder, "Athletic Dressing Room Slogans as Folklore . . ."

13. Eitzen and Sage, *Sociology of American Sport*.

14. W. F. Reed, "Swimming Isn't Everything, Winning Is," *Sports Illustrated*, 32 (March 9, 1970), p. 27.

15. Amati Etzioni, "After Watergate—What?: A Social Science Perspective," *Human Behavior*, 2 (November, 1973), p. 7.

16. Eitzen and Sage, *Sociology of American Sport*.

17. Carroll, Archie B. "Managerial Ethics: A Post-Watergate View." *Business Horizons*, **18** (April, 1975), pp. 75–80.

18. George R. Plagenz, "Cheating Scandals Raise Serious Questions of Morality," *Rocky Mountain News* (June 12, 1976), p. 119.

19. Quoted in Norman Cousins, "A Sense of Values," *Greeley Tribune* (October, 1977).

20. Michael Roberts, *Fans* (Washington, D.C.: *New Republic Books*, 1976), p. 47.

21. Scorecard, *Sports Illustrated*, **46** (March 21, 1977), p. 17.

22. *Newsweek*, (November 24, 1974), p. 69.

23. "The Souring of George Sauer," *Intellectual Digest*, 2 (December, 1971), p. 53.

24. Robert Ward, "The Oakland Raiders' Charming Assassin," *Sport*, **64** (April, 1977), p. 54.

25. Eitzen and Sage, *Sociology of American Sport*, p. 63. Also see for example Joseph Durso, *The Sports Factory* (New York: Quadrangle, 1975); Kenneth Denlinger and Leonard Shapiro, *Athletes for Sale* (New York: Thomas Y. Crowall, 1975); Jim Benagh, *Making it to #1: How College Football and Basketball Teams Get There* (New York: Dodd, Mead, 1976).

26. Richard M. Huber, *The American Idea of Success*, p. 457.

271 Harry Edwards, "Desegregating Sexist Sport," *Intellectual Digest*, **3** (November, 1972), p. 83.

FOR FURTHER READING

1. Betts, J. R., *America's Sporting Heritage: 1850–1950,* Reading, Mass.: Addison-Wesley, 1974.

2. Lewis, G. "Adoption of the Sports Program, 1906–39: The Role of Accommodation in the Transformation of Physical Education," *Quest,* **12** (Spring): 34–46, 1969.

3. Lewis, G., "The Beginning of Organized Collegiate Sport," *American Quarterly* **22** (Summer): 222–229, 1970.

4. Lipsyte, R., *Sportsworld: The American Dreamland,* New York: Quadrangle, 1975.

5. Nixon, H. L., "The Commercial and Organizational Development of Modern Sport," *International Review of Sport Sociology,* **8** (2); 107–135, 1974.

6. Rader, B. G., "Subcommunities and the Rise of Sport," *American Quarterly,* **29** (Fall): 355–369, 1977.

7. Sage, G. H., "The Coach as Management: Organizational Leadership in American Sport," *Quest,* **19** (Winter): 35–40, 1973.

CHAPTER 3

SOCIALIZATION AND SPORT

Socialization is the process by which an individual learns the cultural attitudes, values, and roles of his group and thus acquires a unique personality and becomes a member of society. The activity of socialization is called cultural transmission, which is the means by which a society preserves its norms and perpetuates itself. Every society provides for socialization of its norms and roles, and every society expects its new members to learn the standard rules of conduct and assigns someone the role of teaching these. The primary agents and agencies for socializing the young are the family, peer groups, schools, churches, and the mass media.

Socializing experiences begin at birth and continue throughout life, but the critical years in which the primary and lasting socialization occurs is in childhood and adolescence. For the individual, the socialization process produces attitudes, values, knowledges, and behaviors which are related to cultural norms and the roles which the individual plays in the society.

Each society uses informal as well as formal techniques for cultural transmission. The family, peer groups, and the mass media constitute informal experiences for socialization, while schools and churches provide deliberate institutional means of bringing about socialization. Regardless of the extent of formal agencies for cultural transmission, socialization always depends to a large extent upon informal face-to-face contacts in small groups because culture is not merely conveyed by the written or spoken word—it is acted out in daily activities and becomes an important part of those who are involved.

Out of the infinite array of socializing stimuli in any society, one individual can only experience a few. The individual is given only one set of parents, and, assuming he lives with them, he is socialized by them and not by other parents. A specific set of individuals serve as "significant others" from which the individual learns and whose behavior he emulates. Most individuals live out their lives in a limited geographical part of society—perhaps in a rural or urban area and perhaps in the Midwest, Southwest, or the Pacific Northwest. In any case the residence, or residences, provide the individual with a unique environment in which his socialization takes place. Thus, for each individual, a specific set of socializing agents impinge upon him and draw him into certain activities and away from others. The social experiences into which he is introduced produces social consequences in the form of attitudes, values, and behaviors.

Very little is known about the social dynamics by which persons are socialized into sports. Undoubtedly, the family, peers, the school, and the mass media all are influential social sources in drawing the great numbers of American youth into sport involvement. Certainly, a great deal of interest and effort is devoted to sports by American youth. Social experiences have their consequences, or outcomes, for the participants and there is a popular belief that sports experiences provide an excellent medium for fostering personal-social qualities which are desirable for and functional in the accepted societal norms and roles in America. The readings in this chapter are concerned with two aspects of socialization: socialization into sport and socialization via sport.

Sport involvement socializes members to the specific norms and roles of the activity, but there is a prevailing belief that sport also produces desirable attitudes, values, and behaviors for performing in the diffuse roles of parent, employee, employer, citizen, etc. Eldon Snyder reviews the notion about socialization via sport—that is, whether socialization which occurs in sport results in the development of situational role-specific characteristics or general and diffuse personal-social characteristics. He suggests that there is a considerable body of sociological literature which supports situational contexts unless there are similarities in the situational expectations. He suggests that the analysis of the dimensions of social interaction in the socialization process is necessary to understand the influence of sport for developing specific or diffuse role behavior, and he further points out that the dimensions vary with the situational context within which the experience takes place. He identifies five dimensions and discusses each one with regard to sport. He concludes that although sport may develop only role-specific behavior traits it is no different than many social experiences. In fact, he argues that this is just as well since some behaviors accepted and sanctioned in a sport context might be dysfunctional in the broader society.

In the next reading, George H. Sage identifies briefly the possible ways in which American children may be socialized into sport and then discusses at greater length the social outcomes of sport. He emphasizes that little data exists to clearly delineate the extent to which socialization occurs via sport. The effects of sport involvement on personality development, self-concept development, social status, value orientations, and sportsmanship attitudes are examined from the standpoint of the speculations and research which have been completed on the subject. Sage concludes with a discussion of potential dysfunctional effects of youth sports programs on the participants. Kids' sports programs have been damned and praised; whether they minimize the potential dysfunctional aspects depends to a great extent upon the leadership in such programs, Sage suggests.

In the third reading Christopher L. Stevenson critically reviews the empirical research about the socialization effects of participation in sport. The review is organized around three types of socialization effect: psychological effects, behavioral effects, and attitudinal effects. The results of research are divided between those that support and those that do not support the possibility of socialization effects. Stevenson shows that the results of these studies are contradictory and confusing.

In analyzing the findings from the studies that he reviewed, Stevenson notes several methodological and theoretical problems. For example, the conceptualization of athletes and nonathletes is ambiguous and there is little consistency between studies in the population of athlete and non-athlete. Also, much of the instrumentation is suspect and not comparable between studies. Finally, much of the research is theoretically weak. The author concludes that there is no evidence that participation in sport produces any verifiable socialization effects.

In the last reading George H. Sage discusses the socialization of coaches, with an emphasis on the social milieu as the primary agency for the present beliefs and behaviors which coaches exhibit. Three aspects of socialization are examined: family background, social experiences in youth, and occupational influences. It is argued that the beliefs, and behaviors, and value orientations of coaches are formed through socialization experiences in these settings.

On the basis of predictions which are generated from a review of the typical coaches' life experiences about the beliefs, behaviors and value orientations of coaches, empirical studies are reviewed to ascertain the association between the predictions and the research findings. Sage concludes that there is some support for the predictions that were generated but the research is only suggestive—certainly not conclusive.

ASPECTS OF SOCIALIZATION IN SPORTS AND PHYSICAL EDUCATION

Eldon E. Snyder

In a recent article Kenyon[1] considered the socialization process that takes place within the framework of sports and physical education programs. He pointed out that physical education and sports are valuable areas of social interaction for the analysis of the socialization process. Specifically, he focused on the goals of socialization; for example, does socialization in physical activity result in the development of generalized and diffuse characteristics or does it develop only the ability to play specific roles within the confines of the particular physical activity in question? Frequently, physical education and sports are cited as contributing to the development of desirable traits for playing diffuse roles, such as "democratic citizenship," "moral character," "adjusted personality," "respect for constituted authority," and "the ability to win and lose graciously."[2,3,4]

Kenyon presents a survey of research suggesting that various personality traits are associated with participation in physical activities. Recent research by Schafer and Armer[5] indicates that high school athletes may demonstrate higher academic performances than nonathletes. However, in many cases these studies do not hold constant the possible antecedent and intervening variables necessary to clarify the cause and effect relationships between these activities and the development of personality characteristics. Ulrich noted that, "Although there is always the hope that behavioral patterns can be taught in one place and used in another, it would seem that each behavioral response is specific to the situation, the time, and the place in which it is employed."[6] Sociological literature provides considerable support that situational role-specific expectations and behaviors may not carry over to other situational contexts unless the situational expectations are similar.[7,8,9]

THEORETICAL ASSUMPTIONS

Kenyon concluded with several propositions regarding the development of specific and diffuse roles through the media of physical education and sports. He does not feel that instructional programs in physical education are particularly effective for socialization into diffuse roles; however, in interscholastic and intercollegiate athletics the increased frequency and intensity

Eldon E. Snyder, "Aspects of Socialization in Sports and Physical Education." *Quest*, Monograph XIV (June, 1970), pp. 1–7. Reprinted by permission of the publisher and author.

of social interaction is likely to socialize the athlete into both specific and diffuse roles.

Starting with these propositions, this article extends the discussion of the socialization process and the theoretical assumptions of specific-diffuse role learning. Specifically, the position taken is that by refining the analysis of the situational context within which physical education and sports take place, a greater understanding is likely of the specific-diffuse outcome.

Sociologists and social psychologists have developed a conclusive body of knowledge demonstrating that socialization involves past, present, and anticipated future interaction between the individual and significant others such as parents, siblings, girl friends, peer groups, coaches, teachers, religious educators, etc. These significant others represent the audiences, reference groups, or socializing agents that provide the cues and "feedback" for defining appropriate role behavior. The socialization influence of these groups varies temporally and situationally according to their primacy and control over rewards and punishment.[10] To understand the influence (rewards and punishment) of physical education and sports in developing specific or diffuse roles requires the analysis of the dimensions of social interaction in the socialization process. These vary with the situational context within which the physical activity takes place. Among the most important are:

1. *The degree of involvement in the activity by the participants.* Involvement includes an expressed desire and active engagement through a visible investment of attention and muscular effort.[11] For example, the varsity coach, whose livelihood depends upon successfully carrying out his role as socializer of his players to the skills of the sport, usually is involved deeply in carrying out these expectations. A team captain is usually expected to demonstrate qualities of involvement greater than the other players through his actions in practice, game situations, and on trips. Team substitutes will usually show less involvement by sitting farther down the bench and standing aside from the most actively committed participants during time-outs.

Instructors and pupils in physical education classes are not usually as actively involved as are the participants in varsity sports. They meet fewer times a week and the range of interaction is narrow. Therefore, there is no heavy self-commitment. Playground recreational activities likewise would not ordinarily include a deep involvement. Little League sports, on the other hand, may take on a degree of involvement approximating a school sport. The heavy investment of community recreational resources, parental and coaching involvement, pep talks to get "psyched up," admonitions by the spectators, and auto-suggestions to "get serious" indicates something more than a superficial degree of involvement.

In complex societies, the reference groups and socializing agents may present conflicting demands on individuals. These conflicts help explain some lack of involvement in an activity. The demands of a girl friend may, for example, result in a team member giving little attention to the training rules of his coach; or the desire to spend more time with his friends or to work on a car may become more important than involvement.

In general, the degree of involvement in the socialization relationship would result in variations in acquisition of outcomes. Neither the development of specific nor diffuse traits would be possible, of course, without at least a moderate involvement.

2. *Voluntary or involuntary selection and/or participation.* Closely related to the degree of involvement is the consideration of voluntary or involuntary selection for, and participation in, an activity.[12] For example, participants in a physical education class are often meeting a requirement—their presence is involuntary (though they may in some cases select a particular activity or class section). Also, the instructor has little or no selection of the participants, but is assigned to an activity to be taught at a particular time and place. Conversely, the varsity coach selects the team members and the players voluntarily submit themselves to undergo the rigors of participation.

This discussion of voluntary or involuntary selection and participation could be extended to other forms of physical activity and recreation. The point is that the outcomes of the socialization process may vary depending on the combinations of these variables (the degree of control and discipline the socializer has over the pupil will differ also). We would expect that where both the teacher and pupil voluntarily select and participate in the activity there would be an in-depth involvement, high prestige associated with the activity, and a diffuse level of socialization. Where both the teacher and pupil have no choice but to interact together, we would expect less involvement, less prestige, and the transmission of role-specific skills for fulfilling the activity requirements.

This description has admittedly been overdrawn and is subject to qualification. The purpose here is not to argue that required participation is undesirable; but rather, to achieve an understanding of possible variations in the results.

3. *Instrumental or expressive socialization relationship.* This refers to the quality of the relationship between persons and their socializing agents. A purely instrumental socializing relationship imparts knowledge and skills functionally specific for the achievement of a desired end. The instrumental relationship is affectively neutral* since the relationship *per se* is not expected to be gratifying; the participants are expected to control their personal feelings, emotions, and attitudes lest they interfere with the specific task. In contrast, expressive relationships are affective and personally satisfying ends in themselves; they also allow for broader and deeper levels of communication.[13] Expressive relationships are broad and diffuse; for example, such a relationship with a childhood socializing agent would be "a person to whom the child has general feelings of attachment. Thus he

---

*The terms "effectivity" and "affective neutrality" are attributed to Falcott Parsons, *The Social System.* Glencoe: The Free Press, 1951.

becomes a model for the child, who tends to take over his values, his standards of taste, his fundamental philosophical or ethical outlook."[14]

If physical education and sports are to develop traits necessary for diffuse roles, the socialization process must involve some aspects of an expressive relationship between the teacher and pupil. Expressive relationships are unlikely to develop within the context of the usual school physical education classes; the best the teacher can hope for is the development of specific skills. On the other hand, the social interaction between a coach and his players will usually involve not only the learning of specific skills but a concern for the players' general physical and psychological well-being, their families, girl friends, style of hair, dress, and manners. The coach will often advise his graduating players on the selection of a college and future occupational possibilities. At least for some players the coach is often a consultant and advisor for many years after graduation. Recreational activities such as camping and youth hosteling likewise provide the opportunity for the development of expressive relationships and thus diffuse role characteristics.

A cross-cutting variable influencing the development of expressive relationships is the size of high school or college within which the physical education or sports activity takes place. Frequently, in the small rural community the high percentage of affective relationships both within the school and community will result in an entirely different school climate than in a large metropolitan school situation. Barker[15] found that in large high schools the kinds of extracurricular activities were twice as great as in small high schools, yet the proportion of participants was three to twenty times greater in the smaller schools. The differential influence of sports and physical education in differing school climates, i.e., large and small schools, junior high, high school, and college or university, private and public, needs further exploration.

4. *The prestige and power of the socializer.* Physical educators and coaches vary in their knowledge, skill, success, and prestige. In general, we would expect that the educator or coach with the greatest professional and institutional prestige or esteem will have the greatest influence in developing both specific and diffuse roles. Power, while not conceptually the same as prestige, is closely related and involves the degree of control one person has over another. Usually, a person who is viewed with high esteem because of his knowledge, skill, and past successes will have considerable control and influence over others.

Studies indicate that the greatest likelihood of the inculcation of diffuse values occurs when the socializing agent is prestigeful, powerful, and the affective (expressive) rewards and punishment are great.[16] Childhood socialization usually involves relationships of this type, such as the relationship between parent and child. Conversely, most adult socialization takes place under conditions of low affectivity and little power differential. The most radical shifts of personality among adults usually occur when the socialization process includes conditions of high affectivity and an asymmetrical power relationship, e.g., prisoner of war camps, brainwashing, psychotherapy, religious conversion, intensive graduate programs, etc. Riley and Riley suggested that the "type of expressive relationship which makes for effective teaching is not one of equalitarian friendship, but one of admiration of the teacher as a superior and distant figure."[17] The eminent professional football coach, Vince Lombardi, who maintained a distance from his players and had a great deal of prestige and power in his position, said that his greatest satisfaction in coaching was not in winning but in the rapport and closeness he had with his team.[18] He reported that the essence of his career was that he was more parent than employer and more father than professional coach.

An important consideration for future research is to determine the point on the instrumental-expressive continuum which is optimal for the transmission of specific skills and/or diffuse values. Also, does the transmission of diffuse values interfere (is there a role conflict) with the development of specific skills (and in the case of sports, the winning of contests)? Obviously, there has been no interference in the case of Coach Lombardi but more empirical data is needed.

5. *Personal and social characteristics.* Numerous personal and social characteristics of participants in physical activities are potentially important in socialization. This range of characteristics is too broad to discuss in detail but some areas are suggested for additional analysis.

The participant's talent will be an important aspect of his behavior and self-perception. Self-perception can be an important motivator in the present and a determiner of future aspirations. The student who has the physical and mental abilities to be highly successful in physical education or sports is likely to be receptive to continued participation. Transmission of diffuse traits would seem to be more likely if the participant is talented than if he is not, although this characteristic will also be associated with the degree of involvement.

Social class, racial, and ethnic affiliation also represent important variables. If students see sports and physical education as a way of excelling and achieving social mobility, the possibility of transmitting diffuse traits would seem probable. However, one's racial affiliation and loyalties may present the participant with conflicting loyalties as was indicated by the threatened boycott of the 1968 Olympics and by discontent of black athletes in colleges and universities. Under these conditions of discontent, the socialization outcomes will be affected.

CONCLUSIONS

Kenyon raises some important questions—namely: (1) What are the contributions of sports and physical education as a socialization process? and (2) Does this socialization result in the development of traits suitable for diffuse as well as specific roles? Answers must be found lest physical educators delude themselves into assuming illusory outcomes for physical activities. This paper has attempted to extend the Kenyon discussion to a consideration of several dimensions of socialization seeming to contribute to an understanding of the development of specific and/or diffuse characteristics. It can be concluded that some physical activity results in the development of role-specific characteristics, some contribute to the learning of broader and diffuse roles, and some probably assume a median position. The dimensions outlined above seem to explain some of these differences.

Perhaps something should be said in defense of physical activities that seem to develop only specific skills. It may be that these activities are no different than many other courses. Does a math or foreign language course contribute more to the development of diffuse traits than a physical activity course? In fact, to some extent the development of diffuse role behavior may involve the incorporation of a number of specific roles; thus, "It is obvious that the more roles in an actor's repertoire, the better prepared he is to meet the exigencies of social life."[19] Furthermore, development of specific skills in an activity course may lead to more active participation in an intramural program or eventually into adult recreational activities of a more diffuse nature.

It should be noted that merely because some characteristics are diffuse they are not necessarily desirable. Some diffuse characteristics may be dysfunctional for individual adjustment to the society and for the society itself. For example, a player's behavior on the basketball floor is under constant supervision by the officials. The player is not expected to impose sanctions on himself if he violates the rules. If the player commits a violation he is expected to ignore it, continue playing, and "cover it up." Often, blame is placed on the officials for missing the violation rather than on the player for committing it. Is this socialization of a diffuse attitude toward rules and social control agencies functional to society? Perhaps, there is a relationship between our attitudes toward athletic officials and law enforcement officials.

By focusing attention on the socialization process within physical education and sports, one can better understand what is occurring and what is being achieved. This understanding is necessary to predict and achieve some control over the socialization outcomes. No other consideration is of more importance within the profession. Priority should be given to these matters.

NOTES

1. Kenyon, G. S., "Sociologival Considerations," *Johper,* **39** (Nov.–Dec.), 1968, 31–33.

2. *Ibid.*

3. Reed, W. R., "Big Time Athletics' Commitment to Education," *Johper,* **34** (Sept.), 1963, 29–30, 64–65.

4. Singer, R., "Status of Sports in Contemporary American Society," *The Physical Educator,* **23**, 1966, 147–148.

5. Schafer, W. S., and Armer, J. M., "Athletes are Not Inferior Students," *Trans-Action,* **6** (Nov.), 1968, 21–26, 61–62.

6. Ulrich, C., *The Social Matrix of Physical Education,* Englewood Cliffs: Prentice-Hall, Inc., 1968, 124.

7. Lohman, J. D., and Reitzes, D. C., "Note on Race Relations in Mass Society," *The American Journal of Sociology,* **58**, 1952, 240–246.

8. Strauss, A. *Mirrors and Masks,* Glencoe: The Free Press, 1959, 89–109, 124–129, 144–147.

9. Yinger, J. M. *Toward a Field Theory of Behavior,* New York: McGraw-Hill Book Co., 1965, 103–115.

10. Brim, O. G., Jr., "Socialization Through the Life Cycle," in Brim, O. G., Jr., and Wheeler, S., *Socialization After Childhood,* New York: John Wiley and Sons, 1966, 3–49.

11. Goffman, E., *Encounters,* Indianapolis: Bobbs-Merrill, 1961, 105–110.

12. Barker, R. G., *et al., Big School–Small School: Studies of the Effects of High School Size Upon the Behavior and Expectations of Students,* Midwest Psychological Field Station, The University of Kansas, 1962.

13. Carlson, Richard O., "Environmental Constraints and Organizational Consequences: The Public School and Its Clients," *Behavioral Science and Educational Administration Yearbook,* Part II, edited by Daniel E. Griffiths, National Society for the Study of Education, Chapter 12, 1965. Discusses the variables of selectivity on the part of formal organizations and on the part of the client and their consequences.

14. Riley, J. W., Jr., and Riley, M. W., "Sociological Perspectives on the Use of New Educational Media," *New Teaching Aids for the American Classroom,* Washington, D.C.: Office of Education, U.S. Department of Health, Education, and Welfare, 1960, p. 32.

15. Barker, *op. cit.*

16. Brim and Wheeler, *op. cit.*

17. Riley and Riley, *op. cit.*

18. Johnson, W., "Arararararargh! Vince Lombardi Puts a Legend on the Line," *Sports Illustrated,* **30**, 28–30, 33.

19. Sarbin, T. R., and Allen, V. L., "Role Theory," *The Handbook of Social Psychology,* Lindzey, G., and Aronson, E., Volume I, Reading, Mass.: Addison-Wesley Publishing Company, 1969, 491.

SOCIALIZATION AND SPORT

George H. Sage

Socialization is the process of learning and adapting to a given social system. In the context of society, the activity of socialization is called cultural transmission, which is the means by which a society preserves its norms and perpetuates itself. At birth an infant is certainly a living organism, but he is not a social being. A human raised in isolation develops only his animal nature, while one raised in human society demonstrates the human aspects which derive from social living, and he also shows the impact of society by the wide variations in behaviors which are produced from one society to another. Thus, the process of becoming a member of a social system is called socialization.

Socialization begins at birth and continues throughout the life-cycle, but the years from birth to adolescence are considered the "critical" years for it is in these years that the basic cultural transmission takes place. Numerous people are involved in the socialization of an individual but because of their frequency of contact, their primacy, and control over rewards and punishments, the primary agents and agencies for socialization are the family, peer groups, schools, churches, and the mass media.

For the individual, socialization produces attitudes, values, knowledges, and behaviors which are related to the culture of which he is a part and the roles which he will play in it. Thus, as the child in a society interacts with others—through language, gestures, rewards, and punishments—he learns the attitudes, values, behaviors; and expectations of various individuals and the behavior appropriate to the various social situations of his life.

Now it is rather obvious that a human activity as pervasive as sport in our society is bound to impinge to some extent upon most children in the United States, so the questions about the social sources of involvement and consequences of sport as a socializing agent for American children seem like naturals for the curious minds of social scientists. Remarkable as it may seem, the topic of socialization and sport has been virtually untouched, with regard to hard data, until quite recently. I hasten to add, however, that there are many of essay-type articles on this topic. From the Ancient Greeks to the last Super Bowl, many claims have been made for the socializing function of sport. The Battle of Waterloo is supposed to have been won on the playing

This is revised and updated from the second edition of *Sport in American Society*. Paper originally presented at a Symposium of Colorado Sports, Intermountain Region College of Sports Medicine, February 1973.

fields of Eton, and one of America's most famous generals, Douglas Mac-Arthur, coined the ditty: "Upon the fields of friendly strife are sown the seeds that on other days on other fields will bear the fruits of victory." American physical educators have all been weaned on "social development" as one of the objectives of physical education, but physical education scholars have conducted very little research on it.

The topic of Socialization and Sport may be divided into two sub-topics for analysis: Socialization into Sport and Socialization via Sport. In the former, an analysis is made of the agents and agencies which attract, or draw, children into sports—that is the ways in which children become involved in sports. An analysis of Socialization via Sports focuses upon the consequences, or outcomes, of sports involvement. I want to touch only briefly on Socialization into Sports and give more attention to Socialization via Sports.

The family—its social class, its structure, and its patterning of activities—undoubtedly has a significant influence on socializing youngsters into sports. For example, the lower class origins of many American sports performers is well-documented in the literature. Riesman and Denney's (1951) article on cultural diffusion in American football is a classic, and biographies of famous American athletes frequently describe a lower social class background. In the past decade a sizable body of theoretical and empirical literature has suggested that participation in dangerous sports is a function of birth order, with later-borns being over-represented in dangerous sports. (Nisbitt, 1968; Yiannakis, 1976; Casher, 1977; Landers; 1979) With respect to familial influence, several recent studies have found that parental attitudes toward physical activity and participation in sports were related to the sports involvement of their offspring. (Zeller, 1968; Snyder and Spreitzer 1973, 1976; Melcher and Sage, 1978; Greendorfer, 1977; Greendorfer and Lewko, 1978).

The neighborhood and peer group serve as powerful socializing agents for sports involvement. Axthelm (1970) in his excellent book, *The City Game,* describes how playground basketball in Harlem captures the interest and energies of the young boys, and this phenomenon is duplicated in the inner city of most of our metropolises. In a study examining the influence of socializing agents on the process of socialization of women into sport, Greendorfer (1977) found that peers were the major influence throughout each life-cycle stage (childhood, adolescence, early adulthood).

Of course, the school, with its physical education classes and interschool sports programs, serves a significant socializing role for American children. With universal education and state requirements for physical education, most American children are taught the rudiments of a variety of sports as they pass through the grades and some six million of them participate in interscholastic athletics each year.

Community sponsored sports programs for children exist throughout the country, with some 20 million annual participants. Programs such as Little

League, Pony League, Babe Ruth League, American Legion for baseball, and Pop Warner League football, Bittie Basketball, age group swimming and track, practically engulf young boys, and increasingly girls, from 7 to 18 years of age. These programs serve as another source of socializing youth into sports.

Finally, one must mention the mass media as a sports socializing agency. I'm sure that my suggestion that we are virtually inundated with sports via newspapers, magazines, and television, especially TV, does not need documentation; that the mass media brings sports to the attention of the young is obvious. Few boys do not know the names of the NFL, NBA, and professional baseball teams; a great many boys and girls have idols among the current crop of professional athletes, and the bedroom walls of many youngsters are plastered with sports posters of various types.

These, then, are the sports socializing agents and agencies which impinge on the youth of today. They are powerful influences, and it is a rare youngster who is not touched in some way by sports as he or she passes through childhood and adolescence.

The extent to which American youth are socialized via sport is largely unknown. This is the case because few investigations have been undertaken on this topic. Furthermore, sport constitutes only one set of forces operating on children and youth. It must be recognized that there is a multitude of social experiences to which every youth is subjected which are not sport related. Thus, much of what we "know" about the effects, or consequences, of sports participation is impressionistic, and this fact needs to be remembered in any discussion of this topic.

There are several principles of socialization theory, though, that probably hold true with regard to sports. For example, the degree of involvement, i.e. frequency, intensity, and duration, affects the socialization relationship. Finally, the prestige and power of the socializer is an important factor.[1] With these factors in mind, let me identify some of the possible socializing effects via sport.

To some extent personality is developed through a process of socialization, so presumably sports involvement might influence personality. Research on personality and sport is extensive, but contradictive. Some researchers have suggested that athletes have personalities which are different than non-athletes. Recent research, using more sophisticated statistical procedures than early studies, is not supporting the notion of an "athletic personality." It has even been suggested that athletes possess sport-specific personalities. A recent study of mine (Sage, 1972), using athletes from eight different sports, corroborates other recent research showing no differences in personality profiles across sports groups. There is no convincing evidence at the present showing that athletes possess a unique personality profile or that sport involvement actually produces changes in personality.

Competence in sports skills apparently does influence self-evaluation and social esteem with peers. Sports provide innumerable opportunities to perceive the feelings of others and their judgments about you. Thus, experiences in sports are instrumental in developing a self-image, or self concept. Although with the firing of the first Sputnik, achievement began to replace adjustment as the highest goal of the American way of life, Biddulph (1954) almost 30 years ago reported better personal and social adjustment among school athletes. Recent investigations by Kay (1975) and his colleagues show that sports abilities and interests are related to a positive self-concept. Other research in the past 20 years has consistently shown that young sports participants score higher in a variety of tests which measure "mental health." With regard to social esteem and sport involvement, Cowell once said, "much social interaction centers around physical skill. The child lacking motor skills is often barred or not accepted in social participation." There is a rather extensive literature which shows that athletes, or skilled sports performers, rate high among their classmates. (Coleman, 1961; Clarke and Green, 1963; Broekhoff, 1972; Buchanan et al, 1976)

Before leaving this topic of personal-social development through sports, I must hasten to say that most of the literature to which I have alluded is correlational, and thus not causal. Therefore, differences which exist between athletes, or skilled performers, and the unskilled are not necessarily a consequence of sport involvement.

One major function of socialization is the transmission of values. Values refer to personal and social ideals, beliefs, or standards which may be used to evaluate and regulate one's own or other's behavior. These involve ideals or beliefs about what is good, right, desirable, or true. There are only a few studies which have looked at value orientations of young athletes. Webb (1969) devised an instrument for measuring children's value orientations toward competition and found that as children grow older there is a shift from a high value on fairness and fun in participation to a greater emphasis on skill and victory as the paramount values in sport. Mandel and Vander Velden (1971) extended this work, assessing the values of pre-adolescent boys who participated in organized sports, and found that boys who had played on organized sports teams place higher emphasis on skill and victory than non-participants, who valued fairness more highly. Albinson (1973) administered the same instrument to a group of amateur ice hockey coaches and discovered a potential source of the professionalization of value orientation of youth sports participants. Only one coach out of 117 ranked fairness as the paramount value while 27 percent ranked victory as most important. Eldon Snyder's (1972) excellent paper "Athletic Dressing Room Slogans as Folklore: A Means of Socialization" shows how coaches attempt to socialize youngsters into accepting and internalizing values of success striving, competitive achievement, personal worth based upon sports outcomes, and subjection of self to external control.

Kistler (1957), Richardson (1962), and Corbin (1971) reported studies which show that boys who have participated in organized sports have poorer sportsmanship value orientations than non-sportsmen. In a study not directly related to sports, but one which I think may have implications for socialization via sports, Pearlin and his colleagues (1967) found that parents whose aspirations are high for their children and who pressure them to achieve are contributing, probably unwittingly, to the learning of behavior that is undesirable. They found that cheating by children whose parents were this type was significantly more frequent. Although it is only a hunch, I think that the same consequence may be produced by "win at any cost" and "winning is the only thing" achievement criteria in sport.

Presumably, value orientations of coaches may influence the values of their athletes. Coaches have been characterized by recent radical writers as being highly conservative, even neo-fascistic. I completed research (Sage, 1972) which showed that coaches were indeed more conservative than college students in philosophical, political, economic, educational, social, personal-moral, and religious dimensions of value orientation (as is most of the adult population) but they are more liberal than age cohort businessmen.

I have only scratched the surface of the socialization consequences of sports, but before bringing this presentation to an end, I shall identify several potentially dysfunctional consequences of sports for youngsters. The study of sports dysfunctions has become quite active the past decade, led initially by Jack Scott and a band of former professional athletes but more recently by physical educators and concerned parents. Although the literature is rich with those who have axes to grind or converts to proselytize, they have made some very telling points, and only a head-in-the-sand ostrich, or possibly Woody Hayes, would believe that all is completely well in the world of youth sports.

The first major potentially dysfunctional effect of kids' sports programs is the intrusion of adults on the play of youngsters.[2] The rationale behind the organization of youth sport programs is admirable: to provide young boys and girls a structure for their sports, opportunities for wide participation, proper equipment for their safety, and adult coaching to help them learn the fundamental skills. But since the community, school, parents, and coaches make considerable emotional investment in the young athletes they expect a payoff; the payoff is athletic victories. Consequently, those who are emotionally invested in the youngsters' performance frequently attempt to manipulate the sports activity in order to maximize the likelihood of receiving a payoff. Thus, we see youth sports programs which come to resemble the professionals. They are dressed as pros, coached as pros, have an admiring audience like pros, are taught that "winning isn't everything, it's the only thing" so by God they better win or else! As noted above, Albinson (1973) used Webb's Professionalism Scale to assess the attitude toward play of volunteer amateur ice hockey coaches and found that overwhelmingly the coaches possessed a professional orientation toward playing the sport. The attitude undoubtedly is conveyed to the youth playing under these coaches. While one cannot condemn all youth sports programs, they are all suspect of taking the fun and other play-elements from the youngsters.

When someone is naive enough to inquire the reason behind this "professionalization" of youth sports programs, the almost stock reply is that kids need to prepare for the competitive dog-eat-dog world of adults. Three reactions come to mind: First, apparently many adults haven't noticed that the American frontier closed over eighty years ago. The hard, physical struggle for survival against the elements does not exist today. Furthermore, with anti-trust legislation in effect and various other measures for restraining cut-throat business competition, the adult world "ain't" all that competitive. Indeed, in the field of economics there has been severe criticism of competition (Galbraith, 1968) by some while others have advocated a modified form of competition, with control and fair practices. (Dewey, 1969) Second, there are many American youngsters who never partake of these organized sports programs and no one has ever documented that they are worse off for it in their occupational careers. Third, one might suggest that the "win at any cost" mentality may be dysfunctional in post-industrial society. What this world needs is not highly competitive societies going around trying to blow others up, but cooperative societies dedicated to sustaining and enriching life on this planet. Schickel (1972), writing in *The New York Times,* sums up the effects of sports as preparation idea. He says:

> Aside from their obviously healthy aspects, they [sports] were widely believed to prepare boys for the wins and losses of life—especially the former. And in a way they did, for so many of us are little Nixons, secret sharers of the lunatic notion that life is a succession of game plans and games, a thing that can ideally be quantified in a won-and-loss column. We are prisoners, I think, of middle America's only universal metaphor and we have tried . . . to cram everything into it—politics, wars, careers— and it has stunted me, stunted us all [p. 26].

Adult intrusion into the world of kids' sports is dysfunctional for another reason. It robs the kids of one of the greatest potentials of sports— the opportunity to develop self-discipline and responsibility. George Sauer, former professional football player, hit all the mumbo-jumbo about how sports programs develop an elite of self-disciplined and responsible adults. He said that ". . . coaches know damn well they have never given their jocks a chance to become responsible or self-disciplined. Even in the pros, they tell them when to turn off the lights, when to go to bed, . . . when to eat . . ." [Hoch, p. 112].

Many of these youth sports programs are really adults' programs. The adults (coaches) make all the decisions—they decide who plays and what plays to run. The hired help (the youngsters) carry out the orders, and they do not ask questions, if they don't want to be labeled a "problem athlete."

Although facts are scarce the imposition of adults into kids' programs probably drives some youngsters out of sports (see for example Orlick and Botterill, 1975). The criterion for success—winning—becomes a terrible burden to carry for some. To be labeled a "loser" is the epitome of criticism in our society. For some youngsters, it may be easier to withdraw from sports and just be a spectator. The former long distance runner, Ron Clarke (quoted from Moore, 1973), eloquently summed up this idea by saying, "If youngsters are taught that losing is a disgrace, and they're not sure they can win, they will be reluctant to even try. And not trying is the real disgrace" [p. 42].

The second major dysfunctional potential which I would identify with sport socialization has to do with norm learning. If one accepts the notion that children can learn normative behavior from sports, and if one agrees that social norm deviance is widespread in sport, it becomes clear that American kids' sports programs may be providing patterned reinforcement of attitudes, values, and behaviors which are at variance with our society's norms. I think that it is fair to say that deviation from ideal norms of sports frequently occurs in sports. Thus, we see incidents of brutal attacks upon one athlete by another during games, booing of officials, and even the incorporation of deviance as part of the strategy of the game, i.e., spearing in football, illegal use of body in basketball, etc. Most sports have well planned deliberate violations of the norms to make it difficult for the opponent. The use of deviant normative behavior as acceptable is associated with, I think, the obsession to win. (I am not suggesting that winning should not be an objective of competitive sports. I hasten to add this, because anytime someone suggests that winning is not the only thing in sport, there always are a few who will smugly conclude that the writer is one of those Commies who is trying to poison the minds of Americans.) When I say obsession, I'm talking about the mentality of those who put up locker room slogans which read: "Defeat is worse than death because you have to live with defeat." While one might question the extent to which deviant normative patterns learned in sports are generalized to the larger social relations, one certainly must consider the possible social effects on athletes who play under coaches who encourage unethical behaviors. Moreover, Snyder (1970) has suggested that since it is approved behavior in sport to violate rules and attempt to conceal it from officials or if caught to use various ways of showing disrespect to the officials; there may be, he notes, "a relationship between our attitudes toward athletic officials and law enforcement officials" [p. 6].

A third major dysfunctional potential which I fear lurks in many youth sports programs is what I call the promotion of the Lombardi ethic, which is exemplified in the statement which he is alleged to have made, to wit: "Winning isn't everything, it's the only thing." Now while this notion may have some validity for the big business of professional football, where coaches and players indeed are fired, or disposed of in other ways, if they do not win, this ethic has no place in the sports programs for young boys and girls. It is dysfunctional because it makes conditional persons out of participants. They become defined by won-loss records—the records become the basis for assigning "worthiness" to individuals. Winners are assigned prestige and honor; losers disdain and ridicule. As Jim Tatum, the late football coach once said, "How can anyone be proud of a loser." The expressive nature of sport—fun, joy, etc.—becomes strangled by instrumental concerns. So joy, fun, excitement, and exhilaration in sport comes not from the movement, display of skill, and mastery of self, but from winning, and only winning. The Lombardian ethic separates groups into "our group" and "the enemy." Our group right or wrong must win and prevail; the enemy must be crushed. They are objects to overcome. It seems to me that this ethic is a carryover from the "dog-eat-dog" eras of the past centuries which is obsolete as we move rapidly toward the 21st century. Humankind has the capabilities of obliterating itself on this planet. What is needed is cooperative groups working toward mutual actualization of human potentialities. The old Nation State bickering over territory and nature resources is gradually becoming irrelevant as humankind realizes its destiny demands a new ethical ideal in human relations. If indeed ethical behavior learned in sport generalizes to more general role behavior, sport based upon optimizing expressive values and growth-promoting interpersonal relationships has exciting possibilities.

Let me close on a positive note by saying that sports for young boys and girls have great potential benefits. Whether a given sports program has more functional than dysfunctional socialization effects for its participants depends primarily upon the leadership in the programs. Anyone who really cares about kids' sports programs should become actively involved in some way with them.

NOTES

1. I am indebted to Eldon Snyder for this list of principles. See Eldon Snyder, "Aspects of Socialization in Sports and Physical Education," *Quest,* **14** (June, 1970), pp. 1-7.

2. I am indebted to Emil Bend and his presentation "Some Dysfunctional Effects on Sports Upon Socialization" for some of the ideas which follow.

REFERENCES

1. Albinson, J. G., "Professionalized Attitudes of Volunteer Coaches," *International Review of Sport Sociology*, 8(2): 77–88, 1973.

2. Axthelm, P., *The City Game.* New York: Harper and Row, 1970.

3. Biddulph, L., "Athletic Achievement and the Personal and Social Adjustment of High School Boys," *Research Quarterly*, **25**: 1-7, 1954.

4. Brawley, L. R. and Landers, D. M., "Attitudes and Strategies of Male and Female Athletes and Nonathletes in Playing an Experimental Game." in

Daniel M. Landers and Robert Christina (eds.) *Psychology of Motor Behavior and Sport*, Vol. II, Champaign, Ill.: Human Kinetics Press, 1977, pp. 61–73.

5. Broekhoff, J., "Relationships Between Social Status and Physical Measurements of Boys and Girls from the Fourth Through the Sixth Grade,: Paper presented at the Research Section of the National Convention of American Association for Health, Physical Education, and Recreation, Houston, March, 1972.

6. Buchanan, H. T., Blankenbaker, J., and Cotten, D., "Academic and Athletic Ability as Popularity Factors in Elementary School Children." *Research Quarterly*, **47**: 320–325, 1976.

7. Casher, B. B., "Relationship Between Birth Order and Participation in Dangerous Sports." *Research Quarterly*, **48**: 33–40, 1977.

8. Clarke, H. H. and Green, W., "Relationships Between Personal-Social Measures Applied to 10-year old Boys," *Research Quarterly*, **34**: 288–298, 1963.

9. Coleman, J. S., *The Adolescent Society*. New York: The Macmillan Co., 1961.

10. Corbin, C., "A Study of Spectator Attitudes About Sportsmanship." *Texas Association for Health, Physical Education, and Recreation Journal*, **40** (October): 64, 1971.

11. Dewey, D., *The Theory of Imperfect Competition*. New York: Columbia University Press, 1969.

12. Galbraith, J. K., *The Industrial State*. New York: New American Library 1968.

13. Greendorfer, S. L., "Role of Socializing Agents in Female Sport Involvement." *Research Quarterly*, **48**: 304–310, 1977.

14. Greendorfer, S. L. and Lewko, J. H., "Role of Family Members in Sport Socialization of Children," *Research Quarterly*, **49**: 146–152, 1978.

15. Hoch, P., *Rip Off the Big Game*. New York: Doubleday Co., 1972.

16. Kay, R. S., Felker, D. W., and Varoz, R. O., "Sports Interests and Abilities as Contributors to Self-Concept in Junior High School Boys," *Research Quarterly*, **43**: 208–215, 1972.

17. Kistler, J., "Attitudes Expressed About Behavior Demonstrated in Certain Specific Situations Occurring in Sports," *60th Proceedings of the National College Physical Education Association for Men*, 1957, pp. 55–58.

18. Landers, D. M., "Birth Order in the Family and Sport Participation" in March L. Krotee (ed.) *The Dimensions of Sport Sociology*, West Point, N.Y.: Leisure Press, 1979, 140–167.

19. Loy, J. W., "A Case for the Sociology of Sport," *Journal of Health, Physical Education and Recreation*, **43**(6): 50–53, 1972.

20. Mandel, R. C. and Vander Velden, L., "The Relationship Between the Professionalization of Attitude Toward Play of Preadolescent Boys and Participation in Organized Sports," Paper presented at the Third International Symposium of the Sociology of Sport, Waterloo, Canada, August, 1971.

21. McCraw, L. W. and Tolbert, J. W., "Sociometric Status and Athletic Ability of Junior High School Boys," *Research Quarterly*, **24**: 72–80, 1963.

22. Moore, Kenny, "But Only on Sunday," *Sports Illustrated,* **38** (February 26) 38–42, 1973.

23. Nisbett, R. E., "Birth Order and Participation in Dangerous Sports," *Journal of Personality and Social Psychology,* 8(4): 351–353, 1968.

24. Orlick, T. and Botterill, C., *Every Kid Can Win.* Chicago: Nelson-Hall, 1975.

25. Pearlin, L. I., Jarrow, M. K., and Scarr, H. A., "Unintended Effects of Parental Aspirations: The Case of Children's Cheating," *American Journal of Sociology,* **73**: 73–83, 1967.

26. Richardson, D., "Ethical Conduct in Sport Situations," *66th Proceedings of the National College Physical Education Association for Men.,* 1962, pp. 98–103.

27. Riesman, D. and Denney, R., "Football in America: A Study in Culture Diffusion," *American Quarterly,* **3**: 309–319, 1951.

28. Sage, G. H., "An Assessment of Personality Profiles Between and Within Intercollegiate Athletes From Eight Different Sports." *Sportwissenschaft,* **2**: 408–415, 1972/74.

29. Sage, G. H., "Value Orientations of American College Coaches Compared to Male College Students and Businessmen." *75th Proceedings, National College Physical Education for Men.,* 1972, pp. 174–186.

30. Schickel, R., "Growing Up in the Forties," *New York Times Magazine,* February 20, 1972.

31. Snyder, E., "Athletic Dressing Room Slogans as Folklore: A Means of Socialization." *International Review of Sport Sociology,* **7**: 89–100, 1972.

32. Snyder, E. E., and Spreitzer, E. "Family Influence and Involvement in Sports." *Research Quarterly,* **44**: 249–255, 1973.

33. Snyder, E. E. and Spreitzer, E., "Correlates of Sport Participation Among Adolescent Girls." *Research Quarterly,* **47**: 804–809, 1976.

34. Webb, H., "Professionalization of Attitudes Toward Play Among Adolescents." In Gerald Kenyon (ed.) *Aspects of Contemporary Sport Sociology.* Chicago: *The Athletic Institute,* 1969, pp. 161–187.

35. Yiannakis, A., "Birth Order and Preference for Dangerous Sports Among Males." *Research Quarterly,* **47**: 62–67, 1976.

36. Zeller, J., "Relationships Between Parental Attitudes About Physical Education and Their Children's Performance in Physical Tasks," M.A. Thesis, University of California at Los Angeles, 1968.

SOCIALIZATION EFFECTS OF PARTICIPATION IN SPORT: A CRITICAL VIEW OF THE RESEARCH

Christopher L. Stevenson

The legitimation of physical education and athletics is based essentially upon their efficacy as agents of socialization. In the final analysis, it is the rationale of "character building," of moral development, of citizenship development, of social development, that justifies the existence of physical education and athletics in educational institutions. These rationales, characteristically, are stated as "facts"; they are athletic axioms. Unfortunately, the question of the validity of these axioms is rarely posed. For, no matter how "factually" these axioms are stated, essentially they still fall into the domain of "belief." This troublesome situation behooves us to look at the objective evidence. The purpose of this review of the literature, then, is to determine the extent to which research has demonstrated that beneficial socialization effects do result from participation in sport or sportive activities.

The analysis of the research will be presented in two parts. Initially, the major conclusions of the research will be summarized. Following this description, the validity of these generalizations will be discussed from the perspective of certain theoretical and methodological considerations.

RESEARCH EVIDENCE

This analysis is concerned with the existence of possible cause and effect relationships between participation in sport and the taking-on and the demonstration of certain characteristics by individuals and by populations. A methodological problem is consequently posed. Because of the nature of the socialization claims under investigation, namely alterations in psychological and attitudinal states, and because of the mechanisms of operant conditioning and modeling by which participation in sport is thought to affect these states, an "ideal" approach by such an investigation would be a longitudinal study.

During the course of such a long term investigation a single sample population would be taken from a point in time prior to its initial participation in sport, through an extended period of exposure to sport, and would be culminated upon the population attaining maturity. By means of this ap-

Christopher L. Stevenson, "Socialization Effects of Participation in Sport: A Critical Review of the Research," *Research Quarterly,* Vol. 46 (October, 1975), pp. 287-301. Reprinted by permission.

proach, the development of pertinent characteristics in the population, and the influence which participation has upon this development, could be traced with the use of appropriate instruments. Naturally, the period of time that would be required to complete such an investigation would depend upon a number of factors, including the particular questions under investigation. It can certainly be said, however, that to obtain credible and acceptable information upon the types of socialization claims that are commonly made with regard to sport participation, an acceptable period of time would of necessity have to include preadolescence and adolescence, and would extend into postadolescence. To the author's present knowledge such an ambitious longitudinal investigation has never been accomplished,[1] and clearly there are many obvious practical reasons why this is so.

Because of the nonfeasibility of the long term study of a single population, an alternative approach has typically been the comparison of two or more very similar populations. The basic assumption of this approach is that the different populations under investigation are essentially the same in many significant respects, except for this one feature of sport participation. The populations may differ on this particular feature in a number of ways, for example, they may differ in terms of the extent of their exposure to participative sport, including whether or not such exposure has occurred, or in terms of the type of exposure that they have experienced. In these cases, based upon the assumption of initial similarity, the conclusion might be drawn that any differences between the populations in certain psychological or attitudinal characteristics could be attributed to the fact of, or the extent of, or the type of their participation in sport.

It is the case that the vast majority of the literature upon the educational and psychological effects of sport participation has tended to employ this particular approach. Some of the studies have contrasted samples of populations with respect to the fact of their participation in sport, they have compared athletes with nonparticipants on certain psychological and attitudinal characteristics. Others have concentrated upon the effects of differential degrees of participation, including both the extent and the intensity of participation. Such studies have concerned themselves with comparisons between varsity athletes and nonvarsity athletes, for example, or with comparisons of exceptional athletes versus average athletes versus poor athletes, and, even on occasion, comparison of ninth grade athletes versus twelfth grade athletes. The effects of different types of participation have been the foci of other studies; comparisons have been made between athletes who participate in "team" sport and athletes who participate in "individual" sport, between athletes who participate in different sports, such as wrestlers versus football players, and some studies have concentrated upon the effects of extremely high levels of competition upon exceptional athletes.

It is also the case that the act of participation in sport has been the subject of many claims for a wide variety of socialization effects. Typically, however, the socialization effects thus claimed may be categorized into three broad areas: psychological effects, behavioral effects, and attitudinal effects. In order to facilitate clarity in presentation the research will be reviewed according to each of these three topics.

Psychological Effects

Under this rubric fall those research reports which have concentrated upon the personality characteristics of athletes and nonathletes as determined by a variety of personality inventories. These studies constitute the bulk of the work which may be considered to be concerned with the socialization effects of participation in sport. This review of the personality studies, in part, builds upon the material and the critiques presented in five previously published reviews of the research on personality and sport (1, 5, 16, 39, 46). It is based upon 27 studies, the majority of which were published since 1965.

In the studies reviewed a total of 12 different psychological instruments were used. These instruments ranged from the well known and the well tested, such as Cattell's 16PF and the MMPI, to the individually developed and the untested. The samples in these studies showed a similar dazzling diversity. They included little league baseball players, junior high school, senior high school and college physical education activity classes, youth and adult rugby players, college wrestlers, karate participants, intercollegiate athletes, competitive swimmers, college football players, tennis players, baseball players, fencers, and, of course, the ubiquitous "nonathletes." Clearly, with such diverse experimental conditions it is extremely difficult to arrive at all-embracing conclusions.

Considering, first of all, 18 studies which attempted to compare personality characteristics of samples of different athletic abilities and of different levels of participation. Of these 18, 11 studies were unable to discern any significant personality factor differences between athletes of different abilities, and between athletes and nonathletes (2, 12, 22, 23, 30, 31, 38, 45, 47, 51, 53); the other seven studies, however, were able to conclude that there were significant (.01) sample differences on certain personality factors (3, 15, 17, 26, 32, 43, 44). There were few instances of multiple support for these factors, however; typically each study discovered a different set of factors on which there were sample differences. At best, majority support was given to the finding that the athlete samples were significantly (.01) higher on a "dominance" factor (3, 15, 26, 32, 44).

As for other personality factors, individual support was given to athletes being higher on such factors as cooperation, leadership, extroversion, emotional stability, self-confidence, self-discipline, and aggression. Two studies were also reviewed which concentrated upon female populations (28, 34). The results of these studies were remarkably consistent in suggesting that female athletes were more toughminded and were more emotionally stable than their nonathletic counterparts.

"Champion" athletes were the focus of four other studies, which attempted to produce personality profiles of such athletes using test instrument "norms" as a standard baseline (6, 19, 32, 52). Once more, the personality factors which were seemingly significant closely matched those which were arrived at in the comparisons of athletes and nonparticipants, although one study did conclude that body builders and weight lifters did not differ significantly from the test "norms" (6). One reads results demonstrating significantly (.01) high levels of aggression, dominance, leadership, tough-mindedness, self-sufficiency, and achievement motivation; such factors received the support of individual studies. Multiple support was forthcoming, however, for the factors of self-assurance and of a decreased "need to be nurtured." It is curious that, contrary to some of the results of the studies on athletes and nonathletes, one study of champion athletes found them to be less extrovert than the general population (i.e., the test "norms") (33).

The third subarea of research concentration was the comparison of participants in different sports (18, 24, 26, 28, 34, 36). Two types of comparison were made, participants in team sports were compared with participants in individual sports, and participants in specific sports were compared with each other. Once again, the results of these comparisons are contradictory. While Lakie (26) and Pyecha (36) were unable to detect any differences between participants in different sports, Kroll and Crenshaw (24) demonstrated differences (.01) between football players, wrestlers and gymnasts. Two other studies of female athletes were able to distinguish between team sport participants and individual sport participants, such that team sports seemed to be associated with toughmindedness, sophistication, extroversion, low dominance, and low self-sufficiency (28, 34) while a third study was able to show that basketball players were socially immature compared with three other sports groups (18).

These studies just cited have employed population comparisons as one methodological alternative to the impractical "ideal" of a longitudinal study. There has been some research, however, which has attempted to move methodologically closer to the ideal. These studies deserve extended consideration. Werner and Gottheil (51) in their study of 4 years of "required" college athletics attempted what might be considered a "short term" longitudinal study (51). The conditional "short term" is justified because, as previously discussed, the "ideal" would require an investigation extending from preparticipation in sports through to the attainment of physiological and psychological maturity. Schendel, on the other hand, innovatively has compared cross-sections of athletic groups at different educational levels, at the ninth grade, at the twelfth grade and at college (43, 44). And Ogilvie has reported on his cross-sectional analysis of girl age-group swimmers (33).

Werner and Gottheil conducted a 4-year study of cadets at the U.S. Military Academy at West Point. The regulations at that institution demanded that all cadets participate in athletics throughout their tenure. It was possible consequently, for Werner and Gottheil to attempt to discover the effects of 4 years of sport participation by administering Cattell's 16 PF to the cadets immediately upon their entry into the institution, and again immediately prior to their graduation. The entire sample of 456 cadets was subgrouped for analysis into "athletes" and "nonparticipants" on the basis of their past histories of sport participation. The results indicated that, despite 4 years of regular athletic participation, the designated "nonparticipant" group did not change in personality structure as measured by the 16PF test, (1) to a greater extent than did the "athletes," (2) in a different pattern than the "athletes," (3) nor so as to become more like the "athletes." Thus, on basis of the assumption that if socialization effects could not be demonstrated after 4 years of consistent athletic participation, then such effects would be unlikely from the typical pattern of college athletic participation, Werner and Gottheil concluded that, "no evidence was found to support the view that college athletics significantly influenced personality structure (51:130)."

Schendel administered the California Psychological Inventory to 334 ninth grade, twelfth grade, and college team sport athletes and nonparticipants in athletics (43). The results demonstrated differences between the athlete and nonparticipant groups at each educational level, although the specific differences were not necessarily the same at each level. On the basis of these results Schendel concluded that, while both ninth and twelfth grade athletes generally possessed desirable personal-social psychological characteristics to a greater extent than did the respective nonparticipants, at the college level the situation was reversed and it was the nonparticipant group which possessed the desirable characteristics to a greater extent than did the athletes.

In a related set of conclusions Schendel also suggested that, while there appeared to be few differences between athletes of different ability levels (i.e., outstanding athletes vs. regular players vs. substitutes), the differences which did exist indicated that the relatively less able athlete at the twelfth grade and at college generally possessed desirable psychological characteristics to a greater extent than did the athletes of greater ability. Running consistently through these results there seemed to be two specific characteristics of athletes: (1) Athletes appeared to be more conventional in their responses to social situations, and (2) athletes appeared to be more sociable.

Schendel followed this study with a longitudinal investigation of 91 athletes and nonparticipants (44). Using the same basic format as his previous study, Schendel administered the California Psychological Inventory to his subjects when they were in the ninth grade, and again when they had reached the twelfth grade. The results were very similar to those from his previous study. He found that there were "clear cut" differences between the athletes and the nonparticipants at both grade levels. However, his results also showed that these differences had diminished in number and in degree in the twelfth grade as compared with the ninth grade. This result clearly parallels the reversal from grade 9 to college demonstrated in his 1965 study. The data also documented "striking differences" between athletes of different ability levels. However, while the substitutes did not demonstrate any change over time on the traits of "self-acceptance" and "dominance," the other two categories of players showed dramatic increases.

Ogilvie reported his results on competitive girl swimmers at different age-group levels (33), and was able to indicate certain psychological characteristics in which there were sample differences as the age-group level and consequently the competition level increased. The results indicated that as the girls moved up the competitive ladder, they became: (1) less reserved, (2) more emotionally stable, (3) less self-assertive, (4) more toughminded, (5) more self-assured and self-confident, (6) more self-controlled and self-disciplined and (7) less anxious. There is, however, a problem with the interpretation of these results, as Ogilvie readily admits. There is considerable uncertainty whether these differences are due to an attenuation of the population as the less able physiologically and psychologically drop out, or whether, in fact, the contributing factor has been the continued competitive experience. Another problem with this particular investigation is that the effect of increasing age *per se* on these personality characteristics is not controlled for, and is therefore a confounding variable.

In summary, we may draw the following generalizations from this description of the personality research literature (1). There is a considerable amount of contradictory evidence. Numerically, there is a fairly even dichotomy between those studies ($N = 12$) which were unable to detect differences between athletes and nonparticipants, or between athletes of different ability levels, or between athletes and psychological test "norms," and those studies ($N = 11$) which were able to demonstrate differences between such groups (2). These latter studies gave support to the characterization of athletes as being more toughminded, more dominant, more self-reliant, more extrovert, more emotionally stable, more self-confident, more self-disciplined, more aggressive, more sociable, more conventional in responses to social situations, and as having a lesser need to be nurtured, than nonparticipants.

Behavioral Effects

The literature reviewed under this topic was concerned with the possible relationships between participation in sport and such behavioral features as educational performance, as indicated by grade point average (GPA), mental ability as determined by tests of intelligence, and delinquency, which was determined through the examination of court records.

The literature in this area is not very extensive, but by and large the evidence suggests that participation in sports is associated with greater academic performance. Using athlete vs. nonparticipant comparisons, eight studies have demonstrated the GPA of athletes to be significantly (.01) higher than that of nonparticipants (9, 10, 11, 14, 20, 35, 42, 50). Two of these studies, furthermore, have demonstrated that the GPA of the athletes is greater during the athletic season than it is during the off-season (20, 50). Even when indicators of academic achievement other than grades were used, for example, mental ability as determined by intelligence tests (29), and college aspirations (35), the conclusions remained the same, that a positive correlation exists between participation in sports and academic performance.

There is not, however, a complete consensus. There are at least four disclaiments, two research studies and two reviews of the literature. One research study, conducted in an English public school, was unable to discern any significant relationship between IQ and athletic ability in a sample of the student population (13). The other study at an American college found no significant differences on GPA between college athletes and nonathletes (7). In his analysis of the research, Lowell Cooper felt it necessary to distinguish between tests of intelligence and tests of achievement (5). In athlete vs. nonparticipant comparisons, he found that there was no intellectual difference between the groups when standard tests of intelligence were used. What he did discover, however, was that there were differences in achievement motivation when performances on achievement tests were compared. He thus concluded that, "while there were no clear IQ differences, there was a tendency for athletes to be more achievement oriented (5:18)." Dean Ryan in his analysis of the literature acknowledged that there was a number of studies which indicated significant correlations between motor ability and grades, and between athletic participation and grades, but, he asserted that there was no evidence of a cause and effect relationship. He suggested that "what is probably happening is that the person who is motivated to work in one area is (also) motivated to work in the other (39:73)."

It is indeed an open question whether the academic achievement differences found in the GPA studies were, in fact, related to sports participation. The possibility does exist that the athlete population began high school with a greater academic ability and/or achievement motivation than the nonparticipant population, and so attained the higher grades; and attained them, perhaps, *in spite* of their participation in sports. Two studies did attempt to accommodate this problem by matching their samples. Edwards matched his athlete and nonparticipant samples according to their SES, their IQ scores as freshmen, and their IQ scores as seniors, before making a comparison of their GPA's (9). His results showed the GPA of athletes to be 6 percent higher than that of the nonparticipants. In a control comparison of his two samples against the overall GPA of the high school class, he discovered that his athletes' GPA was the same as that of the overall class, while his nonparticipant GPA was 6 percent lower. This result might well suggest support for

Cooper's conclusion of an association with achievement motivation rather than with intellectual ability *per se.*

Schafer and Armer employed a sample of 585 high school boys, of whom 24 percent were classified as athletes, and found a considerable difference between the GPA of the athletes (2.35) and the GPA of the rest of the sample (1.83). To investigate this finding further, they produced athlete and non-participant samples which were matched on 4 different variables: father's occupation, intelligence test score, curriculum type, and GPA for the final semester of junior high school. The new results showed that the average GPA remained slightly higher for the athletes (2.35 vs. 2.24), but clearly the difference was much reduced (42).

Overall, it must be concluded that there does appear to be a positive correlation between academic achievement and participation in sport. However, it must also be said that a cause and effect relationship has yet to be established. There is the possibility that other factors allied with athletic participation may have had effects upon GPA. After all, one major requirement of participation in athletics is academic eligibility. Academically ineligible students simply do not appear on athletic teams, and often considerable effort is expended through tutorial arrangements, and so on, to maintain the eligibility of athletes.

The research which has concerned itself with the relationship between delinquency and participation in sport has been almost exclusively the work of Schafer and his associates (35, 41, 55). In accordance with the general belief that sport provides a positive moral influence, the research shows that athletes are, indeed, less delinquent than nonathletes. The relationship, however, was shown to be almost entirely the product of a sizable association among blue collar-low achievers. It would seem, therefore, that sport participation is significantly associated with a low delinquency rate in the subpopulation in which delinquency is at its highest. This result may well warrant the conclusion that participation in sport is indeed a positive moral socialization influence. However, there is the ever-present problem of selection. It could be the case that athletics simply do not attract boys who have been or are likely to become delinquent. Also it is highly likely that if an athlete was delinquent, that is, his name appeared on court roles, he would be removed from the team. As Schafer has put it, "the negative relationship between athletic participation and delinquency may not be the result of the deterring influence of athletics at all, but rather to a selection of conformers to the athletic program" (41:100).

Attitudinal Effects

The socialization effects of sport participation upon attitudes and values has been a neglected area of research; there can be no question that there are many procedural and theoretical difficulties with the measurement of attitudes and values. The studies which do exist have been analyzed according to the attitudes upon which they focused. Thus, consideration will be given to studies concerned with "sportsmanship" attitudes, followed by a study of political attitudes, and then in turn by two studies on attitudes toward racial minorities.

Sportsmanship Studies

It is axiomatic that the internalization of the high ideals of "sportsmanship" and of "fair play" accompanies the act of participation in sport. Indeed, the very labels by which this set of attitudes and values is known indicates the very close ideological connection that exists between them and sport activities. It is believed, apparently, that the very nature of the behaviors and attitudinal "sets" which sport demands legislatively and normatively from its participants lead to an internalization of these attitudes and to their transference to other social situations. Whether or not this belief is justified has been the subject of a number of research studies.

In the analysis of this research we once again come across the problem of a diverse array of instrumentation. The six studies in this analysis have used between them four different means of assessing attitudes vis a vis "sportsmanship." These have included the use of a psychometer, a story writing and content analysis, of a "study of values" test, and of a "critical incidents" inventory. In spite of this diversity, however, the results have been remarkably consistent. In studies which contrasted the responses of athletes and nonparticipants, the athletic groups consistently exhibited responses that were considerably less sportsmanlike than those of the nonparticipant population (4, 21, 27, 37). Even in studies of athletes alone, the results demonstrated their responses to be far from the sportsmanship ideal (25, 48). A number of side investigations also produced the following intraathletic comparisons: major sport athletes were lower in "sportsmanship" than minor sport athletes; varsity letter winners showed less favorable "sportsmanship" qualities than did nonletter winners; of a number of athletic groups tested, football players on scholarship were the lowest on "sportsmanship," and a distinction between "sportsmanlike" football players and "unsportsmanlike" players proved to be irrelevant because both sets of responses were so similar and were consistently so far below the ideal.

It is perhaps the case, as Singer has commented, that "there does seem to be some conflict between the ideals of society and the, perhaps realistic (materialistic?) way in which athletes enter competition (46:78)." One may add that there also seems to be some conflict between the socialization beliefs of society and the evidence emanating from studies of "sportsmanship." The question of whether these unsportsmanship attitudes were the result of socialization effects from participation in sport cannot be answered by these studies, however. Clearly, a relationship has been demonstrated, but certainly not a causal relationship.

Political Attitudes

Many national governments and political systems conceive of sport as an important agency for the socialization of political attitudes. Whether the state is an established one interested in maintaining the political and social status quo, or whether it is a recent revolutionary product vitally concerned with inducing massive change in citizens' mores and values, in both cases sport is believed to be a potent instrument in helping to achieve these respective political ends. The only research study that has been concerned with sport participation and political socialization, to our knowledge, is a doctoral dissertation prepared in Chile in 1971 by Barry E. Stern (49).

As evidence of political socialization Stern developed indexes which tapped such attitudes as confidence in the incumbents of political roles, a preference for using legal means rather than illegal means to achieve social or political change, maturity of moral judgment, and political tolerance. Stern concluded that there was "a rather consistent pattern of positive relationships . . . between sports participation and those variables having to do with perceptions of authority figures, in this case coaches and politicians, and with the acceptance of rules in both sports and civic contexts (49:114)."

However, Stern cautions, these relationships, though consistent, were fairly weak. Two other conclusions drawn with regard to political socialization efficacy and the degree of institutionalization of the sport, and the amount of participation in sport, showed that, generally speaking, the more organized the sport and the more systematic the attention given to it then the greater the socialization value it appeared to have, but that the amount of participation did not appear to be a particularly vital factor.

Unfortunately this study, once again, was correlational in nature, and was concerned with macrolevel interrelations between institutions. It is not possible, therefore, to generate any causal statements.

Attitudes Toward Racial Minorities

It is an essential element of the traditional socialization belief that participation in sport generates in the individual positive attitudes toward other cultural, religious, and racial groups. Sport, so the belief goes, cannot tolerate any form of discrimination whatsoever. It is often said that "individuals on the playing field are judged for what they are and what they can do, not on the basis of (the) social, ethnic, or economic group to which their families belong (8:1)."

There are two very different research studies which bear upon this matter. Sargeant investigated the participation of West Indian boys in English school games (40), and Wilson and Kayatani investigated American-Japanese inter-racial attitudes in an experimentally constructed game situation (54). Sargeant discovered that although a significantly greater proportion (.01) of West Indian boys participated on school sports teams, there was very little social interaction effect as a result. He was unable to produce any evidence of increased numbers of "friendships" or other type of interactions between West Indians and whites. He concluded, therefore, that the fact of mutual participation in sport did little to foster interracial relationship.

Wilson and Kayatani contrived an experimental situation in which two-person groups competed against each other in a version of the Prisoner's Dilemma game. They used a number of conditions, racially homogeneous groups versus other groups of the same race, and versus groups of the different race, and racially hetergeneous groups competing against each other. Upon conclusion of the games the participants' attitudes toward the members of the opposing team and toward their own partners were measured. On the basis of these responses the investigators concluded that "race" was not in any way related to the in-game decision making, nor to the postgame attitudes vis a vis partner and opposition.

Naturally there are many issues to be considered before either of these sets of results is taken to be representative of reality. For example, the situations of West Indians in Britain and of Japanese-Americans in Hawaii have very distinct implications in terms of cultural expectations and attitudes, which would tend to affect the results considerably. The best response, therefore, is probably to refrain from drawing any generalizations in this case.

DISCUSSION

The research findings which we have described are somewhat confusing and contradictory. In terms of the psychological socialization effects of participation in sport, half of the studies suggest that such effects might occur, while the other half insist they do not. The studies of behavioral effects, academic performance and delinquency, are consistent in demonstrating a relationship between such features and participation in sport; however, a causal relationship has yet to be established. The attitudinal studies found evidence of a relationship with sport participation, but, once again, causal relationships were not demonstrated. Furthermore, in the case of "sportsmanship" attitudes, the apparent relationship ran counter to popular beliefs relating the playing of sport with good "sportsmanship." Thus, at face value, the evidence is unclear and our opportunities to make generalizations are few and uncertain.

There are some other considerations, however, which are very pertinent to our ability to draw conclusions from the reported research. The validity of these research studies clearly stands and falls upon its methodology, upon the basic assumption of population similarity, and subsequently upon such other methodological concerns as the adequacy of the instrumentation and the adequacy of the definitions of population difference. This latter concern includes both the issue of an adequate operational definition of difference, as well as the issue of the relation of the definition(s) to the theoretical core of the study. The definition must define difference, but must define it in such a manner that the defined differences are also theoretically significant in terms of socialization effect. Thus, a definition may distinguish operationally between, say, different lengths of participation, 1 year, 2 years, 3 years, and so on; but whether or not these are experimentally significant differences can only be determined by reference to the theory under which the study is operating.

Unfortunately, because these considerations may be associated with very real substantive problems, they hang forebodingly over any review of research that is concerned with the socialization effects of participation in sport. Such substantive problems become evident in these studies, for it is clear that, in general, they have neglected the assumption of population similarity, they have employed questionable instrumentation, and they have abrogated their responsibility for maintaining consonance between experimental methodology and theory.

Comparisons have been made, for example, between participants in different physical education activity classes, or between high school students who are on their varsity football team and the remainder of their classmates, without regard to the question of whether or not these populations could be considered to have been initially similar. A number of arguments could be suggested for why they were not. A considerable process of selection occurs with respect to athletic participation. This is not selection simply on the basis of athletic ability.

On the contrary, many other factors are involved in the creation of the athletic population; factors such as academic eligibility requirements, selection on the basis of "promise" rather than present performance, selection on the basis of "attitude," simply the ability to publicly survive the selection rituals, the spring training, the training camps, and so on. This is not to ignore another important factor in athletic participation, the motivations, the likes and dislikes of the individual. As Husman has pointed out "[the] research evidence available still has not told us whether an individual participates in sport because of a psychological need or whether as a result of sport participation his personality is altered" (16:69). Singer has concurred saying "it is difficult to resolve the issue of the extent to which personality profiles are modified due to athletic participation as compared to the influence of personality on activity preference" (47:153). These institutional and individual selection factors suggest that the assumption of initial similarity between populations of athletes and nonparticipants, and between champion athletes and average athletes is a mistaken one, and that a more appropriate assumption would, in fact, be one of initial dissimilarity.

Because the studies reviewed have not made any attempts to control for the possible effects of differential selection factors in the creation of their samples, we must consequently conclude that the discovery of psychological, behavioral, or attitudinal differences between such samples of athletes and nonathletes cannot be attributed to presumed socialization effects of participation. Furthermore, we can argue that because of the individual and institutional selection factors operating in the creation of the athlete and non-athlete populations, differences between such samples should be the norm rather than the exception. The neglect of this consideration of population dissimilarity among the research studies reported in this review effectively prevents the making of any generalizations regarding the socialization efficacy of participation in sport.

The use of invalid and problematic instrumentation has been *the* major consistent criticism in the reviews that have been made of the literature on sport and personality (1, 5, 16, 39, 46). It is the consensus of the reviews that, contemporarily, it is extremely difficult to find instruments that are valid, reliable, and objective. The wide variety of personality and attitude inventories that have been used is somewhat bewildering. Although Cattell's 16 PF seems to have been the most popular psychological test, the gamut has run from the MMPI, through the Athletic Motivation Inventory, the Thurstone Temperament Schedule, the Edwards Personal Preference Schedule, the Gordon Personal Profile, the California Psychological Inventory, and the U.C. Interest Inventory, to the individually developed measures of idiosyncratic investigators. It is, therefore, a very pertinent question when Cooper asks, "is it valid to compare 'social dominance' factors derived from different personality tests administered to different subject populations" (5:20)? Clearly, one cannot be certain that "the presence of a cluster of responses labeled 'social dominance' on several different personality inventories refers to the same behavior and/or feelings for different subject groups." The use of a variety of incomparable psychological instruments makes it difficult to draw any substantive generalizations from these data.

These comments vis a vis instrumentation are not limited purely to personality studies. The research that has looked at attitudes such as "sportsmanship" is subject to the same criticisms, for there is little correspondence between the measures that have been used. While some investigators have derived implications of "sportsmanship" attitudes from responses to personality inventories, others have used a number of quasi-projective techniques. It is difficult, consequently, to have much confidence in individual conclusions and in comparisons of such conclusions.

The correspondence between methodology and theory is, of course, a most important issue. Unfortunately, it is one which the research on the socialization effects of sport participation has woefully neglected. The very fact that socialization effects are at the center of an investigation places certain demands upon the experimental methodology. Very simply, it is necessary that the "treatment" population has experienced sufficient exposure to the socialization agency to ensure that a consequent socialization effect might reasonably be expected. Experimentally, it is not only necessary that socialization should have occurred, but this effect should be significant enough that it can be measured. This demand not only has implications for the length and the intensity of the "treatment," but it also requires that the difference between experimental and control populations with regard to their respective exposures to this "treatment" be theoretically sufficient to produce significant differences in possible socialization effects.

It is on this issue that the research studies are lacking because of the very minimal attention investigators have paid to it. Is it realistic, for example, to expect a required physical education activity class lasting one semester to have a significant socialization effect upon personality characteristics? Is it realistic to go further and to attempt to contrast different activity class populations in order to elicit the different socialization effects of different sports activities? Clearly, on both counts the answer is negative. Furthermore, is it realistic to expect that "superior" athletes and "average" athletes, as two distinct experimental groups on the same college varsity athletic team, have had consistently and sufficiently different socialization experiences? Again the answer must be that it is not realistic. Because this type of methodology— theory inconsistency appears to have been the rule rather than the exception, it is consequently very difficult to accept as valid the conclusions which such socialization studies appear to suggest.

CONCLUSIONS

The basic question of whether sport participation has socialization effects cannot be answered. Although some population differences have been shown between athletes and nonathletes, and although some positive relationships have been demonstrated between certain characteristics and participation in sport, the serious methodological inadequacies of the research effectively damns any attempts at generalization. One very clear conclusion must be, however, that to date there is no valid evidence that participation in sport causes any verifiable socialization effects. The stated educational legitimation of physical education and of athletics must, therefore, remain in the realm of "belief" and should not be treated as "fact."

NOTE

1. It should be noted here that there has been one study which has taken a few tentative steps toward this ideal. Werner and Gottheil investigated the effects of 4 years of required college athletics upon cadets at West Point (51).

REFERENCES

1. Andrews, James C., "Personality, sporting interest and achievement." *Educational Review*, 23:126-34, 1971.
2. Berger, Richard A., and Littlefield, D.H., "Comparisons between football athletes and non-athletes in pesonality," *Research Quarterly* **40**:663-65, 1969.

3. Booth, E.G., "Personality traits of athletes as measured by the MMPI: A rebuttal," *Research Quarterly,* **32**:421-22, 1961.

4. Bovyer, G., "Children's concepts of sportsmanship in the 4th, 5th and 6th grade," *Reserach Quarterly,* **34**:282-87, 1963.

5. Cooper, Lowell, "Athletics, activity and personality: A review of the literature," *Research Quarterly,* **40**:17-22, 1969.

6. Darden, Ellington, "16PF profiles of competitive bodybuilders and weightlifters," *Research Quarterly,* **42**:142-47, 1972.

7. Davis, Billy E., and Berger, Richard A., "Relative academic achievement of varsity athletes," *Research Quarterly,* **44**:59-62, 1973.

8. Educational Policies Commission, *School athletics: Problems and policies.* Washington, D.C., 1954.

9. Edwards, T.L., "Scholarship and athletics," *Journal of Health, Physical Education and Recreation,* **38**:75, 1967.

10. Eidsmoe, R.M., "The academic performance of high school athletes," *Journal of Health, Physical Education and Recreation,* **32**:20, 1960.

11. Eidsmore, R.M., "High school athletes are brighter," *Journal of Health, Physical Education and Recreation,* **35**:53-54, 1964.

12. Hammer, William M., "Anxiety and sport performance," In *Proceedings of 2nd international congress of sport psychology.* Gerald S. Kenyon (Ed.). Chicago: Athletic Institute, 1968.

13. Hockey, S.W., and Murray, G.W., "The role of games in a public school," *British Journal of Physical Education,* **2**:5, 1971.

14. Horine, L. E., "Attendance and scholarship of high school athletes," *Athletic Journal,* **48**:52, 1968.

15. Hunt, David H., "A cross-racial comparison of personality traits between athletes and non-athletes," *Research Quarterly,* **40**: 704-07, 1969.

16. Husman, Burris., "Sport and personality dynamics," National College Physical Education Association of Men, *Annual Proceedings,* **72**:56-69, 1969.

17. Idegami, K., "Character and personality changes in the athlete," In *Proceedings of 2nd international congress of sport psychology.* Gerald S. Kenyon (Ed.). Chicago: Athletic Institute, 1968.

18. Johnson, Patricia A., "A comparison of personality traits of superior skilled female athletes in basketball, bowling, field hockey and golf," *Research Quarterly,* **43**:409-15, 1972.

19. Johnson, William R.; Hutton, D. C.; and Johnson, G. B., "Personality traits of some champion athletes as measured by two projective tests – Rorschach and H-T-P," *Research Quarterly,* **25**:484–85, 1954.

20. Keating, James W., "Character of catharsis," *Catholic Educational Review,* **63**:300–06, 1965.

21. Kistler, J. W., "Attitudes expressed about behavior demonstrated in specific situations occurring in sports." National College Physical Education Association for Men, *Annual Proceedings,* **60**:55–58, 1957.

22. Kroll, Walter., "16PF profile of collegiate wrestlers," *Research Quarterly,* **38**:49–57, 1967.

23. Kroll, Walter, and Carlson, B. R., "Discriminant function and hierarchal grouping analysis of karate participants' personality profiles," *Research Quarterly,* **38**:405–11, 1967.

24. Kroll, Walter, and Crenshaw, W., "Multivariate personality profile analysis of four athletic groups," In *Proceedings of 2nd international congress of sports psychology.* Gerald S. Kenyon (Ed.). Chicago: Athletic Institute, 1968.

25. Kroll, Walter, and Petersen, K. H., "Study of values test and collegiate football teams," *Research Quarterly,* **26**:441–47, 1965.

26. Lakie, William L., "Personality characteristics of certain groups of intercollegiate athletes," *Research Quarterly,* **33**:566–73, 1962.

27. Lakie, William L., "Expressed attitudes of various groups of athletes towards athletic competition," *Research Quarterly,* **35**:497–501, 1964.

28. Malumphy, T. M., "Personality of female athletes in intercollegiate competition," *Research Quarterly,* **39**:610–20, 1968.

29. McIntosh, Peter C., "Mental ability and success in school sports," *Research in Physical Education,* **1**:20–27, 1966.

30. Merriman, J. B., "Relationship of personality traits to motor ability," *Research Quarterly,* **31**:163–73, 1960.

31. Neale, D. C.; Sanstroem, R. J.; and Metz, K. F., "Physical fitness, self esteem, and attitudes towards physical activity," *Research Quarterly,* **40**:743–79, 1969.

32. Newman, E. N., "Personality traits of faster and slower competitive swimmers," *Research Quarterly,* **39**:1049–53, 1968.

33. Ogilvie, Bruce, "What is an athlete," *Journal of Health, Physical Education and Recreation,* **38**:48, 1967.

34. Peterson, S. L.; Weber, J. C.; and Trousdale, W. W., "Personality traits of women in team sports versus women in individual sports," *Research Quarterly,* **38**:686–89, 1967.

35. Phillips, John C., and Schafer, Walter E., "Consequences of participation in interscholastic sports," *Pacific Sociological Review,* **14**:328–36, 1971.

36. Pyecha, J., "Comparative effects of judo and selected physical education activities on male university freshmen personality traits," *Research Quarterly,* **41**:425–31, 1970.

37. Richardson, D. E., "Ethical conduct in sport situations." National College Physical Education Association for Men, *Annual Proceedings,* **66**:98–104, 1962.

38. Rushall, Brent S., "An evaluation of the relationship between personality and physical performance categories," In *Proceedings of 2nd international congress of sports psychology.* Gerald S. Kenyon (Ed.). Chicago: Athletic Institute, 1968.

39. Ryan, Dean, "Reaction to 'Sport and personality dynamics.' National College Physical Education Association for Men," *Annual Proceedings* **72**:70–75, 1969.

40. Sargeant, A. J., "Participation of West Indian boys in English school's sports teams," *Educational Research,* **14**:225–30, 1972.

41. Schafer, Walter E., "Participation in interscholastic athletics and delinquency," In *Schools and delinquency*. K. Polk and Walter E. Schafer (Eds.). Englewood Cliffs: Prentice Hall, 1972.

42. Schafer, Walter E., and Armer, M., "Athletes are not inferior students," *Transaction*, 6:61–62, 1968.

43. Schendel, Jack S., "Psychological differences between athletes and non-participants in athletics at three educational levels," *Research Quarterly*, 36:52–67, 1965.

44. Schendel, Jack S., "The psychological characteristics of high school athletes and non-participants in athletics," In *Proceedings of 2nd international congress of sport psychology*. Gerald S. Kenyon (Ed.). Chicago: Athletic Institute, 1968.

45. Sinclair, E. D., "Personality and rugby football," *Research Papers in Physical Education*, 3:23–28, 1968.

46. Singer, Robert N., "Reaction to 'Sport and personality dynamics.' National College Physical Education Association for Men," *Annual Proceedings*, 72:76–80, 1969.

47. Singer, Robert N., "Personality differences between and within baseball and tennis players," *Research Quarterly*, 40:582–88, 1969.

48. Slusher, Howard S., "Overt and covert reactions of selected athletes to normative situations as indicated by an electric psychrometer," *Research Quarterly*, 37:540–52, 1966.

49. Stern, Barry E., *"The relationship between participation in sports and the moral and political socialization of high school youth in Chile,"* Ph.D. dissertation Stanford University, 1972.

50. Ward, D. S., "A proposal to put intercollegiate athletics in their proper place," *Phi Delta Kappan*, 42:216–18, 1961.

51. Werner, A. C., and Gottheil, E., "Personality development and participation in college athletics," *Research Quarterly*, 37:126–31, 1966.

52. Williams, Jean M., *et al.*, "Personality traits of champion level female fencers," *Research Quarterly*, 40:446–53, 1970.

53. Wilson, P. K., "Relationship between motor achievement and selected personality factors of junior and senior high school boys," *Research Quarterly*, 40:841–44, 1969.

54. Wilson W., and Kayatani, M., "Intergroup attitudes and strategies in games between opponents of the same or a different race," *Journal of Personality and Social Psychology*, 9:24–30, 1968.

SOCIALIZATION OF COACHES: ANTECEDENTS TO COACHES' BELIEFS AND BEHAVIORS

George H. Sage

The behavior of American athletic coaches has come under an avalanche of criticism in recent years. By and large, the critics have focused their attacks on the personality traits and value orientations of coaches.[1,2,3] Coaches have been accused of being authoritarian, dogmatic, insensitive, extremely conservative in value orientation, and demanding obedience to arbitrary and inflexible rules.

The personal trait approach has found congenial reception among sports psychologists because of their interest in individual characteristics. One major problem with this approach is that the coaches are treated as though their background of social experiences was unimportant. There is a suggestion that in some mysterious way persons with certain personal-social characteristics are either attracted to coaching or that the occupation develops persons with a specific set of personal-social attitudes, values, and behaviors. Exactly which of the two processes is operative is never specified. In this regard, Edwards[4] notes, "Information available in the literature is inconclusive as to whether the demands of the coaching role operate selectively to weed out non-authoritarian type personalities, or whether experiences while training to become a coach or while fulfilling the coaching role condition people to react in an inflexible manner." What is overlooked in this view of coaches' beliefs and behaviors is the actual realities of the social milieu which has been part of their lives since birth—their social class background, social activities in youth, and the occupation itself in which they work.

The position of this paper is that coaches' personal-social characteristics are a product of the lifelong socialization which they have undergone. Socialization is the process by which an individual learns attitudes, values, behaviors, and expectations of others which enables him to effectively assume particular roles in society. The foundation for cultural beliefs, behaviors, and expectations is laid in childhood and adolescence, but socialization is a continuous process throughout the life cycle, since the individual is constantly taking on new roles. In the course of the various social experiences, the socializee develops a set of personal-social characteristics which tend to conform to those who have been significant others in his life, and his beliefs and behaviors tend to conform to the expectations of the socializers.

George H. Sage, "Socialization of Coaches: Antecedents to Coaches' Beliefs and Behaviors," *Proceedings of the National College Physical Association for Men*, 1975, pp. 124–132. Reprinted by permission.

Socialization is managed in a variety of formal and informal ways.Formal socialization takes place primarily through the family, school, and the church during childhood and adolescence, and the occupation in adulthood. Informal socialization agents and agencies are more diverse, but relatives, peers, and role models constitute significant others, which induce normative compliance, and typically, an actual sharing of beliefs and behaviors.

The present task is to examine, from a sociological perspective, the antecedent to coaches' personal-social characteristics. This is a contrast to the usual "psychological" explanation of coaches' behavior. The underlying theoretical orientation for this perspective is that the social milieu in which an individual has lived is highly associated with his present beliefs and behavior. Three aspects of socialization will be examined: family background, social experiences in youth, and occupation. It will be suggested that the socialization experiences in these settings lead to predictions about beliefs, behaviors, and value orientations of coaches. Empirical studies will then be reviewed to ascertain the relationships between the predictions which are generated and the research findings.

CHILD REARING PRACTICES AND CONSEQUENCES

The primary role that parents play in the socialization of their children is emphasized in all socialization theories. There is a wealth of research in the psychology and sociology literature which suggests that parental attitudes, values, and behavioral patterns are likely to be transmitted from one generation to another via their offspring through the socialization processes of family living. As Barber says, "Society tends to reproduce itself by the . . . expression of its norms and aspirations through the actions of the parents who socialize the young and thus make new adult members of society."[5]

If we assume that many of the foundations of adult personality, beliefs, and values are laid in the experiences of childhood and adolescence, greater understanding of the differences in attitudes, values and behaviors of adults from different classes might come from knowing something about the differences and similarities in their youth. Children grow up in different social and economic circumstances and in families of varying role structure, and it is clear that the socialization of children in American society is markedly influenced by their parents' position in the social class structure.[6]

It has been repeatedly found that parents from the various social classes differ in their child-rearing practices.[7,8,9] Bronfenbrenner reports that "in matters of discipline, working-class parents are consistently more likely to employ physical punishment, while middle-class families rely on reasoning, isolation, and appeals to guilt" in raising children.[10] Maccoby and Gibbs found that upper-lower class parents employ physical punishment, deprivation of privileges, and ridicule as techniques of controlling their children more commonly than do upper-middle class parents.[11] Elder notes that physical discipline, such as spanking and slapping, are used more frequently by lower-class parents.[12] Finally, McKinley reported that lower-class parents are more rigid in their relationships with children, resulting in higher frequency of punishment.[13]

In conceptualizing the child rearing practices of lower-class parents, the word "authoritarian" is frequently employed.[14] Indeed, several researchers have indicated that lower-class parents have a strong authoritarian orientation. Lipset claims, "Many studies . . . show a consistent association between authoritarianism and lower class status."[15] McKinnon and Centers note, "The working class contains a higher percentage of authoritarians than either the middle class or the upper class."[16] The authoritarian is characteristically punitive and condescending toward inferiors, less sensitive to interpersonal relationships, submissive toward authority, admiring of power and toughness, rigidly conventional, and possesses a general insensitivity to the needs of and motivations of others.[17]

The choice of any particular ideological system and social behavioral orientation emerges out of extremely complex and multiple causes, but parents and their offspring typically obtain positively correlated scores on most measures of individual differences. Again and again, research findings show that social-economic status is highly associated with certain personal dispositions of adults, and that these personal-social characteristics are transmitted to their offspring through the child rearing practices. Both evidence and theory suggest that given the tendency of lower-class parents to treat their children in more authoritarian ways, persons from lower-class backgrounds will exhibit and endorse authoritarian perspectives.

Let us examine briefly the social class background of athletic coaches. Several studies over the past fifty years have shown that public school teachers tend to come from rural and working class families.[18] It is likely that public school coaches are drawn from the same social class pool. Loy and Sage reported that a majority of collegiate football and basketball coaches were from working class families.[19] They say, ". . . the majority of fathers worked at manual jobs."

Given the tendency of lower class parents to treat their children in authoritarian ways, and given the fact that parents and offspring typically obtain positively correlated scores on most measures of individual differences, and given the fact that coaches tend to come from working class social origins, our first prediction is that, as a group, coaches will exhibit and endorse authoritarian perspectives in their personal attitudes and behaviors.

PARENTAL VALUES AND CONSEQUENCES

Few studies have focused directly upon the relationship of social class to parental values, but those which have been concerned with this topic are generally in agreement.[20,21,22,23,24] These studies suggest that working class parents value obedience, neatness, cleanliness, and conformity to external proscriptions to a larger extent than middle-class parents, who value self-control and self-direction more highly. Pearlin and Kohn note, "Middle-class parents value self-direction more highly than do working class parents; working class parents emphasize, instead, conformity to external proscription. Self-control is the pivotal parental value for the middle-class, obedience for the working class."[25]

In addition to parental values emphasizing obedience and respectability among lower-classes, parents in this social stratum display values supporting authoritarian conservatism. Several studies show that authoritarian conservatism is related to social class.[26,27] Kohn and Schooler report, "Class position is linearly related to . . . social orientation. The strongest correlation by a wide margin, is with authoritarian conservatism: the lower the men's social class position, the more rigidly conservative their view of man and his social institutions and the less their tolerance of non-conformity . . . The lower the men's social class positions, the more likely they are to feel that morality is synonymous with obeying the letter of the law; the less trustful of their fellow man they are; and the more resistent they are to innovation and change."[28]

Socialization theories consistently suggest that parental values are transmitted to their offspring and are then internalized to be re-transmitted to their own offspring and others with whom they interact. Given the value orientations which are prominent among working class parents, and assuming that they transmit these values to their offspring, it follows that persons who grew up in the working-class family will themselves tend to possess values stressing political and social conservatism and will show strong support for obedience to authority. Thus, our second prediction is that athletic coaches, as a group, will display and endorse an authoritarian conservative value orientation.

SPORTS PARTICIPATION AND CONSEQUENCES

An enormous amount of social experiences of youth takes place outside the family, and for youth who participate in organized athletics the social environment has the potential to serve as a powerful source of socialization. Snyder[29] has suggested that the greatest likelihood of the inculcation of diffuse attitudes and values occurs when there is a high degree of involvement in an activity, when the activity is done voluntarily, when there is an expressive relationship among participants, and when the socializing agent is prestigeful, powerful, and when his ability to dispense affective rewards and punishment is great. It is obvious that all of these factors are present in the athletic setting and therefore athletic experiences undoubtedly serve as an important source of socialization of attitudes and values for participants.

What are the core attitudes and values of athletics? Assuming some variation from team to team due to the variation in participants and coaches, there is nevertheless what Harry Edwards[30] calls a "sports creed." In essence the sports creed emphasizes competitiveness, obedience to authority, patriotism, loyalty to the group, altruism, self-discipline, and religiosity. Typically, these precepts are forcefully transmitted to the athletes by their coaches and teammates in a variety of ways. In an elegantly conceived study, Snyder showed quite nicely how locker room slogans are used as a means of socializing athletes to the attitudes and values of the sports creed.[31]

To the extent that one has participated in organized sports and to the extent that one has been exposed to the "sports creed," there is a good chance that one will evidence attitudes and values endorsing and supporting the creed. Most current coaches were active participants in interschool and/or age-group sports programs in their youth.[32,33,34,35,36] Thus, they had ample exposure to the "sports creed." Therefore, our third prediction is that coaches, as a group, will evidence strong support for the precepts of the "sports creed," especially such values as obedience to authority and conformity to externally imposed proscriptions, which are core values in the creed.

OCCUPATIONAL SOCIALIZATION AND CONSEQUENCES

Most research into the process of socialization has been concerned with infancy, childhood, and adolescence, but there is a considerable amount of socialization involved in learning and performing occupational roles.[37] According to Moore[38] occupational "socialization involves acquiring the requisite knowledge and skills and also the sense of occupational identity and internalization of occupational norms typical of the fully qualified practitioner."[38] It is clear that for an individual to function in an occupation he must learn a variety of behaviors, attitudes, and values. Numerous studies have demonstrated that occupational affiliation or position in a work organization profoundly affects one's views on various matters as well as one's actual behavior.

An occupational ideology emerges and is sustained through both formal and informal channels of communication and the person who learns the norms, values, and behaviors will emerge not only with an internalized occupational commitment, but also with an identification with the collectivity, the brotherhood. Thus, the main consequence of the various occupational socializing agents and agencies is that there is a relative homogeneity in the employee group—all persons having behaviors and beliefs which are compatible with the demands of the occupation. As Burlingame said, ". . . the intent of socialization is to obviate personalistic, idiosyncratic differences in Freshmen (persons new to the occupation) and replace them with the universalistic, norm-governed behaviors of seniors."[39] Goode also noted, "Characteristic of each of the established professions, and a goal of each aspiring occupation, is the community of profession. Each profession is a community without locus [but it] . . . may nevertheless be called a community by virtue of these characteristics . . . Its members share values in common."[40]

The "sports creed" described above provides a basic underlying philosophy in the coaching profession. Coaching manuals, clinic speakers, and nationally prominent coaches consistently propogate this creed. Its precepts are advanced so regularly and so persuasively and it is so universally endorsed in American sports that it would be almost impossible for a coach not to subscribe to its dictates and accept them as his own.

On the basis of socialization theory and research about an occupational homogeneity of beliefs and behaviors, our fourth prediction is that athletic coaches are indoctrinated to the "sports creed" through various agents and agencies within and external to the coaching occupation, our fifth prediction is that they will endorse the creed and strongly subscribe to values of obedience to authority and conformity to external proscriptions.

EMPIRICAL EVIDENCE FOR PREDICTIONS

To what extent are the predictions which have been generated through a review of the socialization literature sustained by empirical findings? The first thing that becomes quite evident when seeking an answer to this question is that research on the personal-social characteristics of coaches is quite scarce. The presently available data cannot give definitive verification for the predictions, but there are sufficient studies to suggest that they tend to be fairly accurate.

With respect to the prediction that coaches endorse authoritarian perspectives and support high authority structure the findings are incomplete but do suggest support for the proposition. Locke[41] found that a physical education group scored significantly higher on an instrument which measured authoritarian attitudes than did a teacher group who were not physical educators. Although not all physical educators are athletic coaches, a very high percentage of them are. Kenyon[42] assessed several psychosocial and cultural characteristics of aspiring physical educators and reported that physical education majors were more dogmatic and rigid than other prospective teachers. Again, physical education and coaching are not synonymous, but most aspiring coaches major in physical education and most coaches majored in physical education.[43,44] Ogilvie and Tutko described the personality of 64 coaches representing basketball, track, football, and baseball as being quite different in two traits, "The first was the very low tendency to be interested in the dependency needs of others . . . in other words, to give a great deal of emotional support to others . . . The second characteristic . . . was . . . inflexibility or rigidity in terms of utilization of new learning."[45] In a second study of high school coaches, Ogilvie and Tutko[46] suggest that support was found for their previous generalizations; that is that coaches are high in those traits that promote "getting ahead" and succeeding and which do not require personal involvement, but they score low on those personality traits which contribute most to being sensitive and support close interpersonal relationships. Albaugh[47] assessed resentment of college basketball coaches. One high in resentment, demands obedience, denies individual rights, demands that inflexible rules be kept, and commands docile, conforming and spiritless individuals as subjects. He reported that coaches' mean score was approximately one standard deviation higher than teachers.

Scott, one of the most outspoken critics of athletic coaches, has suggested that the value orientations of coaches are so conservative as to be aberrant.[48,49] Ogilvie, another frequent critic of athletic coaches, also believes that coaches are conservative in value orientation. He said: "Traditionally you are going to find in the coaching profession men who are socially and politically conservative."[50] Even some coaches view their colleagues as possessing extremely conservative values. Dr. David Nelson,[51] athletic director at the University of Delaware and formerly the head football coach there, said: "Having been a coach . . . I know that most of us are almost Harding Republicans and three degrees to the right of Ghengis Khan." Unfortunately, there is little research to support these impressionistic observations about coaches but what does exist tends to support these notions.

Sage[52] assessed the value orientations of collegiate football, basketball, and track coaches and found that the three groups hold similar value orientations. Indeed, on twenty items of various dimensions of value difference there were no significant differences on any of these items. In other words, collegiate athletic coaches from several sports hold similar value orientations for a variety of familiar dimensions of value difference, and there was no difference between the values of younger coaches (age 40 and under) and older coaches (over age 40).

With respect to the charge that coaches are conservative, only two studies relate to this question. In a 1969 survey by the Carnegie Commission on Higher Education on the political opinions of over 60,000 full-time college faculty members, physical education faculty (N=1,208) ranked second out of thirty fields in percentage of respondents who characterize themselves as strongly conservative, and also second in percentage of those who characterize themselves as moderately conservative. In apparently the only study specifically concerned with the comprehensive value orientations of coaches, Sage summarized his findings for collegiate coaches in this way: "The total response profile of the coaches showed them to possess moderate-conservative values. . . . Although conservatism is not extreme among coaches, it is more pronounced than it is among college students."[53]

Sage also reported that coaches manifest greater support for "authority structure." That is, they place high value on obedience to authority and standards of good conduct which have been established by religious or societal norms. He says: "This high value for authority structure expressed by coaches will be evident in expectancies that their position culturally accords them the right to direct the actions of their athletes and that the athletes under their jurisdiction agree to accept as the premises of their behavior orders and instructions given to them by the coach."[54]

On the whole, of course, the evidence presented here does not constitute a definitive verification for the predictions nor does it permit a comprehensive assessment of all of the alternative explanations for accounting for the relationship between socialization experiences and various kinds of coaches' attitudes, values, and behaviors. It is hoped, however, that this effort will help make the issue of what accounts for the relationship more salient than previously published literature on this topic.

NOTES

1. J. Scott, *The Athletic Revolution* (New York: The Free Press, 1971).

2. B. Ogilvie and T. Tutko, "Self-Perception As Compared With Measured Personality of Selected Male Physical Educators," in G. S. Kenyon (ed.) *Contemporary Psychology of Sports* (Chicago: The Athletic Institute, 1970) pp. 73–77.

3. B. Ogilvie, Quoted from J. Jares, "We Have a Neurotic in the Backfield Doctor," *Sports Illustrated,* **34** (January 18, 1971) pp. 30–34.

4. H. Edwards, *Sociology of Sport* (Homewood, Ill.: The Dorsey Press, 1973) p. 141.

5. B. Barber, *Social Stratification* (New York: Harcourt, Brace, and World, 1957) p. 265.

6. B. C. Rosen, "Social Class and the Child's Perception of the Parent" *Child Development,* **34** (December, 1964) pp. 1147–1153.

7. E. E. Maccoby, "The Development of Moral Values and Behavior in Childhood," in J. A. Clausen (ed.) *Socialization and Society* (Boston: Little, Brown Co. 1968) pp. 227–269.

8. R. R. Sears, E. E. Maccoby, and H. Levin, *Patterns of Child Rearing* (Evanston, Ill.: Row, Peterson Co. 1957).

9. M. L. Kohn, "Social Class and the Exercise of Parental Authority," *American Sociological Review,* **24** (June, 1966) pp. 352–366.

10. U. Bronfenbrenner, "Socialization and Social Class Through Time and Space," in E. E. Maccoby, T. M. Newcomb, and E. L. Hartley, *Readings in Social Psychology* (New York: Holt, Rinehart, and Winston, 1958) p. 424.

11. E. E. Maccoby and P. K. Gibbs, "Methods of Child-Rearing in Two Social Classes," in W. E. Martin and C. B. Stendler (eds.), *Readings in Child Development* (New York: Harcourt, Brace, and Co., 1954) pp. 380–396.

12. G. H. Elder, "Family Structure and the Transmission of Values and Norms in the Process of Child Rearing," (Unpublished Doctoral Thesis, University of North Carolina, 1961).

13. D. C. McKinley, *Social Class and Family Life* (Glencoe, Ill.: The Free Press, 1961).

14. G. H. Elder, "Structural Variations in the Child Rearing Relationship," *Sociometry*, **25** (September, 1962) pp. 241–262.

15. S. M. Lipset, *Political Man* (Garden City, New York: Doubleday, 1960) p. 105.

16. W. J. McKinnon and R. Centers, "Authoritarianism and Urban Stratification," *American Journal of Sociology*, **61** (May, 1956) p. 616.

17. D. J. Bordua, "Authoritarianism and Intolerance of Nonconformists," *Sociometry*, **24** (June, 1961) p. 199.

18. R. M. Pavalko (ed.), *Sociology of Education* (Itasca, Ind.: F. E. Peacock Publishers, 1968).

19. J. W. Loy and G. H. Sage, "Social Origins, Academic Achievement, Athletic Achievement, and Career Mobility Patterns of College Coaches," Paper presented at the 67th annual meeting of the American Sociological Association, New Orleans, Louisiana, 1972, p. 5.

20. E. M. Duvall, "Conceptions of Parenthood," *American Journal of Sociology*, **52** (November, 1946) pp. 193–203.

21. Bronfenbrenner, *op. cit.* 1958.

22. M. L. Kohn, "Social Class and Parental Values," *American Journal of Sociology*, **64** (January, 1959) pp. 337–351.

23. L. I. Pearlin and M. L. Kohn, "Social Class, Occupations, and Parental Values: A Cross National Study," *American Sociological Review*, **31** (August, 1966) pp. 466–479.

24. M. L. Kohn and C. Schooler, "Class, Occupation, and Orientation," *American Sociological Review*, **34** (October, 1969) pp. 659–678.

25. Pearlin and Kohn, *op. cit.* 1966.

26. Kohn and Schooler, *op. cit.* 1969.

27. A. B. Shostak, *Blue Collar Life* (New York: Random House, 1969).

28. Kohn and Schooler, *op. cit.*, 1969, p. 668.

29. E. Snyder, "Aspects of Socialization in Sports and Physical Education," *Quest*, Monograph XIV, (June, 1970) pp. 1–7.

30. Edwards, *op. cit.*, 1973.

31. E. Snyder, "Locker Room Slogans As Folklore: A Means of Socialization," *International Review of Sport Sociology*, Vol. 7 (Warsaw: Polish Scientific Publishers, 1972).

32. R. C. Havel, "The Professional Status of Head Coaches of Athletics in Colleges and Universities (unpublished Doctoral dissertation, Teachers College, Columbia University, 1951).

33. W. A. Healy, "Administrative Practices in Competitive Athletics in Midwestern Colleges," *Research Quarterly*, **24** (October, 1953) pp. 295–303.

34. O. R. Arms, "The Professional Status of the High School Coach in Arkansas," (unpublished Master's thesis, University of Arkansas, 1965).

35. G. W. Wilcox, "An Analysis of the Professional Preparation of College Head Football Coaches in the Northeast (unpublished Master's thesis, Springfield College, 1969).

36. Loy and Sage, *op. cit.*, 1972.

37. O. G. Brim, Jr. and S. Wheeler, *Socialization After Childhood*, (New York: John Wiley, 1966).
38. W. E. Moore, *The Professions: Roles and Rules*, (Chicago: Rand McNally Co., 1970) p. 71.
39. M. Burlingame, "Socialization Constructs and the Teaching of Teachers," *Quest*, Monograph XVIII (June, 1972) p. 44.
40. W. L. Goode, "Community Within a Community: The Professions," *American Sociological Review*, **22** (April, 1957) p. 196.
41. L. Locke, "Performance of Administration Oriented Educators on Selected Psychological Tests," *Research Quarterly*, **33** (October, 1962) pp. 418–429.
42. G. S. Kenyon, "Certain Psychosocial and Cultural Characteristics Unique to Prospective Teachers of Physical Education," *Research Quarterly*, **36** (March, 1965) pp. 105–112.
43. J. C. Pooley, "The Professional Socialization of Physical Education Students in the United States and England," (unpublished Doctoral dissertation, University of Wisconsin, 1970).
44. Loy and Sage, *op. cit.*, 1972.
45. B. C. Ogilvie and T. Tutko, *Problem Athletes and How to Handle Them* (London: Pelham Books, 1966) pp. 23–24.
46. Ogilvie and Tutko, *op. cit.*, 1970.
47. G. R. Albaugh, "The Influence of Ressentience as Identified in College Basketball Coaches," *75th Proceedings of the National College Physical Education Association for Men*, 1972.
48. J. Scott, *Athletics for Athletes* (Hayword, California: Quality Printing Co., 1969).
49. J. Scott, *op. cit.*, 1971.
50. Ogilvie, *op. cit.*, 1971, p. 33.
51. D. Nelson, Quoted in *The Oregonian* (December 28, 1970) Sports Section, p. 1.
52. G. H. Sage, "Occupational Socialization and Value Orientation of Athletic Coaches," *Research Quarterly*, **44** (October, 1973) pp. 269–277.
53. G. H. Sage, "Value Orientations of American College Coaches Compared to Male College Students and Businessmen," *75th Proceedings of the National College Physical Education Association for Men*, 1972, p. 183.
54. *Ibid.*, p. 184.

FOR FURTHER READING

1. Casher, B. B., "Relationship Between Birth Order and Participation in Dangerous Sports," *Research Quarterly* 48: 33–40, 1977.
2. Greendorfer, S. L., "Role of Socializing Agents in Female Sport Involvement," *Research Quarterly*, 48: 304–310, 1977.
3. Loy, J. W., Birrell, S., and Rose, D., "Attitudes Held Toward Agonetic Activities as a Function of Selected Social Identities," *Quest*, **26** (Summer): 81–95, 1976.

4. Sage, G. H., "Machiavellianism Among College and High School Coaches," *75th Proceeding of the National College Physical Education Association for Men,* 1972, pp. 45-60.

5. Sage, G. H., "Occupational Socialization and Value Orientation of Athletic Coaches," *Research Quarterly,* **44**: 269-277, 1973.

6. Sage, G. H., "American Values and Sport: Formation of a Bureaucratic Personality," *Journal of Physical Education and Recreation,* **49** (October): 42-44, 1978.

7. Snyder, E. E., "Athletic Dressing Room Slogans as Folklore: A Means of Socialization," *International Review of Sport Sociology,* **7**: 89-102, 1972.

8. Mantel, R. C. and Vander Velden, L., "The Relationship Between the Professionalization of Attitudes Toward Play of Preadolescent Boys and Participation in Organized Sport," in *Sport and American Society* (2nd edition) ed. George H. Sage, Reading, Mass.: Addison-Wesley, 1974, pp. 172-178.

9. Yiannakis, A., "Birth Order and Preference for Dangerous Sport Among Males," *Research Quarterly,* **47**: 62-67, 1976.

CHAPTER 4

SPORT AND AMERICAN EDUCATION

The elaborate organization of interscholastic and intercollegiate sports is a uniquely American phenomenon. In most countries of the world there is very little sport in the schools. School sports, or athletics as they are often called, provide countless Americans with excitement and entertainment, and any serious proposal to curtail them is immediately met with a barrage of rebuttals. School teams are the mobilizing force of morale and *esprit de corps* for school, community, and alumni, in the case of college sports, and the athletes are the folk heroes of the subculture of the educational world.

The emphasis on school sports originally developed in the last half of the nineteenth century and began at colleges that were attended mostly by students living away from home. Games and sports were a diversion from the boredom of classroom work. The students played a variety of sports, first as unorganized and impromptu games and later as organized intramural and interclass activities. As the number of colleges and their geographic proximity increased, the next logical step was for the students of one college to challenge the students of a nearby school to a sports contest. The first officially recorded intercollegiate sports contest was a rowing race between Harvard and Yale in 1852. At the beginning, school sports were organized by the students, usually over faculty objection. In time, with increased organization and the proliferation of sports teams, faculties assumed administrative control over sports. Today this control is manifested in national organizations—such as the National Collegiate Athletic Association and the Association for Intercollegiate Athletics for Women—which derive their authority from the colleges and universities.

American high schools mimicked the colleges in the development of sports. Following basically the same pattern as the colleges, high schools initiated interschool sports programs, and by 1900 several states had established high school athletic associations. In 1922 the National Federation of State High School Athletic Associations was founded, indicating the nation-wide scope of high school sports.

American school sports have been praised as the most important factor in the evolution of national character by some and assailed as the "poison ivy" of the schools by others. Supporters of school sports have cited their potential as a developer of better health, socialization, and the learning of moral lessons. Sports critics, on the other hand, have claimed that sports contribute nothing whatsoever to education and that they simply divert the attention and energy of the students and community from the main purpose of education and use up valuable time. For these critics, school sports have become the "tail that wags the educational dog."

The first reading by D. Stanley Eitzen is a replication of James S. Coleman's findings about the status of athletics in American high schools which Coleman reported in his book *The Adolescent Society*. In that book, Coleman asserted that his investigations showed that success in high school sports is valued more highly among high school students than academic achievement. His support for this claim came from responses that students made in comparing the popularity and status of athletes with that of scholars.

Coleman's study was done in the late 1950's and Eitzen wondered whether the popularity and status of athletes and scholars was different in the 1970's, so he collected data similar to Coleman's. The data from students in the high schools studied by Eitzen provides strong support that sports partici-pation is a dominant criterion for popularity and status among high school boys in the 1970's, just as it had been in the 1950's. Eitzen's study also shows that certain variables, such as parents' educational attainment, size of high school, authority structure of the high school, and participation in other school activities, affect the students' perceptions about the importance of sport.

In the second reading, John Phillips and Walter Schafer review the pertinent findings of studies which show that high school athletes tend to exceed nonathletes in their educational expectations and in their achievement of educational goals. First, they review the literature on the relationship between athletic participation and high school academic achievement. They indicate that the research evidence tends to suggest that athletes achieve better grades than non-athletes, notwithstanding the belief of many that athletes are poor students. Second, they review the literature on college expectations and report that the evidence on this topic indicates that athletes aspire to and succeed in attending college more than do non-athletes. Third, they examine the relationship between athletics and delinquency and suggest that athletic participation may be a deterrent to delinquent behavior. Next, they suggest that high school athletics may serve as a means for upward social mobility, especially for athletes from blue-collar backgrounds. Finally, the authors employ the concept of subculture to explain the processes intervening between athletics and various behavioral outcomes.

In the third reading, Snyder conceptualizes the coach as a "significant other" for high school athletes. He examines the role of the coach in advising and counseling players about their educational and occupational aspirations. Snyder reports that high school coaches are indeed influential in helping athletes to form their educational and occupational goals. Coaches are more influential with athletes from lower social class backgrounds than with athletes from upper social class backgrounds.

In the next reading George H. Sage examines intercollegiate athletics. After first acknowledging that there are three general forms of collegiate athletics, each of which has unique characteristics, Sage's essay focuses on "Big Time" intercollegiate sports. First he asks: What do the "Big Time" programs contribute to the goals of the university? His answer is that they contribute very little, and may even be counterproductive to meeting the university's mission. Next Sage examines the validity of the claim that intercollegiate athletics serve a social integrative function. Sage argues that this contention is largely a hoax that is employed by those who wish to promote commercial athletic programs on university campuses. The entertainment function of intercollegiate athletics is examined in the last part of the paper. Sage explains first that there are actually very few athletic events that attract spectators, and second that universities should not be expected to furnish public entertainment, since this is not the function of educational institutions.

It is frequently contended that it is essential for a major university to have a commercial, "Big Time," athletic program. In the final reading John Underwood convincingly shows that such an idea is a myth. Underwood describes the intercollegiate athletic program at Massachusetts Institute of Technology, one of the most esteemed universities in the United States. MIT fields athletic teams in a record 22 sports without granting a single athletic scholarship or charging admission to its sports events.

MIT retains the purpose for which intercollegiate athletics was originally founded—to provide exercise and recreation for the participants. At MIT every student may try out for a team, and if there is enough student interest in forming a team in a sport in which MIT is not presently competing, the athletic department provides funds to have a team.

Maybe not every college and university could have an athletic program like MIT's but many could, and from Underwood's description of the fun and joy that are the outcomes of the MIT program, it would seem to provide a sensible alternative to the commercial athletic programs that are currently popular in most major universities.

ATHLETICS IN THE STATUS SYSTEM OF MALE ADOLESCENTS: A REPLICATION OF COLEMAN'S THE ADOLESCENT SOCIETY *

D. Stanley Eitzen

James Coleman, after studying the adolescent status systems in ten Illinois high schools in 1957 and 1958, concluded that athletic prowess was the single most important criterion for high status.[1] But is this still the case? Significant changes have occurred in American society in the intervening years such as the rise of the counterculture, increased drug usage by youth, heightened racial unrest in schools, and the ever greater tendency to question persons in authority roles (teachers, principals, coaches, ministers, parents, police, and government leaders). Quite possibly, these and other factors have led to the athlete being replaced as the "big man on campus" by student activists, rock musicians, scholars, or some other social category.

The evidence is unclear. Occasional articles appear in the popular press which suggest that boys still want desperately to be athletes because that remains the most highly rewarded activity in their school and community. This has been recently documented, for example, for Benton, Illinois,[5] Yates Center, Kansas,[3] Stockbridge, Michigan,[7] and Tracy, California.[2] At the same time, however, there is evidence that increasing numbers of high school youngsters are becoming disenchanted with sports. This was the conclusion of Frank Jones who made a survey for the Athletic Institute, an organization supported by the sporting goods industry.[4,6] The affluent youngster in the suburbs is also losing interest in sports, according to Talamini. Apathy or antagonism toward athletic programs by the affluent is the result of the regimentation demanded in sports and the denial of creativity and self-expression.[8] While this increased questioning of sports appears to be an urban and suburban phenomenon, high school sports continue to flourish and go relatively unquestioned in rural America, where they are the "only show in town"[2,3,4,5,6,7]

D. Stanley Eitzen, "Athletics in the Status System of Male Adolescents: A Replication of Coleman's *The Adolescent Society*," *Adolescence,* Vol. 10 (Summer 1975), pp. 267–276. Reprinted by permission of Libra Publishers, Inc.

*This is a revised version of a paper presented to the session on Sport and Leisure at the annual meetings of the Midwest Sociological Society, Milwaukee, Wisconsin, April 26–27, 1973. Funds for this study were provided by the General Research Fund of the University of Kansas. The author would like to give special thanks to James Crone and Calvin Broughton for their assistance in the coding and analysis of the data.

This paper will present data that replicates and extends the landmark study by Coleman. Two questions guide this study: (a) Does sports participation remain as the primary determinant of adolescent male status? and (b) Under what conditions is sports participation the most important criterion for status among high school males? In the latter case, we will investigate if there are differences by community, school, and individual characteristics.

Methods

As was the case in Coleman's study, schools were selected for inclusion in the sample not because they were "representative" but because they differed on certain dimensions. The community characteristics considered important because of their potential for affecting the role of athletics in adolescent status systems were: community size, affluence of community, occupational structure, and rural/urban. These data were obtained from the 1970 census data. Relevant school characteristics were size, degree of success in major sports, authority structure, public or private, and proportion of graduates enrolling in college. These data were obtained from a questionnaire completed by school principals. The schools, with the pertinent community and school information, are listed in Table 1.

Questionnaires, including many items from Coleman's original, were completed by a sample of students in each of the nine schools. The questionnaires were distributed to a random sample of sophomores, juniors, and seniors in each school. The number in each class was intended to be 50 to 70 taken from required courses (omitting accelerated and slow classes). Although males and females were included, the study reported here is limited to males.

THE FINDINGS

The first consideration was to determine whether boys are any less interested in sports now than they were when Coleman conducted his study 16 years ago. Four items from Coleman's study were selected to tap the importance of sport now and compare this with the past. The first is probably the most often quoted: "If you could be remembered here at school for one of the three things below, which would you want it to be?" The comparison between Coleman's findings and those for the present study shows: "Athletic star"—Coleman (44 percent), Eitzen (47 percent); "brilliant student"—Coleman (31 percent), Eitzen (23 percent); and "most popular"—Coleman (25 percent), Eitzen (30 percent).

The second item used to determine the degree to which athletes are respected among adolescent boys was "Would you rather be friends with and be like . . ." Coleman's analysis did not include the overall percentages for each of his categories, but it is clear from his discussion that the most popular category was "athlete but not scholar."[1] The results from the present study were: athlete but not scholar (56.1 percent), scholar but not athlete (19.9

Table 1 Characteristics of the Schools and Communities in the Sample

School	State	Community Size	Median Income	% of families with income $3,000	Coaches & Managers	Community Type	School size (3 classes)	Athletic Success	School Authority Structure	Public-Private	% College Bound
A	KS.	76,127	$14,172	1.9	33.8%	Suburb	2,160	Excellent	Middle	Public	65%
B	KS.	20,446	12,143	2.5	29.0	Suburb	290	Excellent	Tight	Catholic	50
C	KS.	10,851	9,363	5.0	24.4	Agriculture	690	Good	Middle	Public	54
D	ILL.	400 app.*	Low*	High*	Low*	Agriculture	92	Poor	Middle	Public	65
E	KS.	13,379	9,240	8.7	14.9	Agri./Ind.	780	Good	Tight	Public	78
F	KS.	11,036	7,717	12.2	22.0	Agri./Ind.	585	Excellent	Tight	Public	60
G	IND.	500 app.*	Low*	High*	Low*	Agriculture	132	Poor	Tight	Public	10
H	IND.	17,604	8,703	8.6	16.6	Business State Capital	1,365	Average	Middle	Public	32
I	KS.	132,135	9,585	8.0	25.0		1,914	Average	Loose	Public	50

*Census data were not available for communities of less than 2,500 persons.

percent), and ladies' man but neither scholar nor athlete (24.0 percent). We added the category "member of the counter-culture" since that may now be a meaningful criterion for status among some adolescents. With this included, the recalculated percentages were 46.3, 16.4, 19.8 and 17.5, respectively.

Clearly, the overall comparisons from the first two items show that adolescents today are just as enthusiastic about sports as they were in the late 1950s. But these first two items only indirectly get at the status system of male adolescents since they ask what the respondents would want to be. This is based on the assumption that teenage boys want to be whatever is highly rewarded by their peers. Thus, it is probably safe to assume that answers to these questions reflect the values of adolescents.

Two additional items from Coleman are more direct measures of the status system of adolescents because they ask the respondent to rank different activities on the basis of the importance of each in achieving status. The first involves the ranking of five possible criteria for status among boys. The second ranks criteria that "make a guy popular with girls around here." Table 2 presents what Coleman found compared to the present findings.

The comparisons in Table 2 show that the relative ranks of the criteria for status among boys and what boys believe it takes to be popular with girls have remained stable over time.

Table 2   The Comparison of Coleman's Findings with Those of the Present Study on the Ranking of Various Criteria for Status

A. Ranking of Criteria to be Popular with Boys

	Average Ranking	
Criteria for status	Coleman*	Eitzen
Be an athlete	2.2	2.06
Be in leading crowd	2.6	2.10
Leader in activities	2.9	2.82
High grades, honor roll	3.5	3.73
Come from right family	4.5	3.98

B. Ranking of Criteria to be Popular with Girls

	Average Ranking	
Criteria for status	Coleman*	Eitzen
Be an athlete	2.2	1.94
Be in leading crowd	2.5	2.12
Have a nice car	3.2	2.81
High grades, honor roll	4.0	3.87
Come from right family	4.2	3.89

*These ranks are approximations extrapolated from a bar graph supplied by Coleman[1]

The overall comparison of the data from Coleman with the present study provides clear support that athletics remain *very* important in the status system of teenage males. If anything, the present data indicate a slightly greater enthusiasm for sports than Coleman found. These data may, however, hide the possibility that some categories of adolescents are disenchanted and apathetic about athletics. Thus, the remainder of this paper will focus on the way boys vary in the importance they attach to athletics by individual, school, and community characteristics. In each case we will assess the differences these characteristics make on only one of Coleman's items—how the individual would like to be remembered.

Individual factors

It could be assumed that boys differ in their enthusiasm for sport by their particular situation. To determine if this is a valid assumption, we selected four individual characteristics for analysis—familial social class, age, college prep or not, and placement in the school status hierarchy.

Table 3 shows that all of the variables but track in school make a difference in the desire to be an athlete. In general, the variables taken one at a time suggest that sons of under-educated fathers, sophomores, and those in the center of the status hierarchy of the school are more inclined toward sports than their counterparts.

Table 3   Individual Factors Related to How One Wishes to be Remembered

| | How Remembered | | | | | | | |
| | Brilliant Student | | Athletic Star | | Most Popular | | Totals | |
Individual Factors	%	N	%	N	%	N	%	N
Father's education								
Non-high school grad	13.7	(28)	56.9	(116)	29.4	(60)	100.0	(204)
High school graduate	27.0	(74)	41.2	(113)	31.8	(87)	100.0	(274)
At least some college	23.7	(70)	47.5	(140)	28.8	(85)	100.0	(295)
Year at school								
Sophomores	21.2	(69)	55.5	(181)	23.2	(76)	100.0	(326)
Juniors	22.7	(64)	47.2	(133)	30.1	(85)	100.0	(282)
Seniors	25.4	(61)	36.3	(87)	38.3	(92)	100.0	(240)
Track in school								
College	31.8	(96)	47.0	(142)	21.2	(64)	100.0	(302)
Non-college	17.8	(93)	47.2	(247)	35.0	(183)	100.0	(523)
Degree of centrality*								
Center	22.8	(18)	50.6	(40)	26.6	(21)	100.0	(79)
Above average	14.3	(25)	59.4	(104)	26.3	(46)	100.0	(175)
Average	20.7	(58)	51.4	(144)	27.9	(78)	100.0	(280)
Below average	29.2	(45)	37.7	(58)	33.1	(51)	100.0	(154)
Fringe	28.3	(47)	34.9	(58)	36.7	(61)	99.9	(166)

*Centrality refers to the perception of the individual to how close he is to the center of activities at his school. To get at this each respondent circled the appropriate circle from among four concentric circles on the questionnaire. The question (taken exactly from Coleman) reads: "Suppose the circle below represented the activities that go on here at school. How far out from the center are you?"

School-related factors

The nine schools were divided into large (1,300 to 2,200 students), medium (500–800) and small (less than 300). Since the proportion of boys participating in interscholastic sports is higher in small schools, one could assume a greater enthusiasm for sports by males there. The data in Table 4 show the highest enthusiasm for sports is in the smaller schools while the interest for sport in the largest schools is decidedly less.

An obvious consideration, but one omitted by Coleman, is the potential impact of a winning or losing tradition in the school on importance of sports. The principal in each school was asked to rate his school over the past five years in football, basketball, and minor sports. An overall composite score was used combining the two major sports to label a school as being successful in sports or not. As expected, students from winning schools had more favorable attitudes toward athletics than students from schools with average or poor athletic success.

The principal of each school in the sample was also asked to rate the formation and administration of rules at his school on a scale from 1 (tight) to 5 (permissive). This was included on the possibility that a rigid authoritarian structure in a school might be an indicator of a non-questioning tradition in which athletics might flourish. Whether this assumption is correct or not remains to be seen, but the data in Table 5 show clearly that students in schools with a "tight" authority structure are much more inclined toward athletics than students in the more permissive schools. Another possibility may be that "tight" schools are more likely to have excoaches as administra-

Table 4   School Related Factors and How One Wishes to be Remembered

School Factors	Brilliant Student		Athletic Star		Most Popular		Totals	
School Size	%	N	%	N	%	N	%	N
Large (2,160–1,365) AHI*	28.8	(78)	35.8	(97)	35.4	(96)	100.0	(271)
Medium (800–500) CEF	22.3	(77)	49.3	(170)	28.4	(98)	100.0	(345)
Small (300) BDG	18.3	(46)	54.8	(138)	27.0	(68)	100.1	(252)
Success in sports								
Good Schools ABCEF	21.3	(125)	47.8	(280)	30.9	(181)	100.0	(586)
Average or Poor DGHI	27.0	(76)	44.3	(125)	28.7	(81)	100.0	(282)
Authority Structure								
Tight Schools BEFG	19.3	(93)	50.8	(245)	29.9	(144)	100.0	(482)
Permissive ACDHI	28.0	(108)	41.5	(160)	30.6	(118)	100.1	(386)

*These initials refer to the schools as labelled in Table 1.

Table 5   Community Related Factors and How One Wishes to be Remembered

Community Factors	How Remembered								
	Brilliant Student		Athletic Star		Most Popular		Totals		
	%	N	%	N	%	N	%	N	
Community Size									
Large (above 15,000) ABHI	24.0	(99)	41.4	(171)	34.6	(143)	100.0	(413)	
Small (below 15,000) CDEFG	22.4	(102)	51.4	(234)	26.2	(119)	100.0	(455)	
Percentage of professionals									
High (22% or above) ABCFI	23.5	(112)	44.7	(213)	31.9	(152)	100.1	(477)	
Low (Less than 22%) DEGH	22.8	(89)	49.1	(192)	28.1	(110)	100.0	(391)	
Percentage of families with incomes less than $3,000									
Low (< 5%) ABC	23.4	(68)	44.1	(128)	32.4	(94)	99.9	(290)	
Medium (8–9%) EHI	24.2	(86)	42.3	(150)	33.5	(119)	100.0	(355)	
High (10% or more) DFG	23.3	(47)	52.5	(106)	24.2	(49)	100.0	(202)	
Percentage of wage earners in manufacturing									
High (>18.2%) ABCFH	23.8	(119)	45.7	(228)	30.5	(152)	100.0	(499)	
Low (< 13.6%) DEGI	22.2	(82)	48.0	(177)	29.8	(110)	100.0	(369)	

tors. It is well-known that successful coaches often become secondary school administrators. Presumably this is because they have not only been successful but perhaps more important to the school board is that they have demonstrated that they are strict. Ex-coaches turned administrators may, and this is speculation, not only be more likely to run a "tight ship" but also give extraordinary encouragement to the school athletic program.

Community-related factors

It is widely believed that small rural communities are especially enthusiastic about their local high school teams. These local teams provide much of the entertainment and are a source of community pride and unity. The data from Table 5 substantiate this claim.

We also examined the proportion of professionals in the community, dividing the sample into those communities exceeding 22 percent and those with a smaller percentage. The data in Table 5 reveal that students from communities with fewer professionals were more inclined to wish to be remembered as an athletic star than students where there were more professional persons.

When the communities were separated by the extent of families living in poverty, the results show that students in the highest poverty communities were more likely than the others to want to be remembered as an "athletic star."

The final community characteristic, the percentage of wage earners in manufacturing, was included to indicate not only the extent of industry in the community but also as an indirect measure of the urban-rural dimension. The results show that boys from communities with relatively little manufacturing were more likely to choose "athletic star" than those who came from more industrialized communities.

Summary

This study was guided by two questions. First, is sports participation as dominant a criterion for status among adolescent males now as it was in the 1950's? The data from students in the nine schools in our sample provide strong support that it continues to prevail.

Although there appears to be widespread acceptance of sports among teenage boys, our second question was: are there certain sectors where support may be breaking down? The data suggest that certain variables appear to affect one's perception of the importance of sport. Our data suggest that the strongest support for sport is found among sons of the undereducated, in small schools, in schools with a strict authority structure, and among students at the center of the schools activities. Conversely, sons of college educated fathers from large urban or suburban schools, affluent and permissive schools are the less enthused about sports (although it should be remembered that they, too, chose sports over the other possibilities but in lower percentages). Thus, several trends lead to the speculation that the enthusiasm for sports may wane in the future. School unification makes schools larger, a larger proportion of youngsters attend suburban schools each year, each generation is better educated, and schools are generally more permissive than in the past. If these conditions lead to somewhat less enthusiasm for sports, as our data indicate, then sports participation as the dominant criterion for social status will diminish in the future.

REFERENCES

1. Coleman, James S., *The Adolescent Society: The Social Life of the Teenager and Its Impact on Education.* New York: Free Press, 1961.
2. Divoky, Diane, and Peter Schrag, "Football and Cheers," *Saturday Review,* (November 11, 1972), pp. 59–65.
3. Johnson, William., "The Greatest Athlete in Yates Center, Kansas," *Sports Illustrated,* (August 9, 1971), pp. 27–31.
4. Jones, Frank B., "Intercollegiate and Interscholastic Athletic Programs in the 1970's," *Sportscope,* (June, 1970), pp. 1–20.
5. Klein, Frederick C., "Hoopster Hoopla: High School Basketball is a Serious Matter in a Small Illinois Town," *Wall Street Journal,* (March 1, 1970).

6. Loyd, F. Glen., "Jack Armstrong is Dead," *Today's Health*, (October, 1970), pp. 47–48; 84–86.

7. Ricke, Tom., "A Town Where Boys are Kings and the Court Business is Basketball," *Detroit Free Press*, (March 14, 1971).

8. Talamini, John T., "Occupational Ideologies and Behavioral Patterns in School Athletics," Ph.D. dissertation, Rutgers University, 1971.

CONSEQUENCES OF PARTICIPATION IN INTERSCHOLASTIC SPORTS: A REVIEW AND PROSPECTUS

John C. Phillips and Walter E. Schafer

Very few sociological studies on the role of athletics in high schools appear to have been done prior to 1960. Since that time, a considerable amount of work has appeared, with generally consistent findings on certain aspects of high school athletics. The research the authors are presently doing involved an effort to explain one of those consistent findings—the fact that athletes tend to exceed comparable nonathletes in their achievement of educational goals. In this paper, we will review the evidence on the academic achievement of high school athletes, discuss our efforts to employ the concept of subculture to explain the advantage that athletes enjoy and, finally, speculate on possible broader applications of the kind of work we have been doing.

"Consequences of Participation in Interscholastic Sports: A Review and Prospectus," by John C. Phillips and Walter E. Schafer, is reprinted from *Pacific Sociological Review*, Volume 14, No. 3 (July 1971), pp. 328–338 by permission of the Publisher, Sage Publications, Inc.

ATHLETES AND ACADEMIC ACHIEVEMENT

As information about high school athletes has grown more and more plentiful, a number of popular myths about the effects of athletic participation have been supplanted. Perhaps the best example of factual information replacing myth is the relationship between athletic participation and high school scholastic achievement. Athletics has been considered an anti-intellectual influence by some authors (Henry, 1963; Coleman, 1960, 1961, 1966), but there is compelling evidence that athletes get slightly better grades than do comparable nonathletes. Schafer and Armer (1968) found that high school athletes got slightly better grades than nonathletes in their matched sample. Athletes from blue-collar homes and boys who were not in a college-preparatory program got even better grades than their nonathlete counterparts. Bend (1968) found substantially the same pattern. Athletes got slightly better grades and the advantage of athletes was most pronounced among "low-endowment" (low-IQ, low-SES) boys.

The fact that "low-endowment" athletes showed the most pronounced difference in achievement could be important to our interest in subculture as an explanation of these differences. Could it be that athletes are·put under special pressure to perform well in the classroom? Perhaps the low-endowment athletes do better than low-endowment nonathletes because they experience pro-educational influences similar to those experienced by middle-class boys.

There is strong evidence to indicate that athletes aspire to and succeed in attending college more than do nonathletes. Bend found that 81.8% of his sample of superior athletes compared to 56.1% of the nonathletes aspired to at least some college education. The figures for low-endowment superior athletes and nonathletes was 39.8% and 13.3% respectively. Over 71% of the superior athletes actually attended college, while 50.0% of the nonathletes attended. Figures for low-endowment athletes and nonathletes were 14.8% and 6.9%. Bend's large sample, longitudinal design, and the fact that the relationship between athletic participation and educational achievement increased as degree of athletic involvement increased inspire confidence in his results. Rehberg and Schafer (1968) and Schafer and Rehberg (1970a, 1970b) found similar patterns in aspirations and expectations for college attendance.

Again, we see blue-collar athletes far exceeding comparable nonathletes in aspirations for college attendance and in the achievement of college attendance. We contend that this difference can be attributed, at least in part, to their experiences as athletes.

Schafer (1969) provides data that indicate that athletes are less likely to be deviant than comparable nonathletes. Again, blue-collar athletes were markedly less likely to be delinquent than blue-collar nonathletes, while the relationship is virtually eliminated among white-collar boys. Schafer argues that, unless some selection factor is working, there must be some influences in athletics that deter boys from engaging in delinquent behavior. We will argue that if potentially delinquent boys were being selected out of athletic participation, then white-collar as well as blue-collar delinquents would be selected. Thus, the negative relationship between athletic participation and delinquency would hold for boys from all socioeconomic backgrounds, not just for lower blue-collar boys.

With the association between athletic participation and educational success especially marked among blue-collar boys, one has firm grounds for expecting more upward social mobility among athletes than among comparable nonathletes. Schafer and Stehr (1968) suggest that, since blue-collar and white-collar athletes are more likely than are nonathletes to associate with the white-collar, college-bound "leading crowd" in high schools (Coleman, 1961: 35–50, 145–151), their mobility chances are enhanced. In a later paper, Schafer and Rehberg (1970a) found that athletes, compared with non-athletes, are more likely to report having been encouraged by teachers and counselors to go on to college. This relationship grows stronger as aspirations for going on to college diminish. Thus it appears that athletes not only attain higher educational achievement, but those who are not disposed toward furthering their education receive special encouragement or sponsorship to do so.

Phillips' (1965) study of college athletes has suggested another possible source of upward mobility among athletes. Phillips found that athletes tended to interact with one another much more than did nonathletes. He argued that this high interaction reduced what Hodges (1964) has termed "the psychic cost of mobility." By having a ready circle of middle-class friends, a blue-collar athlete might better develop the manners, mannerisms, attitudes, and social contacts that facilitate upward mobility. This tendency for athletes to choose other athletes as friends has also been found by Schafer and Rehberg (1970b).

Schafer and Rehberg (1970b:12) also found that athletes "tend to have close friends who are more positive in educational attitudes, aspirations, and behavior than the close friends of non-athletes." While the nature of their data prohibits firm conclusions, they do suggest the possibility that the differences between athletes and nonathletes can, at least in part, be attributed to their greater exposure to pro-educational peer influences.

We may summarize the evidence on differences between high school athletes and nonathletes as follows:

1. Athletes generally receive slightly better grades and are more likely to aspire to and attain more education than comparable nonathletes. This is especially marked among athletes from blue-collar homes.

2. There is some evidence to indicate that athletes are less likely than nonathletes to become delinquent. We do not know whether this relationship is due to selection factors or due to some deterrent effect of athletic participation.

3. Athletes from blue-collar backgrounds are more likely to be upwardly mobile than nonathletes. This can be explained to a great extent by their greater educational attainment, but other factors such as sponsorship and association may also bear on this mobility.

What are the sources of these differences? Schafer and Armer (1968) suggest several possible explanations. First, athletes may receive special assistance in academic matters from teachers, peers, or coaches. Athletes might simply be graded more leniently. Second, there may be certain organizational requirements that might motivate athletes to perform better than nonathletes. Most high schools require a minimum grade-point average for participation. Athletes may work not only to achieve good enough grades for participation, but to qualify for entry into a college to continue their athletic careers. Third, athletes may be favored by "spillover" of certain qualities they have developed through sport. Higher peer status due to the generalization of their athletic status to other areas of social participation may enhance the athletes' self-esteem and, hence, their motivation to succeed in school work. Values of hard work, excellence, and persistence may be developed in sports activities and applied to academic and other activities. Practice and training regimens may influence athletes to use their study time more efficiently. Fourth, it is possible that conforming, ambitious, able boys tend to go out for sports more than do boys who are less "in tune" with the expectations of the school authorities. That is, athletics selects good students and tends to reject bad students (Schafer, 1969).

One recent article has examined the several possible sources of the educational advantages of athletes. Jerome and Phillips (1971) note the evidence of greater attainment of educational goals by athletes in American high schools. They point out the fact that sports programs in American and Canadian high schools are very similar, but that in Canada athletic participation does not receive the same status and esteem it does in American high schools. The authors argue that if good students, more than poor students, tend to go out for and be selected for athletic teams, the educational advantages of American athletes should exist among Canadian athletes as well. Likewise, if values and habits developed in athletics are applied to one's studies, the Canadian athletes should enjoy the same educational advantages that the American athletes enjoy.

Since the Canadian athletes do not appear to be better than their nonparticipating classmates in the achievement of educational objectives, Jerome and Phillips argue that the source of the American athletes' greater achievement lies not in "spillover" or selection but in one or more of the other explanations suggested by Schafer and Armer. These explanations (see above) center on *special experiences that are encountered by athletes* but not by nonathletes.

THE ATHLETIC SUBCULTURE

The evidence that athletes in American high schools appear to have certain special experiences, coupled with evidence of differences of behavior between athletes and nonathletes, has led us to the concept of subculture as a possible explanation of the processes intervening between athletic participation and various behavioral outcomes.

We should note here that two of the crucial conditions for the emergence of a subculture exist among athletes—special experiences and high rates of interaction (Phillips and Schafer, 1970). According to Cohen (1955) and Cohen and Short (1958), persons in like circumstances sharing like experiences should tend to develop values, norms, and beliefs (i.e., a subculture) favorable to those in the special circumstances. Our findings indicate that athletes, who experience special rewards in school, tend to develop a pro-school subculture (Phillips and Schafer, 1970).

In two recent papers, Phillips and Schafer (1971, 1970) have tried to develop a conceptual and methodological approach to the study of sub-cultures. We follow the thinking of Vander Zanden (1970) in conceiving of subculture as values, beliefs, symbols, and norms that are shared among some people but not by the general population. Thus, a subculture exists to the extent that a number of people differ in the norms, values, beliefs, and symbols that they share.

Wolfgang and Ferracuti (1967) point out the problems in measuring the elements of subcultures and point to the salient importance of measuring norms of conduct if we are to study subcultures at all. We contend that, since culture tends "to form a consistent and integrated whole" (Vander Zanden, 1970:35), we can gain an understanding of all the elements of a subculture by studying any single element—in this case, norms. The return potential model for the measurement of norms (Jackson, 1966, 1960) appears to provide a solution to many of the problems that Wolfgang and Ferracuti cite as impediments to the study of subcultures.

Our recent investigations have been concerned with determining the extent to which there exists a distinguishable subculture shared by inter-scholastic athletes, and the extent to which such a subculture might account for the differences between athletes and nonathletes reported earlier in this paper.

In a preliminary study of one high school, we found that athletes interact with other athletes much more than do nonathletes, and, while athletes appear to expect the same kinds of conduct from their friends, the norms shared by the athletes are much more intense and more likely to regulate behavior. That is, athletes appear to be under greater pressure to conform to conventional school standards than are nonathletes (Phillips and Schafer, 1970). This greater pressure to conform to conventional standards of behavior is reflected from time to time in newspaper stories depicting often sharp controversies regarding the misbehavior of athletes (albeit not high school athletes). Few college students need fear reprisals for wearing beards or mustaches, but one can read about athletes being removed from their team rosters for even so minor a transgression.

We are also interested in the role of the coach as a link between the official school culture and the athletic subculture, which, as we have discussed above, reflects the official school culture. We believe that coaches affect not only the norms shared among athletes but the individual athletes themselves. To the extent that we find the official school norms, values, and beliefs being transmitted through the coach to the athletes, and the norms, values and beliefs they share, we will be able to explain the tendency of athletes to conform to the official school goals of academic achievement and conventional conduct.

While we have emphasized the positive outcomes of interscholastic athletics, we are interested in some of the criticisms of highly competitive interscholastic athletics as well. Could it be that the more conventional athletes tend toward intergroup and interpersonal intolerance, uncritical acceptance of existing systems, and a disinterest in public affairs? Since they are rewarded by the "system," athletes may well resist change and reform. We know of one recent incident where high school athletes joined together to suppress an effort by certain other students to challenge a number of school rules.

FURTHER RESEARCH

Until now, we have discussed only the possible existence of subcultural influences on American high school athletes and how those influences might produce the differences we have observed between athletes and nonathletes. We have paid little attention to collegiate athletes, club athletes, and professional athletes. Neither have we sought to investigate the possible impact of the game itself on the participant. These questions promise to be interesting and important if the existing literature is any indication. Weinberg and Arond (1952), Charnofsky (1968), and Scott (1968) respectively provide us with insights on the occupational culture of boxers, baseball players, and jockeys. They discuss the role of superstitions, norms regarding physical courage, beliefs about how one might best win, the athletes' image of themselves, and other matters that suggest the presence of an occupational subculture and, perhaps, certain shared norms, values, beliefs, and symbols that stem from the participants' common interest in the game, but extend to matters external to sports.

Another focus on subcultures in sport might involve participants' commitment to the official value system of a given sports organization or movement. Hans Lenk (1964) has investigated athletes' commitments to the traditional and official aims and values of the Olympic games. He has also examined the implications of the postwar tendency of German athletes to be committed to their clubs only in the realm of sport, not in other aspects of their lives (Lenk 1966). We would expect the degree of athletes' commitment to sports organizations to strongly influence the degree to which the official organizational norms regulate the behavior of club athletes.

It is possible that a national sports movement might enhance certain government efforts toward social change. Wohl (1969a, 1969b) discusses how sports clubs have helped to reduce certain traditional hostilities based on social and geographical origins, as well as replacing certain backward peasant traditions with more open, modern modes of behavior. We would hope to someday examine the condition of peasant and worker sports club participants and nonparticipants to determine if patterns exist that are similar to those we have observed in American high school athletes.

A final aspect of sports that might play a role in the generation of subcultural influences is the meaning of the game to the participants. Webb (1969) discusses the way in which attitudes toward sport are "professionalized." While young children tend to just play at their games, older children appear to place an increasing emphasis on skill and winning. Heinila (1969) employs a similar notion of playing for the sake of a "good match" and playing to win. Whether a team emphasizes the game (good match) or the game outcome (winning) may determine the nature of the interpersonal and organizational relationships among members of the team. These relationships may, in turn, influence the development of subculture among the participants.

In summary, we have convincing evidence that American interscholastic athletes achieve educational goals more than do comparable nonathletes. We have some preliminary evidence that indicates that the athletes share norms that exert a strong pro-school influence on them, and that these norms appear to fit our concept of subculture. We are still investigating the sources and content of this apparent athletic subculture. In the future, we hope to investigate whether subcultures develop among athletes in certain sports, or among members of sports clubs or organizations. We also hope to employ the concepts of professionalization of and commitment to sports and determine their impact, if any, on the development of subcultures in sport. If athletes collectively or individually continue to exert the influence they have in the recent past, the nature of any athletic subculture could take on an increasing importance that extends beyond the world of sport.

REFERENCES

Bend, Emil, *The Impact of Athletic Participation on Academic and Career Aspiration and Achievement*, New Brunswick, N.J.: National Football Foundation and Hall of Fame, 1968.

Charnofsky, Harold, "The major league professional baseball player: self-conception versus the popular image," *International Rev. of Sport Sociology*, 3:39–55, 1968.

Cohen, Albert K., *Delinquent Boys: The Culture of the Gang*, Glencoe, Ill.: Free Press, 1955.

Cohen, Albert K., and James F. Short, Jr., "Research in delinquent subcultures," *J. of Social Issues*, 14:20–37, 1958.

Coleman, James S., "Adolescent subculture and academic achievement," *Amer. J. of Sociology*, 65 (January): 337–347, 1960.

Coleman, James S., *The Adolescent Society*, New York: Free Press, 1961.

Coleman, James S., "Peer cultures and education in modern society," pp. 266–269 in T. M. Newcomb and E. K. Wilson (eds.), *College Peer Groups: Problems and Prospects for Research*, Chicago: Aldine, 1966.

Heinila, Kalevi, "Football at the crossroads," *International Rev. of Sport Sociology*, 4:5–30, 1969.

Henry, Jules, *Culture Against Man*, New York: John Wiley, 1963.

Hodges, Harold M., Jr., *Social Stratification: Class in America*, Cambridge: Schenkman, 1964.

Jackson, Jay, "Structural characteristics of norms," pp. 136–163 in *The Dynamics of Instructional Groups*, Yearbook of the National Society for the Study of Education, Chicago: Univ. of Chicago Press, 1960.

Jackson, Jay, "A conceptual and measurement model for norms and roles," *Pacific Soc. Rev.*, 9 (Spring): 63–72, 1966.

Jerome, Wendy C., and John C. Phillips, "The relationship between academic achievement and interscholastic participation: A comparison of Canadian and American high schools," *C.A.H.P.E.R.J.*, 37 (January/February): 18–21, 1971.

Lenk, Hans, *Werte, Ziele, Wirklichkeit der Modernen Olympischen Spiele (Values, Aims, Reality of the Modern Olympic Games)*, Scharndorf bei Stuttgart: Karl Hoffmann, 1964.

Lenk, Hans, "Total or partial engagement? Changes regarding personal ties with the sports club," *International Rev. of Sport Sociology*, 1:85–108, 1966.

Phillips, John C., "Motivation for participation in athletics: An exploratory study," M.A. thesis, San Jose State College, 1965.

Phillips, John C., and Walter E. Schafer, "The athletic subculture: a preliminary study," presented at the annual meeting of the American Sociological Association, Washington, D.C., 1970.

Phillips, John C., "Subcultures in sport: a conceptual and methodological model," in Publication 2 of the Research Institute of the Swiss Federal School of Gymnastics and Sport, Basel: Birkhauser, 1971.

Rehberg, Richard A., and Walter E. Schafer, "Participation in interscholastic athletics and college expectations," *Amer. J. of Sociology*, 73 (May): 732–740, 1968.

Schafer, Walter E., "Participation in interscholastic athletics and delinquency: A preliminary study," *Social Problems*, 17 (Summer): 40–47, 1969.

Schafer, Walter E., and J. Michael Armer, "Athletes are not inferior students," *Trans-Action* (November): 21–26, 61–62, 1968.

Schafer, Walter E., and Richard A. Rehberg, "Athletic participation, college aspirations, and college encouragement," University of Oregon (unpublished), 1970a.

Schafer, Walter E., "Athletic participation, peer influences, and educational aspirations: Toward a theory of the athletic subculture," University of Oregon (unpublished), 1970b.

Schafer, Walter E., and Nico Stehr, "Participation in competitive athletics and social mobility, some intervening social processes," presented at the meetings of the International Committee on Sociology of Sport, Vienna, Austria, 1968.

Scott, Marvin B., *The Racing Game,* Chicago: Aldine, 1968.

Vander Zanden, James W., *Sociology: A Systematic Analysis,* New York: Ronald Press, 1970.

Webb, Harry, "Professionalization of attitudes toward play among adolescents," pp. 161–178 in Gerald S. Kenyon (ed.), *Aspects of Contemporary Sport Sociology,* Chicago: Athletic Institute, 1969.

Weinberg, S. Kirson, and Henry Arond, "The occupational culture of the boxer," *Amer. J. of Sociology,* 57 (March): 460–469, 1952.

Wohl, Andrzej, "Integrational functions of sport," in Publication 2 of the Research Institute of the Swiss Federal School of Gymnastics and Sport, Basel: Birkhauser, 1969a.

Wohl, Andrzej, "Engagement in sports activity on the part of the workers of large industrial establishment in peoples Poland," *International Rev. of Sport Sociology,* 4:83–128, 1969.

Wolfgang, Marvin E., and Franco Ferracuti, *The Subculture of Violence,* London: Tavistock, 1967.

HIGH SCHOOL ATHLETES AND THEIR COACHES: EDUCATIONAL PLANS AND ADVICE

Eldon E. Snyder

Data gathered from high school basketball coaches and players indicate that the coach is a significant other in advising players about their future educational and occupational plans. Moderate positive correlations exist between advice given by the coach about whether and where to attend college and the players' educational plans after high school. Additionally, many players perceive their coach as influential to them, but this influence is primarily a function of the coach's advice.

A number of investigators have studied the influence of socialization agents upon adolescents. For example, considerable evidence has accumulated to indicate a congruency between parental and children's attitudes, particularly in regard to educational and occupational aspirations. Evidence for parental and familial influences has been presented in the research of Aberle and Naegele (1952); Kahl (1953); Bordua (1960); Straus (1962); Ellis and Lane (1963); Rehberg and Westby (1967); Sewell and Shah (1968); Campbell (1969); and Kandel and Lesser (1969). The importance of the peer group as a socializing agency among adolescents has been emphasized by Coleman (1961) in his study of adolescent behavior and value orientations in ten midwestern high schools; additional studies of peer influence include Haller and Butterworth (1960); Alexander and Campbell (1964); Krauss (1964); and Duncan, et al. (1968). Other socializing agents frequently cited include teachers (Warren, 1968), ministers, family friends, and other adults (Ellis and Lane, 1963; Herriott, 1963; Clausen, 1968; Campbell, 1969; Sewell, et al., 1969; Sewell, et al., 1970; for similar research data on reference groups of Middle Eastern students see Tomeh, 1968, 1970).

Noticeably absent in the above studies, however, are empirical data related to athletic coaches as socialization agents. The objective of this paper is to cite socializing agents influential in the high school athlete's educational and occupational plans, with an emphasis on the importance of the coach in the constellation of reference persons, and also to analyze the player's decision on college attendance as related to: (1) the coach giving advice about whether or not to attend college, (2) the coach giving advice about where to attend college, and (3) the player's perception of his coach's influence on him.

Eldon E. Snyder, "High School Athletes and Their Coaches: Educational Plans and Advice," *Sociology of Education*, 45:313–325 (Summer 1972). Reprinted by permission of the American Sociological Association.

Although empirical data have been lacking, several investigators have noted the theoretical relevance of the coaching role in socialization. Strauss (1959:110–118) has dealt with the function of the coach in the socialization process; more recently, Kenyon (1968) has suggested that physical education and sports provide the necessary conditions for socialization with the existence of agents and models. Elsewhere, Kenyon (1969) has discussed the degrees and types of involvement by participants in a sport and the variations of reference groups that are likely to be important to them. Page (1969:200) has cited the function of coaches as reference persons and educational advisors: "When the kid who at fifteen or sixteen has tremendous promise, coaches are apt to think in career terms: 'you go to Michigan State, we have connections with such and such pro team' [sic]. In this way, coaches become career specialists."

The influence of the coach in the socialization process for athletes is particularly important when several dimensions of the coach-player relationship are analyzed. Since participation in high school athletics is a highly-prized prestige-granting activity, the coach has considerable control—through his use of power and authority—in selecting players and granting rewards and punishments. The players, in turn, voluntarily submit to the coach's control and influence. Brim (1966:27) has noted that "this procedure of selection helps to assure that those who enter the organization [or activity] will not present difficult problems for the socialization program." Additional characteristics of the coach-player relationship that are likely to result in effective socialization include the high degree of participant involvement by players and coaches and the probability that the relationship will be expressive and affective (Snyder, 1970).

The importance of the coach as a reference person is supported by Kemper's (1968) approach to reference groups. He has suggested that there are three types of reference groups: the normative which defines the role the individual is to assume; the role model with whom the actor can compare his performance; and the audience to whom the actor attributes certain values that serve as his behavioral guides. For many athletes, the high school coach embodies all three types of reference groups; he provides normative expectations, a role model, and he promotes value orientations the player uses as guides for his behavior.[1] Kemper (1968:40–41) has noted that the coincidence of these three types of reference groups potentiates the most effective type of socialization.

METHODOLOGY

In the spring of 1969, with the cooperation of the Ohio Association for Health, Physical Education, and Recreation, a sample of 270 Ohio high schools participating in basketball was selected. This sample consisted of one-third of the high schools affiliated with the above association and was a representative cross-section of the schools that participated in the sport. A questionnaire was sent to the basketball coach and to two varsity team members for each of the 270 schools. Since the focus of the study was on the coach-player relationship, the age of the players was a potential extraneous source of variation, particularly with dependent variables such as educational or occupational plans. While variations in the players' ages and the length of time the coach-player relationship had existed may have been valuable data, the present study was limited to varsity players whose reported ages indicated they were likely to be juniors or seniors (96 percent of the players who responded to the sample were juniors or seniors). The response rate to the questionnaires was 64.5 percent for the coaches, 50 percent for the players.[2]

FINDINGS

Influential-Socializing Agents

Since educational and occupational plans are likely to be associated with parental socioeconomic status, this variable was controlled.[3] Table 1 presents the players' responses to the question: "Which of the following persons has been the most important influence on your thinking about your future education and/or occupation?"

In all socioeconomic classifications of players, the coach ranked third in importance. This ranking indicated that for students in the athletic sub-culture, the coach was a significant other. However, players of lower socioeconomic status were more likely than players of higher status categories to indicate the coach was the most important person in their educational/occupational plans. Additional analysis of the data based on mother's educational background likewise showed that the coach ranked third in importance across all educational status categories, though the percentage of players who ranked the coach first was less in the case of players from higher educational backgrounds. The data in Table 1 also suggest that the nonfamilial reference persons, including teachers and coaches, may be more important for players of lower than of upper socioeconomic status backgrounds.

The coaches' responses to a parallel question regarding reference persons who were important in their educational and/or occupational plans are presented in Table 2. For coaches who came from lower socioeconomic status backgrounds, their own coach was their most prominent reference person. Anticipatory socialization may explain this response; the coach served as a role model. As was true of the players, the importance of the coach as an educational/occupational influence declined for the coaches from higher socioeconomic status backgrounds. When the reference persons of coaches were analyzed by mother's educational background, the coach still ranked first (39 percent) in the "Less than High School" category but declined to third (9 percent) in the "Some College or More" group.

Table 1 Reference Persons Cited by Players as Most Important Influence in Their Thinking about Educational and/or Occupational Plans, by Socioeconomic Status of Father (Percentages)

Persons cited as most important	Education of Father			Occupation of Father		
	Less than high school N=80	High school N=145	Some college or more N=64	Semi-skilled, unskilled N=58	Clerical, sales skilled, farm N=153	Professional, executive, proprietor N=68
Mother	33	31	23	22	35	19
Father	21	36	53	26	37	44
Coach	19	9	13	19	12	10
Classroom teacher	10	6	3	9	7	3
Girlfriend	9	6	0	7	5	3
Brother	3	5	3	7	0	9
Minister or priest	3	3	0	3	0	4
Sister	1	1	0	2	1	0
Other relative	1	3	3	3	1	6
Boyfriend	1	0	2	2	0	1

Table 2 Reference Persons Cited By Coaches as Most Important Influence in Their Thinking about Educational and/or Occupational Plans, by Socioeconomic Status of Father (Percentages)

Persons cited as most important	Education of Father			Occupation of Father		
	Less than high school N=83	High school N=52	Some college or more N=38	Semi-skilled, unskilled N=46	Clerical, sales, skilled, farm N=75	Professional, executive, proprietor N=50
Coach	36	31	13	30	37	18
Mother	27	23	26	26	24	28
Father	19	29	58	20	28	46
Brother	5	2	0	0	4	4
Classroom teacher	4	4	0	6	1	2
Sister	2	0	0	2	1	0
Other relative	2	4	0	2	1	2
Girlfriend	2	2	3	9	0	0
Boyfriend	2	4	0	4	1	0
Minister or priest	0	2	0	0	1	0

Table 3   Gamma Correlation Matrix of Variables Used in the Analysis of the Player's Decision on College Attendance, Coach's Advice on Whether and Where to Attend College, and Player's Perception of his Coach's Influence

	(2)	(3)	(4)	(5)	(6)	(7)
1. Father's education	.720	.239	.032	.033	−.163	.328
2. Father's occupation	. . . .	.199	.058	.065	−.070	.311
3. Reported grades		. . . .	.167	.080	.058	.579
4. Coach gave advice: whether to attend college			. . . .	.654	.387	.315
5. Coach gave advice: where to attend college				. . . .	.306	.237
6. Player's perception of coach's influence					. . . .	.150
7. Player's decision on college attendance						. . . .

In the sample of coaches, as with the players, the percentage of non-familial reference persons was greater for the respondents of lower rather than higher socioeconomic status backgrounds. These data may be partially explained by the likelihood that middle and upper status players had fathers present with educational and occupational achievements that the players admired and sought to emulate, while the lower status respondents turned to other reference persons, including their coach, for guidance.[4]

The importance of the coach to the lower socioeconomic status player suggests that the coach represents a reference person who promotes social mobility. This finding provides supportive data for several recent studies (Rehberg and Schafer, 1968; Schafer and Armer, 1968; Rehberg, 1969; Snyder, 1969) that have shown that participation in high school athletics and activities is associated with educational aspirations and achievement. However, the coach's influence is only one of several possible explanations of the social mobility function of athletics (Rehberg, 1969).

**Player's Decision Concerning College Attendance,
Coach's Advice About College Attendance, and the
Player's Perception of His Coach's Influence**

A player's college plans may be associated with (1) the coach giving advice about whether or not to attend college, (2) the coach giving advice about where to attend college, and (3) the player's perception of his coach's influence.[5]

The gamma matrix of Table 3 summarizes the intercorrelations between educational plans, the advice given by coaches about whether and where to attend college, the player's perception of his coach's influence, as well as the additional variables of father's education, occupation, and the player's

reported grades.[6] The last three variables were analyzed since their association with educational plans for college provided a potential extraneous
influence in examining the relationship between the independent variables
and educational plans.

Father's education and occupation were positively associated with a
player's plans to attend college; however, these variables showed little or no
association either with the coach's advice about whether and where to attend
college or the player's perception of his coach's influence. Thus, the player's
socioeconomic status did not seem to be influencing the relationships
between the coach's educational advice or the player's perception of his
coach's influence and the player's college plans. Reported grades did, however, show a slight positive relationship with the coach giving advice about
whether to attend college (.17). Rosenberg's (1962) test factor standardization technique was used to determine whether the relationship between this
advice and educational plans was independent of reported grades. With
reported grades standardized, the relationship was reduced from .31 to .27,
still a significant relationship.

The coach's advice about whether to attend college and his advice about
where to attend college were positively associated with the player's decision
concerning college attendance; advice about whether to attend college
showed approximately the same relationship to educational plans as did the
player's socioeconomic background. The two advice variables also were
associated (.39 and .31) with the player's perception of his coach's influence;
however, the latter variable showed a relationship of only .15 with plans to
attend college. The data in Table 4 display these variables utilizing Rosenberg's (1962) standardization technique as a means of examining their
independent effects on the decision to attend college.

Panel A of Table 4 indicates that the advice coaches gave players about
whether to attend college was not independent of the advice they gave about
where to attend college. When advice about where to attend college was
controlled, the correlation between advice about whether to attend college
and college plans was reduced from .31 to .16. (Note also the correlation of
65 between these two variables in Table 3.) Likewise, panel B shows that the
association between the coach's advice about where to attend college and
college plans was reduced from .24 to .20 when the coach's advice on
whether to attend college was standardized.

The player's perception of his coach's influence had no effect in reducing
the associations between the advice variables and the player's educational
plans. However, an examination of panel C indicates that advice variables
reduce the relationship between the player's perception of his coach's influence and college plans. These data suggest that because the coach is providing
advice about going to college, and perhaps making arrangements with colleges
and coaches for visitations, he is perceived of as influential by the player.

In summary, these data demonstrate moderate positive relationships

Table 4   Player's Decision on College Attendance, Coach's Advice on Whether and Where to Attend College, and Player's Perception of His Coach's Influence (Percentages)

A. Coach gave advice on whether to attend college and player's decision on college attendance

Player's decision on college attendance	Coach gave advice on whether to attend college		
	Often (N=116)	Seldom (N=107)	Never (N=64)
Definitely will attend	78	64	58
Probably will attend	18	20	19
Definitely will not and probably will not attend	4	16	23

Gamma = .31, original relationship
Gamma = .16, with coach's advice on whether to attend college standardized
Gamma = .30, with player's perception of his coach's influence standardized

B. Coach gave advice on where to attend college and player's decision on college attendance

Player's decision on college attendance	Coach gave advice on where to attend college		
	Often (N=66)	Seldom (N=124)	Never (N=97)
Definitely will attend	75	73	59
Probably will attend	17	16	23
Definitely will not and probably will not attend	8	11	18

Gamma = .24, original relationship
Gamma = .20, with coach's advice on where to attend college standardized
Gamma = .24, with player's perception of his coach's influence standardized

C. Player's perception of his coach's influence and player's decision on college attendance

Player's decision on college attendance	Player's perception of his coach's influence		
	Great (N=136)	Some (N=121)	Little, None (N=31)
Definitely will attend	71	69	55
Probably will attend	19	18	19
Definitely will not and probably will not attend	10	13	26

Gamma = .15, original relationship
Gamma = .06, with coach's advice on whether to attend college standardized
Gamma = .12, with coach's advice on where to attend college standardized

between the advice coaches give about whether or not to attend college, where to attend college, and the player's decision on college attendance. However, the two advice variables are not entirely independent in their effects on educational plans. Additionally, while many players perceive their coach as influential, this influence is diffuse (see footnote 5); when examined with regard to educational plans, it seems to be primarily a function of the coach's advice.

SUMMARY AND CONCLUSIONS

In reference group theory, emphasis usually has been placed on the importance of parents, peers, teachers, and other persons and groups. These significant others vary in primacy and salience depending upon the age of the individual. Brim (1966:8) has referred to "the emergence of a series of 'self-other systems' in which the child is oriented toward the role of prescriptions and evaluations of significant others in his environment." The high school coach is not necessarily an important reference person for most high school students, though he probably is a role model for more male students than merely the actual players on his team; however, he is an important reference person for the athletes under his control and influence.

The data presented in this paper indicate that high school coaches are influential reference persons in athletes' future educational and occupational plans. The coach was reported to be influential in these plans by more players from lower than from upper socioeconomic backgrounds; also, the number of reference persons cited was greater for the lower than for the higher status players. This finding seems to support the thesis of Inkeles (1968:121–122) who has pointed out that there is less of a consistency of role models for lower-class than for middle-class youth.

The advice that coaches give their players regarding educational plans beyond high school is positively associated with the players' decisions to attend college. Furthermore, this advice is independent of either parental socioeconomic background or grades. Many players see their coach as influential, but this influence only has a low relationship to educational plans; it is partially a function of the advice given by coaches.

The exploratory findings of this paper suggest that the coach-player relationship is a fruitful area for future research. This relationship usually contains both instrumental and expressive characteristics. The coach's advice to the player often represents a genuine concern and desire to help him. Inherent within the same situation, however, is the potential for self-aggrandizement by the coach. A coach will receive recognition when his athletes continue to receive rewards beyond high school, particularly if they continue their education and participate on a prestigeful college team (many college athletic brochures include the high school from which the players graduated and their high school coaches). A coach's success and self-esteem reflect not only his win-loss record but the number of outstanding athletes he has produced that have continued to distinguish themselves after high school graduation.

NOTES

1. In the present study, 70 percent of the players indicated that their coach gave them advice about personal problems. Additional advice given by coaches, as reported by players, included: whom to date—22 percent, how often to date—49 percent, manner of dress—73 percent, swearing—84 percent, and hair style—88 percent. See footnote 5 for the ways players felt their coaches were influential.

2. While the rate of return for players was not high, an analysis of the early and late returns indicated no significant differences on the following variables that are relevant to the study: (1) players' plans to attend college ($X^2 = 1.38$, 1 d.f.); (2) the coach having given the player advice on whether or not to attend college ($X^2 = 3.05$, 2 d.f.); (3) the coach having given advice on where to attend college ($X^2 = .21$, 2 d.f.); (4) the player's perception of his coach's influence ($X^2 = 2.07$, 2 d.f.). In response to the question: "Would you be willing to continue participation in a follow-up study?" 87 percent of the players who responded indicated their willingness to do so. This datum might be interpreted as a high degree of interest in the study and probable care in answering the items. The research was handicapped by not having access to the players' home addresses. The questionnaires were sent to the players at their respective high schools and it is likely that the letters were not always delivered promptly to the players. Furthermore, the questionnaires were sent during the last month of the school year when the end of school activities might have interfered with answering the questionnaires. In general, the factors that seem to best explain the rate of return appear to be randomized rather than reflecting a response bias.

3. The occupational level was operationalized by asking: "What sort of work does your father (or stepfather) do? If retired or dead, what sort of work did he generally do when he was working?" Responses were trichotomized as in the tables. The educational level was operationalized by the question: "How much formal education does your father or stepfather have?" and categorized as in the tables.

4. Incidental to the present study is the relative influence of the parents presented in Tables 1 and 2. The greater importance of the mother than the father among the lower status respondents is apparently a function of using the father's educational and occupational background for classification. Such a classification may be unrealistic for lower status respondents. When the respondents (both players and coaches) were classified by their mother's educational background, the father's influence was equal to, or greater than, the mother's influence at all educational levels.

5. These items were operationalized by the following questions: "Have you decided whether or not to go to college? Definitely decided to go. . . . ? Definitely decided not to go. . . . Not decided, but probably will go. . . ." Not decided, but probably will not go . . . ." For statistical analysis,

players were classified on educational plans as: Definitely will attend college; Probably will attend college; Probably will not; and will not attend college. "Does your basketball coach ever give suggestions or advice about whether or not you should go to college? Often . . . . , Seldom . . . . , Never . . . ." "Does your basketball coach ever give suggestions or advice about where you might go to college? Often . . . . , Seldom . . . . , Never . . . ." "Has your basketball coach been an influence to you? Great deal of influence . . . . , Some influence . . . . , Little or no influence . . . ." "If he has been an influence, in what ways?" The percentage distribution of the players' perceptions of their coaches' influence was: (a) a great deal of influence–47 percent, (b) some influence–42 percent, and (c) little or no influence–11 percent. To illustrate the breadth of influence, the answers to the open-ended question on the ways the coach had been influential yielded the following categories: helped with personal problems, helped develop basketball proficiency and discipline, taught pride, teamwork, and sportsmanship, showed the value of hard work, accepted me as an individual, and provided understanding. Three percent of the players indicated the coach had been a negative influence.

6. Reported grades were operationalized by the question: "What would you say is your average grade in high school subjects? Mostly A's . . . . , Mixed A's and B's . . . . , Mostly B's . . . . , Mixed B's and C's . . . . , Mostly C's . . . . , Mixed C's and D's . . . . , Mostly D's . . . ." For analysis, the grades were trichotomized into the categories: (1) Mostly A's, Mixed A's and B's, and Mostly B's, (2) Mixed B's and C's, and (3) Mostly C's, Mixed C's and D's, and Mostly D's.

REFERENCES

Aberle, D. F., and K. D. Naegele, "Middle-class father's occupational role and attitudes toward children," *American Journal of Orthopsychiatry*, 22 (April): 366–378, 1952.

Alexander, C. N., Jr., and E. A. Campbell, "Peer influences on adolescent educational aspirations and attainments," *American Sociological Review*, 29 (August): 568–575, 1964.

Bordua, D. J., "Educational aspirations and parental stress on college," *Social Forces*, 38 (March): 262–269, 1960.

Brim, O. G., "Socialization through the life cycle," pp. 3–39 in Orville G. Brim, Jr., and Stanton Wheeler (eds.), *Socialization After Childhood: Two Essays*, New York: John Wiley and Sons, 1966.

Campbell, E. Q., "Adolescent socialization," pp. 821–859 in David Goslin (ed.), *Handbook of Socialization Theory and Research*, Chicago: Rand McNally and Company, 1969.

Clausen, J. A., "Perspectives on childhood socialization," pp. 132–181 in J. A. Clausen (ed.), *Socialization and Society*, Boston: Little, Brown and Company, 1968.

Coleman, James S., *The Adolescent Society*, New York: The Free Press, 1961.

Duncan, O. D., et al., "Peer influences on aspirations: A reinterpretation," *American Journal of Sociology*, 74 (September): 119–137, 1968.

Ellis, R. A., and C. Lane, "Structural supports for upward mobility," *American Sociological Review*, 28 (October): 743–756, 1963.

Haller, A. O., and C. E. Butterworth, "Peer influences of levels of occupational and educational aspirations," *Social Forces,* 39 (May): 287–295, 1960.

Herriott, R. E., "Some social determinants of educational aspiration," *Harvard Educational Review,* 33 (Spring): 157–177, 1963.

Inkeles, A., "Society, social structure, and child socialization," pp. 74–129 in Clausen, J. A., (ed.), *Socialization and Society,* Boston: Little, Brown and Company, 1968.

Kahl, J. A., "Educational and occupational aspirations of 'common man' boys," *Harvard Educational Review,* 23 (Summer): 186–203, 1953.

Kandel, D. B., and G. S. Lesser, "Parental and peer influences on educational plans of adolescents," *American Sociological Review,* 34 (April): 213–223, 1969.

Kemper, T. D., "Reference groups, socialization, and achievement," *American Sociological Review,* 33 (February): 31–45, 1968.

Kenyon, G. S., "Sociological considerations," *Journal of Health, Physical Education, and Recreation,* 39 (November–December): 31–33, 1968.

Kenyon, G. S., "Sport involvement: A conceptual go and some consequences thereof," pp. 77–84 in Gerald S. Kenyon (ed.), *Aspects of Contemporary Sport Sociology,* Chicago: The Athletic Institute, 1969.

Krauss, I., "Sources of educational aspirations among working class youth," *American Sociological Review,* 29 (December): 867–879, 1964.

Page, C. H., "Symposium summary, with reflections upon the sociology of sport as a research field," pp. 189–209 in Gerald S. Kenyon (ed.), *Aspects of Contemporary Sport Sociology,* Chicago: The Athletic Institute, 1969.

Rehberg, R. A., "Behavioral and attitudinal consequences of high school interscholastic sports: A speculative consideration," *Adolescence,* 4 (Spring): 69–88, 1969.

Rehberg, R. A., and W. Schafer, "Participation in interscholastic athletics and college expectations," *American Journal of Sociology,* 73 (May): 732–740, 1968.

Rehberg, R. A., and A. Westby, "Parental encouragement, occupation, education, and family size: Artifactual or independent determinants of adolescent educational expectations," *Social Forces,* 45 (March): 362–374, 1967.

Rosenberg, M., "Test factor standardization as a method of interpretation," *Social Forces,* 41 (October): 53–61, 1962.

Schafer, W. E., and J. M. Armer, "Athletes are not inferior students," *Trans-Action,* 6 (November): 21–26, 61–62, 1968.

Sewell, W. H., et al., "The educational and early occupational attainment process," *American Sociological Review,* 34 (February): 82–92, 1969.

Sewell, W. H., et al., "The educational and early occupational status attainment process: Replication and revision," *American Sociological Review,* 35 (December): 1014–1027, 1970.

Sewell, W. H., and V. P. Shah, "Social class, parental encouragement, and educational aspirations," *American Journal of Sociology,* 73 (March): 559–572, 1968.

Snyder, E. E., "A longitudinal analysis of the relationship between high school student values, social participation, and educational-occupational achievement," *Sociology of Education,* 42 (Summer): 261–270, 1969.

Snyder, E. E., "Aspects of socialization in sports and physical education," *Quest,* **14** (June): 1–7, 1970.

Straus, M. A., "Work roles and financial responsibility in the socialization of farm fringe, and town boys," *Rural Sociology,* **27** (September): 257–274, 1962.

Strauss, A., *Mirrors and Masks,* New York, The Free Press, 1959.

Tomeh, A. K., "The impact of reference groups on the educational and occupational aspirations of women college students," *Journal of Marriage and the Family,* **30** (February): 102–110, 1968.

Tomeh, A. K., "Reference-group supports among middle-eastern college students," *Journal of Marriage and the Family,* **22** (February): 156–166, 1970.

Warren, R. L., "Some determinants of the teacher's role in influencing educational aspirations: A cross-cultural perspective," *Sociology of Education,* **41** (Summer): 291–304, 1968.

THE COLLEGIATE DILEMMA OF SPORT AND LEISURE: A SOCIOLOGICAL PERSPECTIVE — A REACTION

George H. Sage

Can you identify the source of this statement?:

Athletics are taken seriously in most American colleges . . . There is not much fun or freedom in the life of the candidate for the . . . team . . . intense rivalry smothers the spirit of fair play and leaves the game short of one of its greatest attractions. . . . The newspapers make capital of this in exaggerated paragraphs, and football [games] assume the appearance of a gladiatorial show. . . . The money making value of the game is dragging sports down from its true place as a recreation, and, together with the rivalry before alluded to must tell against its best interests. But the evil does not stop here, for smaller colleges, like small boys, try to imitate their big brothers, and so offer distinguished players large salaries to coach their football teams that they may compete with some hope of success; and thus many of the men who become noted in college athletes have professionalism thrust upon them.

This is not a speech that was made last week nor last year. It is not something that was written by some sport radical. It was written by a professional physical educator, but not a contemporary one. It is part of a speech

George H. Sage, "The Collegiate Dilemma of Sport and Leisure: A Sociological Perspective—a Reaction," *Proceedings of the National College Physical Association for men,* 1976, pp. 186–203. Reprinted by permission.

made by R. Tate McKenzie (1893) to the American Association for the Advance of Physical Education in 1893!

Let's try another one:

> When intercollegiate athletics are conducted for education the aims are: 1) to develop all the students and faculty physically and to maintain health; 2) to promote moderate recreation, in the spirit of joy, as a preparation for study; and 3) to form habits and inculcate ideals of right living. When athletics are conducted for business, the aims are 1) to win games—to defeat another person or group being the chief end; 2) to make money—as it is impossible otherwise to carry on athletics as business; 3) to attain individual or group fame and notoriety. These three—which are the controlling aims of intercollegiate athletics—are also the aims of horse-racing, prize-fighting, and professional baseball.

It may not surprise you at this point to learn that the statement comes from a 1915 issue of the *Atlantic Monthly,* authored by William T. Foster (1915).

I think these two excerpts make quite clear that we are dealing with a dilemma in higher education that has been with us for a long time. It is, nevertheless, a phenomenon that needs thoughtful analysis, and hopefully, action toward resolving the dilemma.

Snyder and Spreitzer have very eloquently contrasted the relationships of the athletic and the leisure-recreation sub-systems within universities, and, in general, I agree with their analysis.[2] But I shall eschew academic-like weighing of the pros and cons of their paper and will instead use it as a basis to make a more direct approach to the dilemma; let the chips fall where they may: What in the hell is a commercial entertainment enterprise doing on a university campus. Big-time intercollegiate sports is a business enterprise that is part of a cartel, a form of corporate organization for which there are a number of federal laws prohibiting such structure, but, as James V. Koch (1973), writing in *Law and Contemporary Problems,* says, "Despite the claims of the National Collegiate Athletic Association (NCAA) that it is a champion of amateur athletics and physical fitness in colleges and universities, the NCAA is in fact a business cartel composed of university-firms which have varying desires to restrict competition and maximize profits in the area of intercollegiate athletics."

Any serious notion that the NCAA is dealing with amateur athletics is quickly dispelled in its own *Manual* (1979). On page 9 of the 1979–1980 edition the following statement appears: "An amateur student-athlete shall not be eligible for participation in an intercollegiate sport if: 1) He takes pay, or has accepted the promise of pay, in any form, for participation in that sport. . . ." But, incredible as it may sound 8 pages later, the *Manual* contains a section on *financial aid* to intercollegiate athletes! It reads: "Financial aid, including a grant-in-aid . . . may be awarded for any term . . . during which a student-athlete is in regular attendance. . . . Financial aid awarded by an institution to a student-athlete shall conform to the rules and regulations of the awarding institution. . . ." So much for amateur athletics! And so much for the notion that intercollegiate athletics is primarily an educational function of the universities!

Not only are big-time intercollegiate athletic programs a commercial business enterprise, functioning as part of a cartel, and employing athletes, but the programs are operated with employees (athletes) who are being paid slave wages. Whereas, professional football players earn an average of around $65,000 per year, the average collegiate football player earns around $5,000 for doing essentially the same job—entertaining spectators. Even granting that collegiate football teams play only half the number of games as the pros, the collegiate players are vastly underpaid. A university that reports that its athletic program showed a million-dollar profit need not be too proud; it was accomplished at the expense of exploiting its employees.

Now, I realize that there are several forms of intercollegiate athletic programs, each having somewhat unique characteristics, so what is true of one form is not necessarily true of another. I group the types of programs into three categories: the amateur-educational, the big-time-professional, and the semi-professional. The first comes close to serving a truly educational function on the campus. Athletes are not given financial aid *just* because they are athletes; and they do not receive special favors. Many colleges operate programs of this type. They should be commended. There is no intercollegiate athletic dilemma at these institutions.

Everybody knows who the big time-professionals are: They are grouped into conferences such as the Big Eight, Big Ten, PAC-10, etc. The group which I call the semi-professionals is made up mostly of middle-sized universities who are trying to emulate the big timers. They are schools without much academic stature who are trying to get visibility through sports. In many cases they offer the full-ride scholarship, but some offer only partial athletic scholarships, even if they have to take it out of OEO federal money or out of the general student's pockets. Since nationwide attention is devoted to the big time-professional programs, and it is here where the greatest dilemma exists, as far as I am concerned, my remarks will be directed towards them.

Snyder and Spreitzer are right, of course, the contemporary university is a many-splintered thing; but, as they note, we certainly might suppose that its main goals are the transmission of knowledge, the discovery of new knowledge, and the pursuit of truth. What does big-time sports contribute to the goal attainment function? I suspect that they contribute very little; as I pointed out earlier, a big-time program is a business—the business of making money through sports contests. The coaches themselves acknowledge that they have little commitment to the academic goals of the University. "Bear" Bryant of Alabama noted:

> I used to go along with the idea that football players on scholarship were student-athletes which is what the NCAA calls them. Meaning a student

first, an athlete second. We are kidding ourselves, trying to make it more palatable to the academicians. We don't have to say that and we shouldn't. At the level we play, the boy is an athlete first and a student second (Bryant and Underwood, 1974).

Sonny Randle, (1975) former football coach at the University of Virginia, said: "We've stopped recruiting young men who want to come here to be students first and athletes second." Denny Crum, (McDermott, 1977) basketball coach at Louisville University said: We're . . . in the business of filling the gym. . . ." Finally, Frank Kush, football coach at Arizona State University argued: "My job is to win football games. I've got to put people in the stadium, make money for the university, keep the alumni happy, and give the school a winning reputation" (Michener, 1976).

The athletes also understand the purpose of the athletic programs. Heisman Trophy winner, Steve Owens (1969) said, while he was at Oklahoma: "In high school the game was almost entirely fun. Here it's a business. We're supposed to fill the stadium with 60,000 fans and win . . . I still love the game, but there's so much pressure, sometimes it makes me wonder." Andre McCarter (1974), a UCLA basketball player, noted: "There's no rahrah stuff about the game. . . . We look at it like a business, a job. . . . It's like the pros, except you don't have any income." Oakland Raider quarterback, Kenny Stabler, describes how he viewed the educational mission of the college for him. He said: "I went to college to play football, not for education" (Jones, 1977).

The notion that a big time intercollegiate athletic program has anything to do with the educational goals of a university is absolutely bizarre when you consider the fact that some of the most esteemed universities in the world do not have intercollegiate sports: Oxford, Cambridge, University of Heidelberg, etc. Even in the United States, some of the most prestigious universities have an amateur-educational program: University of Chicago, MIT, Cal Tech, and some others.

This is not to say that there may not be some indirect impact on the academic programs because of successes in sports. As Snyder and Sprietzer say: ". . . The favor resulting from such a program does promote political and economic support." Presidents at state universities feel that a successful athletic program yields greater support from the legislature, and several universities have documented that alumni contributions fluctuate with the successes and failures of the teams.

Frankly, I have several reactions to this state of affairs. First, it should not be too surprising that legislators and alumni judge the success of a university by its athletic teams. After all, the public relations milieu of the universities are devoted to projecting the athletic teams as the symbols of the quality of the university. Offices of sports information directors and their staff of assistants make a persistent and consistent effort to get the public to identify with the teams. If the athletic teams falter, what can one expect in the way of financial support. It's easy to see how the thinking of legislators and alumni could go: "The university is failing; let it know you don't like it—withhold funds." The way to resolve this problem is to turn the sports information offices into academic information offices and promote the ongoing scholarly activities on the campuses. Who knows, perhaps the several publics who financially support a university could be persuaded to evaluate the institution by its contributions to education. As one University of Nebraska professor noted: "If we were able to make our presentations [to the state legislature] without the distraction of football ratings, we could fare well with the legislators. Reason usually prevails" (Budig, 1972).

Another reaction I have to using sports to generate funds for academic purposes is related to the exploitation of student-athletes. I question the morality of using student-athletes to hustle money for the university—the university profits from the sweat of the athletes. At least the student-athlete should be paid a decent wage by the employers, if one of his functions is to produce capital, either directly or indirectly.

Another reaction: At what cost to the athlete, not in financial terms but in academic terms, do these big time programs squeeze money out of the alumni, legislators, and spectators? Some of the best collegiate athletes have been involved in sad endings to their collegiate careers—not athletically, but academically. Allen Brenner (1969), a captain of Michigan State's football team, said: "Playing college football is becoming a delusion. It takes too much of your time. There are fall meetings, fall practice, spring practice, weight programs. The plight of the player-student is almost impossible. He doesn't have enough time to study."

At what cost to the athlete in psychological terms is the university treasury supplemented? Gary Shaw (1972), a former Texas football player, says: "What they do to those kids is nothing short of criminal. When a boy doesn't measure up, they put him out there 'head knocking' until he quits. They've left cripples all over the state of Texas." Several years ago at Florida State, the football coaches conducted illegal practices during the winter in which they placed athletes in a room with a false ceiling of chicken wire about 4-5 feet high and made them fight and wrestle until they collapsed (Putnam, 1973). The next time you hear that a winning football or basketball team has been responsible for favorable legislation or increased alumni giving, consider at what cost in human terms this was achieved.

Moving away from the relationship between the educational goals and big time sports, another favorite claim of apologists for intercollegiate athletics is that they serve a social integrative function—that athletics develops a loyalty and identification with the institution on the part of students, faculty, and alumni. Indeed, Snyder and Spreitzer make this point. They state: "It is clear that the realization of community on campus is facilitated through athletic contests and their associated pageantry." Recently an editor of the Notre Dame student newspaper made the case for the integrative nature of intercollegiate football at that university (Grasser, 1975). He wrote: "What is the value of the fiction of football? . . . Perhaps most importantly, football at Notre Dame is a ritualistic event that more than any other single activity helps to unite all the people that have been, are, and will be connected with Notre Dame."

Well, how can anyone doubt the argument that universities need big-time sports to keep everyone loyal and identifying with the institution. It is, of course, very difficult because we have all been so thoroughly indoctrinated by the sports establishment who have hammered this theme so persistently, using the "big lie" technique, that we have all internalized this as truth. The big lie technique was eloquently articulated by Adolf Hitler, to wit: "The great masses of people . . . will more easily fall victims to a big lie than to a small one."

The idea that universities need big time programs for loyalty and identification maintenance is easily exposed for the hoax that it is, if we can pull ourselves away from the propaganda to which we have been exposed. Many of the great universities do not have big time programs, but they do not seem to suffer from an integration problem. Indeed, their pride and loyalty seems to be directed to the academic programs. The student editor at Notre Dame says that, ". . . football . . . more than any other single activity helps to unite all the people that [are] connected with Notre Dame." United them for what? Is there an enemy out there preparing to attack Notre Dame? It makes one wonder about the academic climate of a university which must depend upon a game for its unity. It is curious that an institution of higher education cannot find support, nourishment, intellectual stimulation, and even unity, if that is necessary, from its scholars—its students and faculty.

But, of course, the whole idea that a major university must depend upon its athletic teams for social integration is absolute nonsense when one gives the idea a few moments of objective thought. It is true, of course, that for some students their identification with their institution comes from the athletic teams, but most students at a major university have little direct or indirect association with the athletic program, so it can hardly be said to bind them to the organization.

Let's look briefly at one final supposed function of big time intercollegiate programs—the entertainment function. It is often contended that athletic contests provide wholesome entertainment for students, but at the most there are five home football games and 12 to 14 home basketball games per year, and these are typically the sports that provide the most spectator interest. Seventeen to twenty days of entertainment in a normal 200-day collegiate academic year hardly constitutes a major form of entertainment, especially when the costs to the students, state, alumni, etc., are considered.

As to entertaining the public, we do not insist that banks, factories, department stores, and other businesses provide entertainment for their employees, clientele, customers, present or past, or the general public. Universities are institutions of equal importance to society, insofar as they attend to their main purposes. There is no compelling reason why universities should be in the professional sports industry. Lord knows we have enough of these—120 businesses that may be called major-league professional teams.

The intercollegiate dilemma, in essence, is how can we reconcile commerical athletic enterprises on collegiate campuses? I believe we can't, and we ought to take steps to remove these operations from our campuses. Time prohibits me from enumerating the various ways that this might be accomplished, but I will say one thing—this Association ought to formulate a clear and unequivocal statement against professional collegiate athletics and support for educational-based athletics in colleges. The leisure-recreation programs that Snyder and Spreitzer talk about are the educational programs which we have on campus, and these might include an intercollegiate program, providing that it is conducted for the students' welfare. The cards are only "stacked toward the extrinsic world of athletics and against the intrinsic sphere of leisure," to use Snyder and Spreitzer's words, because of the past and present dealers. There is no reason why the cards cannot be removed from one dealer's hand and placed in another's. This could very well result in a re-stacking, hopefully, in favor of educational recreation and sport.

NOTES

1. This is a revised edition of a paper that was presented as a reaction paper to a presentation by Eldon Snyder and Elmer Spreitzer made at the annual convention of the National College Physical Education Association for Men, Hot Springs, Arkansas, 1976.

2. Published in *the Proceedings of the National College Physical Education Association for men,* 1976, Eldon Snyder and Elmer Spreitzer, "The Collegiate Dilemma of Sport and Leisure: A Sociological Perspective: pp. 186–203.

REFERENCES

Brenner, A., Quoted in "Scoreboard," *Sports Illustrated,* March 24, 1969, pp. 16–17.

Bryant, P. W. and Underwood, J. *Bear: The Hard Life and Good Times of Alabama's Coach Bryant* Boston: Little, Brown, 1974.

Budig, G. A., "Grid Stock Up—Academic Stock Down," *Phi Delta Kappan,* LIV (September): 56, 1972.

Foster, W. T., "An Indictment of Intercollegiate Athletics," *The Atlantic Monthly,* 116 (November): 577–587, 1915.

Grasser, J., *Scholastic,* (Notre Dame, Indiana: Notre Dame University) vol. 116, No. 8, January 24, 1975, p. 50.

Jones, R. F. "Getting Nowhere Fast." *Sports Illustrated.* September 19, 1977, pp. 88–102.

Koch, J. V., "A Troubled Cartel: The NCAA," *Law and Contemporary Problems,* **38** (Winter-Spring); 135–150, 1973.

McCarter, A., In Barry McDermott, "After 88 Comes Zero," *Sports Illustrated,* January 28, 1974.

McDermott, B., "Dunkers Are Strutting Their Stuff." *Sports Illustrated,* March 14, 1977, pp. 22–27.

McKenzie, R. T., "The Regulation of Athletic Sports in Colleges," *Department Congress of Physical Education, Proceedings and Reports,* American Association for the Advancement of Physical Education, July, 1893.

NCAA Manual 1977–80, NCAA, Shawnee Mission, Kansas, 1979.

Owens, S., "Intercollegiate Athletics," *Sport,* November, 1969, p. 94.

Randle, S., Quoted in "Scoreboard," *Sports Illustrated,* September 1, 1975, p. 12.

Shaw, G., *Meat on the Hoof,* New York: St. Martin's Press, 1972.

BEATING THEIR BRAINS OUT

John Underwood

During one of those chatty interludes in a televised college football game the other season (no matter which), Sportscaster Chris Schenkel cut rather merrily to the subject of intercollegiate athletics at the Massachusetts Institute of Technology, and how—wow!—Old Brainy had more teams (22) competing in NCAA sports than any other school. There are 697 participating colleges and universities in the three divisions of the National Collegiate Athletic Association. Some of them are named Southern Cal and Ohio State. Schenkel's discovery was smugly noted in the MIT student newspaper, *The Tech,* with the comment that this was actually better publicity for the NCAA than for MIT because association with such a "well-known academic institution" was "obviously good for the NCAA's image."

On the premise that it is hardly news once it is intoned by Chris Schenkel, the fact that MIT sends 22 squads of geniuses out to slay the opposition with fastballs, hook shots and backhand volleys instead of coefficients and loga-

John Underwood, "Beating their Brains Out," *Sports Illustrated,* **42,** (May 26): 84–96, 1975. Reprinted by permission.

rithms is not in itself a revelation here. However, 22 is a goodly number regardless of whose image is served or how good the teams are. MIT's, mostly, are patsies.

What you may not know is that:

1. MIT equips and fields all these teams without offering or granting a single athletic scholarship; without recruiting a single athlete, be he blue, red or white chip; without charging a nickel for admission to any event; without caring, really, if anybody shows up to watch, which is always a possibility. Some of its teams do very well, and some merit the inattention.

2. MIT will spend $820,000 this year on its athletic program—$345,000 for the 22 intercollegiate sports, featuring this spring baseball, lacrosse, tennis and so forth; the rest for five women's varsity sports, physical education, intramurals and club sports, and a modestly priced stray special or two such as Hatha yoga and Frisbee—with nary a discouraging word from faculty or administration about "how much all this is costing." The expenditure is, in fact, quite modest compared, say, with Michigan's $4.1 million budget or UCLA's $3.3 million, but it should be remembered that there is no hope whatsoever of breaking even at MIT. In the economic pinch, "break even" has become the rallying caterwaul of college athletic programs across the country. At MIT you don't even hear a groan.

3. Not a penny of the $820,000 is derived from or expended for the MIT football team. There is no MIT football team. Nor is there evidence that anyone wants one. Athletic Director Ross H. (Jim) Smith says that the subject is broached "in cycles, every five years or so," usually by fiery-eyed stars of the Class A intramural football league (the ones who are coordinated) itching to get their mitts on the likes of Colby and Bates. At MIT, the cyclic phenomenon is treated as if it were an open jar of smallpox virus, and soon routed. Peter Close, the sports information director, notes that the school fielded a football team from 1882 to 1893. In 13 games with Harvard it was outscored 555–5.

4. Twenty-six of MIT's 132 hallowed acres, a vertical slash of oak-lined real estate hard by Memorial Drive on the Charles River in Cambridge, are devoted exclusively to athletics. The complex includes two baseball fields, a lacross-soccer-track stadium, 10 tennis courts, a tennis bubble, a rugby field, a gymnasium, a field house, an indoor track-basketball "cage" made of two former U.S. Navy airplane hangars, a swimming pool, a boathouse, a sailing pavilion and various spaces in between for intramurals. They are in constant use. The light in the tennis bubble burns nightly past midnight. It is not unusual for a squash match to start at 2 a.m. Eight intramural softball diamonds are filled in three daily shifts and six football fields are lined off to accommodate 68 intramural teams. Howard W. Johnson, chairman of the MIT Corporation, the school's governing body, says woe unto the department head who tries to lay a finger on a square inch of those 26 acres.

As part of a recently unveiled plan for new development, $6.1 million *more* has been earmarked for a double-decker indoor ice rink-track facility to be completed in two years. Clint Murchison Jr. (class of '44), the Texas sports mahout, will be the funding ramrod. One might assume that such a grand addition was a proud response to the success of the MIT ice hockey team, which now labors on a junky, well-scarred, 20-year-old "temporary" outdoor rink next to Kresge Auditorium. Games there have been called off when the snow piled up. Toes freeze as does the wooden ball in the referee's whistle. During one varsity game played at 7° below zero the referee dropped the frozen puck on the ice and it broke in two.

This assumption, however, would be wrong. The hockey team has lost a record 33 straight games, including the last four of the 1975 season by a combined score of 44–3. Assume, rather, that the love of sport at MIT, though not new, has nothing to do with traditional American won-lost values. Winning is not everything, and it is certainly not the only thing, and coming in second is not considered so bad. When the women's rowing team finished third in a three-team race with Princeton and Yale recently the coach was elated. "You don't realize how good Princeton and Yale are," he said.

Be assured before going further that this is the same MIT you have always imagined it to be: 110 years of feeding a hungry world (and its laboratories, industries and space agencies) prize-winning scientists and engineers, their feet not quite touching the ground as they emerge from the famed architectural hodgepodge just across the river from Back Bay Boston. MIT is as independent, richly endowed and cocky as ever. The names Aristotle and Copernicus are engraved in stone below the great dome of the engineering library. It is said that students think this to be "the center of the universe"— a place "for men to work, and not for boys to play," quoth MIT President Francis Walker in 1892. Noses at MIT are grindstone oriented. Labs sometimes drag on for seven hours, and a male student averages 1.3 dates a year.

But a center of athletic excellence? Yes, in a way, and not hardly. All the hoary jokes about "hearing their brains ticking" are revived when MIT boys come out to play. As well they should. Says a student adviser who divides his time with the Apollo program at nearby Draper Laboratories, "There are those who, when they come out to play basketball, cannot turn the ball loose to dribble it. A lot of them are just terribly smart young men who have developed no physical dexterity or practical sense. I had one who sheared the bolts off his muffler unscrewing them the wrong way. I had another who could make nitroglycerin in the eighth grade. In his senior year in high school he was able to formulate plastic explosives, the most complicated kind. One weekend he blew up the high school cafeteria."

But come out to play they do. In multiples. In increasing, staggering droves, spurred on by an energetic, yes, even enlightened athletic department and by their own logical quest for grindstone respite. Beyond the standard physical education requirement (a dose of eight credits in two years), 68% of the students compete in some form of organized athletics, including those on the 800 teams in 19 intramural sports. One thousand of the total undergraduate enrollment of 4,000 make up the 22 intercollegiate teams, an astounding one in four. These squads usually are larger than the opposition's because players are not cut at MIT—for practical as well as humanitarian reasons. An MIT varsity coach, traditionally, is ignorant of his material. His unsung, unrecruited athletes sign in as total strangers on registration day. A coach cannot be too careful under those conditions. When John Barry, now assistant athletic director, was basketball coach, he said he "lived with the single nagging fear that someday no one would show up for practice."

In such an insulated, catch-all environment, many who reach varsity status—the upper crust—"think they're better than they are," says Peter Close, an angular, goateed, lyric, ex-Olympic distance runner from St. John's who doubles as the assistant track coach. A conscientious SID, he enjoys telling the whimsical anecdotes about his charges. As a coach he is not so sure. "I had a boy collapse near the finish of a two-mile relay. I said, "You run out of gas?' He said, 'No, I fainted.' What's the difference?

Coaches at MIT go bananas answering 'why.' *I* go bananas. They ask, 'Why four laps? Why not five? Or three?' We practice till 7:30, then I have to stand around an hour explaining the workout we just had.

"It's the MIT way. When the basketball team refused to stand for the national anthem a few years ago, MIT quit playing it. Most of them are great kids, strong Middle America types. I had one mother in Skokie, Ill. send a walnut tray of caviar and cheese, she was so grateful to the department. But some of these kids—face it—are snobs. Especially the younger ones. They had a job getting here, and they're proud of it. They walk around with their noses up, making fun of people. I took a team to Columbia, into Spanish Harlem, and I was scared to let them out of their rooms. I was afraid they would get killed with their attitudes.

"We never have trouble getting opponents. Everybody wants to beat MIT. They think when they beat us they're beating us in the classroom. It ain't so. They beat us because we're bad."

But, ah, says Close, the dawn comes up like thunder over the Charles River. Encouraged to leave their intellectual cocoons, given time and opportunity, the true scholar-athletes emerge at MIT. Except that the order is reversed from the way you may have remembered it at your neighborhood football factory. "The professionals," as MIT athletes call those on scholarships at big-time football schools, ride in on the best deal a recruiter can buy them and, it is to be hoped, eventually discover the classroom. At MIT a straight-A student stumbles, blinking, into the sunlight—and discovers athletics. And this, says Close, is *really* the fun of it: some of them actually get good.

Exhibit A

John Wesley Pearson, class of '74, mechanical engineering, Six three, 220 pounds, brown hair, brown eyes, a graduate student with a research grant in nuclear thermo design. President of the MIT Varsity Club. Two-time All-America hammer thrower, Division III NCAA Personal best, 175'6".

This is John Pearson talking: "I weighed 250 pounds when I came here. Not fat, but overweight. My size, you play football in high school. I wasn't good at football. I didn't play anything. I was into music, I sang. And I was smart, so nobody hassled me. I came to MIT to study, period. I thought that's what everybody did. How was I to know?

"There are three well-defined groups at MIT. First, the ones who study all the time. They wind up hating it. And griping. A lot of chronic complainers are intellectuals. They *need* to gripe. The second group coasts through, never really getting involved, skimming over studies and barely trying the activities. The third group jumps into everything. Really get involved. You won't believe this, but some guys here have more activities than they do studies.

"Anyway, I was a fairly big guy. I must have stood out. When I went in for PE the trainer asked me to come out for track. He said, 'You can throw the hammer.' I didn't know what a hammer was, much less how to throw it. You never see one in high school. But Coach [Gordon] Kelly is an unbelievable teacher. For the next four years the hammer was a big thing in my life. I threw three hours every day, and lifted weights. When I won the NCAAs in 1974 it was a first for MIT.

"I believe I'd never have made it here without athletics. If I'd gone to Cal Tech, say, or Stanford, where the varsity sports program is limited or the athletes are handpicked, I'd have studied, period. And probably flunked out. I didn't do well as a freshman and sophomore. I still don't know why I wasn't put on notice, except that MIT bends over backward to keep you in school. They're so meticulous about admissions they feel the ones they choose should make it.

"Athletics gave me a reason to stay. A commitment. And a release from the academic crunch. In athletics you make your own pressure. The coaches here don't come around dragging you out of bed to practice. But if you want attention, they'll go with you every step.

"I found that athletes at MIT actually become the better students. They organize their time better. They have to. Most of them get their best grades during the season of their sport. Sounds crazy, right?

"It's not just sports at MIT, it's everything. There's something like 170 activities on campus. The rule is, if a group of kids wants something, it's made available. We had the world Frisbee champion here giving classes. A couple years ago somebody wanted to start a tiddly-winks team. They went to the student government. They got the money for it."

(When asked about the latter, Publicist Close looked as though he had been hit with a cream pie. "Oh, don't mention that," he said, grinning sheepishly. Why not? "It's embarrassing. *Tiddly-winks.*" What prompted it? "The world championships. In London. Please don't mention it." The team went to London? "Yes." How'd it do? Subdued voice: "They won." How'd they get the money to go? "MIT is very soft shouldered. Get a guy who wants to enter a Ping-Pong tournament in Hong Kong, and Jim Smith will scrape up the money. Get *two* guys and he'll find a coach.")

Exhibits B, C. et al.

Al Dopfel, class of '72, marketing major, baseball pitcher. Dopfel pitched the first no-hitter in MIT history. In 1972 he led the nation with 15.4 strikeouts a game. He was voted the Most Valuable Player in the Greater Boston League. He signed, for a bonus estimated at $15,000, with the California Angels. "I think it will be easier to get a job in baseball than in the business world," he said. Dopfel dropped out of baseball this spring rather than be assigned to the Angels' AA farm team in El Paso. He was convinced that he was not going to make the big leagues, though at MIT he is still proudly referred to as "the only guy in our history who could have."

Bill Young, class of '74, aeronautics and astronautics. Tennis captain. The 1973 New England singles and doubles champion. Coach Ed Crocker, who has been at MIT 19 years (MIT coaches do not discourage easily and are usually given every opportunity to die with their boots on), says Young was "the best we ever had, good enough to make the pro league right now if he wanted." Young has entered the Air Force instead. "I have a thing about height," he said. He once took a special mountain climbing course at MIT.

George Braun, class of '75, oceanography. MIT's current lacrosse captain and consistent winner in the 600-yard run. He was the lacrosse team's leading scorer the last three years, though the team went 0–11 and 0–14 the first two. It was 3–9 this year. Braun is the first MIT man in anyone's memory who came right out and said that he would like to chuck engineering and become a coach. Blasphemy. To that end he plans to do graduate work at Springfield. "Engineering," he says, "isn't much fun."

Erland van Lidth de Jeude, class of '76, computer science. A 6'6", 330-pound wrestler. The Greater Boston champion as a freshman, the year the coach's wife stitched two size-44 uniforms into one for him. He gets a lot of forfeits in wrestling, he says, because 190-pounders take one look and change their minds. De Jeude has a slight Dutch accent, a brown belt in judo and a baritone voice that makes walls tremble. In an MIT production of *Man of La Mancha* he played Dr. Carrasco because, he told Joe Concannon of *The Boston Globe*, "I make a very imposing figure in armor." He got rave reviews.

De Jeude says he finds solutions to his engineering problems "in the middle of the night. I wake up and write them down." Though he wants to be an opera singer as well as a computer analyst, he also wants to wrestle as long as he can. "It is a very sportsmanlike pastime. You're not thinking of killing anyone. In football [which he played without distinction in high school], they always said you had to hate the guy in front of you. On what basis?"

The party line in team sports at MIT is "to be competitive," maybe win as many as you lose. In 10 years the baseball and basketball teams have had eight winning seasons. The hockey team has had none, the wrestling team nine. It evens out. This year the 22 teams have a combined 124–144 record to date. Yet, seeking .500 or mediocrity, some manage to rise above it. The 1974 heavyweight crew finished second to Wisconsin in the intercollegiate championships and two weeks ago the heavyweights were second to national champion Harvard in the Eastern Sprints. The 1974 baseball team represented New England in the NCAA championships. Johan Akerman led MIT to the 1974 Intercollegiate Fencing Association Foils title. The 1974 pistol team had two All-Americas in Karl Seeler and Stephen Goldstein and won the NRA collegiate championship. The women's sailing team won the nationals in 1971 and 1973.

But for all these slightly breathtaking feats and the emergence of what could be called legitimate MIT athletes, one might still miss the point here if it were not for . . . well, if it were not for 6-foot, 170-pound Lawrence D. David, known around the locker rooms and playing fields of MIT as LD^2.

David—LD^2—is a senior in organic chemistry, "the one," he says, "with all those funny-colored compounds." He delves daily into the private lives of water molecules, hoping to extract fuel, and the blue blood of crabs. He is a Phi Beta Kappa (4.9 average out of 5.0). "I like school," says LD^2.

He also likes athletics, but he is not an athlete. In his four years as an undergraduate he went out for the intramural softball team but did not play. "What I'm good at," he says, "is walking. I'm a terrific walker. I'm better than anybody I know at walking."

David is an only child. "In high school in Dover, N.H. I was a turkey. I studied all the time. I shut myself away. The basketball coach knew my parents. He asked if I'd come out and do some statistics. I did statistics for football, basketball and baseball. I got good at it. I developed a system where you could chart an entire football game on two sheets of paper, 80-by-100 grids."

At MIT, LD^2 introduced Head Basketball Coach Fran O'Brien to the advantages of the "assist chart" and the "turnover chart." He became the basketball team manager, and when baseball started, he managed that team, too. He provided O'Brien (also the baseball coach) with an "on-base percentage chart," the "best way," he said, "to structure your lineup, though in college the reference frame is too short because there aren't enough games."

LD^2 managed the baseball and basketball teams four seasons. "Athletes aren't pieces of meat at MIT," he says. "Coaches aren't dictators. Coach O'Brien and I practically lived together nine months a year, so we had to get along. He's a great guy. But we had our moments. Mostly he'd argue over my scoring of base hits. I tried to score on a major league level. Did the ball hit the fence before the guy dropped it or after? Sometimes I suggested who should hit in what position. I don't say he always listened, but he never said, " 'You're just the manager. Managers should be seen and not heard.' "

LD^2 calls the athletic program at MIT "a great catalyst. I know I wouldn't have the depth of education without it. I learned to love the guys on the teams. Adversity is a great leveler."

Peter Close says he believes David would rewrite the Ten Commandments if he thought them lacking. "LD^2 doesn't look at you when he's talking." Close says, "but his eyes roll behind those glasses, and when he's onto something and whipping himself into a frenzy, he gets very satisfied with what he's saying. His eyes really roll then."

David says he does indeed get exercised when the cause is right. For example, he says he got very upset about the caliber of opposition the basketball team faced. "Way out of our league—teams like *Howard,* for crying out loud. It was ridiculous." He wrote a two-page "prospect for change," recommending that MIT coaches have more to say about scheduling. Athletic Director Smith made copies and filed it away.

In a week when the Associated Press was running a series of articles on the athletic dilemma of such schools as the University of Wisconsin, where Athletic Director Elroy (Crazylegs) Hirsch was portrayed as a modern Jacob wrestling a killer $3 million budget, MIT's Smith tended his unthreatened $820,000 program without a hitch. From hour to hour he tooled around the facilities, usually on foot, sometimes in his ancient yellow Volkswagen, through the rusted front fender of which an inspired auto dealer had stuck a key in an attempt to impress on Smith his need for a new car. Smith resisted the pitch.

MIT that week was alive with goings-on. On Tuesday the baseball team lost its annual big game with Harvard 9–2. Julia Child came to speak in Kresge Auditorium, rocking gently in a sea of mushrooms and bell peppers as she sliced and sautéed. There was a flea market in the student center and a science fair at the Rockwell Cage where, during fall registration, MIT coaches are allowed to set up booths to entice prospects. In the wrestling and fencing rooms, faculty and students submitted themselves to Maggie Lettvin for overhauls. Maggie is svelte, black-haired and 48, "The Beautiful Machine" of Boston educational television. Her roly-poly husband is an MIT biology and electrical engineering professor.

Jim Smith is 60, no longer svelte, a wide-lipped, round-faced man with dark eyebrows and light, almost stoic good humor. He uses the latter to convert minimums to maximums in his athletic budget.

He has been MIT athletic director 14 years, coming from Cornell, where he coached lacrosse, soccer and freshman basketball. He is his department's only full professor. He says that the 68 people on his current payroll actually boil down to 41.2 positions (the Frisbee instructor was on campus, and got $250 for a short-term deal), and only 20 of the staff are full-time varsity coaches. Smith juggles. He is inventive and very opportunistic.

"How, you might ask, does MIT justify having a skiing coach?" he said as he slipped the Volkswagen behind the fence near the outdoor rink and stepped onto the spongy grass. It had been raining on Greater Boston, a bleak spring day. MIT was seen in a curiously depressing perspective, like the heaths in a Constable oil. "Well, we found a guy who was a certified ski professional *and* an All-America soccer player at Springfield. He coached both. Unfortunately, he hasn't worked out. The new skiing coach will probably be a graduate student from Harvard Business School. We'll probably wind up hiring a combination rink operator-hockey coach when the new rink is completed. See? It's a constant juggle. The current hockey coach is a part-time civil engineering instructor. Sometimes you get lucky. The rugby club team doesn't even want a coach."

The MIT athletic program was student controlled until 1947. A student committee had full power to fire coaches and buy equipment. The students themselves asked for the change. Smith is only MIT's third athletic director.

"When President [Julius] Stratton hired me," Smith said, "he told me he wanted a program for the students, not for the glory of the school or financial gain. Athletics were never intended to make money here. Our intercollegiate sports were never intended to be dependent on gate receipts. It's the root of most problems at other schools.

"The only reason we go beyond the intramural level and field all those teams is that there are young men and women who want to compete at a higher level, as high as we can provide. That's the way intercollegiate competition began years ago. It's not that way anymore, of course."

Smith watched the track team's progress against Bowdoin for a while, then moved downfield, pulling his rain jacket around him and letting his uncovered balding head take its chances.

"We try to treat everybody the same. Our most expensive program is crew, which costs about $14,000 a year exclusive of salaries and overhead. Our full-time coaches make $15,000 to $20,000. The important thing is that we create no jealousies. That's how you get cooperation. If nobody or no team is getting a free ride, they're all willing to help. When a school gives one sport, say football, the lion's share, and that sport subsidizes all the others, you're bound to have jealousies. I'm not knocking college football you understand. I love it and love to watch it. I wish we could have a team. It's a game people are naturally drawn to. If you can handle it, it's certainly worthwhile. But what we have is an alternative. Another way to go. I think there's room for both."

Smith walked past the empty baseball field (the varsity was down at Wesleyan losing for the eighth time in 16 games) to where, under the looming presence of a giant Cain's mayonnaise sign, the rugby team was being cheered on by a vest-pocket crowd, most of them wielding bumbershoots. The ruggers were holding their own in a game with Dartmouth, but their red-and-white uniforms were losing to the muck. An occasional ball popped loose from the scrum and floated dream-like over the chain-link fence, bouncing into the front of the Chaffin Optical Company across the street.

Smith worked his way back toward the tennis pavilion, which glistened like a huge blister against the seal-gray sky. MIT's match with Williams had been moved indoors. With his own key Smith let himself into the bubble through the back door, bringing with him a giant whoosh of air that stopped play on all four courts and drew stares from a knot of spectators huddled at the far end. Smith apologized to Coach Ed Crocker for the interruption. Crocker was having his own problems. Williams was leading on all four courts.

"We want to be competitive," said Smith, outside again and moving, "We want to win. Too many people think we don't try. We do. We feel in Division III, where there are no scholarships, we've a 50-50 chance in every sport." He smiled, raising his dark eyebrows. "In some our 50-50 chances are better than in others."

He walked past the lacrosse field, where MIT had beaten Holy Cross the day before, and onto the track, where the meet with Bowdoin was winding to an anticlimax. The wet crowd in the bleachers could have been carried home in one car. Peter Close intercepted Smith. "We're getting clobbered," said Close, his head dripping. "It's 95–55."

Smith returned to his office. He took off his raincoat and patted the head of a stuffed beaver near his desk. "That's our mascot," he said. "The idea is we work like beavers around here. The students hate it, just like they hate all those references to slide rules." He looked at the beaver. "It *is* a pretty goofy-looking thing."

Smith said that every MIT coach is concerned with getting better athletes and more publicity, and this is natural. "A lot of academically qualified athletes don't think they can hack it at MIT what with the grades and the tuition, which is around $6,800 a year, including books and board. They just aren't aware of what's here. Sixty percent of our student body gets some kind of scholarship help. It's available.

"The hard part is that our applicants often overlap with Princeton's and Yale's, and a kid with athletic ability who is accepted by all three will go to Princeton, maybe, because he doesn't think we've got enough sports for him. Just the opposite may be true.

"Enrollment is down everywhere. Ours isn't, but applications are. We're trying something new this year. The admissions office is putting a card in with every form, requesting applicants to advise us if they are interested in an intercollegiate sport. That way a coach can mail some literature to them about our program, let them see what's here before they decide to go else-where. It's the closest we've ever come to recruiting."

Smith said he had indeed made budget cuts, doing what Chancellor Paul Gray calls "getting a good deal of bang for the dollar." There are fewer overnight trips; the freshman schedules have been reduced. Equipment Manager John Murphy never throws anything away. Some MIT rugby shoes are 12 years old and still in use. Smith juggles on. He was able to help finance Florida trips for baseball and lacrosse teams mostly out of a zealously guarded reserve fund, which also provided $120,000 for a pistol and rifle range and an automatic timer with electric touch pads for the pool.

Especially gratifying, he said, was the way large donations always seemed to arrive in the nick of time. "A lot of people give a lot of money to MIT because they've had some good feeling about the place—the activities, the athletics," Smith said. George Leness ('26), retired chairman of the board of Merrill Lynch, won 41 medals as an MIT middle-distance runner. The medals glisten on Smith's office wall. Leness' $100,000 endowment fund glows from MIT's balance sheet. David Flett du Pont ('56) left $1 million for athletic development in his will—he was killed in an auto accident after his junior year. Harold Whitworth Pierce's $300,000 gift made completion of the splendid Pierce Boat House possible in 1966. Pierce did not even go to MIT. "In fact," said Smith, "he dropped out of Harvard after his freshman year."

As Smith left his office Close brought news that the tennis team had pulled it out against Williams 5–4. The heavyweight crew race with Northeastern and Boston U had been postponed by high winds. The Charles, said Close, looked as if it had been fed from a crankcase. The MIT team had wanted to race, anyway, but the others had chickened out.

Jim Smith moved 400 pounds of fertilizer in his Volkswagen on Sunday, piling the bags on the floor and seats. Thus encumbered, he volunteered to drive a visitor to the airport. The visitor sat with his legs propped up on the bags.

The crew race was postponed once more. Finally, at 8:30 Monday morning Peter Close and a few MIT fans stood and cheered as the crew beat Northeastern by four lengths. "It was the biggest clobbering we ever gave them," beamed Close.

The Lambda Chi chapter at MIT is housed in a 75-year-old, six-story building on the opposite shore of the Charles from the school. It is within walking distance, via the 85-year-old Harvard Bridge. The Lambda Chis rank just above the SAEs and the Black Student Union as the all-jocks of MIT. They were the winners of the coveted intramural Class A football championship last fall.

The Lambda Chis have gone a long way to establishing campus standards, athletic and otherwise. Some years ago it was decided that a freshman pledge named Oliver Smoot, a 5'5" rugby player, should be used to measure the length of the Harvard Bridge. After a festive day and night in the frat house, he became stiff as a tongue depressor and was hoisted on the shoulders of his brothers and taken to the Charles. The distance was marked off in "Smoots" as he was conveyed end-over-end across the bridge—it being exactly 364.4 lengths of Smoot's body from one side to the other. A Smoot is now an accepted (if unofficial) unit of measure at MIT.

By whatever measure, the Lambda Chis are indeed jock infested, and proud of it. On a recent Friday evening President John Cavolowsky, a tall, handsome, short-haired junior from Dedham, Mass. and a two-sport letterman (baseball and basketball), led members in an informal postdinner discussion on the whys and why nots of the non-existent MIT varsity football team. Dinner had been coat and tie. A polite, to-the-point blessing was said, and a bawdy—though dated—table song sung to enliven the stew. Some of the members brought dates.

A cluster of boys and a few of the girls (none of them MIT coeds) repaired to a large comfortable den with a well-stocked bar and, over it, a plaque that read: "On Thursday, August 16, 1962, at 12 noon, while preparing a dry martini cocktail, the bartender of this establishment succeeded in isolating the vermouth molecule."

It was Cavolowsky's belief (he did not realize, he admitted later, that he was in the throes of the five-year-cycle tremors) that MIT could field a football team. Peter Close, one of the dinner guests, said the wild thing about MIT intramural football players was that they think they can slap on a set of pads and go out and play Harvard.

"What's the difference?" said Cavolowsky. "I practice two hours a day for the intramural team. It might as well be in pads."

"We don't have the size," said a brother. "All the big guys are out for crew."

"Yeah, where will we get our guards and tackles?"

Another brother said the problem was image. MIT had one to live up to. "The other schools have professionals. Like the ones who play for Harvard and Yale. Here there's no way."

"There's always Bowdoin and RPI."

"Yeah."

Close said this kind of talk actually produced results in the 1940's. A team called the MIT Non-Vars (for non-varsity) managed to get itself coagulated, almost entirely from 28-year-old veterans of the V-12 program. A kind of club team. "But they couldn't even beat Belmont High," said Close, "and had no chance whatsoever against Exeter."

"The real problem," said one older boy with a beard, "is money. It would throw the whole athletic program out of whack here if you spent the kind of money you need for a football team. And it would be chaos trying to find field time. Nobody wants to give up a minute of their precious field time."

"And we couldn't get on Tufts' or Bates' or anybody's schedule for 10 years," said Close. "They make those things up so far in advance."

"Who'd want to, anyway? We get to watch the good games on Saturday afternoon, then we get to play ourselves."

"You can't compete with the professionals," said the beard. "No gate receipts, no recruiting, no scholarships, no spring practice, no four-hour practice sessions. It would be a disaster."

"I still say it'd be fun to try. There are a hell of a lot of good football players on this campus."

"Good *touch* football players."

"A football team is great for school spirit."

"Not if it loses. Watch a team lose 26 in a row and see what happens to school spirit. We may lose the spirit we already have. Hell, no. Football would corrupt the entire program."

"And that," said a brother, "would be a shame."

The student adviser was flying down to Miami for a vacation from the Draper labs and from his work at MIT, where he has gotten his Master's. He said he loved it there because he'd become involved in the sports program. He'd actually learned to play squash and was running every day and allowing Maggie Lettvin to streamline him.

He said, too, that the more he got to know the MIT kids, the more he came to realize a remarkable thing, almost a phenomenon about the kids.

"After they've been exposed to MIT a few years," he said, shaking the ice in his empty scotch and soda glass, "and get into activities and athletics, a lot of them really blossom. I mean, the change is remarkable. It seems that they're a lot more normal as seniors than they were as freshmen."

FOR FURTHER READING

1. Denlinger, K. and Shapiro, L., *Athletes for Sale,* New York: Thomas Y. Crowell, 1975.

2. Durso, J. **The $ports Factory**, New York: Quadrangle, 1975.

3. Gilbert, B. "Imagine Going to School to Learn to Play," *Sports Illustrated,* **43** (October 13): 86–98, 1975.

4. Hanks, M. P. and Eckland, B. K. "Athletics and Social Participation in the Educational Attainment Process," *Sociology of Education,* **49** (October): 271–294, 1976.

5. Hauser, W. J. and Lueptow, L. B., "Participation in Athletics and Academic Achievement: A Replication and Extension," *The Sociological Quarterly,* **19** (Spring); 304–309, 1978.

6. Landers, D. M. and Landers, D. M., "Socialization Via Interscholastic Athletics: Its Effects On Delinquency," *Sociology of Education,* **51** (October): 299–303, 1978.

7. Rehberg, R. A. and Cohen, M., "Athletes and Scholars: An Analysis of the Compositional Characteristics and Image of These Two Youth Culture Categories," *International Review of Sport Sociology*, **10** (1): 91–107. 1975.

8. Otto, L. B. and Alwin, D. F., "Athletics, Aspirations, and Attainments," *Sociology of Education*, **50** (April): 102–113, 1977.

9. Westby, D. L. and Sack, A., "The Commercialization and Functional Rationalization of College Football," *Journal of Higher Education*, **47** (November-December): 625–647, 1976.

CHAPTER 5

SOCIAL STRATIFICATION AND SPORT

Social stratification is the arrangement of any social system into a hierarchy of positions which are unequal with regard to valued characteristics such as power, property, social evaluation, and/or psychic gratification. The stratification system is impersonal and involves only the ranking of positions or the assignment of status to them rather than the ranking of persons as individuals. Thus all occupants of a position with about the same value will be viewed as equal and occupants of positions of different value will be viewed as higher, lower, superior, inferior. Persons who occupy the highly valued positions in a social system are considered to have high status. A commonly used label for strata power within the context of a society is social class. A social class is a set of persons who share similar valued characteristics of that society. The factors which show up most consistently in American social class differentiation are occupation, income, education and race. The most commonly used indices in research on social class are occupational position and educational attainment (Hollingshead, 1957; Warner, et al., 1949; Blau and Duncan, 1967). Of course, while the terms upper and lower classes are used to designate positions in the social class structure, these are not meant by sociologists to reflect value judgments; they refer, for the most part, to power and prestige, and not to moral worth.

Every social system has rules, written or unwritten, which determine how power, property, social prestige, and psychic gratification are allocated and valued. Every social system has, therefore, a stratification system. Although there are no universal criteria for status differentiation, those positions which are functionally essential to a social system and which require special aptitudes and/or skills and which require relatively full-time participation are conferred with higher evaluation. Typically, greater rewards, both material and psychological, power, and prestige are associated with these positions.

Since its beginnings, Americans have cherished the notion that this is a classless society, and this belief has become known as the American creed of equality. Hodges (1964) emphasizes the extent of this belief:

The creed of classlessness is imbedded in American folklore. It is part and parcel of the very American heritage, so much so, in fact, that to publically deny it is perilously close to blasphemy. Nor is this surprising. Much of our heritage and its accompanying ideology is premised on the compelling assumption that our worth is determined not by ancestry, but by what we, as individuals, accomplish in our own lifetimes by our own efforts. [p. 1]

Even a cursory review of American history vividly confirms the fact that this society has never been "classless" and the social ferment of the past decade has dramatically illustrated that we are indeed "class-bound" which in some respects even approaches caste characteristics, at least for a segment of our population.

If the American creed of equality is pervasive in our society, the notion of equalitarianism is even more pronounced in sport. The notion of social stratification in sport is anathema to many. Sport, many claim, is where you "make it on your own." You make it on your achievements. While there is no question that sports has many equalitarian aspects, social stratification is exemplified in various ways through sport.

Social class linkage is evident in many sports. It has been observed that sport, like fashion, tends to propagate downward in the social classes. Many sports were initially popularized by the upper classes and then adopted by the lower classes; i.e., tennis, baseball, golf, pool. School sports were started in England in the Great Public School, which were not public at all but instead were private and exclusively for the education of children of upper-class families.

There is a variety of ways in which social class is displayed through sport involvement. For example, while the upper classes purchase yachts and large cabin cruisers, the lower classes make do with small motor boats and row boats. The wealthy may own golf carts, the lower classes, if they can afford to golf at all, carry their clubs and walk. The wealthy wear expensive tennis, ski, golf, etc. sport clothing while the poor make do with the less extravagant apparel. The wealthy go on expensive hunting safaris or follow their favorite collegiate or professional team across the country while the less affluent are content to watch these events on television. Wealthy sports fans purchase box seats costing, sometimes, thousands of dollars while the poor watch on television or, if they attend the game, sit in the outfield or in the end zone.

Social stratification is evident within and between sports groups. Boxing is stratified by weight classifications; and the heavier the weight, the higher the status of the boxers. Judo has its system of "belts." Football has a neatly organized stratification system: the interior linemen play in "the pit" and are referred to as the animals. The backs, especially the quarterbacks, occupy the high-status positions—here is where the power, prestige, and rewards are in football. For anyone who doubts this, all he has to do is observe who wins the Heisman Trophy each year and which players are invariably chosen "most valuable." Social stratification is evident between sports teams since some sports are referred to as "major" and some as "minor." In some high schools the letter awards given are different for the so-called major and minor sports.

One important aspect of social stratification is the pattern of movement from position to position, and thus from one social class to a higher or lower one. Social systems differ in the processes by which movement, or social mobility, from one class to another occurs, the amount of such movement, and the different methods of institutional or internalized norms that influence these processes of mobility (Rothman, 1978). Social systems are considered to be closed or open, in terms of social mobility, depending upon the extent to which positions in the system are available to its members. In a closed, or caste, system the positions of members are fixed for a lifetime because of the possession of hereditary traits of some kind. In an open system, positions are available to be filled by the best qualified and, theoretically, one can raise or lower his position in the status hierarchy by his achievements.

A part of the American creed is that the social class structure is open— that one may go from one stratum, or class, to another. This is manifested in the so-called "equality of opportunity" or "land of opportunity" principle. Wright (1951) selected "the Horatio Alger 'rags to riches' story" as one of the basic beliefs which forms the underlying faith of American democracy. Smith (1940) describes the Horatio Alger hero as:

> A boy who was born in the slums of a great city with a very low social position, becomes a bootblack, works hard, applies himself to his studies saves his money, and rises through sheer effort to a position of social economic, and occupational importance" [p. 99].

It is often contended that sports participation is an important avenue for upward social mobility in the United States, and the "rags to riches" stories of some of the great athletes such as Joe Louis, Willie Mays, and Mickey Mantle are often cited as examples of this process. Moreover, some sociologists have advanced the idea that sports serve as an avenue for mobility of lower social class boys. For example, Havighurst and Neugarten (1957) assert that "athletic prowess combined with education often provides a very good base for mobility in a lower class boy" [p. 45]. In his text on social stratification, Hodges (1964) states that "college football has functioned as a highly effective status elevator for thousands of boys from blue-collar ethnic backgrounds" [p. 167] .

Aside from the examples of famous athletes from lower-class origins and the "off the cuff" statements of some sociologists, almost nothing is known about the actual extent to which sports participation facilitates upward social mobility, nor about the ways in which this occurs. Furthermore, there is a general impression that most athletes come from lower social class backgrounds but definite information on high school, college, and professional athletes is not plentiful.

In the first reading Walter A. Zelman examines the social class factor of occupational prestige on involvement in leisure activities, especially sports activities. It is Zelman's thesis that differences in sport participation between persons in the upper and lower social classes are not simply differences based on the costs to play them. Sports of the upper and lower classes are, according to Zelman, different social experiences, and they are differences in terms of personal needs, opportunities, and environment.

In general, lower class sports tend to be inexpensive to play, involve lots of physical contact, and are played with a high degree of competitiveness. On the other hand upper class sports tend to be expensive, do not involve much physical contact, and the competition in the contest may be irrelevant, since the participation may be viewed as a sociable event. Other differences that Zelman points out are the tendencies for the sports of the lower class to be played by the young much more than the old and by men much more than women, while upper class sports attract old as well as young and relatively large numbers of women play them.

The reading by Rabel J. Burdge extends Zelman's discussion of differences in participation in leisure activity, and focuses especially on sport participation. Though sports permeates American life, sports interest and participation are not identical in the various socioeconomic classes. Lifestyles —the kind of house and neighborhood one lives in, the kinds of books and magazines one reads, the cultural products one enjoys, and one's sports pursuits—vary from one social class to another. The author's basic proposition is that there is a relationship between occupational prestige and involvement in specific leisure activities. Although the concept "leisure activities" encompasses activities other than sports, a great deal of leisure activity is sport related, and, in fact, the author focuses specifically upon sports involvement as one prominent form of leisure activity. Burdge found several interesting relationships between sports activity involvement—both participant and spectator—and occupational prestige.

The idea that sports serve as a vehicle for upward mobility is firmly embedded in the conventional wisdom of America. Persons from lower social class backgrounds and ethnic and racial minorities are the most frequently mentioned beneficiaries of the "upward mobility through sport" belief. As noted above, there is very little empirical research to confirm this rather commonly held belief. The last reading is one of the few studies that have examined this issue. Allen Sack examined the social origins and occupational mobility of Notre Dame University football players who graduated between 1946 and 1965. He found that the football players came from lower socio-economic backgrounds than the non-football graduates. Notre Dame football players from lower middle class backgrounds were no more occupationally successful than non-players from similar origins. Former first team football players were more occupationally successful than second teamers and reserves, regardless of social origin.

REFERENCES

Blau, P. M., and Duncan, O. D., *The American Occupational Structure,* New York: John Wiley & Sons, 1967.

Havighurst, R., and Neugarten, B., *Society and Education,* Boston: Allyn & Bacon, 1957.

Hodges, H. M., *Social Stratification—Class in America,* Cambridge, Schenkman Publishing Company, 1964.

Hollingshead, A. B., "Two-Factor Index of Social Position," New Haven: privately printed, 1957.

Rothman, R. A. *Inequality and Stratification in the United States.* Englewood Cliffs, N.J.: Prentice-Hall, 1978.

Smith, M. B., *Survey of Social Science,* New York: Houghton Mifflin Co., 1940.

Warner, W. L., Meeker, M., and Eels, K., *Social Class in America,* Chicago: Social Research Associates, 1949.

Wright, D. McC., *Capitalism,* Chicago: Henry Regnery, 1951.

THE SPORTS PEOPLE PLAY

Walter A. Zelman

IN A MANHATTAN bank a dentist calculates how much money he needs for the family's ski weekend in Vermont. He does not worry about equipment; he already has $1,000 worth of that. But there are still lift tickets, transportation, lodging, lessons, and the unexpected. At the teller's window he writes $350 on a withdrawal slip. "If I'm short, he figures, "I can always use credit cards."

Seventy-five blocks uptown, on a crowded Harlem basketball court, a teenager waits for "winners." His equipment is a sweatshirt, a pair of jeans, and chain store sneakers. It is what he wears to school every day. He does not own a basketball.

Some sports are expensive to play, and some are cheap, and people with different amounts of money tend to play different ones. That much certainly must be obvious to all.

What is less obvious is that expensive and cheap sports are not simply different athletic activities; they are different social experiences as well. And as such they are more than the mere reflection of athletic tastes and pocketbook dimensions; they are integral components of vastly different sets of needs, opportunities, and environments.

No doubt, the teenager in the previous example is playing basketball primarily because he wants to play basketball. In the words of Pete Axthelm, basketball is the "city game," and he might have added inner-city game. Its best talent and its best legends (e.g., Hawkins in New York, Chamberlain in Philadelphia) come from the cities; its asphalt nature is a city nature; and because of its multitude of inner-city pros, it holds out, as does no other sport, a compelling urban dream of rocketlike social and economic mobility.

So the lower-income city youth—and especially ghetto youth—plays basketball in large part because he wants to; indeed, he loves to.

But he plays it for another reason as well. He can afford to. For him, skiing is economic fantasy. So too is golf, horseback riding, yachting, or sailing. If he occasionally dreams of venturing out into this suburban sports world, dreaming is as far as he gets.

Even tennis is probably out of his range.

Walter A. Zelman, "The Sports People Play," *Parks and Recreation Magazine,* Vol. 11 (February 1976), pp. 27–39. Reprinted by permission of the National Recreation and Park Association.

These, after all, are upper-income games. All involve some initial and continuing investments, and all are played by society's better off.

The teenager in question, though, is hardly without athletic opportunities. He can box, or run (track), and in places where it is popular, play hockey. Running and boxing will cost him nothing, and hockey nothing but a pair of skates and a stick.

He can also take up, and most likely will, any one or all of the three games that constitute the athletic bread and butter of lower-income America —baseball, basketball, and football. These, after all, are America's most popular, visible, and accessible of sports. Their countless variations—touch, flag, one-on-one, punchball, stickball, slapball, etc.—can be played anywhere, on any surface, and on any street.

And what is most important, basketball, baseball, and football are cheap. Schools and local sponsors usually pick up equipment costs when necessary, and short of that, playing these games costs next to nothing.

They are, in other words, lower-income games. Upper-income groups, to be sure, play them as well. But they do not do so as exclusively, as intensely, or as long. Indeed, there is an unquestionable and direct relationship between money and these sports. The less the athlete has of the former, the more he is likely to play the latter.

All of which might mean little were it not for the fact that upper-income and lower-income games are such dramatically different social experiences.

*Coach Tom Fears of the (*now defunct*) World Football League's Southern California Sun is talking with a reporter about training camp problems. "I got 140 men coming to camp," he says, "and beds for only 90. I got to get rid of 50 men in two days."*

"How are you going to do that?" the reporter asks.

"Mostly," says Fears, "I'm gonna see how they hit. It's a hittin' game. If you can't hit you can't play."

The most dramatic difference between lower-income and upper-income games is that the former involve physical contact, and the latter do not.

Skiing may involve courage. Sailing may entail the highest in adventure and heroics. Golf, with its miniscule margin of error, may demand the greatest control under the greatest of athletic pressure. But none of these upper-income games involves "hittin' " anybody.

Nor do they necessarily involve competition with other individuals. In upper-income games winning and losing may be relatively unimportant or even completely irrelevant.

Not so with the bread-and-butter lower-income games. One can practice— but one cannot play—basketball, baseball, or football without a human opponent. These are, almost by definition, competitions against other people. Even when two youngsters in a playground throw grounders at each other they imagine themselves to be the players who are hitting the balls.

These differences exist, in large part, because of different environments.

For youngsters raised in poorer communities, "hittin' " is often a way of life. The streets are rough. Like it or not, one gets used to physical contact with others and used to the reality that survival and getting ahead frequently depend on fast feet, strong hands, and the ability to use them.

But for youngsters in more affluent suburban areas, things are likely to be different. Be it blessing or handicap, upper-income children tend to be more sheltered and less accustomed to physical contact. The result is often less of an attraction to sports that demand such contact and a tendency, when they do play them, to do so less aggressively. As one observer of Los Angeles basketball put it, "The more south in the city you go (the more poor and black), the rougher the game gets. Basketball in the valley (suburban, white, middle class) ain't nothing like basketball in the jungle."

Lower-income youngsters may also have more need to express themselves physically and aggressively. There are more tensions in the communities they come from—more people, more poverty, more unemployment, more racial tension. Sports, especially physical contact sports, are one means of dealing with those tensions, one outlet for emotions (hostility?) which sorely need release.

One New York City high school football player expressed it in these terms: "I tried golf, but I couldn't get off. I felt all cramped up and uptight. I kept trying to hit the ball with everything I had. But the game doesn't work that way."

Standing on the other side of the football tracks, an upper-middle-income Los Angeles youth saw things rather differently. He had once loved football, he explained, at least as played in his own community and with his own friends. "We hit each other hard," he recalled, "But somehow there seemed to be limits. Then I started playing varsity football in high school, and often the limits weren't there anymore. Some guys, especially when we played some of the ghetto schools, just went too all out. They wanted to win too bad." It was not, he continued, that the game was less fun; it was "scary."

This leads to the question of competition and the myriad of sociological studies suggesting that lower-income athletes tend to take sports competition more seriously than do society's wealthier athletes.

No doubt this is because they are more likely to see sports as an avenue of social and economic mobility, and a sorely needed one at that. And undoubtedly they are aware that according to society's endless varieties of educational, social, and economic rankings, they are already far down in the loss column.

As a result, many lower-income youths experience a particularly strong need to prove and test themselves athletically and physically. Only here, in a sense, is the test a fair one. Explained one basketball player from Brooklyn's Bedford Stuyvesant area, "Basketball is the most important thing in my life.

It's a way of defining myself. When I play I play to win, and I'll do almost anything to win. You got to recognize, I ain't winning anywhere else."

In the world of the upper-income athlete, by contrast, sports competition is usually unrelated to the profundities of self-definition and self-worth. Upper-income athletes may take their sports seriously, but rarely *that* seriously. For them athletic fields are more playgrounds than proving grounds, and the sportsmanship that penetrates all of the upper-income games does so, in part because winning really is not everything and because losing really is not all that painful. Win or lose on the playing fields, the money will still be in the bank, the college education still available, and above all, the ego still intact.

Sam Snead is still competing with the best at age 63. Ted Hood captained Courageous *to victory in the America's Cup at age 47.*

But Jerry West thought he had to retire at 35. Willie Mays was over the hill at 38. Few pro football players last much beyond 35.

Most upper-income sports demand relatively little in the way of speed, strength, and contact. As a result, they can be played at all ages, as long, in fact, as the player can walk, and sometimes even after that.

In fact, a trip to the local golf course, mountain ski resort, or local marina will support the conclusion that participation in these sports not only continues into the middle ages, but actually increases. Partly, this is a direct result of money factors. These sports cost money, and the middle-aged individual who has "made it" has more of it (and more time) than the younger man or woman who is still only on the road to "making it."

But participation in upper-income games by a high percentage of middle-aged people is also a function of the physical nature of those games. They may demand exertion, coordination, and some conditioning, but they rarely involve power, great physical stress, or—as noted earlier—"hittin."

The relationship between age and participation in lower-income sports is just the opposite. In these games it is quite apparent that as the participant ages, participation decreases, eventually to the point of non-existence.

Baseball, basketball, and football, in short, can be played only as long as the player can run, and run fast. The nature of these games precludes their being played at a middle-aged half speed.

It is a sad athletic reality. Everyone today is preaching the virtues of physical recreation. But masses of football-, baseball-, and basketball-mad Americans find that after the age of 35—if not earlier—their athletic lives come to a dead end. So, they stay at home and turn on the tube. Soon they are ex-athletes, avid watchers rather than avid doers.

There is nothing to prevent them, to be sure, from taking up other games (tennis, golf, etc.) and many of them do, especially when they have come into some money. But these are not their favorite games, and learning them at 40, without too much time, poses a sizeable psychological as well as physical challenge. Many prefer to remain on the spectator side.

A young man is working hard at learning the game of golf. But after weeks of studying the great swings and practicing his own, his game shows little improvement. An elderly friend finally suggests, "You'll never learn this game until you take some lessons."

On a city playground a 13-year-old sets a pick for an older teammate. But he does it poorly, and the teammate is annoyed. "Damnit, kid," he barks, "can't you set a decent pick?" Quickly, he demonstrates the maneuver. A few minutes later the youngster does it a little better.

Different games are learned in different ways—upper-income games often in lessons with professionals, lower-income games on the street. By the time the basketball, football, and baseball players get some formal coaching, usually in high school, their skills are already well developed. Indeed, if they are not, the athlete will not make the team and, consequently, will not get any coaching at all.

Part of this difference, of course, is money. Wealthy people can afford professional lessons; poorer people cannot.

But something else is involved—the nature of the games and the skills they demand. Baseball, basketball, and football place great importance on speed, strength, and agility, skills and gifts associated with natural athletic ability. They are, in a sense, body language sports. They demand fluidity of motion and they allow for the expression of considerable physical individuality. There is no "proper" way to perform them or to learn them and, at least in the early learning stages, no dire need for "proper" instruction.

By contrast, many upper-income sports, especially golf, involve more precise and disciplined body movements. Skill in these games will depend less on natural ability and more on the development of form and the repetition of very specific movements. There is then, a "proper" way to perform these games. Lessons are almost mandatory. Otherwise, the slice will never get corrected, the topspin will never get enough kick, and the parallel turn will remain a parallel jerk.

All of which is much more than mere coincidence. Many lower-income athletes, confined in factories, small apartments, and crowded schoolrooms and streets, have little use for games which do not allow for the fullest amount of physical expression, in other words, for games which entail excessive repetition, form, and precision. Where there is a great need for the release of physical energy, the sports people play are likely to reflect that need; and such sports are likely to be unconfining, free flowing, and relatively imprecise.

Upper-income athletes rarely find their environments so physically confining. As a result, their sports may not have to provide the same degree of release or physical self-expression. Their environments are more likely to emphasize mental and physical discipline, and the sports they play reflect that emphasis.

The owner of a set of eight tennis courts on Long Island is talking about how he makes his living. "On weekends," he says, "I rent courts mostly to men. But during the week I make much more money off women."

The American sports world has always been a predominantly male world. But it is less so among the rich and more so among the poor.

Many women ski, play golf or tennis, ride, and sail. Many also participate in swimming, gymnastics, skating, track and field, and bowling. But the great majority of female participants in these sports are upper-income women, or at least middle-income women. Lower-income women are a strikingly non-participatory lot. With the exceptions of bowling and track and field, their sports universe is a very limited one.

There are a number of possible explanations for this situation, the first among them being the fact that the chauvanism of the male sports world has hit lower-income women with particular force.

The games in which women are least likely to be accepted—strenuous, contact, and highly competitive games ("unladylike" games)—are the very games which are most accessible to lower-income women. In other words, they are the games that many lower-income women would be most likely to play, and yet they are also the games in which female participation has been most discouraged.

On the other hand, sports in which female participation has been more acceptable—tennis, golf, skiing, etc.—are largely upper-income games. Most lower-income women are not very familiar with them and cannot afford to play them.

There is also the question of leisure time. Lower-income women have much less of it than upper-income women, at least in the post-school years. They work more, they tend to have more children, and they rarely have domestic help.

Finally, there is the depressing reality that the environment in which lower-income women live has always been one in which male chauvanism tends to reach particularly oppressive heights. Relative to wealthier women, few lower-income women are encouraged to break down social barriers, pursue careers, or venture into the male-dominated world of sports.

Today, more and more people are recognizing that the world of sports is a mirror of society. In the case of sports and income, the sports people play reflect the size of their pocketbooks, their needs, their opportunities, and the environments in which they live.

On the whole, lower-income sports tend to be cheap, rough, always competitive, and physically strenuous; they stress the attributes of power, speed, and natural athletic ability; and they are played by the young much more than by the old, by men much more than by women.

Upper-income sports tend to be expensive, noncontact, not necessarily competitive, and not too physically strenuous; they involve more precise, disciplined movements; and they are played by the old as much as by the young, and by relatively large numbers of women.

These overall patterns are likely to persist for some time. If the mirror analogy is accurate, radical changes in the sports world will only come with radical changes in the social, political, and economic worlds. And despite Watergate, inflation, recession, Vietnam, and all the rest, radical change in America seems to have only a distant past and a distant future.

Until these distances grow smaller, upper-income and lower-income sports will continue to be different sports experiences played by different people from different places.

LEVELS OF OCCUPATIONAL PRESTIGE AND LEISURE ACTIVITY

Rabel J. Burdge

Many sociological variables are related to leisure participation. For instance, people in high income brackets, young age categories, high educational levels, and having positions with paid vacations generally have been found to be the most active participants in structured leisure activity.[1]

For the purposes of this paper, leisure is defined as activity occurring during periods free from obvious and formal duties of a paid job or other obligatory occupation.[2] Occupational prestige is the variable here used to explain differences in the use of leisure. Membership in an occupation provides social recognition in the form of status. Society assigns higher status to individuals who are willing to acquire the necessary skill and education for complex occupations. The work experience also provides an opportunity for identity and meaningful life experience. Many of the experiences and associations gained during preparation for work and participation in it carry over to leisure time.

The general proposition guiding this study, then, is that a person's position in the occupational prestige structure is a determinant of how leisure

Rabel J. Burdge, "Levels of Occupational Prestige and Leisure Activity," *Journal of Leisure Research*, 1(3):262–274, 1969. Reprinted by permission of the National Recreation and Park Association.

is used. In short, the accruement of rewards—monetary and status—will determine the variety of leisure outlets.[3] Participation in leisure is designated as the dependent variable and occupational prestige as the independent variable. In keeping with previous research studies dealing with status evaluations the North-Hatt Occupational Prestige Scale was used as the empirical method of assigning prestige evaluations to specific occupations.

PREVIOUS RESEARCH

The most influential study relating occupational prestige levels and leisure activity was completed by Clarke (1956, p. 301). This researcher studied the relationship between social status levels as measured by the North-Hatt Occupational Prestige Scale and participation in specific leisure activities. Clarke mailed questionnaires so as to obtain at least 100 completed schedules in each of the five occupational prestige categories. He found that most of the relationships were linear or near linear; that is, participation in specific forms of leisure were common to persons in either the highest or lowest occupational prestige level. Watching television, fishing, playing poker, attending drive-in movies, spending time in a tavern, and attending baseball games were activities common to persons in the lowest occupational prestige level. Working on automobiles was associated with level IV, playing golf with level III, and weekend trips, football games, and attending parties associated with persons in level II. Most other forms of leisure such as attending concerts, playing bridge, reading books, and working in a flower garden were found to be common to persons in prestige level I. Leisure activities found to be distributed among all prestige levels include hunting, bowling, gardening, listening to the radio, and picnicking. Reissman also found differences between occupational prestige groups on such items as reading and watching television (1965, p. 76).

Other investigations, which include the research of Outdoor Recreation Resources Review Commission (1962), White (1955, p. 145), Havighurst and Fiegenbaum (1959, p. 396, Burdge (1962), and Hollingshead (1949, p. 302), have found differences in the use of leisure time among occupational prestige groups and social class levels.

METHODOLOGICAL PROCEDURES

Data for use in this study come from a random, stratified sample of persons living in Allegheny County, Pennsylvania (which includes the city of Pittsburgh). This county typifies most metropolitan areas in that it is characterized by a large central city with a declining population, an expanding suburban area, and a hinterland of mixed rural and urban influences. The employment patterns of Pittsburgh may be classed as industrial, devoted predominantly to basic metal manufacturing.

A representative sample of 1,635 individuals was drawn from the 1,628,587 people in Allegheny County. The investigation was limited to individuals eighteen or older. Thus, for the age group selected, the sample includes about one in approximately 700 people eighteen and older living in Allegheny County. The sample was stratified utilizing a series of social, income, ethnic, racial, and residential variables taken from census data. From the 1,635 persons in Allegheny County selected for personal interview, 1,562 completed schedules were obtained. This represents a completion rate of 95.3 percent. Seventy-three people, including three persons who discontinued the interview, would not cooperate in completing the scheduled list of questions. No substitutions were permitted for those who refused to answer or were not at home.

In sampling validity checks reported in detail elsewhere, it was found that the sample of respondents obtained adequately reflected the racial, age, and occupational characteristics of Allegheny County (Burdge 1963, p. 27). It therefore appears reasonably safe to generalize the findings of this study to Allegheny County and perhaps to similar metropolitan areas in the Northeast. Although the inland Ohio Valley location of Allegheny County depresses the amount of participation in both deep water and mountaineering types of recreation, it is not anticipated that the basic relationships uncovered would be altered greatly at more favored locations.

North-Hatt Occupational Prestige Categories. The North-Hatt Scale was used as a measure of occupational prestige. This scale ranks occupations according to their relative prestige in relation to other occupations. The initial rating of occupational prestige was done by a nationwide sample of adults interviewed by the National Opinion Research Center (1947, p. 10). Respondents were instructed to assign scores from zero to one hundred to a series of occupations. The higher scores were to be assigned to the higher prestige occupations. The list of occupational prestige scores from the original study has been expanded to include most common occupations.

For purposes of analysis, the North-Hatt occupational prestige scale was divided into four broad categories—functionally labeled as levels of occupational prestige. Class I includes professional and high-level management; Class II includes other white-collar workers; Class III includes skilled workers; and Class IV includes unskilled workers. These levels of occupational prestige are similar to categories developed by Clarke from the North-Hatt Occupational Prestige Scale.[4]

In selecting occupational prestige as the measure of social class, such variables as income and education are explicitly excluded. Occupation, however, generally quite accurately reflects levels of income and education. There may be some deviant cases such as the high-status college professor drawing a low salary or the blue-collar truck driver making $17,000 a year, but the normative pattern suggests that occupation is a defensible choice.

Leisure Activity. The respondents were asked if they had participated in certain leisure activities within the past year. The responses were categorized as "participation" or "no participation." Information on annual frequency of participation was obtained for certain outdoor and urban recreation activities, but this analysis is not included in the present paper.

Outdoor recreation is here referred to as that activity taking place in an outdoor setting. Urban activities refer to types of leisure that generally are done at home or in an organized commercial setting.

ANALYSIS

Two important questions are explored in this section:

Are specific leisure activities associated with a particular occupational prestige level?

What, if any, clustering of leisure activities exists for a particular occupational prestige level?

The chi-square test for significant differences was used to determine if any significant disporportionality exists between participation in a specific leisure activity and levels of occupational prestige. The analysis examines six categories of leisure activity: outdoor recreation, urban recreation, playing sports, attending sports events, hobbies, and a collection of other recreation and activity orientations of interest to planners, developers, and administrators of recreation areas.

Outdoor Recreation Activities. Table 1 shows which occupational prestige level participated most frequently in sixteen types of outdoor recreation. With the exception of picnicking, canoeing, and hiking the analysis indicates that all the relationships were significant and that persons in prestige levels I and II were the most active in the listed sixteen forms of outdoor recreation. No outdoor recreation activities were found to be most common to persons in the class III and IV prestige levels. These data also indicate that winter sports and most water-related activities were more common to persons in prestige level I, while activities such as hunting and fishing were more common to prestige level II.

These findings disagree somewhat with those of other researchers. Fishing was found to be associated more with persons in the middle prestige groups than with the lower prestige groups as reported previously by Clarke (1956, p. 301) and Burdge (1965, p. 27). Hunting, which was previously reported to be associated with the lowest prestige category, was found to be more common among persons in Class II. Picnicking appears to be common to all prestige levels. Clarke and Burdge may have reached different conclusions due to the nature of their sampling procedures. Both used mailed questionnaires which yielded low return rates and required extensive remailings. It is suggested that persons responding to a mailed questionnaire about

Table 1   Outdoor Recreation Activities by Prestige Level Participating Most Frequently*

Activity	Prestige level participating most frequently				Level of significance
	I (N = 157)	II (N = 586)	III (N = 519)	IV (N = 253)	
Picnicking	X				.10
Swimming or to the beach	X				.01
Camping	X				.05
Sailing	X				.01
Water skiing	X				.01
Nature walks	X				.05
Snow skiing	X				.01
Ice skating	X				.01
Tobogganing or coasting	X				.01
Fishing		X			.01
Hunting		X			.05
Bicycling		X			.05
Horseback riding		X			.05
Canoeing		X			NS
Other boating		X			.01
Hiking		X			NS

* The Chi-Square test of significance was used to test for disproportionality between leisure activity and the four levels of occupational prestige. In all cases a 2 x 4 table resulted with a level of significance of .10 or less being reported. The X shown in the analysis tables indicates which prestige level had the highest percentage of persons participating in the particular leisure activity. Persons in other prestige levels may also participate to a lesser degree. For example, all four groupings went picnicking, but Class I's went most often. This format for analysis and presentation follows also for Tables 2 through 6.

leisure might be more active in leisure. Nonrespondents in the present study tended to be older and unemployed.

Except for certain activities, such as canoeing which showed little response, and hiking, which was sometimes taken by respondents to mean simply walking around the block, the statistical evidence strongly suggests that persons in the higher social classes are the major users of outdoor activities. Almost 60 percent of the sample households reported participation at least once during the year, although the percentage was most frequent for Class I persons.

The significant finding for the outdoor recreation activities, with the exception of the large amount of nonparticipation by the two lower occupational prestige classes, is the syndrome of activities associated with the two upper prestige classes. There appears to be a difference based on routinely available and moderately priced recreation versus the more exclusive and expensive. Activities that might be classed as more expensive and less generally available include camping, sailing, snow skiing, water skiing, and tobogganing. Activities which are generally accessible include fishing, hunting, bicycling, and boating.

Urban Activities. Twelve types of urban recreation activity in relation to occupational prestige level are shown in Table 2. With the exception of driving for pleasure, all chi-square relationships were significant.

Urban leisure activities were most common to persons in prestige level I, with the exception of bowling and working in a vegetable garden, which were characteristic of persons in Class II and Class III, respectively. For persons in prestige level IV, no urban recreation activities were the most popular.

Another term for urban activities might well be after-work activities. Most are readily available within the immediate living environs of urban dwellers. Skill is a limitation only for the golfer and the bowler, although for the casual participant this is not a problem. A more realistic block to participation in some urban activities such as golf might be lack of money or

Table 2   Urban Recreation Activities by Prestige Level Participating Most Frequently

Activity	Prestige level participating most frequently				Level of significance
	I	II	III	IV	
Driving for pleasure	X				.10
Walking for pleasure	X				.01
Work in flower garden	X				.01
Play golf	X				.01
Go dancing	X				.01
Attend the movies	X				.01
Attend concerts and plays	X				.01
Play cards	X				.01
Spend time in a tavern, bar, club	X				.01
Attend parties	X				.01
Go bowling		X			.01
Work in vegetable garden			X		.01

perhaps lack of prior socialization in the activity. As an activity becomes more popular, it would be expected that appeal would increase for persons in all class levels. Bowling seems to be undergoing such a transition, but golf continues to be the exclusive domain of persons in the higher-status occupations.

The findings shown in Table 2 are rather consistent with status expectations. We expected and found that persons in the highest prestige category played golf, went dancing, attended concerts and plays, drank at cocktail lounges and clubs, and attended parties.[5] Some of these activities, such as golfing, spending time in a bar or club, and parties might well be dictated by occupational demands. The surprising finding is that activities such as flower gardening, dancing, attending the movies, and card playing were most common to a greater percentage of persons in the upper prestige levels. This finding appears to indicate that participation in a variety of even the more mundane leisure activities is most common among the higher prestige groups.

The activities of bowling and working in a vegetable garden were found to be common for persons in prestige levels II and III, respectively. Bowling certainly has the connotation of middle class or lower-middle class. While recreational bowling is quite popular, this sport has been sustained by bowling leagues that keep the alleys full during otherwise slack recreational periods. Working in a vegetable garden, while undeniably a relaxing activity, has certain economic value to families on a limited budget. The conclusion that status differences affect the type of gardening and that the importance of gardening for production would increase for lower-status persons appears reasonable.

Sports Activity. Table 3 shows the results of the chi-square analysis between playing certain sports and games and occupational prestige levels. Many of the results are not statistically significant, due to the small number of people who reported participation in some of the sports activities.

The results indicate that playing sports was generally most common to the two highest occupational prestige levels. Playing softball, basketball, and touch football were common to Class III, with no participation in sports common to level IV.

Although most of the statistical relationships were not significant, a general clustering of sports activity around different prestige levels appears to exist. The sports requiring individual skill and execution appear to be popular for persons in the highest prestige level. Team sports appear to be generally more popular with persons in prestige level III. This relationship, however, is not statistically significant. Persons in prestige level II have an interest in a mixture of team as well as individual sports, although only in the case of miniature golf and the driving range was the relationship significant. The finding that playing miniature golf or frequenting the driving range is a middle class to lower-middle class activity supports the earlier finding that

Table 3   Sports Activity by Prestige Level Participating Most Frequently

Activity	Prestige level participating most frequently				Level of significance
	I	II	III	IV	
Played soccer	X				NS
Played tennis	X				.01
Played badminton	X				.01
Played croquet	X				.01
Played chess	X				.01
Played checkers	X				NS
Target shooting or variation	X				NS
Played baseball		X			NS
Played volleyball		X			NS
Played archery		X			NS
Played miniature golf		X			.01
Played at the driving range		X			.01
Played wrestling		X			NS
Played softball			X		NS
Played basketball			X		NS
Played touch football			X		NS

golf—actually playing on a course—is predominantly the domain of higher-income persons.

Attending Sports Events. Attendance at sporting events was compared with occupational prestige levels using chi-square analysis as shown in Table 4. Most of the relationships were significant and indicate that persons in the highest prestige level were the most likely to attend sporting events.

Attendance at sports events follows the popular conception of high and low prestige activities. For example, high-status persons reported minimal attendance at stock car races, or boxing and wrestling matches (with the possible exception of amateur wrestling), but were most likely to watch football, soccer, or golf. Watching basketball was found to be most common to persons in prestige level II. Since the sample area was without a professional basketball team, it can be assumed that attendance was at secondary and collegiate level games.

These results differ radically, but not unexpectedly, from those of other researchers. Clarke found attendance at baseball games and the zoo common

Table 4   Attendance at Sporting Events by Prestige Level Participating Most Frequently

Sporting event	Prestige level participating most frequently				Level of significance
	I	II	III	IV	
Football games	X				.01
Baseball games	X				.01
Hockey games	X				.01
Zoo	X				.01
Soccer matches	X				NS
Golf matches	X				.01
Horse races	X				.01
Go-cart races	X				NS
Basketball games		X			.01
Stock car races			X		NS
Boxing matches			X		NS
Wrestling matches				X	NS

to the lowest prestige level, while the present study found these activities to be characteristic of persons in the highest prestige level (Clarke 1956, p. 304). The syndrome of upper middle class activity includes football games, hockey, golf, and betting on the horse races. Most of these sporting events are expensive and admission charges, with the exception of horse races, are enough to exclude lower income groups. Attendance at the zoo could very likely be part of the socialization process of upper middle and middle class persons. Attendance at soccer matches and go-cart races was so small for the entire sample to make comparison almost impossible. The general finding is that persons in the higher prestige categories tend to be the greater participants in specator sports.

A major finding in this study that runs counter to popular conception regards baseball. Most people have thought, and popular literature supports the notion, that baseball is the working man-laborer sport. According to this study most frequent attendance, and significantly so, is for the highest prestige categories. Data on the number of times respondents attended baseball games was not obtained in the questionnaire. It may be that certain members of the working class attend many games throughout the year and that many persons in the higher prestige classes attend only once a year.

Hobbies. Table 5 shows the results of the chi-square analysis between levels of occupational prestige and participation in hobbies. The results provide many instances of nonsignificance, although this was due in part to

Table 5   Hobbies by Prestige Level Participating Most Frequently

| Activity | Prestige level participating most frequently | | | | Level of significance |
	I	II	III	IV	
Sketching	X				.05
Decorating	X				.01
Refinishing furniture	X				NS
Painting	X				NS
Flower arranging	X				NS
Photography	X				.01
Music	X				.01
Reading books	X				.01
Collections	X				.01
Ceramics		X			NS
Carving		X			NS
Woodworking			X		NS
Home improvement			X		NS
Automobiles			X		NS
Motorcycles			X		NS
Cooking				X	.01
Sewing				X	NS

the small numbers of persons reporting activity in hobbies. More than half of the respondents did not report even one hobby. Persons in prestige level I generally had the greatest variety of hobbies.

Respondents in Class IV indicated cooking and sewing as hobbies. Unfortunately, the analysis did not determine if the cooking was recreational or done from necessity. Gourmet cooking, which is generally classed as a hobby, is popularly thought to be the exclusive domain of the highest prestige individuals. Woodworking, home improvement, automobiles, and motorcycles were found to be common as hobbies to persons in prestige level III. The occupations in this category mostly include persons with some technical skills that were being transferred to leisure use. The hobbies common to persons in Class I require some special talent as well as financial support and educational background.

Other Recreation Activities and Activity Orientations. Table 6 shows the relationship between levels of occupational prestige and certain forms of leisure which are of special interest to persons concerned with the future development of outdoor recreation facilities.

Persons in the higher prestige occupations appear to be among those most interested in private recreation facilities. Those who have fished at a fee

Table 6   Other Recreation Activities and Activity Orientations by Prestige Level

Activity	Prestige level participating most frequently				Level of significance
	I	II	III	IV	
Fished at fee fishing lake	X				NS
Would like to visit fee fishing lake	X				NS
Would like to hunt at commercial area	X				NS
Would like to rent a cabin or cottage	X				NS
Would like to go on a farm vacation	X				NS
Would like to camp at private camp- grounds	X				.01
Took vacation	X				.01
Took overnight trip	X				.01
Took vacation at home			X		NS
No hobbies				X	.01
Played no sports				X	.01
Attended no sports events				X	.01

fishing lake, would like to fish at a fee fishing lake, would like to hunt at a commercial hunting area, would like to and do rent cottages or cabins, would like to go on a farm vacation, and would like to camp at a private camp-ground, are more likely to come from the highest prestige occupations. These are the same people who took the most vacations and weekend trips. Those in prestige level III, however, were the most likely to have taken a paid vacation at home. Persons in prestige level IV did not have any hobbies, did not participate in sports, and did not attend sporting events.

The analysis indicates that persons in the highest prestige level would be a potential market for any type of private recreation. These persons, however, represent only about 10 percent of the families. Also, it should be remembered that verbalizing a desire and actual participation are quite different; but since persons in Classes I and II, which make up about half of the sample, were the most active in other forms of outdoor recreation, they seem to offer the best prospect for any future private development.

CONCLUSIONS

This paper has examined the relationship between specific leisure activities and levels of occupational prestige as measured by the North-Hatt Occupational Prestige Scale. It was found that persons in the highest occupational prestige level were the most active in all major types of structured leisure. Of the 82 specific forms of leisure activity here reported, persons in the highest prestige level were the most active in 57, followed by 17 for level II, 11 for level III, and 3 for level IV. Although some class differences in types of leisure behavior were found, the persons in the highest prestige classes were found to participate in the greatest variety of leisure activities.

For the outdoor recreation activities, winter and water sports, such as snow skiing, water skiing, and sailing, were significantly associated with persons in Class I. Persons in Class II were more likely to be active in such forms of outdoor recreation as fishing, hunting, and bicycling. None of the outdoor recreation activities were related statistically to persons in Classes III and IV.

Urban recreation, with the exception of bowling and working in a vegetable garden, was found to be most common to persons in prestige level I. Bowling was common to persons in level II and working in a vegetable garden common to level III.

Participating in sports activities was found to have occupational prestige differences based on whether the sport was of an individual or team nature. The higher the occupational prestige, the more likely the person was to engage in individual sports. The finding that golfing (on a golf course) was common to Class I persons with miniature golf and the driving range common to Class II persons suggests that one of the ways people prepare for entrance into a higher social class is to imitate the leisure behavior of that group.

Attendance at sports events followed a rather common-sense pattern. Events such as stock car races, boxing and wrestling matches, which have not enjoyed widespread popularity, were found to be attended most frequently by individuals in the lower prestige occupations. Most other sports events included in this study were attended by persons in the higher prestige occupations.

Hobbies were found to vary by prestige levels. Hobbies that require aesthetic and educational background were common to persons in Class I. Hobbies that require a special occupational skill, such as woodworking and automobiles, were common to the prestige levels that include skilled workers. Finally, hobbies that have a daily, functional application were common to persons in the lowest prestige groups.

Questions concerning the desire to utilize private recreation facilities were analyzed in relation to levels of occupational prestige. Persons in the highest occupational prestige level were the most likely immediate prospects for future participation in private outdoor recreation.

This study indicates that the concept that various forms of leisure or free-time activity are associated with specific social classes should be re-examined. The data presented here show that for almost every type of leisure activity the probability is that, proportionately, the participants will come from the middle or upper classes. Persons in these occupations, while not generally experiencing a decline in the length of the work week, are afforded sufficient income to pursue leisure in their free moments. Another reason for greater participation by the upper prestige occupations is that their life experience opens up a variety of opportunities. Education tends to broaden one's perspective and the income from better-paying jobs allows opportunity to explore a variety of leisure pursuits. Persons in the working or lower occupational groupings tend to have limited education and life experience. They tend to interact with other persons of limited perspective, and they may also feel that many forms of leisure are not open to them simply because of their class position.

By including only "structured" forms of leisure activity in the interview schedule certain types of free-time activity common to persons in lower prestige occupations may have been excluded. It may be that unstructured activity such as "sitting" and "talking" is more common to persons in this prestige level. A detailed investigation focusing on this particular group would be helpful in better understanding their leisure styles.

This paper does not suggest that most structured forms of leisure activity are the exclusive domain of the two highest class levels. Except for the activities of snow skiing, sailing, attending golf matches, and ceramics, some frequency of participation was noted in each activity for each class. The normative styles of persons in Classes I and II suggest, however, that they are the present participants in leisure activity. The long-term trend in American society is for professional, business, and white-collar occupations to increase, and for blue-collar and semi-skilled occupations to decline. It is suggested that the leisure styles found to be associated with Class I and II persons will become more widespread as the occupational composition of American society becomes more like persons represented in this study by Class I and II persons. As the general level of affluency increases, however, leisure and recreation styles may diffuse more rapidly from upper to lower classes.

NOTES

1. Structured leisure refers to that activity which is specifically named and has societal recognition to the extent that persons derive status from the social structure for participating in the activity. Structured leisure is the opposite of activity that is nondescript and provides no specific status for the participant.
2. This definition, with some slight rewording, is similar to that proposed by Lundberg, et al. These researchers noted that "leisure is popularly defined as the time we are free from the more obvious and formal duties which a

paid job or other obligatory occupation imposes upon us." George A. Lundberg, Mirra Komarovsky, and Mary Alice McInery, *Leisure: A Suburban Study* (New York: Columbia University Press, 1934), p. 2.

3. The effect of work or occupation on other types of nonwork behavior has not been ignored in sociological thought. Sorokin points out that in a society with a complex division of labor, the occupation exerts influence in the form of occupational selection and in "molding the body, mind, and behavior of its members." On this last position he notes that "the occupation group is one of the most indispensable coordinates for a definition of the sociocultural position in an individual. . . ." See Pitirim A. Sorokin, *Society, Culture, and Personality* (New York: Cooper Square Publishers, Inc., 1962), pp. 211 and 215.

4. See Alfred C. Clarke, "The Use of Leisure and Its Relation to Levels of Occupational Prestige," *American Sociological Review,* Vol. 21 (September, 1956), pp. 301–312. The present study utilized the following ranges in the North-Hatt scores for the four levels of occupation prestige: Class I, 93–75; Class II, 74–65; Class III, 64–54; and Class IV, 53–35. These categories were developed on the basis of the normal curve which ideally places 16 percent of all respondents in Class I, 34 percent in Class II, 34 percent in Class III, and 16 percent in Class IV. However, due to frequent cases of many persons receiving the same score (107 steel workers received the North-Hatt score of 60) it was not possible to achieve these ideal divisions. The empirical categories yielded 10.4 percent of the sample in Class I ($N = 157$), 38.7 percent in Class II ($N = 586$), 34.3 percent in Class III ($N = 519$), and 16.6 percent in Class IV ($N = 253$). This measure of occupational prestige was found to correlate with education +.470, family income +.468, and with a measure of social class—based on social and economic data from census tracts—of +.374.

5. Unfortunately, these data did not distinguish between the separate establishments of taverns, cocktail lounges, and clubs. It might be expected that different status groupings would frequent different surroundings. However, most of the responses to this question came from persons in Class I.

REFERENCES

Burdge, Rabel J., "Occupational Influences on the Use of Outdoor Recreation," Ph.D. dissertation, The Pennsylvania State University, 1965.

Burdge, Rabel J., and others, 1962, *Outdoor recreation research: a pilot study of the economic, sociological and physical aspects of private and public outdoor recreation in a selected Ohio county,* Columbus: The Natural Resources Institute, The Ohio State University.

Clarke, Alfred C., 1956, "The use of leisure and its relation to levels of occupational prestige," *American Sociological Review,* **21**:301–7.

Department of Agricultural Economics and Rural Sociology, The Pennsylvania State University, 1963, "The North-Hatt Scale," mimeographed.

Havighurst, R. J., and Fiegenbaum, K., 1959, "Leisure and life style," *American Journal of Sociology,* **64**: 396–404.

Hollingshead, A. B., 1949, *Elmtown's Youth,* New York: Wiley.

Lundberg, George A., Komarovsky, Mirra, and McInery, Mary Alice, 1934, *Leisure: A Suburban Study,* New York: Columbia University Press.

North, Cecil C. and Hatt, Paul K., 1947, "Jobs and occupations: A popular evaluation," *Opinion News* (September).

Outdoor Recreation Resources Review Commission, 1962, *National Recreation Survey,* Study Report No. 19, Washington, D.C.: Government Printing Office.

_____ , 1962, *Outdoor Recreation for America,* Washington, D.C.: Government Printing Office.

_____ , 1962, *Participation in outdoor recreation: Factors affecting demand among American adults,* Study Report No. 20, Washington, D.C.: Government Printing Office.

Reissman, Leonard, 1954, "Class, leisure, and social participation," *American Sociological Review,* **19**: 76-84.

Sorokin, Pitirim A., 1962, *Society, Culture, and Personality,* New York: Cooper Square Publishers.

White, R. C., 1955, "Social class differences in the use of leisure," *American Journal of Sociology,* **61**: 145-50.

COLLEGE FOOTBALL AND SOCIAL MOBILITY: A CASE STUDY OF NOTRE DAME FOOTBALL PLAYERS

Allen L. Sack and Robert Thiel

It is a widely held belief that college football has been an effective avenue for upward social mobility. Thousands of boys, so the argument goes, would never have risen above their humble origins if they had not received athletic

*This is a revised version of a paper delivered at the annual meeting of the American Sociological Association at San Francisco, September, 1978. The authors are indebted to the University of New Haven for providing financial support for this study and to Gina R. Sack, Thomas Mordecai and Cynthia Kranyik for assistance in gathering, coding, and processing the data.

Allen L. Sack and Robert Thiel, "College Football and Social Mobility: A Case Study of Notre Dame Football Players," *The Sociology of Education,* Vol. 52 (January 1979), pp. 60–66. Reprinted by permission of The American Sociological Association and the authors.

scholarships. One has only to point to such parvenu celebrities as Joe Namath, O. J. Simpson, or Franco Harris for evidence in support of this view. The main purpose of this study is to determine whether conventional wisdom concerning big time college football and social mobility holds up under empirical investigation.

There are a number of empirical studies which show that athletic participation in high school is positively related to academic achievement (Schafer and Armer, 1968; Phillips and Schafer, 1971) and to educational expectations (Bend, 1968; Rehberg and Schafer, 1968; Schafer and Rehberg, 1970; Spreitzer and Pugh, 1973; Snyder and Spreitzer, 1977). All of this research suggests that sport involvement in high school in some way enhances an athlete's chances of attending college and of becoming upwardly mobile later in life. Few studies, however, have examined the consequences of sport participation at the college level for an athlete's career mobility.

It is hard to deny that commercialized college football, as played at schools like Notre Dame, Texas, or the University of Nebraska, makes far greater demands on an athlete than is typically the case in high school. Thus, it is reasonable to expect that athletes will face many obstacles in obtaining their college educations they did not encounter at high school level. In other words, even if athletes benefit in a number of ways from high school sport, their experiences might be quite different at the big time college level.

Sage (1967) and Webb (1968) provide evidence that college athletes are less successful academically than non-athletes. Sage compared two groups of former high school athletic stars; one group chose to play college sport while the other did not. Sage found that non-athletes received better grades, were more occupationally oriented, and were less concerned about fraternities and campus social life than athletes. Webb, in a study of Michigan State athletes, found that only 49 percent of the team athletes as opposed to 70 percent of the regular Michigan State students had actually graduated when five years had lapsed since the graduation of their original college classes.

The argument that college sport often interferes with an athlete's intellectual development is supported by a number of former college athletes (e.g., Meggysey, 1970; Scott, 1971; Shaw, 1972; Edwards, 1973; Sack, 1977). All of these writers found the demands of "big time" college sport to be incompatible with the pursuit of a first rate education. While the views of former athletes and the work of Sage and Webb do not provide enough solid empirical evidence to make firm conclusions, they do at least suggest that participation in college sport might in some way hinder career mobility.

Many of the studies of college athletes, as Loy (1969) points out, have either focused on their social origins (McIntyre, 1959; Webb, 1968) or on their careers after graduating from college (Coughlan, 1956; Litchfield and Cope, 1962; Crawford, 1962). There have been few attempts, however, to compare an athlete's status of origin with his status later in life.

Loy (1969), in his study of athletes from UCLA, attempted to correct this shortcoming. By using mailed questionnaires, Loy was able to gather data on the social origins as well as the present social statuses of 845 life pass holders at UCLA. To obtain a life pass, an athlete must have competed at the college level for 4 years and have earned at least 3 varsity letters. Loy utilized the Duncan Socioeconomic Index (SEI) to rate an athlete's first job after graduation (status of entry), present job (status of destination) and his father's job when the athlete entered college (status of origin). By comparing the mean SEI scores for fathers and sons, Loy was able to derive a measure of social mobility.

Loy's use of data on origins and destinations was a marked improvement over earlier studies, but he failed to deal adequately with a number of other important methodological problems. Most importantly, he failed to use a control group of college students who were not varsity athletes. Thus, there is no way of knowing whether the mobility experienced by ballplayers in his study was a consequence of athletic participation or whether ballplayers and non-ballplayers alike experienced mobility during this period due to factors unrelated to athletic involvement.

Loy's study was also deficient in that it only included subjects who had at least three varsity letters. Thus, average and reserve ballplayers were excluded. The tendency to focus on star athletes when discussing sport and social mobility is a major problem with many studies in this area. An adequate study of how participation in college football affects social mobility must include all ballplayers who experienced the rigors of commercialized college sport. It is important to emphasize that most big time college ballplayers never reach the star category and many never earn a letter. There is also a sizeable number of athletes who receive scholarships, attend practice for 4 years, but never dress for a game. To exclude such ballplayers would be a gross oversight.

METHODS

In the present study, the social origins and career mobility of 2 groups of college graduates were examined—former Notre Dame football players and Notre Dame students who were not varsity athletes. Social rank was measured in a number of ways. The Hollingshead Two Factor Index of Social Position (ISP) and the Duncan SEI were used as measures of social status. In addition, income and educational attainment helped to locate respondents in the stratification system. Social mobility was measured by examining the status, educational and income attainment of respondents who came from similar social origins. By social origin was meant the father's social rank when the respondent entered Notre Dame.

The sample consisted of 344 Notre Dame football players who graduated between 1946 and 1965. It also included 444 randomly selected regular students who graduated from Notre Dame during that same period.[1] The years 1946-1965 were chosen because graduates during that era should now be well established in their careers. A twenty-year span was chosen to insure that a large number of football players could be included. The oldest subjects in the study were around 55, the youngest 35. Care was taken to include first team, second team and reserve ballplayers in the sample. It should be noted that Notre Dame was an all-male university during this period.

Data were gathered by use of a mailed questionnaire. Current mailing addresses of ballplayers and regular students were obtained from the Alumni Records Office at Notre Dame. Lists of football players were derived from rosters in football *Dopebooks* that were published yearly during the period under investigation. Only seniors were taken from each roster. A systematic sample of regular students was drawn from names in alumni files. Of the 788 questionnaires mailed out, 759 actually reached the respondents. The returned questionnaires numbered 482, with 218 coming from ballplayers and 264 from regular students. The overall response rate of 64 percent was about equal for both ballplayers and regular students.[2]

FINDINGS

It is clear from Table 1 that Notre Dame players came from lower socio-economic backgrounds than average Notre Dame students. In education, income and in social status (Hollingshead ISP), the fathers of ballplayers rank much lower than the fathers of regular students.

Table 1   Percentage Distribution of Indicators of Social Origin by Type of Student

Father's Education	Players (N = 215)	Students (N = 261)	Total
16 years or more	15.8	36.7	130
12-15 years	29.3	33.3	150
Less than 12	54.9	30.0	196
Father's Income*	Players (N = 202)	Students (N = 238)	Total
$40,000 +	15.9	39.5	188
$20-39,000	28.2	29.0	126
Less $20,000	55.9	31.5	126
Father's Class (ISP)	Players (N = 205)	Students (N = 248)	Total
Upper	23.4	53.2	180
Middle	25.4	25.4	115
Lower	51.2	21.4	158

*Father's income is based on 1977 dollars.

Note: In this and in all subsequent tables, the total number of ballplayers and students should be 218 and 264 respectively. Where this is not the case, it is because of missing data.

X^2 is significant at .001 for all three indicators.

Table 2 indicates that both ballplayers and regular students have experienced considerable status mobility. The mean Hollingshead ISP scores of respondents whose fathers were from classes IV and V reveal that both ballplayers and regular students have moved well beyond their social origins.[3] A two way analysis of variance indicates that the main effect of student type on respondents' ISP is not statistically significant, nor are there any significant interactions. Thus, ballplayers were no more or less mobile than regular students. The main effect of father's status on son's status, however, is statistically significant at the .03 level.[4]

It is obvious that the rather high social status enjoyed by the respondents can be largely attributed to their being college graduates. The fact that the Hollingshead ISP as well as other indices of social status rely heavily on education as a factor impairs somewhat their usefulness in assessing differences in social rank within a sample of college graduates. It should be noted, however, that the use of educational attainment, independent of the occupational factor in Hollingshead's index, reveals some important differences among Notre Dame graduates.

Table 3 indicates that Notre Dame football players were less likely than regular students to have earned graduate or professional degrees, regardless of father's educational attainment. Of the regular students whose fathers did not graduate from high school, 44 percent earned advanced degrees. This was true of only 29 percent of the ballplayers from similar origins. This would suggest that the former experienced greater educational mobility. It would also appear that for players and regular students alike, there was a positive relationship between father's and son's educational attainment.

A two way analysis of variance examining the effects of father's income and student type on son's income found no statistically significant main effects or interactions. It is clear, however, that both ballplayers and regular students experienced considerable income mobility. Even respondents whose fathers made less than $15,000 a year (adjusted to 1977 dollars) now have a mean annual income of over $30,000 (see Table 4). A three way analysis of variance using father's income, father's education, and rank on football team, i.e., first team, second team or reserve, as independent variables and son's income as the dependent variable, uncovered only one statistically significant main effect. That was the effect of rank on team. The absence of any statistically significant interactions means that the relationship between rank on team and son's income holds up regardless of father's education and income.

Table 5 clearly illustrates this relationship between a ballplayer's rank on the football team in his senior year and his present income. Whereas 41 percent of the first team ballplayers are now making $50,000 or more, this is true of only 30 percent of the second teamers and 13 percent of the reserves. Table 5 also indicates that there is very little difference in income attainment when regular students are compared with ballplayers as a whole.

Table 2   Mean Hollingshead ISP Scores of Ballplayers and Regular Students Controlling Father's ISP*

	Father's ISP Score					
Student Type	I (11–17)	II (18–31)	III (32–47)	IV (48–63)	V (64–77)	Total
Players	15.3(12)	19.5(35)	19.9(51)	20.3(74)	19.5(31)	19.6(203)
Students	16.6(57)	18.5(74)	18.0(63)	17.4(46)	18.2(6)	17.7(246)
Total	16.4(69)	18.8(109)	18.9(114)	19.2(120)	19.0(37)	18.6(449)

*In Hollingshead's ranking system, ISP scores range from a high of 11 to a low of 77.

Table 3   Percentage of Respondents Who Earned Advanced Degrees by Type of Student and Father's Education

	Father's Education							
Student Type	16 or more years	(N)	12–15 Years	(N)	Less than 12 Years	(N)	Total	(N)
Players	38.2	(34)	34.9	(63)	28.8	(118)	32.1	(215)
Students	55.2	(96)	50.6	(87)	43.6	(78)	50.2	(261)
Total	50.8	(130)	44.0	(150)	34.7	(196)	42.0	(476)

Table 4 Mean Income of Ballplayers and Regular Students Controlling Father's Income (In Thousands of Dollars)*

Student Type	Father's Income					Total
	-$15,000	$15-$19,999	$20-$29,999	$30-$39,999	$40,000+	
Players	35 (70)	33 (42)	37 (46)	41 (11)	44 (31)	37 (200)
Students	36 (35)	35 (40)	36 (43)	36 (24)	38 (94)	36 (236)
Total	35 (105)	34 (82)	36 (89)	38 (35)	36 (125)	37 (436)

*The means in this table were calculated on the basis of midpoints of intervals. Income categories ranged from 1 to 8 with 1 being 0–$4,999 and 8 being $50,000+. All entries are rounded to nearest thousand.

Table 5 Percentage Distribution of Respondent's Present Income by Type of Student and Rank on Football Team

Income	Student Type		Rank on Team		
	Players	Students	1st	2nd	Res.
$50,000–	29.6	24.3	41.0	29.8	13.1
$30–49,999	29.2	35.2	25.3	26.3	36.1
Less $30,000	41.2	40.5	33.7	43.9	50.8
Total	(216)	(259)	(95)	(57)	(61)

X^2 for student type and income is not significant at .05.
X^2 for rank on team and income is significant at .05.

A player's rank on the team, while influencing income, had little effect on a player's social status or educational attainment. A two way analysis of variance examining the effect of father's ISP and rank on team on son's ISP revealed that only father's ISP had a statistically significant main effect. Furthermore, while 42 percent of the second teamers, 33 percent of the reserves and only 29 percent of the first team ballplayers earned advanced degrees, this difference was not statistically significant at the .05 level.

DISCUSSION

From the above findings it can be concluded that both Notre Dame football players and regular students have experienced considerable upward social mobility. Only in educational attainment beyond a college degree do the two groups differ significantly. The fact that the respondents were all at least college graduates has undoubtedly contributed to their general success. Among ballplayers, rank on the team appears to have had a marked impact on income mobility.

The finding that ballplayers earned fewer advanced degrees than other students may indicate that athletes set a lower priority on academic accomplishment. Then again, the demands of commercialized college football may force even academically oriented ballplayers to do only enough studying to get by. What many people fail to realize, or refuse to acknowledge, is that big time college football demands as much time and energy as professional football. When presented with the statement, "playing football at Notre Dame is as physically and psychologically demanding as playing in the National Football League," 64 percent of the respondents who had actually played pro ball agreed or strongly agreed. Only 32 percent were in disagreement and 4 percent were undecided.

Given the fact that big time college athletes work as hard as professionals, it is not surprising that many of them take academic shortcuts. When asked if they cheated in school work while at Notre Dame, 69 percent of the ballplayers and only 43 percent of the regular students admitted having done so. Ballplayers were also found to be under-represented in fields that require considerable scholarly commitment (such as science and engineering) and had lower grade point averages than regular students. As a result of the lower priority athletes are often forced to give to education, it is to be expected that they would earn fewer advanced degrees than other students.

The finding that first team ballplayers experienced greater income mobility than second teamers and reserves, while not surprising, is nonetheless open to a variety of interpretations. One could argue that the fame the first team athletes receive gives them entree to high paying positions which demand people with celebrity status. This fame is even enhanced if an athlete has a successful career in professional football. Paul Hornung, Daryl Lamonica, Myron Pottios, and Nick Pietrosante are just a few of the many Notre

Dame graduates in the sample who were able to capitalize on their stellar careers in professional football.[5]

It might also be argued, however, that the interpersonal skills and character traits which make successful athletes are precisely those which make successful entrepreneurs. Athletes who rise to the top in the often brutal competition of big time college football may be best suited for careers in business. This study uncovered no significant status differences among first team, second team and reserve ballplayers. Likewise, the careers pursued by all three categories of ballplayers were fairly similar. There is one occupational difference though that is worth noting. Of the first team ballplayers, 34 percent are presently top executives in their companies, i.e., presidents, vice presidents, assistant vice presidents, or treasurers. This was true of only 13 percent of the second teamers and 14 percent of the reserves.

Whether the income and business success of first team athletes is the result of their celebrity status or their ability to thrive in highly competitive situations is a question worthy of further research. Further research should also explore in greater detail other differences among star, journeyman, and marginal college athletes. This is especially important in studies of sport and social mobility. An issue that was not raised here is how do ballplayers fare who do not graduate from college? It would also be useful to compare the career mobility and academic accomplishments of athletes who attend a wide variety of academic institutions. A comparison of big time college athletes with athletes in the Ivy League might be particularly revealing in this regard. These are just a few of the many possibilities for further research in this area.

NOTES

1. Of the 482 respondents who returned the questionnaires, 12 reported that they never received their degrees. Only one of those was a former football player.
2. It should be noted that the age distributions for football players and regular students who returned the questionnaires were almost identical.
3. The use of Duncan's SEI yielded very similar results. The mean SEI scores of ballplayers and regular students who came from lower status origins were 74 and 78 respectively. Given the fact that the mean SEI scores for the fathers of both groups were in the 30's, it is clear that the respondents have experienced considerable status mobility.
4. In this and all subsequent ANOVA, effects have been estimated using the least squares approach to unequal cell N's. Post-hoc between-group comparisons were made using the Scheffe approach, a conservative test appropriate to the non-orthogonal design.
5. It should be noted that 59 percent of first team athletes, 28 percent of second teamers and only 8 percent of the reserves went on to play pro ball. Nonetheless, a two way analysis of variance examining the effects of team rank and playing pro ball on present income revealed that only team rank had a statistically significant main effect.

REFERENCES

Bend, E., 1968, *The Impact of Athletic Participation on Academic and Career Aspiration and Achievement*. New Brunswick, N.J.: The National Football Foundation Hall of Fame.

Coughlan, R., 1956, "What happens to football players?" *Sports Illustrated* (September 24) (October 1).

Crawford, A. B., 1962, *Football Y Men: 1872-1919*, Men of Yale Series. New Haven: Yale University Press.

Duncan, O. D., 1961, "A socioeconomic index of all occupations." Pp. 109-138 in Albert J. Reiss, et al., *Occupations and Social Status*, New York: Free Press.

Edwards, H., 1973, *Sociology of Sport*. Homewood, Ill.: Dorsey.

Litchfield, E. E., and M. Cope, 1962, "Saturday's hero is doing fine."*Sports Illustrated* (July 8):66-80.

Loy, J. W., 1974, "The study of sport and social mobility," Pp. 249-268 in George H. Sage (ed.), *Sport and American Society*. (2nd ed.) Reading, Ma.: Addison Wesley.

McIntyre, T. D., 1959, *Socio-economic Background of White Male Athletes from Selected Sports at The Pennsylvania State University*. Unpublished M.Ed. thesis. The Pennsylvania State University.

Meggysey, D., 1970, *Out of Their League*. Berkeley: Ramparts.

Phillips, J., and W. E. Schafer, 1971, "Consequences of participation in inter-scholastic sports: A review and prospectus," *Pacific Sociological Review* 14 (July):328-338.

Rehberg, R., and W. E. Schafer, 1968, "Participation in interscholastic athletics and college expectations," *American Journal of Sociology* 73 (May):732-740.

Sack, A. L., 1977, "Big time college football: Whose free ride?" *Quest* 27 (Winter):87-96.

Sage, J. N., 1967, "Adolescent values and the non-participating college athlete." Paper presented at the convention of the Southern Section of the California Association of Health, Physical Education, and Recreation. San Fernando, CA.

Schafer, W. E., and J. J. Armer, 1968, "Athletes are not inferior students." *Trans-Action* 5 (November):21-26, 61-62.

Schafer, W. E., and R. Rehberg, 1970, "Athletic participation, college aspirations, and college encouragement," *Pacific Sociological Review* 13 (Summer): 182-186.

Scott, J., 1971, *The Athletic Revolution*. New York: Free Press.

Shaw, G., 1972, *Meat on the Hoof.* New York: St. Martin's.

Snyder, E., and E. Spreitzer, 1977, "Participation in sport as related to educational expectations among high school girls," *Sociology of Education* **50** (January):47-55.

Spreitzer, E., and M. Pugh, 1973, "Interscholastic athletics and educational expectations," *Sociology of Education* **46** (Spring):171-182.

Webb, H., 1968, "Social backgrounds of college athletes." Paper presented at the National Convention of the American Association of Health, Physical Education, and Recreation. St. Louis, Mo.

FOR FURTHER READING

1. Berryman, J. W. and Loy, J. W., "Secondary Schools and Ivy League Letters: A Comparative Replication of Eggleston's 'Oxbridge Blues'," *British Journal of Sociology* **27** (March): 61-77, 1976.

2. Dubois, P. E., "Participation in Sports and Occupational Attainment: A Comparative Study," *Reseearch Quarterly* **49**: 28-37, 1978.

3. Gruneau, R. S., "Sport, Social Differentiation and Social Inequality," in *Sport and Social Order,* Donald W. Ball and John W. Loy (eds.), Reading, Mass.: Addison-Wesley, 1975, pp. 117-184.

4. Loy, J. W., "Social Origins and Occupational Mobility Patterns of a Selected Sample of American Athletes," *International Review of Sport Sociology* **7**: 5-26, 1972.

5. Martin, T. W. and Berry, K. J., "Competitive Sport in Post-Industrial Society: The Case of the Motocross Racer," *Journal of Popular Culture* **8** (Summer): 107-120, 1974.

6. Massengale, J. D. and Farrington, S. R., "The Influence of Playing Position Centrality on the Careers of College Football Coaches," *Review of Sport and Leisure* **2** (June): 107-115, 1977.

CHAPTER 6

WOMEN AND SPORT

The personal-social aspects of women's life in American society is currently one of the most lively topics in the social sciences. College classes on Psychology of Women, Sociology of Women, etc. are becoming commonplace, and some colleges have even initiated programs leading to a major in "Women's Studies." While the "Women's Liberation" movement has been omnipresent in recent years, there is no area of human activity that has experienced a greater transformation of women's roles than sports.

Until recent years, women have played a minor role in the history of sport. Women were literally excluded from sports in ancient Greece (except in Sparta). Indeed, women were strictly barred from even viewing the Olympic Games, and punishments were prescribed for any woman caught at the Games. The women did, however, create their own program of sports— The Heraea Games, in honor of Hera, the wife of Zeus. These were athletic events, held every four years, for women only. This might be called the beginning of women's sports. But only in the past fifty years, with the emancipation of women from home responsibilities and their securing of equal status with men in most spheres of life, have women begun to take a prominent part of the world of sport.

Several factors account for the insignificant position of women in sports history. First, in most societies, the woman's cultural tasks have been child rearing and "home making." These tasks leave little time for participation in sports. Even the play pastimes of young girls have been largely limited to "playing house"—taking care of dolls, cooking mud pies, and dressing up like mother. Also, girls have been expected to take care of younger siblings, thus limiting their own play time. Second, there has been a deep-seated suspicion that vigorous sports were a health hazard for women. Folklore about how sports might be injurious to the child-bearing ability of women has persisted for centuries. Finally, social mores of masculine-feminine sex roles have been a powerful influence in discouraging women from participating in sports, particularly highly competitive activities. Boys have been encouraged to develop sports prowess, while girls have been restrained from sports activities and urged to act "feminine," that is, to show dignity and charm. This lack of encouragement has, of course, had the effect of destroying interest in sports performance for women.

Prior to 1860 very few women were active in American sports; then in the latter years of the nineteenth century archery, croquet, tennis, golf, and cycling began to attract women. With the rise of sports interest in the United States in the early years of this century, sports enthusiasm of girls and women increased, interschool sports teams flourished until, by 1930, many of the excesses of men's sports became the excesses of women's sports. Educators and physicians rose to protect women against sports. And protect them they did, not only from the evils of highly organized competition but also from competition itself. For a number of years, school competition in many forms was forbidden for girls and women. New leadership in the physical education and sports fields in the past ten years has caused the pendulum to swing back to a greater encouragement of sports participation for girls and women.

Probably the greatest impetus to women's sports has been the Olympic Games. Women's events first appeared in the modern Olympics in 1912 in Stockholm, Sweden, and were confined to swimming and diving competition. In 1928, women were allowed to compete in track and field events. But the participation of American women in the Olympics remained at a low ebb until success in the 1956 and 1960 Games sparked a widespread enthusiasm for women's sports competition. The interest generated by the Olympics is reflected in other recent developments. The Division of Girls' and Women's Sports of the American Alliance for Health, Physical Education, and Recreation has begun to actively promote interschool sports programs, and since 1963, has developed policies for competition in girls' and women's sports on all educational levels. An annual schedule of national intercollegiate championships in sports for college women was initiated in 1969. In the past ten years the Association for Intercollegiate Athletics for Women (AIAW) has become the most powerful organization for the promotion of female athletics.

The history of sport has been the history of male domination. In the first reading Mary E. Duquin examines the heritage of female involvement in sport by first reviewing social and psychological motivations about the general perceptions of sex roles. This is followed with a careful examination of three distinct cultural perspectives of sport: sport perceived and conducted as an agent of masculine orientation, sport perceived and conducted as an instrumental activity appropriate for both sexes, and sport perceived and conducted as an androgynous activity. In the latter, sport is viewed "as an activity in which both instrumental and expressive behaviors are experienced, where agency and communication can merge."

In the second reading Janet Lever focuses attention on how play and games serve as avenues for informal learning, and specifically on how social skills emerge as a consequence of a particular style of play. Lever used a variety of techniques to ascertain the play activities cf elementary school children. Her data show that there are significant differences in the organization of play between boys and girls, and that the primary difference is in the complexity of the social setting in which play occurs. Lever found that boys' play is more complex than girls' play. She suggests that the differences in the play forms engaged in by boys and girls may give males an advantage in the adult occupational world that share structural features with complex games.

The final reading is a critical essay on the emerging interscholastic and intercollegiate athletic programs for girls and women. First, Sage suggests that the leaders of revolutionary movements often get co-opted into the mainstream of a social system. Sage claims that the early trends of the growing female sports programs give every indication that these programs are adopting all of the features of the traditional male programs. Rather than developing an alternative sports model emphasizing equal sports opportunities for *all* females, the female sports programs are becoming just as elitist and discriminatory as male programs. The author argues that the "educational" potential of school athletics for females is being sacrificed in the quest to make the programs exactly like the male programs.

THE ANDROGYNOUS ADVANTAGE

Mary E. Duquin

Within the past decade, sport has undergone a variety of judicial analyses. Critics have explored the areas of sport ethics, economics, politics, racism and sexism.[18,25] Currently, one of the most controversial and dramatic issues in sport is that of female equality in opportunity and involvement in the sport experience.

The history of sport is generally one of masculine domination.[47] Such domination results from cultural patterns and perceptions which determine not only who participates in sport but how sport is conducted and experi-

Mary E. Duquin, "The Androgynous Advantage," *Women and Sport: From Myth to Reality*, Carole A. Oglesby (ed.), pp. 471–483, published by Lea & Febinger, 1978. Reprinted by permission of author, editor, and publisher.

enced. However, male dominated sport is becoming an antiquated concept in many corners of the sport world, and today's emphasis on the growth and expansion of women's involvement in sport has important implications for how sport will be perceived and conducted in the future.

The more interesting areas of investigation involve questions concerning how sport involvement could affect women, how female involvement in sport could change society's perception of sport, and how society's perception of sport influences the number of women attracted to the sport experience.

The basic issues of how cultural perception and psychological motivations relate to the general perception of sex roles and psychological well-being will be explored. Then three different cultural perceptions of sport, sport perceived and conducted as an agent of masculine orientation, sport perceived and conducted as an instrumental activity suitable for both sexes and sport perceived and conducted as an androgynous activity, will be examined in greater detail.

SOCIO-PSYCHOLOGICAL PERCEPTIONS OF SEX ROLES

The socially distinct roles played by men and women lead societies to label certain behaviors and traits as masculine and certain others as feminine. This bipolar view of behavior has both historical and cross-cultural significance.[37] Generally, the traits needed to fulfill a given sex role are considered desirable for that sex.[3] Thus, for example, in many cultures the child-rearing domestic female must be able to perform expressively. Expressive behavior is characterized by the capability to be understanding, sympathetic, affectionate, compassionate and tender. These traits, together with others such as sensitivity, warmth and shyness, combine to form a social image of femininity. Likewise, in many cultures the publicly oriented male must perform instrumentally, that is, be independent, assertive, ambitious, aggressive, and willing to take risks. Thus, a socially "masculine" or instrumental image is described in terms of leadership, dominance and competitive tendencies.

The fact that societies generally ascribe instrumental traits to males and expressive traits to females does not assure the validity or desirability of such ascriptions. Nevertheless, the subsequent belief that sex-typed socialization of individuals contributes to psychological well-being and healthy social adjustment has usually followed.[5] In some societies such segregation of sex roles may function efficiently. However, the more complex the society is, that is, the greater number of roles which must be learned, the more dubious the efficiency of such a system, and the greater the likelihood of sex-typed role conflict.

The participation of women in sport has often been cited as an example of this role conflict.[24] Various writers have claimed that the role of the expressively-oriented female is in conflict with the role of the instrumentally-oriented athlete.[53] Some writers have even proposed that female participation in sport robs males of the right to sport as an agent of masculine orientation.[19,50] The implicit assumption here is that psychological health and social adjustment rests on the maintenance of instrumentality as a male preserve and expressiveness a female preserve. Recent developments in social psychology, however, have stressed the need to reassess the definition of psychological well-being as it relates to the practice of sex-typing.[3,10,31] Research on highly sex-typed individuals has provided evidence which supports the belief that a high degree of sex role development is not conducive to behavioral flexibility and does not necessarily facilitate general social or psychological well-being.[4]

Studies on females have shown that high femininity is associated with poor adjustment, low social acceptance, and high anxiety.[14,22,49] Research on high masculine adult males has shown them to have high anxiety, and neuroticism and low self-acceptance.[23,34,35] Maccoby[31] has summarized the research on the effect of sex-typing on intellectual development and has found that greater intellectual development seems to be associated with cross sex-typing. In describing cross sex-typing Bem[2] states, "In girls, impulsiveness and aggressiveness are positive factors, whereas fearfulness and passivity are negative factors. In boys, the pattern of correlations is exactly the reverse." Cross sex-typed individuals have been found to have higher creativity, higher spatial abilities and higher overall intelligence.[31]

The benefits of cross sex-typing have important implications for interpreting the research regarding female participation in a culturally perceived cross sex-typed activity such as sport. High scores on the personality dimensions of autonomy and achievement orientation so often reported for female athletes provide evidence as to the ability of these women to be instrumentally oriented.[9,17,36] Further research suggests, however, that although female athletes see themselves as instrumental in sport situations, they see themselves as typically feminine (expressive) in social situations.[32,38] Although some research has found female athletes to score below the norm on some feminine traits,[26] typical measures of masculinity and femininity tend to polarize male and female attributes, rendering impossible the recognition of individuals who perceive themselves as both instrumental *and* expressive, (i.e., androgynous).[4] The psychological rubric "androgyny" describes those persons who perceive themselves as being both instrumental *and* expressive, both assertive *and* yielding, both masculine *and* feminine.[4]

Proceeding with a firm belief in the existence of androgynous persons, Bem[6] constructed the Bem's Sex Role Inventory (BSRI) which places masculinity and femininity in two dimensions, thus allowing for the identification of the androgynous individual. On the BSRI scale individuals score masculine, feminine or androgynous according to the degree of difference between their masculinity and femininity scores. Using the BSRI to classify individuals masculine, feminine or androgynous, Bem[4] tested the assumption that sex-typing contributes to psychological well-being and behavioral flexibility. Bem tested the hypothesis that sex-typed individuals would tend to exhibit defensive trait-like consistency in their responses to situations which call for behavior in conflict with their perceived sex role expectations (i.e., feminine, or masculine). Androgynous individuals as Bem hypothesized are expected to exhibit behavioral flexibility by performing effectively in both the instrumental and expressive domains.

The experimental results of Bem's research[5,8] found that given an instrumental task, males and females who scored androgynous or masculine on the BSRI performed significantly better than males and females who scored feminine. When given an expressive task, Bem found that androgynous and feminine individuals performed better than masculine individuals.

In a further study on the avoidance of cross-sex behavior, Bem[7] found that sex-typed individuals were more likely than sex-reversed or androgynous individuals to prefer sex-appropriate activity and to resist sex-inappropriate activity. Results also indicate that when required to perform a cross sex-typed activity, the sex-typed individuals experienced the most discomfort and felt the worst about themselves.

As a whole, Bem's research shows that individuals with androgynous capabilities are more likely to possess behavioral flexibility and psychological well-being in today's complex society.

An important sports education problem, stemming from androgyny research, concerns the vital need to develop in feminine females a sense of instrumentality. In addressing this problem three important issues must be raised. The first concerns how females might come to feel instrumental. An understanding of this issue is suggested by self perception theory which states that,

"Individuals come to 'know' their own attitudes, emotions and other states partially by inferring them from observation of their own overt behavior and/or the circumstances in which this behavior occurs."[3]

This suggests that the process of socialization can work in both directions, i.e., "I am what others tell me I should be" and "I am the way I see myself behave."

According to self-perception theory, females may come to view themselves as being capable of instrumental activity if they observe themselves engaging in instrumental activities.

The second issue concerns what activities may facilitate instrumental development. Assuming sport provides instrumental experiences and research shows that females benefit psychologically if their sense of instrumentality is nourished, then sport could and should make a significant contribution to the development of female instrumentality.

The final problem concerns how to induce females to engage in instrumental activities given that "feminine" females avoid participation in such cross sex-typed activities.

In attracting females to the sport experience, one of the more important aspects to consider may be the way sport is perceived. Such perception may influence both the type and number of females attracted to the sport experience. In addition, how sport is conducted influences the kind and quality of experience provided by the sport encounter.

As a result of various social forces (e.g., the Women's Movement, Civil Rights Movement) U.S. culture is slowly evolving its view of sport, especially as it relates to female participation. The direction of change is from a perception of sport as an "agent of masculine orientation" to a perception of sport as an "instrumental" activity open to and desirable for both sexes. A third and more desirable perception of sport as "androgynous" activity, that is, an activity which requires and fulfills both instrumental and expressive tendencies is proposed.

The following sections explore these three cultural perceptions of sport, and the effects of these perceptions on the type and number of females attracted to the sport experience.

SPORT AS AN AGENT OF MASCULINE ORIENTATION

Literature in the fields of psychology and sport psychology give much support to the view that sport and athletics are generally perceived as a male sex-typed activity.[15,27] Everything from children's textbooks to the toys parents buy for their children attests to the perceived masculine orientation of sport.

Experiments on parents indicate that male infants are physically stimulated, thrown about and played with more roughly than their female counterparts. Although there is no physical rationale to justify differential treatment, parents treat female infants as if they were more fragile. Research involving older children finds that parents give male children more autonomy and freedom to explore the environment than female children. These freedoms correlate highly with non-verbal and spatial abilities in which boys, on the average, excel girls.[16,27]

One of the most extreme sex differences found in childhood occurs in play behavior. Boys and girls discover early what are considered appropriate games, toys and playmates for their sex. In nursery school boys tend to play in larger groups than girls and tend to aggress and roughhouse more than girls. By second grade both girls and boys classify athletics as a masculine activity.[45]

Parents also encourage and reward sex-typed behavior as illustrated in the types of toys they buy for their girls and boys and the kind of clothing in which they dress their children. Little girls are often clothed in dresses which are inappropriate for vigorous physical play.

In elementary textbooks the masculine image of activity is reinforced. Child, Potter and Levine[13] discovered that girls in these books risk little and gain little. The passivity ascribed to females causes them to be portrayed as lazy far more often than males. Investigating California State Series texts, Kidd[28] found sexual role dramatized in the following way:

"Mark! Janet. . . .!" said Mother
"What is going on here?"
"She cannot skate," said Mark
"I can help her.
I want to help her
Look at her, Mother.
Just look at her.
She is just like a *girl*.
She gives up."

Mother forces Janet to try again.

"Now you see," said Mark.
"Now you can skate.
But just with me to help you."

These books reinforce in the minds of girls *and* boys that sport, vigorous activity and risk-taking are appropriate behaviors for males but not for females. As Bem[3] states, "When females appear, they are noteworthy primarily for what they do *not* do. Boys in these stories climb trees and fish and roll in the leaves and skate. Girls watch, fall down, and get dizzy."

Within the framework of this perception the female psyche is perceived as too weak or nervous for the strain of sport competition and the female body is described as inefficient or unsuited for sports.[11] Participation of females in sport is seen somehow to lower the quality of sport participation and spectatorship.[20] The results of perceiving sport as an agent of masculine orientation has serious consequences for the conduct of sport programs.

The primary indication that sport is being conducted as a male sex-typed activity is the greatly different status accorded male and female sport programs. The higher priority given male sport programs as regards facilities, equipment, publicity, coaches' salaries, training, awards, and budget indicates that sport is being perceived as an activity considered primarily for males.

Perceiving and conducting sport as a sex-typed activity has significant effects on both males and females as well as on the profession of physical education itself. Much professional time has been devoted to discussing, debating, deciding and then dictating what females should and should not be allowed to do in the realm of sport. Certain sports and sport events are deemed inappropriate or even illegal for female participation.[33] For example, females are restricted from pole vaulting, high hurdles, hammer-throw and

long distance Olympic swimming and running events. Inappropriate sports
include wrestling, football and ice hockey.

Females are artificially limited, before the fact, by rules based on preconceived notions of what is appropriate or even what is humanly possible for
them to achieve. Males, however, are allowed to repeatedly redefine their
human limits by striving to achieve beyond known boundaries.

Physical education curricula are also affected by sex role expectations.
Typical of curricula which espouse a philosophy based on fulfilling pupil
needs, the California State Department of Education's Physical Education
Framework[12] advocates that girls spend a greater percentage of their time in
dance than boys and that boys spend a greater percentage of their time in
team sports and physical fitness activities. Conditioning exercises for "figure
control" and improvement of "posture" are also a special recommendation
for girls.

These curricula recommendations are usually suggested without the
benefit of any substantiating physiological research data. Why boys need
sports more than girls and why girls need dance more than boys is not explained. What does seem to be a logical result of this lopsided curricula,
however, is that physical education programs produce many rhythmical
females who bemoan the fact that they are destined to dance alone!

Such sex biased curricula are based on traditional notions of what males
and females should learn. This curriculum bias is akin to a U.S. history course
which requires that only the girls learn about the suffrage movement and
the boys learn about the World Wars, because that is where their interests lie.
As Wilson[51] so aptly questions, "Do we or do we not have a subject matter"
in physical education.

Wherever sex bias infiltrates, curricula and teachers alike are affected.
Another effect of sex typing sport as masculine is that physical abilities and
coordinations become associated with males and, as a result, teachers often
expect much less of their female pupils in the early grades and, in turn, come
to offer less to them in the upper grades. Although the literature does not
support physiological sex differences which would significantly affect physical skill performance in the pre-pubescent child, teachers and tests will often
set much lower standards for girls or expect less from them.[52] And as teacher
expects of a child is exactly what occurs, be it good performance or poor
performance.[40]

Within the sex-typed view of sport, girls are more likely to come to view
their bodies as passive objects to be adorned rather than as active and able
agents to be used to control and direct their destiny. Consequently, females
are less likely to develop their physical potentials. Sex-typing sports and
sport proficiency as masculine tends to set up the masculine standard as the
norm. Thus if a girl runs or bats a ball correctly, she is said to "Run like a boy"
or "Bat like a guy." Females come to learn that correct and coordinated
movement patterns are associated with males and that uncoordinated and

inefficient movement patterns are associated with females i.e., "He runs like a girl—help him." Some girls come to accept this standard for feminine movement and ability as normal and consequently have a poor concept of themselves in sport performance situations.[42] This attitude can detrimentally affect movement patterns and physical attributes and thus severely handicap women with regard to their perceived or actual ability to operate, by choice or by chance, independently without the protection or assistance of a male.

Sport perceived and conducted as an agent of masculine orientation thus appears to have a number of negative consequences for females. However, one final characteristics of this sport perception is important to mention. Sport perceived as an agent of masculine orientation is conducted as a highly instrumental activity characterized by a strong emphasis on the participant's autonomy-power capabilities and the end results achieved. Sport conducted with such extreme instrumental orientation is likely to develop the characteristic of high masculinity. That is, sport, untempered by a sufficient concern and sensitivity to people and processes, is likely to be characterized by arrogance, exploitation and callosity. The traditionally unexpected involvement of women in sport has resulted in women avoiding the roles of sport victim or victimizer, roles which often characterize activities conducted with extreme instrumental orientations.

IMPLICATIONS FOR FEMALE PARTICIPATION

The major result of perceiving sport as an "agent of masculine orientation," that is an instrumental activity suitable only for males, is that a majority of females will not desire prolonged or serious participation in such an activity. This fact has been substantiated by research which has found that the importance of participating in sport declines drastically for girls around puberty.[16,46] The important issue of female performance in sport and female attraction to sport must be considered when evaluating the effects of sport perception.

Using Bem's psychological categories, predictions can be made about how psychologically predisposed each group of females is toward high performance in sport. Holding physical potential constant, both androgynous and masculine females should be able to perform well on a cross sex-typed activity like sport. The psychologically "feminine" female, however, given the same physical potential for performance, would not be expected to perform as well. Because of her sex typing she would likely experience psychological conflicts which would inhibit her performance.

If one assumes that people are attracted to those activities they perceive as being compatible with their own psychological frameworks, then it is possible to determine how attracted each female group is to the sport experience. Bem's data suggest that "feminine" females, when given a choice, would reject sport as an activity they would enjoy performing because they perceive sport as a cross sex-typed activity and would therefore feel uncomfortable performing instrumentally.

Table 1 illustrates the expected female attraction to and performance in sport perceived and conducted as a masculine activity. Masculine and adrogynous women are expected to be moderately attracted to such sport and are expected to perform well. Feminine women, however, are expected to have a low attraction and low performance in sport.

In summary, sport, when perceived as an instrumental, cross sex-typed activity has little overall appeal to women and has a low appeal to the feminine female who, in fact, has the greatest need for experiencing such instrumental activities.

SPORT AS AN INSTRUMENTAL ACTIVITY FOR BOTH SEXES

The cultural perception of sports as an instrumental activity open to and desirable for females is a growing but not yet established perception. This perception enlarges upon the sex-typed perception of sport as an agent of masculine orientation by advocating that females can and should benefit from the instrumental sport experience. An important aspect of this perception of sport is the right of women to develop their physical potentials, appreciate their physical abilities and enjoy the mastery of their bodies in sporting activity.

Another aspect is the equalitarian approach to sport which claims that *if* participation in sport is going to mold leaders, build stamina, heighten competitive spirit, produce physical fitness, create mental toughness and put students through college, then girls, as well as boys, should have equal opportunity to participate in sport and gain such benefits. However, sport perceived as an instrumental activity for both sexes is based upon and includes more than just the value of equalitarianism. Viewing sport from this perspective affects the sex-typed value of instrumentality.

The effect of changing the perception of sport from a sex-typed activity to a sex neutral activity has some intriguing psychosocial consequences.

Society has traditionally expected males to be instrumental, not expressive and females to be expressive, not instrumental. Perceiving sport as an

Table 1   Sport Perceived as an Agent of Masculine
Orientation

Females Classified on the BSRI	Expected Performance	Expected Attraction
Masculine	High	Moderate
Androgynous	High	Moderate
Femine	Low	Low

instrumental activity open to and desirable for both sexes in effect says instrumentality is a valuable trait for both males and females. This neutralization of instrumentality as a male preserve does not in any way neutralize expressivity as a female preserve. Thus, under this perception males are still expected to be solely instrumental, while females are expected to be both instrumental and expressive. The perception that instrumentality is important for both sexes has the effect of elevating the status of instrumental traits and behaviors over expressive traits and behaviors. One further step results in the subtle assumption that instrumentality is *the* only "orientation for a healthy adult to possess." [10]

As an instrumental activity, sports focus is a product versus process orientation. Instrumental sport is primarily concerned with the ends achieved. This instrumental perspective is successfully portrayed in common locker room slogans such as those reported by Snyder.[43] These slogans deal with themes of aggressiveness, competitive spirit, stamina, and discipline, all important aspects of instrumental sport.

> Win by as many points as possible
> Give 100 percent or get out
> We issue everything but guts
> Be good or be gone
> Winning beats anything that comes in second
> No one likes a loser
> A moral victory is like kissing your sister
> Live by the code or get out
> They ask not how you played the game but whether
>   you won or lost
> No one ever drowned in sweat
> Be a doer not a tryer
> We don't want excuses we want results

Women's orientation to sport has traditionally not been this highly instrumental. In fact, research on sex differences in achievement motivation and task competence[48] indicates that women "do not especially learn to value assertive competence above other goals" especially those of affiliation or acceptance by others. Females are more oriented toward "doing something for its own sake without concern for payoff values, becoming absorbed in the task whatever its difficulty," whereas the male orientation is toward "power of winning over the demands of an external task," toward "performance that requires assertiveness via power, autonomy and achievement." Researchers do, however, suggest that given consistent exposure to socially evaluative settings, females are likely to adopt the more instrumental orientation.[48]

Sport conducted as an instrumental activity valuable to both sexes is as stated previously, a philosophically equalitarian approach to sport and is characterized by a sexually equal apportionment of sport opportunities and materials. Recent legislation, such as Title IX of the Educational Amendments Act of 1972, reflects the legal efforts to bring about comparable sport programs in terms of curricular offerings, facilities, equipment, scholarships, competitive opportunities, budget, training and coaching.

Because the perception of sport as an instrumental activity for both sexes is an evolving cultural perception, implications of this perception must necessarily be predictive in nature.

One significant consequence an instrumental orientation of sport for both sexes has, is that programs for women would be created where previously no sport programs existed. Institutions which do provide programs for females may have to alter their programs to establish parity with the existing men's programs. Men's programs *may* be comparable with the women's programs; however, given the greater instrumentality, higher status and culturally valued support of men's programs, legal pronouncements would likely have the effect of requiring women's programs to model themselves on the men's programs or show just causes for the differences in their programs.

Sport, conducted as an instrumental activity, would give primary attention to the more talented and serious sport pursuer as opposed to the less instrumental more expressive participant. Thus inter-scholastic and inter-collegiate sport programs would have higher priority than intramural sport programs. Whereas, in the preceding perception, sports was pursued by nearly all boys as a masculinizing experience, instrumental sport for both sexes would patronize those highly talented individuals of both sexes. Thus poorly skilled boys may find less pressure and possibly less opportunity to participate in intramural sport when financial limitations require assessment of program importance. Conducting sport as an instrument activity open to females would tremendously alter the present sport establishment. Institutions would support women in their desire to explore and expand their physical potentials, pursue sport careers and exhibit pride in their physical capabilities.

Society would construct reward systems for women who have the capabilities and talent to "make it" in the realm of instrumental sport. Physical abilities would be rewarded for both sexes. However, with instrumentality the overriding principle of sport, males may still be considered to be more instrumental in sport because of their general ability to outperform females in those sporting activities involving power, speed and strength. In any case, instrumental sport will require that women, like men, be able to "sell" their sport ability to the public. Finally, sport conducted from this perspective would be likely to enlighten men to the sporting abilities of women, upgrade the quality of female sport performance and improve the overall physical potential of those women attracted to the sport experience.

Table 2   Sport Perceived as an Instrumental Activity for Both Sexes

Females Classified on the BSRI	Expected Performance	Expected Attraction
Masculine	High	High
Androgynous	High	High
Feminine	Low	Low-Moderate

IMPLICATIONS FOR FEMALE PARTICIPATION

Again the assessment must be made as to which females would be attracted to sport perceived as an instrumental activity and how well they would perform. Bem's data[5,7] would support the hypotheses that masculine and androgynous women would react as they did to sport as a cross sex-typed activity. Both androgynous and masculine women should perform well and be attracted to sport as an instrumental activity for females. Given that sport is defined as an instrumental activity open to *both* sexes, the "feminine" females should have a low to moderate attraction to sport but their actual performance in sport would still likely be low in comparison to masculine and androgynous women. Table 2 is a synopsis of these implications.

The feminine female perceiving sport as an instrumental experience would still have a difficult time finding her way into the sporting experience. If participation in sport becomes part of the social identity of a girl's peer group, then the feminine girl may be pressured into participating and may thus be exposed to instrumental experiences. However, if only successful participants are given the rewards of sport and her level of performance is low, she may decide to change her friends in order to avoid the unrewarding sport experience. In any case, repeated failure in sport would not be conducive to maintaining her involvement. The status of sport in the individual peer group, the individual's ability to perform instrumentally and the attraction of the sport experience all mediate in determining the feminine females' involvement in sport.

THE FUTURE OF SPORT: ANDROGYNY

Androgynous sport is perceived as an activity in which both instrumental and expressive behaviors are experienced, where agency and communion can merge.[6] Western culture perceives sport as primarily instrumental. The question to ask is whether only instrumental qualities are inherent in sport or whether Western societies have merely inhibited or ignored what might be termed the more expressive aspects of the sport experience. According to an androgynous perspective, sport can involve the following expressive experiences:

1. Moving with child-like joy and cheerfulness

2. Experiencing passive, defensive, yielding movements

3. Moving and responding to others by understanding what they are communicating non-verbally

4. Moving delicately, tenderly, gently

5. Becoming aware and sensitive of others, their presence, their movements, their emotions

6. Creating beauty with movement, sensing the aesthetic nature of human movement

7. Sensing the introspective quality of becoming absorbed in one's bodily movements and feeling at one with one's body.

Perceiving sport this way is possible because sport is basically human movement and human movement has an infinite variety of qualities. The instrumental view of sport does not necessarily encourage the recognition or emphasis of these other experiences. An androgynous view of sport recognizes the importance of both the sport process and the sport product.

Historically and philosophically the majority of women leaders in physical education have directed their programs for girls from what may be termed an expressive perspective. Product (i.e. winners, stiff competition, high level performance, dedicated training) was ideally to play a subordinate role to process.[11] Given this expressive ideal as the goal, but aware of the product orientation of sport as males played it, (in practice), many female sport encounters were probably quite androgynous.

Some present day organizations are attempting to combine this process-product orientation of sport. The Escelen Sport Institute is one example of an organization which is conducting sport from a more androgynous perspective. An expert from the *Escelen Sport Center News* states:

Western Culture is goal and competition oriented. Many of us overemphasize these aspects and in the process lose the sense of present-time involvement. With it we lose the intense joy of immediacy and the kind of focus that allows for supreme performance, no matter what the activity. One of the greatest challenges to modern man is finding personal balance."

The traditional Eastern orientation to sport is also a more process-product approach which emphasizes body awareness, sensitivity, meditation, and joy. The path of sensitivity to the expressive element in sport culminates in quality performance.[41] Authors writing on the humanistic movement in sport have also urged that present day instrumental sport become more attuned to the individual, to the expressive element in sport, and to the zestful process of sport itself.[39]

There are many indications that sport is being experienced as an androgynous activity. The participant feels a sense of fulfillment when participating, as well as when winning. She feels joy, strength, thrill, competence and control when sporting whether in practice or competition. She performs ethically, drawing her ethics from her own self-conscience, with standards which if necessary could rise above a coach's instructions. She performs with confidence and comradeship. She thinks deeply of the balance between means and ends, between seriousness and play. And she thinks it important to live fully all moments in sport. This kind of sport may be difficult to experience if teammates, opponents and coaches approach sport from a totally instrumental perspective. It may also be difficult to experience given the research on overjustification effects,[30] if money, scholarships and extrinsic incentives are perceived as improving the total sport experience. Extrinsic motivations may benefit instrumental sport but may retard the experience of androgynous sport.

Critics may fear that conducting sport as an androgynous activity may result in a deterioration of the quality of sport performance. However, the Eastern perspective and writers, such as Leonard[29] who are familiar with Eastern philosophy, do not predict a lower performance but rather a higher quality more harmonious sport response. The quality of the sport experience would also be enhanced by a mutually respectful and honest relationship between athlete and coach. In addition, sport programs would provide for social as well as competitive experiences between teams and participants. Androgynous sport would provide a mechanism by which the values and viewpoints of the athlete could be recognized and considered in decisions which affect the sport participant and the conduction of sport. Finally, the sport experience would be conducted so as to make operational both instrumental and expressive values thereby providing an enticing and creative medium of human expression for both sexes.

IMPLICATIONS FOR FEMALE PARTICIPATION

Bem's research would support the hypothesis that androgynous and masculine women would both be able to perform well in androgynous sport, although depending upon the specific sport's expressive requirements, androgynous females may perform better. In considering attraction to sport, both masculine and androgynous females should be attracted to sport with the androgynous females being likely to exhibit the stronger attraction. Finally, the feminine woman, who at last has found a substantial expressive component in sport, would for the first time, be expected to perform moderately well. Feminine females would also be expected to show a moderate attraction to androgynous sport (Table 3).

Table 3   Sport Perceived as an Androgynous Activity

Females Classified on the BSRI	Expected Performance	Expected Attraction
Masculine	Moderate-High	Moderate-High
Androgynous	High	High
Feminine	Moderate	Moderate

Androgynous sport would be expected to appeal to the largest number of female participants. Those females who perceive themselves as highly expressive would be able to feel that sport is an activity which could fulfill expressive needs. Likewise, androgynous sport would also appeal to those females who enjoy seeking out instrumental activities.

Returning once again to Bem's conclusion,[6] if it is true that "what separates women from one another is . . . whether their sense of instrumentality or agency has been sufficiently nourished . . ." then, as a means of attracting feminine females to engage in instrumental activities, androgynous sport would appear to be the most attractive perception of sport.

EPICENISM: A STEP BEYOND ANDROGYNY

The androgynous person is one who is able to perform and feel instrumentally and expressively. And sport, viewed androgynously, allows for both instrumental and expressive activity. However, as Bem[6] states:

> The concept of androgyny contains an inner contradiction and hence the seeds of its own destruction . . . the concept of androgyny necessarily presupposes that the concepts of masculinity and femininity themselves have distinct and substantive content. But to the extent that the androgynous message is absorbed by the culture the concepts of masculinity and femininity will cease to have such content and the distinctions to which they refer will blur into invisibility. Thus when androgyny becomes a reality, the concept of androgyny will have been transcended.

Thus, the step beyond androgyny is epicenism, the quality of being held in common by both sexes. When society reaches the perceptual point of epicenism, behavior, including sport behavior, will have no gender. Sport will then be perceived as human activity.

REFERENCES

1. Bem, D.: *Self Perception Theory,* New York, Academic Press Inc. 1972.

2. Bem, S. and D. Bem: *Homogenizing the American Woman: The Power of an Unconscious Ideology.* Unpublished manuscript, 1972, P. 8.

3. Bem, S.: Psychology looks at sex roles: Where have all the androgynous people gone? Paper presented at the UCLA Symposium on Women, Los Angeles, May 1972.

4. Bem, S.: The measurement of psychological androgyny. *J. Consulting and Clinical Psychology,* **42,** 155, 1974.

5. Bem, S.: Sex role adaptability: One consequence of psychological androgyny, *J. Personality and Social Psychol.,* **31,** 634, 1975.

6. Bem, S.: Beyond androgyny: Some presumptuous prescriptions for a liberated sexual identity. Paper presented at the National Institute of Mental Health Conference on New Directions for Research in the Psychology of Women, Madison, Wisconsin, May, 1975.

7. Bem, S. and E. Lenney: Sex typing and the avoidance of cross-sex behavior. *J. Personality and Social Psychol.,* **33,** 48, 1976.

8. Bem, S., W. Martyna and C. Watson: Sex typing and androgyny: Further explorations of the expressive domain. *J. Personality and Social Psychology,* **34,** 1016, 1976.

9. Bird, E. J.: A review and evaluation of the assessment of aggression among women athletes as measured by personality inventories. Proceedings of the fourth Canadian symposium on psycho-motor learning and sport psychology. Waterloo, Ontario, Canada, October, 1972, Pp. 353–364.

10. Broverman, I. K., D. M. Broverman, F. E. Clarkson, P. S. Rosenkrantz and S. R. Vogel: Sex role stereotypes and clinical judgments of mental health. *Journal of Clinical and Consulting Psychology,* **34,** 1, 1970.

11. Burchenal, E.: A constructive program of athletics for school girls: Policy, method and activities. *American Physical Education Review,* **24,** 272, 1919.

12. California State Physical Education Framework, Sacramento, California, 1973.

13. Child, S., E. Potter and E. Levine: Children's textbooks and personality development: An exploration in the social psychology of education. In J. Posenbleth and W. Allensmith, (Ed.), *Causes of Behavior: Readings in Child Development and Educational Psychology.* Rockleigh, New Jersey, Allyn, 1960.

14. Cosentino, F. and A. Heilbrun: Anxiety correlates of sex-role identity in college students. *Psychology Reports,* **14,** 729, 1964.

15. Cratty, B.: *Social Dimensions of Physical Activity.* Englewood Cliffs, New Jersey, Prentice-Hall Inc., 1967.

16. Cratty, B.: *Psychology and Physical Activity.* Englewood Cliffs, New Jersey, Prentice-Hall, Inc., 1968.

17. Dayries, J. and R. Grimm: Personality traits of women athletes as measured by the Edwards Personal Preference Schedule. *Perceptual and Motor Skills,* **30**, 229, 1970.

18. Edwards, H.: *Sociology of Sport.* Homewood, Illinois, The Dorsey Press, 1973.

19. Fisher, A.: Sports as an agent of masculine orientation. *The Physical Educator,* **29**, 120, 1972.

20. Gilbert, B. and N. Williamson: Sport is Unfair to Women. *Sports Illustrated.* May 28, 1973, Pp. 88–98.

21. Gilbert, B. and N. Williamson: Are you closed minded? *Sports Illustrated.* June 4, 1973, Pp. 45–55.

22. Gray, S.: Masculinity-femininity in relation to anxiety and social acceptance. *Child Development,* **28**, 203, 1957.

23. Harford, T., C. Willis and H. Deabler: Personality correlates of masculinity-femininity, *Psychological Reports,* **21**, 881, 1967.

24. Hart, M.: Stigma or prestige: The all American choice. In G. McGlynn (Ed.), *Issues in Physical Education and Sports.* Palo Alto, California, National Press Books, 1974, Pp. 214–220.

25. Hoch, P.: *Rip Off the Big Game.* Garden City, New York, Doubleday and Co., Inc., 1972.

26. Ibrahim, H.: Comparison of temperament traits among intercollegiate athletes and physical education majors. *Research Quart.,* **38**, 615, 1967.

27. Kagan, J. and H. Moss: *Birth to Maturity.* New York, John Wiley and Sons, Inc., 1962.

28. Kidd, V.: Now you see, said Mark. *New York Review of Books.* September, 35, 1970.

29. Leonard, G.: Winning isn't everything, it's nothing. *Intellectual Digest,* October, 1973.

30. Lepper, M. R., D. Greene and R. Nisbett: Undermining children's intrinsic interest with extrinsic reward: A test of the overjustification hypothesis. *Journal of Personality and Social Psychology,* **28**, 129, 1973.

31. Maccoby, E. E.: Sex differences in intellectual functioning. In E. E. Maccoby (Ed.), *The Development of Sex Differences.* Stanford, California, Stanford University Press, 1966, Pp. 25–55.

32. Malumphy, T.: Personality of women athletes in intercollegiate competition. *Research Quarterly,* **36**, 610, 1968.

33. Metheny, E.: Symbolic forms of movement: The feminine image in sports. In *Connotations of Movement in Sport and Dance.* Dubuque, Iowa, Wm. C. Brown Co., 1965, Pp. 43-56.

34. Mussen, P.: Some antecedents and consequents of masculine sex-typing in adolescent boys. *Psychological Monographs, 75,* No. 506, 1961.

35. Mussen, P.: Long-term consequents of masculinity of interests in adolescence. *Journal of Consulting Psychology, 26,* 435, 1962.

36. Neal, P.: Personality traits of US women athletes who participated in the 1959 Pan-American Games as measured by EEPS. Master's thesis, University of Utah, Salt Lake City, Utah, 1963.

37. Ortner, S.: Is female to male as nature is to culture? In M. Rosaldo and L. Lamphere, (Eds.), *Woman, Culture and Society.* Stanford, California, Stanford University Press, 1974, Pp. 67-87.

38. Rector, J.: Selected personality variables in social and competitive situations as perceived by female athletes. Masters of Science thesis. Pennsylvania State University, 1971.

39. Scott, J.: Sport and the radical ethic. In G. McGlynn, (Ed.), *Issues in Physical Education and Sport.* Palo Alto, California, National Press Books, 1974, Pp. 155-162.

40. Silberman, C.: *Crisis in the Classroom.* New York, Random House, 1971.

41. Smith, A.: The Zen approach to sports. *Psychology Today, 9,* 48, 1975.

42. Smith, H. and M. Clifton: Sex differences in expressed self concepts concerning the performance of selected motor skills. *Perceptual and Motor Skills, 14,* 71, 1962.

43. Snyder, E.: Athletic dressing room slogans as folklore; a means of socialization. *International Review of Sport Sociology,* 7:89-100, 1972.

44. Spino, M.: Sports and the energy body. *Escelen Sports Center News,* I, 1973.

45. Stein, A. and J. Smithells: Age and sex differences in children's sex role standards about achievement. *Developmental Psychology, 1,* 252, 1969.

46. Tyler, S.: Adolescent crisis: Sport participation for the female. In D. Harris (Ed.), *DGWS Research Reports: Women in Sports, 2,* 27, 1973.

47. Van Dalen, M. and B. Bennett: *A World History of Physical Education.* Englewood Cliffs, New Jersey, Prentice-Hall, Inc., 1958.

48. Veroff, J., L. McClelland and D. Ruhland: Varieties of Achievement Motivation. In M. Mednick, S. Tangri, and L. Hoffman (Eds.), *Women and Achievement.* Washington, D.C., Hemisphere Publishing Corp., 1975, Pp. 172-205.

49. Webb, A.: Sex role preferences and adjustment in early adolescents. *Child Development, 34,* 609, 1963.

50. Werner, P.: The role of physical education in gender identification. *The Physical Educator*, **29**, 27, 1972.

51. Wilson, B.: The battle between the sexes in physical education. *The Physical Educator*, **29**, 139, 1972.

52. Wyrick, W.: The physiological support system. In E. Gerber, J. Felshin, P. Berlin and W. Wyrick (Eds.), *The American Woman in Sport*. Reading, Massachusetts, Addison-Wesley Publishing Co., 1974, P. 475.

53. Zobel, J.: Femininity and achievement in sports. In D. Harris (Ed.), *Women and Sport: a National Research Conference*. Pennsylvania State HPER Series No. 2, 1972, Pp. 203-224.

SEX DIFFERENCES IN THE COMPLEXITY OF CHILDREN'S PLAY AND GAMES

Janet Lever

The cognitive development theorists in psychology, most notably Jean Piaget, have traced the growth in knowledge and perceptions through the various stages of childhood. To date, little has been done to chart the parallel development of interpersonal skills needed as the child moves from the egocentric orientation of the family to the community of children found in the school. George Herbert Mead (1934) initiated this line of thought with his classic essay on the child's learning to regard the "self as object" and "take the role of the other." Unfortunately, few have followed Mead's example.

Significantly, both Mead and Piaget recognized the rich learning environment provided in play. Mead credits the child's shift from aimless play to the realm of structured games as a crucial step in the development of role taking. Piaget (1965), through a close study of the game of marbles, meticulously

*This research was supported by an N.I.M.H. dissertation fellowship. I would like to thank Stanton Wheeler, Louis W. Goodman, and R. Stephen Warner for their guidance and criticism, and the Yale Child Study Center for its help in securing access to the public schools. I also thank John Meyer, Allan Schnaiberg, Marshall Shumsky, and the anonymous reviewers for their careful reading and discussion of an early draft of this paper.

Janet Lever, "Sex Differences in the Complexity of Children's Play and Games," *American Sociological Review*, Vol. 43 (August 1978), pp. 471–483. Reprinted by permission of the author and The American Sociological Association.

explains how children develop moral values while they play rule-bounded games. Aside from Mead and Piaget, little attention has been paid to the world of play and games in the study of childhood socialization.[1]

This study follows in the Mead and Piaget tradition by focusing on play and games as situations in which crucial learning takes place, but it goes beyond Mead's and Piaget's work in three important ways. First, Mead and Piaget each rests his analysis on a single game, whereas this study is based on a wide range of play and game activities. Second, both Mead and Piaget ignore sex differences in play. Mead's solitary example is the boys' game of baseball, but he does not tell us how girls, who are less familiar with team play, learn the same role-taking lessons. Piaget mentions, almost as an afterthought, that he did not find a single girls' game that has as elaborate an organization of rules as the boys' game of marbles, but he too fails to draw out the implications of his observation. A central concern of this study is to explore sex differences in the organization of children's play and to speculate on the sources as well as the potential effects of those differences.

Third, the paper highlights a specific dimension of play hitherto disregarded, namely, the *complexity* of the learning experience. I shall define complexity in more detail below, but it includes many of those attributes associated with the emergence of modern industrial society, such as division of labor, differentiation, heterogeneity, and rationalization (Simmel, 1955; Tonnies, 1955; Durkheim, 1893; Weber, 1967; Parsons and Smelser, 1956). My basic thesis is that the play activities of boys are more complex than those of girls, resulting in sex differences in the development of social skills potentially useful in childhood and later life.

METHODOLOGY

A variety of methods was used to gather as much data as possible in one year, 1972. In total, 181 fifth-grade children, aged 10 and 11, were studied. Half were from a suburban school and the other half from two city schools in Connecticut. The entire fifth grade of each school was included in the study. Three schools were selected whose student populations were predominantly white and middle-class—a choice made deliberately because of the possibility that race and class distinctions would confound the picture at this stage of exploratory research.

Four techniques of data collection were employed: observation of schoolyards, semistructured interviews, written questionnaires, and a diary record of leisure activities. The diary was a simple instrument used to document where the children had actually spent their time for the period of one week. Each morning, under the direction of the researcher, the children filled out a short form on which they described (1) what they had done the previous day after school, (2) who they did it with, (3) where the activity took place, and (4) how long it had lasted. Half the diaries were collected in the winter and half in the spring. The questionnaire, designed to elicit how children spend their time away from school, also was administered by me inside the classroom. I conducted semistructured interviews with one-third of the sample. Some were done in order to help design the questionnaire and diary; others were done later to help interpret the results. I gathered observational data while watching children's play activity during recess, physical education classes, and after school.[2]

MEASURING COMPLEXITY

In common usage, the word "complex" means something that is made up of a combination of elements. Sociologists similarly have applied the term to describe the amount of functional differentiation in any social unit, from a small group or a large organization, to society as a whole. Based on the ideal type of complex organization, regardless of the scale of the collectivity, there is general agreement that increases in any of the following six attributes constitute greater complexity (Etzioni, 1969; Blau and Schoenherr, 1971):

1. Division of labor based on specialization of roles;

2. interdependence between individual members;

3. size of the membership;

4. explicitness of the group goals;

5. number and specificity of impersonal rules; and

6. action of members as a unified collective.

Borrowing from the work of some contemporary students of games (Roberts et al., 1959; Redl et al., 1971; Avedon, 1971; Eifermann, 1972), I developed operational definitions for these six dimensions of complexity as they apply to the structure of play and games:

1. Role differentiation. For the purposes of this study, activities are to be considered low in role differentiation if the same behavior is required or expected from all players. For example, in the game of checkers, each player is equipped with the same number of pieces and is expected to move them in accordance with the same rules. Role differentiation is to be scored medium if one player has more power and acts differently from the undifferentiated group of other players. This describes all central-person games such as tag and hide-and-seek. An activity is to be scored high on role differentiation if three or more distinct game roles are present. For example, in the game of baseball, the pitcher has a different task to perform than the shortstop whose task is different from the center fielder and so on.

2. Player interdependence. An activity is to be judged low on the dimension of interdependence of players when the performance of one player does not immediately and significantly affect the performance of other players. For example, in the game of darts, one person's score does not interfere with the next player's score for the round. On the other hand, in the game of tennis, each player's move greatly affects the other's so that game has high interdependence of players.

3. Size of play group. This is a simple count of the number of players engaged in an activity. In this analysis, a group of three or fewer children is considered low on this dimension of complexity.

4. Explicitness of goals. The explicitness of goals is found in the distinction between play and games. *Play* is defined as a cooperative interaction that has no stated goal, no end point, and no winners; formal *games,* in contrast, are competitive interactions, aimed at achieving a recognized goal (e.g., touchdown; checkmate). Goals may involve tests of physical or mental skills, or both. Formal games have a predetermined end point (e.g., when one opponent reaches a specified number of points; end of ninth inning) that is simultaneous with the declaration of a winner or winners. The same basic activity may be either play or games. For example, riding bikes is play; racing bikes is a game.

5. Number and specificity of rules. Sometimes the word "rule" is broadly used to refer to norms or customs. Here the term is used in a narrower sense and refers to explicit rules which (a) are known to all players before the game begins, (b) are constant from one game situation to the next, and (c) carry sanctions for their violation. Play as defined above never has rules, whereas games always are governed by them. But games do vary by the number and specificity of their rules. Some games, like tag and hide-and-seek, have only a few rules; other games, like baseball and monopoly have numerous well-established rules.

6. Team formation. A team is a group of players working collectively toward a common goal. Play, as defined above, is never structured by teams. Games, on the other hand, are to be divided into those requiring team formation when played with three or more persons and those prohibiting or excluding team formation. Within the category of games with team formation are included both those games where teammates play relatively undifferentiated roles, as in tug-of-war or relay races, and those that require coordination between teammates playing differentiated positions, as in baseball.

In order to test the hypothesis that boys' play and games are more complex in structure, I examine closely the type and frequency of the play activities of both sexes as they occur in public and private places. The evidence for private play is in the diary data, reporting after school and weekend play. Diary data are important because they reflect a large number of incidents, a wide range of activities, and a free choice of both games and playmates. The evidence for public play, based on observational data collected mostly during recess and gym periods, reveal the rich texture of the play world, replete with dialogue that helps the researcher understand the meanings children attribute to different play forms.

Diary Data

The diary responses reflect activities played inside or around the home in the hours after school. From over two thousand diary entries, 895 cases of social play were isolated for this analysis.[3] They represented 136 distinct play activities which were then scored by the author and three independent coders.[4] The operational definitions of the six dimensions of complexity were presented to the coders, along with descriptions of play activities derived from the children's interviews. The activities were then rated along each of the six dimensions. All games were given ratings based on the children's own reports of how a game is played most typically at the fifth grade level.[5]

Table 1 presents the basic data. To develop an overall complexity score, five of the dimensions were dichotomized and assigned either a low or high value (0,1).[6] (The sixth dimension, size of group, varied from one play situation to the next and was tabulated independently.) The five dichotomous attributes yield thirty-two possible combinations; however, only nine occurred empirically. In Table 1 they are organized from lowest to highest complexity (scores from 0 to 5). Only the forty-eight activities that appeared in the diaries ten or more times are used to exemplify this scoring procedure, but all social play activities, even those less frequently mentioned, are included in the tabulations.[7] By age ten, play activities are generally known to be sex segregated. The "g" or "b" after each activity in Table 1 indicates whether it is played predominantly by girls or boys; the absence of a letter implies that the sexes engage in the activity with roughly equal frequency.

Table 1 yields two important findings. First, it shows the great variety regarding levels of complexity in the games played by children of similar age. Mead and Piaget, by focusing on only a single game, could not show the range of experiences available within the play world. Fully a third of the activities were low on all the measured dimensions of complexity. Another fifth were high on all. Children exposed to one or the other of these types of play are likely to be learning very different skills. Second, if we can agree that games provide differential learning environments, then we must assume differential effects for boys and girls. Boys experience three times as many games at the highest level of complexity and over twice as many boys' activities are located in the top half of the complexity scale.[8]

Table 2 views the data from a different perspective by showing the sex distribution separately for each of the six dimensions. Although greater complexity in boys' activities is demonstrated for all six, the major finding

Table 1   Coding and complexity scores of the most frequently listed diary activities

	Girls	Boys	Total
Type I. Complexity Score=0			
one role (0); low interdependence (0); play (0) no rules (0); no teams (0).			

1. listen to records (g)	11. exploring woods (b)
2. listen to radio (g)	12. hiking (g)
3. drawing (g)	13. horseback riding (g)
4. painting (g)	14. grooming horses (g)
5. work with clay (g)	15. take a walk (g)
6. build things (b)	16. jump roofs (b)
7. ice skating (g)	17. climb trees (b)
8. roller skating (g)	18. sled ride (b)
9. bike riding	19. launch rockets (b)
10. mini-biking (b)	20. fly kites (b)

	Girls	Boys	Total
Type I:	42% (179)	27% (126)	34% (305)

Type II. Complexity Score=1

A. one role (0); high interdependence (1); play (0);
no rules (0); no teams (0).

21. cheerlead practice (g)	23. dancing (g)
22. singing (g)	24. catch (b)

	Girls	Boys	Total
	(13)	(14)	(27)

B. one role (0); low interdependence (0); game (1);
few rules (0); no teams (0).

25. bowling (g)	28. paddle pool (b)
26. skittle bowl (b)	29. race electric
27. pool (b)	cars (b)

	Girls	Boys	Total
	(17)	(42)	(59)
Type II:	7% (30)	12% (56)	10% (86)

Type III. Complexity Score=2

A. two or more roles (1); high interdependence (1);
play (0); no rules (0); no teams (0).

30. dolls (g)	32. jumprope (g)
31. indoor fantasy (g)	33. outdoor fantasy (b)
(e.g., school, house)	(e.g., Army, FBI,
	Batman)

	Girls	Boys	Total
	(72)	(19)	(91)

Table 1 (continued)

B. two roles (1); low interdependence (p); game (1);
   few rules (0); no teams (0).

34. tag, chase (g)	36. kick the can (b)			
35. hide-and-seek (g)		(38)	(23)	(61)

C. one role (0); high interdependence (1); game (1);
   few rules (0); no teams (0).

37. simple card games (g)	38. 2-square;	(21)	(29)	(50)
	4-square Type III:	31%	15%	22.5%
		(131)	(71)	(202)

Type IV: Complexity Score=3

one role (0); high interdependence (1); game (1);
many rules (1); no teams (0).

39. chess (b)	41. board games (g)			
40. checkers (b)	(e.g., Monopoly,			
	Parchesi)			
	Type IV:	8%	15%	12%
		(35)	(70)	(105)

*Type V: Complexity Score=4

one role (0); high interdependence (1); game (1);
many rules (1); team formation (1).

Type V:	2%	1%	1.5%
	(9)	(5)	(14)

Type VI: Complexity Score=5

two or more roles (1); high interdependence (1);
game (1); many rules (1); team formation (1).

42. football (b)	46. soccer (b)			
43. ice hockey (b)	47. kickball (g)			
44. baseball (b)	48. punch ball (b)			
45. basketball (b)	Type VI:	10%	30%	20%
		(43)	(140)	(183)
	Total Social Play:	100%	100%	100%
		(427)	(468)	(895)

*Infrequently played activities, exemplified by Newcombe (g) and Capture the Flag (b).

Table 2   Sex differences on the six dimensions of
complexity in play and games

Dimensions of complexity	Girls	Boys
1. Number of roles (3 or more roles)	18% (427)	32% (468)
2. Interdependence of players (high interdependence)	46% (427)	57% (468)
3. Size of play group (4 or more persons)	35% (427)	45% (468)
4. Explicitness of goals (game structure)	37% (427)	65% (468)
5. Number of rules (many rules)	19% (427)	45% (468)
6. Team formation (teams required)	12% (427)	31% (468)

of Table 2 is seen on the fourth dimension, explicitness of goals. Sixty-five percent of boys' activities were competitive games compared to only 37% of girls' activities. In other words, *girls played more* while *boys gamed more*. This difference is not merely a function of boys' playing more team sports. Only 140 of the 305 games played by boys were team sports. Eliminating team sports for both sexes, we would still find 54% of the boys' activities and 30% of the girls' activities competitively structured. Sedentary games, like chess and electric race cars, are as important as sport in reflecting boys' greater competitiveness.

Nor is it the case when girls do participate in competitive games that they experience the same level of complexity as their male peers. The games girls play have fewer rules, and less often require the formation of teams.[9] In summary, the data from children's diaries show strongly that boys, far more often than girls, experience high levels of complexity in their play and games.

Observational Data

Observations of children at play during recess, gym classes, and after school also indicate very distinct play patterns for boys and girls. As in the diary data, boys' activities were found to be more complex. The following descriptions of a few selected play activities illustrate the way in which each of the dimensions of complexity is expressed. Greater attention is given to girls' games as they are less familiar to adults. Some implications of differential organization of play are suggested, but their elaboration awaits the discussion section.

1. Role differentiation. The largest category of girls' public activity was the same as their private activity, namely, single-role play. These were cooperative activities with both or all parties doing basically the same thing such as riding bikes, roller skating, or ice skating. A minority of girls' activities were competitive games. Observing recess periods for a year, I saw only one instance of a spontaneously organized team sport, namely, kickball. The activities that appeared most regularly during recess were the traditional girls' games, like hopscotch, which are turn-taking games with only one game role present at a given time. Each player, in specified sequential order, attempts to accomplish the same task as all other players. A few turn-taking games have two distinct roles: for example, in jumprope there is the role of rope turner and that of rope jumper. The other girls' games I observed frequently at recess were central-person games, the most popular being tag, spud, and Mother May I. These games also have only two roles—the "it" and the "others." Power is usually ascribed in these games through "dipping rules" like "odd-man-out."

Boys at this age have largely stopped playing central-person games except as fillers; for example, they might play tag while waiting for a bus or after so many team members have been called home to dinner that their previous game has disintegrated. The great majority of observed games were team sports with their multiple roles. Besides distinctions based on positions and assigned tasks, there were also distinctions in power between team captains and their subordinates. Sometimes the leaders were appointed by teachers, but more often the children elected their captains according to achievement criteria.[10] After school especially, I observed boys in single role activities, some noncompetitive, like flying kites and climbing trees, but most competitive like tennis, foot races, or one-on-one basketball.

2. Player interdependence. There are many types of player interdependence: (1) interdependence of action between members of a single group; (2) interdependent decision making between single opponents; (3) simultaneous interdependence of action with one's own teammates and an opposing group of teammates.

Very little interdependence was required of those girls engaged in single role play; coaction rather than interaction is required of the participants. Also, little interdependence was required of those playing turn-taking games. Even though the latter activity is competitive, the style of competition is indirect, with each player acting independently of the others. That is, one competes against a figurative "scoreboard" (Player A→norm←Player B). Participation in such games is routinized and occurs successively or after the previous player's failure; that is, opponents do not compete simultaneously. Interdependent decision making is not necessary in turn-taking games of physical skill as it may be in some of the popular board games.

When girls do play interdependently, they tend to do so in a cooperative context where there is interdependence of action between members of a single group. This type of interaction is best exemplified (but rarely observed) in the creation of private fantasy scenarios. One public example occurred when seven girls from one school took the initiative to write, produce, and act out a play they called "Hippie Cinderella." They stayed indoors at recess and rehearsed almost daily for three weeks in preparation for presentation to the entire fifth-grade class.

When boys compete as individuals, they are more likely to be engaged in direct, face-to-face confrontations (Player A $\leftrightarrows$ Player B). Interdependent decision making between single opponents is necessary in games like tennis or one-on-one basketball that combine strategy with physical skill. More often, boys compete as members of teams and must simultaneously coordinate their actions with those of their teammates while taking into account the action and strategies of their opponents. Boys interviewed expressed finding gratification in acting as representatives of a collectivity; the approval or disapproval of one's teammates accentuates the importance of contributing to a group victory.

3. Size of play group. Observations made during recess periods showed boys playing in much larger groups than girls to a far greater extent than appeared in the diary data. Boys typically were involved in team sports which require a large number of participants for proper play. Boys in all three schools could play daily, depending on the season, in ongoing basketball, football, or baseball games involving ten to twenty-five or more persons. Girls were rarely observed playing in groups as large as ten persons; on those occasions, they were engaged in cooperative circle songs that seemed to emerge spontaneously, grow, and almost as quickly disintegrate. More often, girls participated in activities like tag, hopscotch, or jumprope, which can be played properly with as few as two or three participants and seldom involve more than five or six. In fact, too many players are considered to detract rather than enhance the fun because it means fewer turns, with longer waits between turns. Indeed, Eifermann (1968), after cataloging over 2,000 children's games, observed that more girls' games, like hopscotch and jacks, can be played alone, whereas the great majority of boys' games need two or more players.

4. Explicitness of goals. In the recess yards, I more often saw girls playing cooperatively and boys playing competitively. Some girls engaged in conversation more than they did in play (see Lever, 1976:481). Others, like those who initiated the circle songs and dances, preferred action governed by ritual rather than rules. For example, the largest and most enthusiastic group of girls witnessed during the year of research was involved in a circle chant called "Dr. Knickerbocker Number Nine." Twenty-four girls repeated the chant and body motions in an outer circle, while one girl in the center spun around with eyes closed. She then stopped, with arm extended, pointing out someone from the outer circle to join her. The ritual chant began again while the new arrival spun around; this procedure continued until nine persons had been chosen in similar random fashion to form the inner circle. Then the ninth person remained in the circle's center while the others resumed their original positions and the cycle would begin anew.

Although this activity appeared monotonous to the observer because it allowed the participants little chance to exercise physical or mental skills, these ten-year-olds were clearly enjoying themselves. Shouts of glee were heard from the circle's center when a friend had been chosen to join them. Indeed, a girl could gauge her popularity by the loudness of these shouts. For some the activity may provide an opportunity to reaffirm self-esteem without suffering any of the achievement pressures of team sports.

Even when girls engaged in presumably competitive games, they typically avoided setting precise goals. In two schools, I observed girls playing "Under the Moon," a popular form of jumprope. The first person hops in and jumps once, in any fashion of her choosing, and then hops out. She then enters again and does two jumps, usually though not necessarily, different from the first. She increases her jumps by an increment of one until she has jumped ten times. Her turn over, she then becomes a rope turner. There was no competition exhibited between players. They participated for the fun of the turn, not to win. Even if the jumper trips the rope, she is allowed to complete her turn. If the jumper competes, it is with herself, as she alone determines whether to attempt an easy jump or a more difficult one.

The point is that girls sometimes take activities in which a comparison of relative achievement is structurally possible (and sometimes normatively expected) and transform them into noncompetitive play. Girls are satisfied to keep their play loosely structured. For example, in the game of jacks, girls can say before beginning, "The first to finish 'double bounces' is the winner." More often, however, they just play until they are bored with the game. Players may or may not verbalize "you won," and recognize who has advanced the most number of steps. Boys grant much more importance to being proclaimed the winner; they virtually always structure their games, be it one-on-one or full team basketball, so that the outcomes will be clear and definite.

5. Number and specificity of rules. This investigator also observed, reminiscent of Piaget, that boys' games more often have an elaborate organization of rules. Girls' turn-taking games progress in identical order from one situation to the next; prescriptions are minimal, dictating what must be done in order to advance. Given the structure of these games, disputes are not likely to occur. "Hogging" is impossible when participation is determined by turn-taking; nor can fouls occur when competition is indirect. Sports games, on the other hand, are governed by a broad set of rules covering a wide variety of situations, some common and others rare. Areas of ambiguity which demand rule elaboration and adjudication are built into these games. Kohlberg (1964) refines Piaget's thesis by arguing that children learn the greatest respect for rules when they can be used to reduce dissonance in ambiguous situations.[11]

Because girls play cooperatively more than competitively, they have less experience with rules per se, so we should expect them to have a lesser consciousness of rules than boys. On one of those rare occasions when boys and girls could be watched playing the same games, there was striking evidence for a sex difference in rule sensitivity. A gym teacher introduced a game called "newcombe," a simplified variation of volleyball, in which the principal rule is that the ball must be passed three times before being returned to the other side of the net. Although the game was new to all, the boys did not once forget the "3-pass" rule; the girls forgot it on over half the volleys.

6. *Team formation.* Team formation can be seen as a dimension of complexity because it indicates simultaneously structured relationships of cooperation and conflict. In turn-taking games, girls compete within a single group as independent players, each one against all others. Boys compete between groups, acting interdependently as members of a team. Team formation is required in all of their favorite sports: baseball, football, basketball, hockey, and soccer. Only a few girls in each school regularly joined the boys in their team sports; conversely, only a few boys in each school avoided the sports games. Questionnaire data support these observations. Most boys reported regular participation in neighborhood sports games. In addition, at the time of the study 68% said they belonged to some adult-supervised teams, with a full schedule of practice and league games. In fact, some of these fifth graders were already involved in interstate competitions.

The after-school sports program illustrates boys' greater commitment to team competition. Twenty girls from the third, fourth, and fifth grades elected captains who chose teams for newcombe games. Only seven of those girls returned the following week. In contrast, after-school basketball attracted so many boys that the fifth graders were given their own day. The teacher called roll for the next two weeks and noted that every boy had returned to play again.

Thus observational data, like the diary data, support the basic hypothesis that boys' play activities are more complex in structure than those of girls. Boys' play more frequently involves specialization of roles, interdependence of players, explicit group goals, and larger group membership, numerous rules, and team divisions. This conclusion holds for activities in public as well as in private. It suggests a markedly different set of socialization experiences for members of each sex.

DISCUSSION

Sources of the Sex Difference

What is it that produces these distinct play patterns for boys and girls? The answer is mostly historical and cultural and holds true for much of Europe as well as the United States. While the rise of recreational physical activities in the late nineteenth century was enjoyed by women and men alike, the organized team sports which flourished at the same time were limited to participation by males (Paxson, 1917). The combined beliefs in the masculine nature of sport and the physiological inferiority of females led early twentieth century educators to lobby for competitive athletics for boys while restricting the physical education of girls to gymnastic exercises and dance. The emphasis on competitive athletics for males was reinforced by the view that sport served as a training ground for future soldiers ("the battle of Waterloo was won on the playing fields of Eton") and by the growing interest in spectator sports in which the dominant performers were young men (Cozens and Stumpf, 1953). Despite some outstanding individual female athletes in golf, tennis, and track and field, there was no development of interest in women's team sports. This situation is only now beginning to change.

Evidence generated in connection with Title IX of the Education Amendments Acts shows the extraordinary sex difference with respect to the allocation of funds for athletic programs from the primary grades through college. In 1969 the Syracuse New York School board allocated $90,000 for boys' extracurricular sports compared to $200 for girls' sports. In rural Pennsylvania, the Fairfield area school district set its 1972–73 budget at a ratio of 40:1 in favor of male athletes whose interscholastic competition begins in earnest by fifth grade. Even at Vassar, where sports for women are given great attention, the boys' athletic budget was double that of girls, although they comprised only one-third of the student body (Gilbert and Williamson, 1973).

Of course, it is not only the schools that encourage boys' and restrict girls' athletic participation. Parents act as the conveyor belts for cultural norms, and it is no less the case for norms pertaining to sport. Male children are quick to learn that their demonstrations of athletic skill earn the attention and praise of adults. Many fathers show more emotion and enthusiasm for professional sports than anything else. Girls at young ages may not be actively discouraged from sports participation, but they are told that they are "tomboys" which is understood to be a deviant label. In the recent Little League debate, psychologists, parents, and coaches voiced their concern for the masculinization of female athletes, and the possible damage to young male egos when girls defeat boys in public (Michener, 1976). This cultural legacy is still with us, even though we now appear to be on the verge of radical change.

Historical analysis of children's games confirms that boys are playing more team sports now than ever before. Equally important, boys have drifted away from loosely structured play towards more formally organized competitive games (Sutton-Smith and Rosenberg, 1971). Evidence presented here supports this picture. It appears that the growing cultural emphasis on sports and winning has carried over to nonphysical activities and made them more competitive, and that, to date, it has had this effect to a far greater extent for boys than for girls.

Consequences of the sex differences

Boys' games provide a valuable learning environment. It is reasonable to expect that the following social skills will be cultivated on the playground: the ability to deal with diversity in memberships where each person is performing a special task; the ability to coordinate actions and maintain cohesiveness among group members; the ability to cope with a set of impersonal rules; and the ability to work for collective as well as personal goals.

Team sports furnish the most frequent opportunity to sharpen these social skills. One could elaborate on the lessons learned. The rule structure encourages strategic thinking. Team sports also imply experience with clear-cut leadership positions, usually based on universalistic criteria. The group rewards the individual who has improved valued skills, a practice which further enhances a sense of confidence based on achievement. Furthermore, through team sports as well as individual matches, boys learn to deal with interpersonal competition in a forthright manner. Boys experience face-to-face confrontations—often opposing a close friend—and must learn to depersonalize the attack. They must practice self-control and sportsmanship; in fact, some of the boys in this study described the greatest lesson in team sports as learning to "keep your cool."

Girls' play and games are very different. They are mostly spontaneous, imaginative, and free of structure or rules. Turntaking activities like jumprope may be played without setting explicit goals. Girls have far less experience with interpersonal competition. The style of their competition is indirect, rather than face to face, individual rather than team affiliated. Leadership roles are either missing or randomly filled.

Perhaps more important, girls' play occurs in small groups. These girls report preferring the company of a single best friend to a group of four or more.[12] Often girls mimic primary human relationships instead of playing formal games, or they engage in conversation rather than play anything at all. In either case, there are probable benefits for their affective and verbal development. In Meadian terms, it may be that boys develop the ability to take the role of the *generalized other* while girls develop empathy skills to take the role of the *particular other*.

That the sexes develop different social skills in childhood due to their play patterns is logical conjecture; that those social skills might carry over and influence their adult behavior is pure speculation. Indeed, the weight of evidence indicates that life experiences are vast and varied; much can happen to intervene and change the patterns set during childhood. Still, there is so much continuity between boys' play patterns and adult male roles that we must consider whether games serve a particular socializing function.

This idea is now popular. In a recent best seller on managerial leaders, Maccoby (1976) describes the 250 executives he studied as gamesmen who organize teams, look for a challenge, and play to win. The same social skills may be equally helpful in lower level bureaucratic jobs or other settings, like trade unions and work crews, where complexity of organization is also found. One need not endorse the world or organizations, bureaucracy, sharp competition, and hierarchy to recognize it as an integral part of modern industrial society.

The unfortunate fact is that we do not know what effect playing games might have on later life. We do not know, for example, whether the minority of women who have succeeded in bureaucratic settings are more likely to have played complex games. A recent study offers a modicum of supporting data. Hennig and Jardim (1977) portray their small sample of twenty-five women in top management positions as former tomboys. It is also the case that elite boarding schools and women's colleges, many of which stress team sports, have been credited with producing a large portion of this nation's female leaders. I would not want to argue that competitive team sports are the only place to learn useful organizational skills. Surely, the skills in question can be learned in nonplay settings in both childhood and adulthood. Nevertheless, it can be argued that complex games are an early and effective training ground from which girls traditionally have been excluded.

CONCLUSION

Children's socialization is assumed to have consequences for their later lives. Sociologists have looked to the family and the school as the primary socializing agents. In contrast, this analysis focused on the peer group as the agent of socialization, children's play as the activity of socialization, and social skills as the product of socialization. The data presented here reaffirm Mead's and Piaget's message that during play children develop numerous social skills that enable them to enjoy group membership in a community of peers.

The data also demonstrate that some games, when analyzed structurally, provide a highly complex experience for their young players while others do not. By itself, the notion of complexity adds to our appreciation of games as important early training grounds. However, the evidence of differential exposure to complex games leads to the conclusion that not all children will learn the same lessons. Here the approach to play and games differs dramatically from that of Mead and Piaget who presumed social and moral development as a normal part of the growth process and, therefore, did not make problematic the different experience of boys and girls. One implication of this research is that boys' greater exposure to complex games may give them an advantage in occupational milieus that share structural features with those games. At the very least, the striking similarity between the formula for success in team sports and in modern organizations should encourage researchers to give serious attention to play patterns and their consequences.

NOTES

1. Among others who have recognized the importance of play in childhood socialization are Roberts and Sutton-Smith, 1962; Stone, 1971; Bruner et al., 1976.

2. See Lever (1974:65–108) for a detailed description of the methodology.

3. There were 2,141 activities recorded in the children's diaries. Five hundred eight entries were eliminated from this analysis because they were descriptions of nonplay activities like attending church services, doing homework or household chores, or going to the doctor. Another 527 items were eliminated because they reflected pastimes rather than actual play. This category included: watching television; reading books, comics or newspapers; going to the movies; going for an auto ride; and talking on the telephone. Television viewing, by far, accounts for most of the entries in this category. Of the remaining 1,106 play activities, 211 were not included because they were instances of the child's playing alone rather than in the company of others. Because the complexity dimensions reflect interpersonal skills, pastimes and solitary play are not relevant. However, it should be noted that there was no sex difference in the number of leisure hours spent with the television (15 to 20 hours/week) or playing alone (about 20% of all play).

4. The coders included the headmistress of a private elementary school who previously had taught fifth-graders for over a decade, a graduate student who had been a camp counselor for ten-year-olds for several years, and an assistant professor of sociology. Overall, the judges agreed on over 90% of the items coded.

5. Such reports were especially needed because separate groups of children may play the same game somewhat differently, while even the same children do not necessarily play a game in identical fashion from one occasion to the next. It is also important to note that children modify adult games, so that a game like pool, which has complicated rules for adults, usually is played according to simple rules by children.

6. To justify linking the six dimensions, a factor analysis was run on the 136 activities. There was only one factor present, and all six dimensions were a part of it (the lowest degree of communality was .60); I have referred to this single factor as "complexity." While it may be argued that some dimensions add more complexity than others, the absence of guidelines encourages equal weighting at this time.

7. See Lever (1974:394–7) for a complete list of games recorded in the children's diaries.

8. Because some children reported more activities than others, there is the

possibility that these results, based on activities as the units of analysis, reflect the extreme scores of a few individuals and are not representative of the sample as a whole. To guard against such misinterpretation, I made the individuals the units of analysis. To do so, I used the same dichotomization and point system displayed in Table 1 and added the sixth dimension, size of play group, as it appeared in each of the 895 entries. Once each activity could be given a complexity score (now zero to six), an average complexity score could be ascertained for each child based on the entire week's social play report. Seventy percent of the boys, compared with 36% of the girls, had average complexity scores of 3.0 or higher—a fact which further sustains the hypothesis.

9. Fifty-one percent of the games girls play (n = 158) contain many rules, compared with 69% of the boys' games (n = 305). Looking only at games with three or more participants, we note that boys played 26% more games which called for team formation.

10. In response to the interview question "Who are the fifth-grade leaders?" the boys in all three schools answered that the best athletes/team organizers rightly held that position. In contrast, most girls hesitated with the question, then named persons who had power, but credited their aggression rather than particular valued skills. They equated giving directives with assertiveness and gave that behavior negative labels like "bossy" or "big mouth." Some openly stated that leaders acted less than ladylike and were not envied for their power. Attitudes that underlie Kanter's (1977: 201) "mean and bossy woman boss" stereotype obviously are set at a very young age.

11. See Lever (1976:482–3) for a description of sex differences in the handling of quarrelling in games.

12. It is important to note that, according to their questionnaire responses, the minority of thirty girls who reported playing complex games during the diary week also indicated a preference for larger friendship groups. The fact that the sex difference in size of friendship cliques disappears when controlling for complexity of game experience is one indication of importance of this classification scheme.

REFERENCES

Avedon, Elliott M., 1971, "The structure elements of games." Pp. 419–26 in Elliott M. Avedon and Brian Sutton-Smith (eds.), *The Study of Games.* New York: Wiley.

Blau, Peter and R. A. Schoenherr, 1971, *The Structure of Organizations,* New York: Basic Books.

Bruner, J. S., A. Jolly, and K. Sylva, 1976, *Play: Its Role in Development and Evolution.* New York: Penguin.

Cozens, Frederick and Florence Stumpf, 1953, *Sports in American Life,* Chicago: University of Chicago Press.

Durkheim, Emile, [1893] 1964, *The Division of Labor in Society,* New York: Free Press.

Eifermann, Rivka, 1968, "School children's games." Final Report, Contract No. OE-6-21-010. Department of Health, Education and Welfare; Office of Education, Bureau of Research. Unpublished paper.

Eifermann, Rivka, 1972, "Free social play: a guide to directed playing." Unpublished paper.

Etzioni, Amitai, 1969, *A Sociological Reader on Complex Organization*. New York: Holt.

Gilbert, Bil and Nancy Williamson, 1973, "Sport is unfair to women." *Sports Illustrated* **38** (May 28):88–98.

Hennig, Margaret and Ann Jardim, 1977, *The Managerial Woman*. New York: Doubleday.

Kanter, Rosabeth Moss, 1977, *Men and Women of the Corporation*. New York: Basic Books.

Kohlberg, Lawrence, 1964, "Development of moral character and moral ideology." Pp. 383–431 in M. L. Hoffman and L. W. Hoffman (eds.), *Review of Child Development Research*, Vol. 1. New York: Russell Sage.

Lever, Janet, 1974, *Games Children Play: Sex Differences and the Development of Role Skills*. Ph.D. dissertation, Department of Sociology, Yale University.

Lever, Janet, 1976, "Sex differences in the games children play." *Social Problems* **23**:478–87.

Maccoby, Michael, 1976, *The Gamesman*. New York: Simon and Schuster.

Mead, George Herbert, 1934, *Mind, Self, and Society*. Chicago: University of Chicago Press.

Michener, James A., 1976, *Sports in America*. New York: Random House.

Parsons, Talcott and Neil J. Smelser, 1956, *Economy and Society: A Study in the Integration of Economic and Social Theory*. London: Routledge.

Paxson, Frederic L., 1917, "The rise of sport." *Mississippi Valley Historical Review* **4**:144–68.

Piaget, Jean, 1965, *The Moral Judgment of the Child*. New York: Free Press.

Redl. F., P. Gump, and B. Sutton-Smith, "The dimensions of games." Pp. 408–18 in Elliott M. Avedon and Brian Sutton-Smith (eds.), *The Study of Games*. New York: Wiley.

Roberts, John M., M. J. Arth, and R. R. Bush, 1959, "Games in culture." *American Anthropologist* **61**:597–605.

Roberts, John M. and Brian Sutton-Smith, 1962, "Child training and game involvement." *Ethnology* **1**:166–85.

Simmel, Georg, 1955, *The Web of Group Affiliations*. Trans. by Reinhard Bendix. New York: Free Press.

Stone, Gregory P., 1971, "The play of little children." Pp. 4–17 in R. E. Herron and Brian Sutton-Smith (eds.), *Child's Play*. New York: Wiley.

Sutton-Smith, B. and B. Rosenberg, 1971, "Sixty years of historical change in the game preference of American children." Pp. 18–50 in R. E. Herron and B. Sutton-Smith (eds.), *Child's Play*. New York: Wiley.

Tonnies, Ferdinand, 1955, *Community and Association*. Trans. by Charles P. Loomis. London: Routledge.

Weber, Max, 1967, From Max Weber: *Essays in Sociology*. Trans. and ed. by H. H. Gerth and C. Wright Mills. New York: Oxford University Press.

THE FEMALE ATHLETE AND ROLE CONFLICT

George H. Sage and Sheryl Loudermilk

Every person occupies a number of positions in the society in which he or she lives. For each position there is a set of expectations comprising the rights, privileges, and obligations of an occupant of that position; the set of expectations which are held by an individual and others in the society about appropriate behaviors for occupants of a particular positions are often incompatible. When a person perceives or experiences his or her role expectations as being incompatible to some degree, role conflict is said to exist. Thus, role conflict exists when the role expectations placed upon an individual are incompatible, making it impossible for the person to conform to both sets of expectations at the same time (Thomas, 1968). Conflicting role expectations associated with discrepant positions are thought to lead to ambiguous self-definitions and conflicting role directives, as well as to intrapsychic strain (Lenski, 1954, 1956).

Male and female constitute ascribed social positions and in every society there is a set of role-appropriate attitudes and behaviors for males and females; severe sanctions are imposed on those who violate those role expectations. Thus a major part of the socialization process consists of learning the separate activities of males and females. Sex-role differentiation becomes established by the age of 3 and beliefs about sex-appropriate abilities, attitudes, and behavior begin to be acquired by the 5th year (Flerx, Fidler, & Rogers, 1976; Maccoby & Jacklin, 1974; Thompson, 1975).

George H. Sage and Sheryl Loudermilk, "The Female Athlete and Role Conflict," *Research Quarterly*, Vol. 50, No. 1, (1979), pp. 88–96.

The traditional message in American society has stressed that desirable qualities for males are aggressiveness, independence, and achievement striving, while desirable qualities for females are passivity, affiliation, nurturance, and dependence. Sport participation and vigorous physical pursuits have been positively associated with the male role and negatively associated with the female role. The existence of bipolar sex-role norms is well documented (Birns, 1976; Lunneborg, 1970).

One of the most salient differences in male and female role expectations involves sports participation. For the male, sports involvement is expected and rewarded; it is perhaps the most visible means for validating the internalization of the male sex role. Boys learn at a young age that sports and games are socially defined as an important means of recognition. On the other hand, the little girl is encouraged to play with dolls, help mother with housework, and is rewarded for being a "little lady." Girls learn that "tomboy" activities, though possibly tolerated in the prepubescent girl, are not really considered "ladylike" and are expected to be discarded with maturity. Thus, females have different socially acceptable means for recognition.

Indeed, females who have persisted in sports activities have often been stigmatized as "masculine" (Eitzen & Sage, 1978). One of the oldest and most persistent folk myths, and one of the main deterrents to female sports participation, has been the notion that vigorous physical activity tends to masculinize girls and women. Women of physical competence have been stigmatized as masculine by a tradition that taught that women who have excellent physical competence must be unfeminine. The stereotype of the female athlete as aggressive, frustrated, and unfeminine is well described by Malumphy (1971). Thus, consciously or unconsciously, athletic achievement has been equated with loss of femininity.

A dichotomy appears to exist between society's stereotypic view of acceptable female behavior and the qualities necessary for successful participation in competitive sport. Participation in sport in a serious way is inconsistent with society's view of femininity. The young woman who participates in sport risks her feminine image. According to Felshin (1974), sport serves as a feedback system for the ideological values of society. It confirms the social assumption that doing and being, asserting and overcoming, striving and fulfilling aspirations are the appropriate models and motivations of males, and participation in vigorous sports is the prerogative only of the male. Felshin asserts that the female athlete is a social anomaly and female athletes use a variety of means to maintain and emphasize their own femininity and thus avoid threatening their image. Emphasizing femininity may take the form of dressing in sex-appropriate ways, pursuing the so-called more acceptable sports, not taking sports seriously, etc. All these artifacts of femininity assist in reducing the threat of sports to the revered feminine image and seem designed to reduce role conflict.

Evidence from a variety of sources suggests that since athletic participation has traditionally been viewed as a male prerogative and the female participant often faced social stigma and endangered her feminine image it is likely that female athletes perceive and actually experience role conflict (Hart, 1974; 1976; Scott, 1974). Harris (1975) reported that the female athlete experiences dissonance between her social self and her competitive self. Griffin (1973), using the semantic differential technique, found that the least valued roles judged by college students were the female athlete and the female professor. In examining the semantic space between concepts she found the most distance between female athlete and ideal woman. Snyder and Kivlin (1977) found that over 50% of intercollegiate female basketball and track and field athletes reported that social stigma was attached to women participating in those sports, while 65% of a group of nonathletes felt there was a stigma attached to women's participation in sports.

According to a number of investigators, in addition to the potential role conflict that all female athletes may encounter, the degree of role conflict is likely to be related to the sport in which one participates, since acceptability of female participation varies according to type of sport. Sports in which strength, bodily contact, and endurance are emphasized have traditionally had low social approval, and women participating in sports of these types have been socially stigmatized, while sports emphasizing skill, grace, and beauty, and not involving touching one's opponent, have been more socially approved (Malumphy, 1968; Metheny, 1965; Snyder, Kivlin, & Spreitzer, 1975). Moreover, a consistent finding with regard to attitudes toward female athletic participation is that individual sports are more socially acceptable than team sports (Debacy, Spaeth, & Busch, 1970; Garman, 1969; Harres, 1968; Sherrif, 1969; Snyder & Kivlin, 1975).

Although many persons have speculated that role conflict likely exists for the female athlete, there has been little empirical research on this topic. The major objective of this study was to investigate the overall levels of *perceived* and *experienced* role conflict among female athletes. It was expected that female athletes would perceive and experience considerable social negativism and role conflict. A second expectation was that there would be differences in perceived and experienced role conflict between athletes according to the type of sport in which they participate.

METHOD

Subjects

The subjects of this study were 268 female varsity intercollegiate athletes from 9 sports, representing 13 colleges. They ranged in age from 18 to 24, with a modal age of 19. The subjects were not a random or necessarily representative sample of the population of collegiate female athletes but the issue of representativeness of the sample is not considered critical since the purpose of this study was to obtain a sufficient number of diverse respondents to test the relationship between variables rather than parameter estimation (Nunnaly, 1967). All of the subjects who were asked to participate in the study agreed to do so.

That the subjects had an extensive physical activity background is confirmed by the fact that over 90% reported that between the ages of 14 and 17 they were either above average or well above average in sports activities compared to age cohorts, and 92% indicated that they had been members of high school teams.

Procedure

Data were collected during the 1976–77 academic year by a personally administered questionnaire. The instrument was a 20-item inventory that assessed perceived and experienced role conflicts of the subjects in enacting their roles as female and female athlete. Approval to administer the inventory was obtained from coaches and athletes. The instrument contained a set of directions for responding to the questions and the investigators or their trained aides remained in the room to answer any individual questions while the subjects completed the inventory.

The instrument was based upon a model of role conflict developed by Grace (1972) and extended by Massengale and Locke (1976), with questions about role conflict modified to deal with relating the roles of female and female athlete. The areas of conflict included a general attitude of society toward females and athletic participation; physical appearance and skills of the female which may seem incompatible with athletic participation; incompatibility of expectations of parents, friends, and others regarding sex roles and athlete role; and stereotyped female nonphysical characteristics which may conflict with desirable traits of the competitive athlete.

The 20-item inventory actually consisted of two parts, with the same 10 items used for both parts. The first part was designed to measure role conflict perception (RCP) and the second was designed to measure role conflict experience (RCE) (Getzels & Guba, 1955; Grace, 1972). The operational definition of perceived role conflict was the role occupant's *perception of conflicting expectations* or orientations. The 10 role conflict items were therefore presented to the respondents as role problems which female athletes might encounter during the course of their participation. On the RCP part the athletes were asked to respond to each item on a 5-point scale from "Not at all" (1) to "A very great extent" (5), in terms of their *perception* that this was a role conflict problem. The operational definition of experienced role conflict was the extent to which the role occupant *had personally experienced* role incompatibilities in enacting the roles of female/female athlete. For the RCE part the 10 items of the RCP part were repeated but the subjects were asked to respond to each item on a 5-point scale ranging from "Not at all" (1) to "A very great extent" (5) in terms of their actually having experienced this as a role conflict problem.

The conflict areas employed in the present instrument are not intended to represent the true population of all role-related problems for the female/ female athlete. The conflict areas surveyed were selected because cultural sex-role prescriptions and previous research led to a theoretical expectation that they would be appropriate.*

RESULTS

It was apparent from the responses to both the RCP and the RCE sections that many respondents neither perceived nor experienced extreme role conflict in fulfilling the position of female athlete. The percentage of respondents in each part responding "not at all" or "of little importance" was: RCP, 44%; RCE, 56% (Table 1).

On the other hand it was also apparent from the analysis of responses to the suggested role conflict areas on both the RCP and RCE parts that they were accepted by the subjects as actual problem and conflict situations which female athletes perceived and encountered. The percentage of respondents in each part responding that the extent of conflict was "great" or "very great" was: RCP, 26%; RCE, 20%.

The chi square analysis of RCP and RCE for the total set of subjects indicated that the athletes perceive greater role conflict than had actually been experienced (X^2 (4) = 138.74, $p < .01$). The average of the sum of responses to RCP was 2.70, and the average of the sum of responses to RCE was 2.38.

When perceived and experienced conflict were examined by dividing groups into traditionally "Not socially approved" (softball, basketball, volleyball, field hockey, track and field) and traditionally "Socially approved" (tennis, golf, swimming, gymnastics) sports, there were no significant differences in perceived role conflict (X^2 (4) = 2.55, $p > .05$) (Table 2). The average sum of responses for the "Not socially approved" group was 2.71 and the "Socially approved" group was 2.69. The percentage of respondents in both groups indicating that the extent of perceived role conflict was a problem "not at all" or a problem "of little importance" was 44%. The percentage of

Table 1   Percentage of perceived and experienced role conflict reported by female athletes

	N	Not At All	Very Little	Mod-erate	Great	Very Great	Mean of Re-sponses
Perceived Role Conflict	268	19.4	24.3	29.9	18.5	7.7	2.70
Experienced Role Conflict	268	32.2	24.1	22.8	12.7	7.3	2.38

$$X^2(4) = 138.74, p < .01.$$

*A complete description of the validation and reliability techniques that were employed may be found in the original article.

Table 2   Percentage of perceived and experienced role conflict for female athletes in traditionally socially approved and not socially approved sports

	Not At All	Very Little	Mod-erate	Great	Very Great	Mean of Re-sponses
Perceived Role Conflict						
Not socially approved[a] ($N = 212$)	19.5	24.1	29.9	18.1	8.0	2.71
Socially approved[b] ($N = 56$)	19.1	25.0	30.0	19.6	7.6	2.69
$X^2(4) = 2.55, p > .05.$						
Experienced Role Conflict						
Not socially approved ($N = 212$)	30.5	23.5	23.9	13.6	7.6	2.43
Socially approved ($N = 56$)	38.4	27.3	18.4	9.5	6.3	2.17
$X^2(4) = 23.34, p < .01.$						

[a] Softball, basketball, volleyball, field hockey, track and field.
[b] Tennis, golf, swimming, gymnastics.

respondents indicating that the extent of perceived role conflict was "great" or "very great" was 25% for the "Not socially approved" group and 27% for the "Socially approved" group.

Chi square analysis of RCE indicated that the "Not socially approved" athletes had experienced significantly greater role conflict than "Socially approved" athletes (X^2 (4) = 24.34, $p < .01$). The average sum of responses on experienced role conflict was higher for the "Not socially approved" group, 2.43, than for the "Socially approved" group, 2.17. The percentage of re-spondents indicating that the extent of experienced role conflict was a problem "not at all" or a problem "of little importance" was 54% for the "Not socially approved" group and 66% for the "Socially approved" group. The percentage of respondents indicating that the extent of experienced role conflict was "great" or "very great" was 20% for the "Not socially approved" group and 16% for the "Socially approved group."

On both the RCP and the RCE sections the item on which the respond-ents expressed the highest degree of role conflict was: "Because American society traditionally places little value on girls' participation in sports, the female athlete receives little recognition for her skills and accomplishments." The item which they perceived as presenting the least role conflict was: "Girls are expected to look attractive and dress well, but participation in athletic activities often results in sweat, tousled hair, and broken fingernails." And the item in which they had actually experienced the least role conflict was: "Parents may encourage their daughters to participate in many kinds of activities but an athlete often devotes a great deal of attention to sport."

DISCUSSION AND IMPLICATIONS

As predicted, college female athletes perceive and experience role conflict in enacting their social roles as female and athlete. Twenty-six percent of the respondents reported perceiving role conflict to a great or very great extent and 20% reported experiencing role conflict to the same extent. However, the extent of role conflict did not reach the level that was anticipated by the investigators, since some 44% of the respondents indicated they perceived role conflict very little or not at all, while 56% had experienced little or no role conflict.

There are several possible explanations for these findings. First, it is possible that girls who either perceived or had experienced role conflict may have withdrawn from athletic participation before they reached college; thus, the findings may be somewhat biased by a sample of women who have elected to participate in sport because they do not perceive or have not experienced conflict. A second possible explanation is that the female athlete, through her skill acquisition and through other positive social approval that she obtains from participation, may have a more positive feeling about herself. Research by Snyder et al. (1975) and Harris and Jennings (1977) also supports the present finding and suggests that female athletes do not display perceived dissonance in their roles of female and athlete. In both the previous studies the subjects were reported to have significantly higher self-esteem than non-athletes, which would suggest that they felt competent and self-determining in their roles as athletes in the face of sex-role expectancies contrary to their role as females. Snyder and Kivlin (1975) and Snyder and Spreitzer (1976) found that high school and collegiate female athletes tended to manifest a more favorable self-concept than their non-athlete peers. These findings suggest that the social costs of sports participation by females are not as great as they once were due to the broadening definitions of sex-role behaviors.

The finding that perceived role conflict was higher than experienced role conflict is similar to findings for teachers (Grace, 1972) and physical educator-coaches (Massengale & Locke, 1976). It appears that regardless of the position one occupies, role incompatabilities that may exist are not manifested in others' actual behavior toward the role occupant to the extent that they are perceived as conflicting expectations.

The finding that female athletes participating in traditionally not socially approved sports experienced greater role conflict than those participating in more socially approved sports was expected. There is substantial evidence that persons actually behave differently toward those female athletes in the less socially approved sports than they do toward other female athletes.

The finding that society's attitude toward and recognition of the female athlete was perceived and experienced as the greatest conflict area probably reflects the fact that opportunities for females to participate in a variety of quality programs have been quite recent. There has not been sufficient time for either the high level skills to be developed or the recognition of those skills to be given. In the past, females have been content to participate, despite the lack of attention and recognition. However, recent legislation along with widespread media coverage of the emerging female athlete has no doubt made women more aware of the sex discrimination that has existed.

We would like to conclude with the optimistic observation that rapidly increasing sports opportunities for females may make the problem of role conflict among female athletes one of merely historical interest. One might speculate that it will exist only so long as society supports the stereotype of female role-appropriate behavior which is in conflict with the requirements of sports participation.

REFERENCES

Birns, B., "The emergence and socialization of sex differences in the earliest years," *Merrill-Palmer Quarterly,* 1976, **22**, 229-254.

Cronbach, L. J., & Meehl, P. E., "Construct validity in psychological tests," *Psychological Bulletin,* 1955, **52**, 177-193.

Debacy, D. L., Spaeth, R., & Busch, R., "What do men really think about athletic competition for women?" *Journal of Health, Physical Education, and Recreation,* November-December 1970, **41**, 28-29.

Del Rey, P., "In support of apologetics for women in sport," *International Journal of Sport Psychology,* 1977, **8**, 218-224.

Eitzen, D. S., & Sage, G. H., *Sociology of American sport.* Dubuque, Iowa: Wm. C. Brown, 1978.

Felshin, J., "The social view," in E. R. Gerber, J. Felshin, P. Berlin, & W. Wyrick (Eds.), *The American woman in sport.* Reading, Mass. Addison-Wesley, 1974.

Flerx, V. C., Fidler, D. S., & Rogers, R. W., "Sex role stereotypes: Developmental aspects and early intervention," *Child Development.* 1976, **47**, 998-1007.

Garman, E. W., *A study of attitudes toward softball competition for women.* Unpublished master's thesis, University of California, Santa Barbara, 1969.

Getzels, J. W., & Guba, E. G., "The structure of roles and role conflicts in the teaching situation," *Journal of Education Sociology,* 1955, **29**, 30-38.

Grace, G. R., *Role conflict and the teacher.* London: Routledge and Kegan Paul, 1972.

Griffin, P. S., "What is a nice girl like you doing in a profession like this?" *Quest,* 1973, **19**, 96-101.

Harres, B., "Attitudes of students toward women's athletic competition," *Research Quarterly,* 1968, **39**, 278-284.

Harris, D. V., "Psychosocial considerations," *Journal of Physical Education and Recreation,* January 1975, **46**, 32-36.

Harris, D. V., & Jennings, S. E., "Self-perceptions of female distance runners," in P. Milvy (Ed.), *The marathon: Physiological, medical, epidemiological, and psychological studies.* New York: Academy of Sciences, 1977.

Hart, M., "Stigma or prestige: The all-American choice," in G. H. McGlynn (Ed.), *Issues in physical education and sport.* Palo Alto, Calif.: National Press Books, 1974.

Hart, M., "On being female in sport," in M. Hart (Ed.), *Sport in the sociocultural process* (2nd ed.). Dubuque, Iowa: Wm. C. Brown, 1976.

Kerlinger, F. N., *Foundations of behavioral research* (2nd ed.). New York: Holt, Rinehart and Winston, 1973.

Lenski, G., "Status crystallization: A non-vertical dimension of status," *American Sociological Review,* 1954, **19**, 405-415.

Lenski, G., "Social participation and status crystallization," *American Sociological Review,* 1956, **21**, 458-464.

Lunneborg, P., "Stereotypic aspect in masculinity-femininity measurement," *Journal of Consulting and Clinical Psychology,* 1970, **34**, 113-116.

Maccoby, E., & Jacklin, C. N., *The psychology of sex differences.* Stanford, Calif.: Stanford University Press, 1974.

Malumphy, T. M., "Personality of women athletes in intercollegiate competition," *Research Quarterly,* 1968, **39**, 610-620.

Malumphy, T. M., "Athletics and competition for girls and women," in D. V. Harris (Ed.), *DGWS research reports: Women in sports.* Washington, D.C.: American Association for Health, Physical Education, and Recreation, 1971.

Massengale, J. D., & Locke, L. F., *The teacher/coach in conflict: A selective analysis of perceived and experienced dysfunction within the occupational role.* Paper presented at the National Convention of the American Alliance for Health, Physical Education and Recreation, Milwaukee, Wisconsin, April 1976.

Metheny, E., *Connotations of movement in sport and dance.* Dubuque, Iowa: Wm. C. Brown, 1965.

Nunnaly, J., *Psychometric theory.* New York: McGraw-Hill, 1967.

Scott, J., "Men and women in sport: The manhood myth," in G. H. McGlynn (Ed.), *Issues in physical education and sport,* Palo Alto, Calif.: National Press Books, 1974.

Sherrif, M. C., "The status of female athletes as viewed by selected peers and parents in certain high schools of central California," unpublished master's thesis, Chico State College, 1969.

Snyder, E. E., & Kivlin, J. E., "Women athletes and aspects of psychological well-being and body image," *Research Quarterly,* 1975, **46,** 191-199.

Snyder, E. E., & Kivlin, J. E., "Perceptions of the sex role among female athletes and non-athletes," *Adolescence,* Spring 1977, **45,** 23-29.

Snyder, E. E., Kivlin, J. E., & Spreitzer, E., "The female athlete: Analysis of objective and subjective role conflict," in D. M. Landers (Ed.), *Psychology of sport and motor behavior.* University Park: Pennsylvania State University, 1975.

Snyder, E.-E. & Spreitzer, E., "Correlates of sport participation among adolescent girls," *Research Quarterly,* 1976, **47,** 804-809.

Spence, J. T., Helmreich, R., & Stapp, J., "A short version of the attitudes toward Women Scale, (AWS)." *Bulletin of the Psychonomic Society, 1973,* **2,** 219-220.

Thomas, E. J., "Role theory, personality, and the individual," in E. F. Borgatta & W. W. Lambert (Eds.), *Handbook of personality theory and research.* Chicago: Rand McNally, 1968.

Thompson, S. K., "Gender labels and early sex role development," *Child Development,* 1975, **46,** 339-347.

WOMEN IN SPORT: COOPTATION OR LIBERATION?

George H. Sage

Liberation movements have a way of promising more than they deliver. The underlying idealism and optimism produces an aura of excitement and anticipation. People expect that justice is about to prevail and that social oppression is about to be eliminated for another group of people. It turns out, however, that the liberationists were only after a piece of the existing pie rather than striving for truly alternative modes of living for large blocks of humanity. Never mind that the pie has many ingredients that are spoiled, sour, or downright hazardous to health. The important thing is "getting a piece of the action," "getting what's coming to one." The idealism and the potential for "real" change—change that promotes human growth throughout the broad spectrum of human life—gets blunted and diffused as the liberationists get absorbed into the mainstream of the social system; they are co-opted.[1]

Granted, the mainstreamers may have to make some accommodations and concessions to the liberationists, but gradually, as the latter begin to obtain the "goodies" of the mainstream, they adopt and internalize most mainstream orientations, thus becoming a "new class" of powerful persons with limited perspectives of equalitarianism and very protective of the power and influence they now hold.

What does this have to do with women's sports? Well, I think that it is obvious that the field of sport has witnessed a liberation movement within the past ten years—women's sports liberation. The women's sports movement has been one of the most significant liberation activities of the century. We really must applaud it. God knows that females need the same opportunities as males to engage in healthful sports. The female sex stereotyping which has discouraged female sports involvement has been an integral part of Western Civilization for over 2,000 years, and the need to break this cultural bondage was long overdue.

What has been its consequences? Well, surely it has opened up unprecedented opportunities for girls and women to engage in sports. While social attitudes do not change overnight, or even in a decade, female achievements in sport have produced new attitudes among both males and females about females' potential as athletes and as human beings. In many ways, it has given females a new respect for themselves.

George H. Sage, "Women in Sport: Cooptation or Liberation?" *Colorado Journal of Health, Physical Education, and Recreation*, 1, No. 2, (March, 1975).

Like most liberation movements, the women's sports movement has not achieved some of the outcomes that many had hoped and wished for. When it began a few years ago, there was an excitement and an anticipation that women were not only going to move into greater sport involvement but that they were going to develop a new model for interscholastic and intercollegiate sports. A model that would contain the best features of the male programs but that would exclude the worst features, a model that would add new, exciting, humane features.

It was reasoned that for over fifty years women had the opportunity to observe, sometimes with horror, as male high school and collegiate athletics, in the process of fostering healthful, educational sports, entered the field of professional entertainment. For the male coaches, marketplace criteria became virtually the only measure of coaching ability, and "win" became synonymous with success, and "lose" became associated with failure. Prestige in coaching was based upon won-loss records. This system tended to emphasize the treatment of athletes for what they could do for the coach—win— rather than the treatment of athletes based upon what coaches could do for the personal-social growth of athletes as persons.

Surely, many thought, leaders of female inter-school sports programs would, in their wisdom and with their years of observing male sports programs, advance an alternative educational sports model. It is now clear that there is no intention on the part of women physical educators and coaches of doing this at all. The main thrust of the women's sports movement is to mirror the men's programs in virtually every respect in the name of equality of opportunity. The opportunity to observe the strengths and weaknesses of male programs over the past half century and to select the strengths for emulation and reject the weaknesses as unwanted has been sacrificed in the quest to have exactly what the males have, regardless of the consequences (and historians say we learn from history!).

I am being facetious now, but it almost makes one wonder if the women's sports movement has not been a very subtle and clever scheme of male chauvinists. If male chauvinists in sports had intentionally set out to co-opt females into the mainstream orientations of the sport social system they could not have been more successful. Their grand strategy would have gone like this:

Give them (female sports leaders) a piece of the action. Of course, we will have to make some concessions, but basically we will continue to operate as usual. But once the females are in the business, there will be at least two benefits for male sports programs. First, the females will have to stop belly-aching about the enormous sums of money and human resources that are expended in male programs because the females will now be part of the problem—that is, they'll be spending large sums too. Second, in order to protect their own newly-won empires, the females will be supportive of male programs because they know that their programs depend on the health of male programs. Neat, the entire effect is to reinforce the existing mainstream school sports system, the one that has serious problems which are acknowledged by coaches such as Joe Paterno and Frank Broyles, football coaches at Penn. State and Arkansas, as well as by thoughtful educators throughout the country.

Earlier in this essay, I mentioned that once a liberation group secured its immediate demands and became co-opted by the mainstream of the social system, its members tend to adopt a rather narrow perspective of equalitarianism. Let me use one example of how this notion is related to the women's sports movement. It quickly became evident that when women sports leaders spoke of equality of women's intercollegiate sports with men's collegiate sports they included the granting of athletic scholarships. Oh, there was a brief show by the AIAW denying the desire for athletic scholarships, but few really took this seriously, and many women physical educators and coaches did not agree with this position. Besides, it was clear that this policy would be tested in court rather quickly. And so it was.

Now, the stage was set. If men give athletic scholarships, women could too. But surely a stronger argument than that is needed, and sure enough, it was available; the men have been using it for years. It goes like this: Athletic scholarships can be justified on the basis that they are "talent" scholarships. Athletes have a special talent and one way of rewarding talent is to give some monetary reward—it's the All-American way. Female sports leaders had their justification. Female athletes, like male athletes, possess a talent—a talent that has been developed through years of practice. Why shouldn't colleges award scholarships to these talented athletes—females as well as males?

Fine, but, and here is where we get into the limited perspectives of liberationists' notions. If we are going to award "talent" scholarships to football, field hockey, basketball and track athletes, why not soccer, table tennis, billiards, judo, figure skating and sky diving athletes? Are not skilled performers in these latter sports, and many others, as "talented" as those in the former group? How about modern and contemporary dancers? Are they not skilled? Athletic? Dedicated? Talented? Why are not the dance teachers at collegiate institutions given a specific number of athletic scholarships just as the coach of football, field hockey, basketball, etc.?

Let's face it, at every college in the country there are many students who possess talents for which they receive no financial remuneration from the institution. Why are they less worthy to receive talent scholarships? My guess is that most coaches would say that their talent is not marketable; that is, it cannot be used to entertain or amuse. Or it might be contended that the scholarship group practices long hours to maintain the award. Thus, athletic scholarships are justified on the moral basis of rewarding the talented, but the exclusive nature of the awards is based upon financial, entertainment, and public relations considerations. I wonder if this is consistent with a real liberation, or equalitarian, perspective?

I want to note, in concluding this essay, that I don't want to seem to be overcritical of the emerging women's sports program. Men have lived with a number of serious programs in their inter-school sports programs for the past half century and have made little effort to correct these problems. It may be too much to expect that women will be able to develop an ideal sports model in the first decade of intensive inter-school sports involvement. But we can hope for better things because an alternative sports structure which stresses cooperation, participation, expressiveness, fun, intrinsic motivation, and self-actualization would be a refreshing substitute for the current emphasis in interscholastic and intercollegiate programs. What is needed is a better model for these sports programs to make them truly "educational."

NOTES

1. Phillip Selznick defines co-optation as "the process of absorbing new elements into the leadership or policy-determining structure of an organization as a means of averting threats to its stability or existence." (Selznick, P., *TVA and the Grass Roots*, New York: Harper Torchbook 1966).

FOR FURTHER READING

1. Gerber, E. R., Felshin, J., Berlin, P. and Wyrick, W. (eds.), *The American Woman in Sport,* Reading, Mass.: Addison-Wesley, 1974.

2. Hannon, K., "Too Far Too Fast," *Sports Illustrated* **48** (March 20): 34–45, 1978.

3. Huckle, P., "Back to the Starting Line: Title IX and Women's Intercollegiate Athletics," *American Behavioral Scientist* **21** (January-February): 370–392, 1978.

4. Oglesby, C. A., (ed.), *Women and Sport: From Myth to Reality* Philadelphia: Lea and Febiger, 1978.

5. Snyder, E. E. and Spreitzer, E., "Correlates of Sport Participation Among Adolescent Girls," *Research Quarterly* **47** (December): 804–809, 1976.

6. Snyder, E. E. and Spreitzer, E., "Perceptions of the Sex Role Among Female Athletes and Nonathletes," *Adolescence* **12** (Spring): 23–29, 1977.

7. "Comes the Revolution," *Time Magazine* June 26, 1978, pp. 54–59.

CHAPTER 7

RACE AND SPORT

It is often argued that sports have been the most responsive of the many integrating social agencies in American society for enculturalizing and providing personal-social opportunities to the polyethnic and multi-racial groups in it. Indeed, sport is frequently called the greatest democratizing institution in this country, in this regard, Boyle (1963) states:

> Sport has often served minority groups as the first rung on the social ladder. As such, it has helped further their assimilation into American life. It would not be too far-fetched to say that it has done more in this regard than any other agency, including church and school (p. 100).

Riesman and Denney (1951) in their classic paper on the role of football for cultural diffusion suggest that the linkage between football and various ethnic groups has been pronounced since the 19th century. They say, with reference to football:

> . . . its rationalization as a sport and as a spectacle has served to bring out more openly the part it plays in the ethnic, class, and characterological struggles of our time—meaning by "Characterological struggle," the conflict between different styles of life. The ethnic significance of football is immediately suggested by the shift in the typical origins of player-names on the All-American Football Teams since 1889. In 1889 all but one of the names (Heffelfinger) suggested Anglo-Saxon origins. . . . After 1895, it was a rare All-American team that did not include at least one Irishman. . . . By 1927, names like Casey, Kipke, Oosterbaan, Koppisch, Garbisch, and Friedman were appearing on the All-American list with as much frequency as names like Channing, Adams and Ames in the 1890's (pp. 309–310).

Although individuals and groups from a variety of origins have been prominent in American sports—DiMaggios and Pepitones of the Italians, Nagurskis of the Poles, Greenbergs and Koufaxs of the Jews, Joe Louis and Willie Mays of the Blacks—it would be highly inaccurate to describe the sports world as completely equalitarian. The most infamous example of racial discrimination is professional baseball which excluded Blacks for over fifty years (see Robert Peterson's book, *Only the Ball Was White,* for an account of this).

Racial prejudice against Blacks has been with us since slaves were imported into this country. But even in the days of slavery, several sports were open for Black participation. Boxing was generally open to Blacks; horse racing had many Black jockeys in the nineteenth century; and Blacks were prominent in the early years of professional baseball up to 1888, when an unwritten law of professional baseball barring Blacks was introduced. This law was effective until 1945, when Jackie Robinson became the first modern Black to sign an organized baseball contract.

Although racial discrimination has always been incompatible with the ideals of American sports, widespread sports opportunities for the Black emerged only when discrimination became incompatible with good financial policy. In those team sports in which the profit motive has come to dominate, the contribution of outstanding Black athletes to winning championships and holding public interest has opened up opportunities to Blacks in college and professional sports. Sports more social in nature and with less spectator interest have been slow to attract and integrate the Black.

In the past twenty-five years the Black has assumed a remarkably prominent role in American sports. In 1956, 14 percent of the professional football players were Blacks; today more than 40 percent of all players in the NFL are Blacks. In baseball's major leagues, about 30 percent of the players are Blacks. And a recent count of professional basketball teams shows that Blacks represent 70 percent of the total players. Thousands of Blacks are playing on college athletic teams, and today the basketball teams of many high schools, especially in the big cities, often have five non-whites in the five starting positions.

American Black athletes have dominated recent Olympic Games in the short races and the jumping events. Moreover, Blacks are champions in many boxing weight classifications.

Sports opportunities have undoubtedly improved for Blacks in the past two decades, but discrimination appears to persist, albeit in a more subtle form. Rosenblatt (1967) reported that an analysis of Major League batting averages over two different three-year periods (1958-61 and 1962-65) showed that the Black ballplayer, to be treated equally, must be better. Loy and McElvogue (1970) reported apparent racial segregation, based upon the positions which they play, for both professional football and baseball players.

The Black's success in sport has led many to seek an explanation for this phenomenon. Some have claimed that the Black possesses physical characteristics which are advantageous for athletic performance (see Kane, 1971). Anthropologists have identified several structural differences in Blacks and Caucasians, but no proof has been given that these differences actually do provide motor skill advantages, and investigations of various physical factors comparing Blacks and Caucasians have yielded inconclusive results.

Many social scientists are of the opinion that sociological and psychological factors are the primary reason for the Black's rise to eminence in sports. They note that most Black athletes come from the low socioeconomic classes; here recreational outlets for the young are mainly sports, so many hours are spent playing in the streets, recreation centers, and playgrounds (see Axthelm, 1970). Furthermore, it has been emphasized that excellence in sports provides an opportunity for Blacks to escape from the slums and ghettos. Thus, the desire to escape from their childhood environments seems to have caused many Black youths to approach sport with greater motivation to excel than is found in middle-class whites.

In the first reading, Harry Edwards forcefully attacks the notion that Blacks have physical advantages which enable them to excel in sports. He suggests that in fact the propagation of the notion that Blacks are physically superior to whites is a racist guise to advance the old stereotype that Blacks are not as phylogenetically advanced as whites, that they are closer to lower animals. Edwards warns those who accept the notion of the genetic theory of Black physical superiority that they are falling into the trap set by white racists. For Edwards, the conditions which are responsible for the current Black prominence in American sports are mainly social. Since a great majority of Blacks are in the lower social classes, and since there are only one or two avenues for upward social mobility based on personal achievement—one being sports—these conditions produce a strong motivation among young Blacks to achieve and excel in sports.

In the second reading D. Stanley Eitzen and Norman R. Yetman focus on three components of the sports world where discrimination against Blacks is alleged to occur: the assignment of playing positions, reward and authority structures, and performance differentials. The three major professional team sports of baseball, basketball, and football are the subjects of this analysis, since it is in these sports where Blacks are most prominent.

Eitzen and Yetman convincingly show that Blacks have been stacked into the peripheral positions, and while it cannot be proven that prejudice against Blacks was responsible for this phenomenon, it raises some serious issues about equalitarianism in sports. The authors describe how discrepancies in the reward and authority structure of professional sports has worked to the disadvantage of Blacks. The final issue, that of performance differentials between Blacks and whites, is dealt with by the authors by showing that one form of discrimination in sport has been unequal opportunity for equal ability, that is, Black players have had to be superior in performance to their white teammates to gain entrance into sports.

Several studies of Black athletes in professional baseball and football show them to be under-represented in the central positions and over-represented in the peripheral positions, and several explanations have been advanced for this phenomenon. One of these explanations has been proposed by Barry McPherson. In the last reading McPherson argues that stacking of Black athletes into peripheral positions may not be deliberate discriminatory acts by white coaches. Instead, according to McPherson, Black athletes may segregate themselves into particular playing positions because they use Black athletic stars as their heroes and wish to model their athletic experiences after the Black stars. Since the Black professional athletes have tended to play the noncentral positions, these are the positions that Black youth play, and the result is that Blacks are overrepresented in these positions today.

REFERENCES

Axthelm, P., *The City Game,* New York: Harper & Row, 1970.

Boyle, R. H., *Sport: Mirror of American Life,* Little, Brown, and Company, 1963.

Kane, M., "An Assessment of 'Black is Best'," *Sports Illustrated,* **34** (January 18); 72–83, 1971.

Loy, J. W., and McElvogue, J. F., "Racial Segregation in American Sport," *International Review of Sport Sociology,* **5**: 5–25, 1970.

Peterson, R., *Only the Ball was White,* Englewood Cliffs: Prentice Hall, 1970.

Riesman, D., and Denney, R., "Football in America: A Study of Culture Diffusion," *American Quarterly,* **3**: 309–319, 1951.

Rosenblatt, A., "Negroes in Baseball: The Failure of Success," *Trans-Action,* **4** (September): 51–53, 1967.

Weinberg, S. K., and Arond, H., "The Occupational Culture of the Boxer," *American Journal of Sociology,* **57** (March): 460–469, 1952.

THE MYTH OF THE RACIALLY SUPERIOR ATHLETE

Harry Edwards

While there can be little argument with the obvious fact that black performances in sports have been and continue to be superior, on the whole, to those of whites, there is room for considerable debate over the identity and character of the factors that have determined that superiority and contributed to its perpetuation.

The myth of the black male's racially determined, inherent physical and athletic superiority over the white male rivals the myth of black sexual superiority in antiquity. While both are well fixed in the Negrolore and folk beliefs of American society, in recent years the former has been subject to increasing emphasis due to the overwhelmingly disproportionate representation of black athletes on all-star rosters, on Olympic teams, in the various "most valuable player" categories, and due to the black athletes' overall domination of the highly publicized or so-called "major sports"—basketball, football, baseball, track and field. But seldom in recent times has the myth of racially linked black athletic prowess been subject to so explicit a formulation and presentation as in the January 18, 1971 issue of *Sports Illustrated* magazine.

In an article entitled "An Assessment of 'Black is Best' " by Martin Kane, one of the magazine's senior editors, several arguments are detailed, discussed and affirmed by a number of widely known medical scientists, athletic researchers, coaches and black athletes. In essence, the article constitutes an attempt to develop a logical and scientifically defensible foundation for the assertion that black athletic superiority in sports is due to racial characteristics indigenous to the black population in America but not generally found within the white population.

Clearly there is no argument that black society is contributing more than its 11% share of athletes and star-status performers to professional sports. And where blatant racism and discrimination do not keep blacks from participation almost completely—such as in the Southeastern Conference [no longer true] —a similar pattern of black domination prevails in colleges and at other amateur levels where major sports endeavors are pursued.

Harry Edwards, "The Myth of the Racially Superior Athlete," *Intellectual Digest,* 2:58–60 (March 1972). Originally published in *The Black Scholar,* 3:16–28 (November 1971). Copyright © by *The Black Scholar.* Reprinted by permission of *The Black Scholar* and *Intellectual Digest.*

Attempting to explain this disproportionate representation, Kane mentions, almost in passing, the probable influences of contemporary societal conditions and then launches into a delineation and discussion of the major factors giving rise to black athletic superiority. They are:

Racially linked physical and psychological characteristics:

1. Proportionately longer leg lengths, narrower hips, wider calf bones and greater arm circumference among black athletes than among whites.

2. A greater ratio of tendon to muscle among blacks, giving rise to a condition typically termed "double jointedness," a relatively dense bone structure.

3. A basically elongated body structure among black athletes enabling them to function as more efficient heat dissipaters relative to whites.

Race-related psychological factors:

1. The black athlete's greater capacity for relaxation under pressure relative to the capacity of the white athlete.

Racially specific historical occurrences:

1. The selectivity of American slavery in weeding out the hereditarily and congenitally weak from among those who came to be the forebears of today's black population.

Let us now turn to a general consideration of these major factors.

RACIALLY LINKED PHYSICAL AND PHYSIOLOGICAL CHARACTERISTICS

Kane's attempt to establish the legitimacy of this category of factors as major contributions to the emergence of black athletic superiority suffers from two basic maladies—one methodological, the other arising from a dependence upon scientifically debatable assumptions and presumptions concerning differences between the "races" of men and the impact of these differences upon capacity for physical achievement.

Simply stated, one grossly indefensible methodological tactic is obvious in virtually every case of "scientific" evidence presented in support of a physical or physiological basis for black athletic superiority. *In no case was the evidence presented gathered from a random sample of subjects selected from the black population at large in America.* Thus, supporting data, for the most part, were taken from black athletes of already proven excellence or from blacks who were available due to other circumstances reflective of some degree of uncontrolled social, political, or otherwise contrived selectivity. Therefore, the generalization of the research findings on these subjects to the black population as a whole—even assuming the findings to be valid— constitutes a scientific blunder of the highest magnitude and invalidates the would-be scientific foundations of this component of the author's argument.

With regard to the alleged physical traits supposedly characteristic of black athletes, the question can justifiably be posed, "What two outstanding black athletes look alike or have identical builds?" One of Kane's resource persons answers this question: "Lloyd C. 'Bud' Winter makes it quite obvious that black athletes differ from each other physically quite as much as whites do." He notes that Ray Norton, a sprinter, was tall and slender with scarcely discernible hips, that Bobby Painter, a sprinter, was squat and dumpy with a swayback and a big butt, that Dennis Johnson was short and wiry, that Tommy Smith was tall and wiry, and so on.

Further evidence is plentiful: What physical characteristics does Lew Alcindor [Kareem Abdul-Jabbar] have in common with Elgin Baylor, or Wilt Chamberlain with Al Attles, etc? The point is simply that Wilt Chamberlain and Lew Alcindor have more in common physically with Mel Counts and Henry Finkel, two seven-foot white athletes, than with most of their fellow black athletes.

Even excepting the hyperbolic illustrations just documented, what emerges from any objective analysis of supposed physical differences between so-called races is the undeniable fact that there exist more differences between individual members of any one racial group than between any two groups as a whole.

Recognition of this essential fact precludes the type of incredible qualification that Kane is forced to make when faced with exceptions that do not fit the framework he has developed. A case in point is his assertion that the physical differences between white and black racial groupings predispose blacks to dominate the sports requiring speed and strength while whites, due to racially linked physical traits, are predestined to prevail in those sporting events requiring endurance. When confronted with the fact that black Kenyans won distance races and defeated highly touted and capable whites in the 1968 Olympic Games, the author makes the ridiculous post hoc assertion that (the Kenyans) Keino and Bikila have black skin but a number of white features.

RACE-RELATED PSYCHOLOGICAL FACTORS

The academic belief in the existence of a national or a racial "character" was supposedly disposed of by scholars decades ago. Their persistence among the ranks of coaches and other segments of the American population only indicates the difficulty with which racial stereotypes and caricatures are destroyed or altered to comply with prevailing knowledge. Kane and his resource persons, mostly coaches, recreate a portrait of the black athlete as the happy-go-lucky, casual, "What—me worry?" Negro made so familiar to Americans through history books, Stepin Fetchit movies and other societal outlets. But besides the fact that the overall portrayal is inappropriate, not even the psychological traits attributed to black athletes are substantiated.

Kane quotes Lloyd C. Winter, former coach of a long line of successful black track and field athletes as stating: "A limber athlete has body control, and body control is part of skill. It is obvious that many black people have some sort of head-start motor in them, but for now I can only theorize that their great advantage is relaxation under stress. As a class, the black athletes who have trained under me are far ahead of whites in that one factor— relaxation under pressure. It's their secret."

In data collected by Bruce C. Ogilvie and Thomas A. Tutko, two athletic psychologists whose work was ironically featured in the same issue of *Sports Illustrated* in which Kane's article appears, a strong case is made for the fact that black athletes are significantly less relaxed than white athletes in the competitive situation. (I am intimately familiar with this data as a result of my Ph.D. dissertation, *Sport in America: Its Myths and Realities*.) Using an Institute for Personality and Ability Testing (IPAT) test that is generally considered to have a high degree of reliability in both cross-cultural and simple comparative investigations, the following findings emerged when the psychological orientations of successful black and white athletes were compared:

1. On an IPAT test, successful black athletes showed themselves to be considerably more serious, concerned and "uptight" than their white counter-parts as indicated by their relative scores on the item "Sober/Happy-go-lucky." Blacks had a mean stern score of 5.1 as compared to a mean score for whites of 5.5 (level of significance of differences between scores is .01; N = 396 whites, 136 blacks).

2. On the IPAT item of "Casual/Controlled," successful black athletes indicated a more controlled orientation. Blacks had a mean stern score of 6.6 as compared with the whites' mean score of 6.2 (level of significance of differences is .01; N = 396 whites, 136 blacks).

Sociologically, this pattern of differences among black athletes is perhaps to be expected, given the fact that they are aware that they operate at a decided disadvantage competing against whites for highly valued positions and rewards in an admittedly white racist society. Furthermore, sports participation holds the greatest promise of escape from the material degrada-tion of oppressed black society. Thus, the assertion that black athletes are more "relaxed" than white not only lacks scientific foundation but is ludicrous as even a commonsense assumption.

RACIALLY SPECIFIC HISTORICAL OCCURRENCES

Kane states that "it might be that without special breeding the African has a superior physique." The statements of Kane and his resource persons evi-dence confusion as to the scope of characteristics involved in the selectivity process as it has affected mankind. Natural selection or "the survival of the fittest" has been predicated upon relative strength and physical attributes to a lesser degree in mankind than in any other form of animal life. This has been due largely to man's tremendously developed mental capabilities. The same would have held for the slave. While some may have survived as a result of greater physical strength and toughness, many undoubtedly also survived due to their shrewdness and thinking abilities.

The major implication of Kane's argument for the black population at large is that it opens the door for at least an informal acceptance of the idea that whites are *intellectually* superior to blacks. Blacks, whether athletes or nonathletes, must not give even this passing credence to the possibility of white intellectual superiority. By a tempered or even enthusiastic admission of black physical superiority, the white population of this racist society loses nothing. For it is a simple fact that a multitude of even lower animals are physically superior, not only to whites, but to mankind as a whole: gorillas are physically superior to whites, leopards are physically superior to whites, as are lions, walruses and elephants. So by asserting that blacks are physically superior, whites at best reinforce some old stereotypes long held about Afro-Americans—to wit, that they are little removed from the apes in their evolutionary development.

On the other hand, intellectual capability is the highest-priced commodity on the world market today. If in a fit of black identity, or simple stupidity, we accept the myth of innate black superiority, we could be inadvertently recognizing and accepting an ideology which has been used as the justification for black slavery, segregation and general oppression.

What then are the major factors underlying black athletic superiority? They emerge from a complex of societal conditions. These conditions instill a heightened motivation among black male youths to achieve success in sports; thus, they channel a proportionately greater number of talented black people than whites into sports participation. Our best sociological evidence indicates that capacity for physical achievement (like other common human traits such as intelligence, artistic ability, etc.) is evenly distributed throughout any population. Thus, it cuts across class, religious, and, more particularly, racial lines. For race, like class and religion, is primarily a culturally determined classification. *The simple fact of the matter is that the scientific concept of race has no proven biological or genetic validity.* As a cultural delineation, however, it does have a social and political reality. This social and political reality of race is the primary basis of stratification in this society and the key means of determining the priority of who shall have access to means and thus, valued goods and services.

Blacks are relegated in this country to the lowest priority in terms of access to valued goods and services. This fact, however, does not negate the equal and proportionate distribution of talent across both black and white populations. Hence, a situation arises wherein whites, being the dominant group in the society, have access to *all* means toward achieving desirable valuables defined by the society. Blacks, on the other hand, are channeled into the one or two endeavors open to them—sports, and to a lesser degree, entertainment.

Bill Russell once stated that he had to work as hard to achieve his status as the greatest basketball player of the last decade as the president of General Motors had to work to achieve his position. The evidence tends to indicate that Russell is quite correct. In short, it takes just as much talent, perseverance, dedication and earnest effort to succeed in sports as to become a leading financier, business executive, attorney or doctor. Few occupations (Music and art being perhaps the exceptions) demand more time and dedication than sports. A world-class athlete will usually have spent a good deal of his youth practicing the skills and techniques of his chosen sport.

The competition for the few positions is extremely keen and if he is fortunate he will survive in that competition long enough to become a professional athlete or an outstanding figure in one of the amateur sports. For as he moves up through the various levels of competition, fewer and fewer slots or positions are available and the competition for these becomes increasingly intense because the rewards are greater. Since the talents of 25 million Afro-Americans have a disproportionately higher concentration in sports, the number of highly gifted whites in sports is proportionately less. Under such circumstances, black athletes naturally predominate. Further, the white athletes who do participate in sports operate at a psychological disadvantage because they believe blacks to be inherently superior as athletes. Thus, the white man has become the chief victim of his own lie.

IMMUNE FROM RACISM?

D. Stanley Eitzen and Norman R. Yetman

No other aspect of sport in America has generated more sociological interest than race relations. The research interest in race undoubtedly has been influenced by the turmoil of the late fifties and sixties that generated increased academic and critical attention to all phases of black life in America. At the same time the American sports world became increasingly open to black participation during the civil rights era.

D. Stanley Eitzen and Norman R. Yetman, "Immune from Racism?" *Civil Rights Digest,* Vol. 9 (Winter 1977), pp. 3–13. Reprinted by permission of the authors.

Since the early 1960's the percentage of black competitors in each of the major professional team sports (football, basketball, and baseball) have exceeded blacks' proportion (11 percent) of the total U.S. population. In baseball, for example, the 1957–58 season was the year that blacks achieved a proportion equivalent to their percentage in the U.S. population. The watershed year in professional football was 1960 (see Table 1); in professional basketball it was 1958 (see Table 3).

By 1975, blacks comprised better than 60 percent of all professional basketball players, 42 percent of all professional football players, and 21 percent of major league baseball players. An additional 11 percent of major league baseball players were Latin Americans.

The large proportion of blacks and the prominence of black superstars such as Kareem Abdul-Jabbar, Hank Aaron, and O. J. Simpson have led many Americans—black and white—to infer that collegiate and professional athletics have provided an avenue of mobility for blacks unavailable elsewhere in American society. Sports, thus, seems to have "done something for" black Americans. Many commentators—social scientists, journalists, and black athletes themselves—have argued, however, that black visibility in collegiate and professional sports has merely served to mask the racism that pervades the entire sports establishment. According to these critics, the existence of racism in collegiate and professional sports is especially insidious because sports promoters and commentators have projected an image of athletics as the single institution in America relatively immune from racism.

In a previous article (*Civil Rights Digest* August 1972) we examined racial discrimination in American sports—in particular, college basketball. This article examines three aspects of the athletic world alleged to be racially biased—the assignment of playing positions, reward and authority structures, and performance differentials. The analysis will focus primarily on the three major professional team sports (baseball, basketball, and football) where blacks are found most prominently, and therefore slights the obvious dearth of blacks in other sports (e.g., hockey, tennis, golf, and swimming).

STACKING TEAM POSITIONS

One of the best documented forms of discrimination in both college and professional ranks is popularly known as stacking. The term refers to situations in which minority-group members are relegated to specific team positions and excluded from competing for others. The result is often that intrateam competition for starting positions is between members of the same race (e.g., those competing for running back slots are black, while those competing for quarterback slots are white). For example, Aaron Rosenblatt noted in *Transaction* magazine that while there are twice as many pitchers on a baseball team as outfielders, in 1965 there were three times as many black outfielders as pitchers.

Examination of the stacking phenomenon was first undertaken by John Loy and Joseph McElvogue in 1970, who argued that racial segregation in sports is a function of "centrality" in a team sports unit. To explain racial segregation by team position in sports, they combined organizational principles advanced by Hubert M. Blalock and Oscar Grusky.

Blalock argued that:

1. The lower the degree of purely social interaction on the job . . . , the lower the degree of [racial] discrimination.
2. To the extent that performance level is relatively independent of skill in interpersonal relations, the lower the degree of [racial] discrimination.

Grusky's notions about the formal structure of organizations are similar:

All else being equal, the more central one's . . . location: (1) the greater the likelihood dependent . . . tasks will be performed, and (2) the greater the rate of interaction with the occupants of other positions. Also, the performance of dependent tasks is positively related to frequency of interaction.

Combining these propositions, Loy and McElvogue hypothesized that "racial segregation in professional team sports is positively related to centrality." Their analysis of football (where the central positions are quarterback, center, offensive guard, and linebacker) and baseball (where the central positions are the infield, catcher, and pitcher) demonstrated that the central positions were indeed overwhelmingly manned by whites, while blacks were overrepresented in noncentral positions.

Examining the data for baseball in 1967, they found that 83 percent of those listed as infielders were white, while 49 percent of the outfielders were black. The proportion of whites was greatest in the positions of catcher (96 percent) and pitcher (94 percent), the most central positions in baseball.

Our analysis of data from the 1975 major league baseball season showed little change from the situation described by Loy and McElvogue in 1967. By 1975 the percentage of infielders who were white had declined slightly to 76 percent, but the outfield was still disproportionately manned by blacks (49 percent). Moreover, pitcher (96 percent) and catcher (95 percent) remained overwhelmingly white positions.

Table 1 compares the racial composition of positions in football for the 1960 and 1975 seasons. The conclusions to be drawn from these data are clear. While the proportion of blacks has increased dramatically during this 15-year period, central positions continue to be disproportionately white. One difference between 1960 and 1975 is that blacks have increasingly supplanted whites at noncentral positions.

Table 1   The Distribution of White and Black Players by Position in Major League
Football

| | 1960 and 1975 (in Percentages) | | | | | |
| | 1960* | | | 1975 | | |
Playing position	% of all whites	% of all blacks	Percent black by position**	% of whites	% of blacks	Percent black by position
Kicker/Punter	1.2	0	0	9.0	.2	1.3
Quarterback	6.3	0	0	9.7	.5	3.5
Center	5.3	0	0	6.7	.5	4.9
Linebacker	11.5	3.6	4.2	17.4	8.6	26.0
Off. guard	8.0	1.8	3.0	8.7	4.5	26.9
Off. tackle	8.3	23.2	28.3	8.6	5.7	31.8
Def. front four	11.0	14.3	15.4	12.3	15.7	47.6
End/flanker	22.6	7.1	4.6	11.6	20.2	55.3
Running back	16.5	25.0	17.5	8.1	21.1	65.2
Def. back	9.3	25.0	27.5	8.1	23.2	67.3
	100.0	100.0		100.2	100.2	
Total number	(199½)	(27)	12.3	(870)	(620)	41.6

*The 1960 data were compiled by Jonathan Brower who obtained them from the
media guides published annually by each team. Whenever a player was listed at two
positions, Brower credited him as one-half at each position. 1975 data are taken from
1975 *Football Register* published annually by *The Sporting News*. Since both the
media guides and the *Football Register* are published before each season, they
include only information on veterans. The total N for 1960 is smaller than one
would expect, presumably because Brower was unable to obtain media guides for
all teams.

**Since blacks were 12.3 percent of the player population in 1960, those playing
positions with a black percentage less than 12.3 were underrepresented. In 1975
those positions less than 41.6 percent black were underrepresented.

On the other hand, blacks appear to have made some inroads in the
central offensive positions—for example, a shift from 97 percent white to 87
percent white from 1960 to 1975. But when length of time in the league is
held constant, the overwhelming proportion of whites in these positions
remains. Among those players in the league 1 to 3 years, 79 percent were
white in 1975; 4 to 6 years, 80 percent white; 7 to 9 years, 80 percent white;
and 10 or more years, 96 percent white. (The latter may be a consequence of
the league's having a small proportion of black players in the past.)

The effects of stacking in noncentral positions are far reaching. In 17 of
the 26 pro football teams surveyed, approximately three-fourths of all 1971
advertising slots (radio, television, and newspapers) were alloted to players in
central positions.

Second, noncentral positions in football depend primarily on speed and quickness, which means in effect that playing careers are shortened for persons in those positions. For example, in 1975 only 4.1 percent of the players listed in the *Football Register* in the three predominantly black positions—defensive back, running back, and wide receiver (65 percent of all black players)—had been in the pros for 10 or more years, while 14.8 percent of players listed in the three predominantly white positions—quarterback, center, and offensive guard—remained that long. The shortened careers for noncentral players have two additional deleterious consequences—less lifetime earnings and limited benefits from the players' pension fund, which provides support on the basis of longevity.

ASSIGNMENT BY STEREOTYPE

The Loy and McElvogue interpretation of these data rested primarily upon a position's spatial location in a team unit. However, Harry Edwards argues that the actual spatial location of a playing position is an incidental factor in the explanation of stacking. The crucial variable involved in position segregation is the degree of leadership responsibility found in each position. For example, quarterbacks have greater team authority and ability to affect the outcome of the game than do individuals who occupy noncentral positions.

Thus, the key is not the interaction potential of the playing position but the leadership and degree of responsibility for the game's outcome built into the position that account for the paucity of blacks at the so-called central positions. This is consistent with the stereotype hypothesis advanced by Jonathan Brower (specifically for football, but one that applies to other sports as well):

> The combined function of . . . responsibility and interaction provides a frame for exclusion of blacks and constitutes a definition of the situation for coaches and management. People in the world of professional football believe that various football positions require specific types of physically- and intellectually-endowed athletes. When these beliefs are combined with the stereotypes of blacks and whites, blacks are excluded from certain positions. Normal organizational processes when interlaced with racist conceptions of the world spell out an important consequence, namely, the racial basis of the division of labor in professional football.

In this view, then, it is the racial stereotypes of blacks' abilities that lead to the view that they are more ideally suited for those positions labelled "noncentral." For example, Brower compared the requirements for the central and noncentral positions in football and found that the former require leadership, thinking ability, highly refined techniques, stability under pressure, and responsibility for the outcome of the games. Noncentral positions, on the other hand, require athletes with speed, quickness, aggressiveness, "good hands," and "instinct."

Evidence for the racial stereotype explanation for stacking is found in the paucity of blacks at the most important positions for outcome control in football (quarterback, kicker, and placekick holder). The data for 1975 show that of the 87 quarterbacks in the league only three were black; of the 70 punters and placekickers mentioned in the *Football Register,* only one was black; and of the 26 placekick holders, not one was black.

It is inconceivable that blacks lack the ability to play these positions at the professional level. Placekick holders must, for example, have "good hands," an important quality for pass receivers, two-thirds of whom were black, but no black was selected for the former role. Kicking requires a strong leg and the development of accuracy. Are blacks unable to develop strong legs or master the necessary technique?

The conclusion seems inescapable: blacks are precluded from occupying leadership positions (quarterback, defensive signal caller) because subtle but widely held stereotypes of black intellectual and leadership abilities still persist in the sports world. As a consequence, blacks are relegated to those positions where the requisite skills are speed, strength, and quick reactions, not thinking or leadership ability.

Another explanation for stacking has been advanced by Barry D. McPherson, who has argued that black youths may segregate themselves in particular positions because they wish to emulate black stars. Contrary to the belief that stacking can be attributed to discriminatory acts by members of the majority group, this interpretation holds that the playing roles to which black youths aspire are those in which blacks have previously attained a high level of achievement. Since the first positions to be occupied by blacks in professional football were in the offensive and defensive backfield and the defensive linemen, subsequent imitation of their techniques by black youths has resulted in blacks being over-represented in these positions today.

Although his small sample makes his findings tentative, Brower has provided some support for this hypothesis. He asked a sample of 23 white and 20 black high school football players what athletes they admired most and what position they would most like to play if they had the ability and opportunity. The overwhelming majority of blacks (70 percent) had only black heroes (role models) whereas whites chose heroes from both races. More important for our consideration is the finding that black high school athletes preferred to play at the "noncentral" positions now manned disproportionately by blacks in the pros.

Brower concluded that "Since the young blacks desire to perform at the 'standard' black positions, these findings make plain the impact and consequences of the present football position structure on succeeding generations of professional football players." Although the role model orientation does not explain the initial discrimination, it helps to explain why, once established, the pattern of discrimination by player position tends to be maintained.

Since McPherson produced no empirical support of his explanation, others sought to determine whether black athletes changed positions from central to noncentral more frequently than whites as they moved from high school to college to professional competition. Data from a sample of 387 professional football players indicated a statistically significant shift by blacks from central positions to noncentral ones.

That blacks in high school and college occupied positions held primarily by whites in professional football casts doubt on McPherson's model. Athletic role models or heroes will most likely have greater attraction for younger individuals in high school and college than for older athletes in professional sports, but professional players were found distributed at all positions during their high school playing days.

The socialization model also assumes a high degree of irrationality on the part of the player—it assumes that as he becomes older and enters more keenly competitive playing conditions, he will be more likely to seek a position because of his identification with a black star rather than because of a rational assessment of his own athletic skills.

It is conceivable, however, that socialization does contribute to racial stacking in baseball and football, but in a negative sense. That is to say, given discrimination in the allocation of playing positions (or at least the belief in its existence), young blacks will consciously avoid those positions for which opportunities are or appear to be low (pitcher, quarterback), and will select instead those positions where they are most likely to succeed (the outfield, running and defensive backs).

Gene Washington, all-pro wide receiver of the San Francisco Forty-Niners, was a college quarterback at Stanford through his sophomore year, then switched to flanker. Washington requested the change himself. "It was strictly a matter of economics. I knew a black quarterback would have little chance in pro ball unless he was absolutely superb. . . ."

STACKING IN BASKETBALL

Although social scientists have examined the stacking phenomenon in football and baseball, they have neglected basketball. They have tended to assume that it does not occur because, as Edwards has put it:

> . . . in basketball there is no positional centrality as is the case in football and baseball, because there are no fixed zones of role responsibility attached to specific positions. . . . Nevertheless, one does find evidence of discrimination against black athletes on integrated basketball teams. Rather than stacking black athletes in positions involving relatively less control, since this is a logistical impossibility, the number of black athletes directly involved in the action at any one time is simply limited.

However, two researchers reasoned that positions in basketball do vary in responsibility, leadership, mental qualities of good judgment, decisionmaking, recognition of opponents' tactics, and outcome control. To confirm this judgment, they undertook a content analysis of instructional books by prominent American basketball coaches to determine whether there were specific responsibilities or qualities attributed to the three playing positions—guard, forward, and center—in basketball.

They discovered surprising unanimity among the authors on the attributes and responsibilities of the different positions. The guard was viewed as the team quarterback, its "floor general," and the most desired attributes for this position were judgment, leadership, and dependability. The center was pictured as having the greatest amount of outcome control because that position is nearest the basket and because the offense revolves around it; the center was literally the pivot of the team's offense.

Unlike the traits for other positions, the desired traits mentioned for forwards stressed physical attributes—speed, quickness, physical strength, and rebounding—even to the point of labeling the forward the "animal."

Given this widespread agreement that varied zones of responsibility and different qualities are expected of guards, forwards, and centers, the researchers hypothesized that blacks would be over-represented—stacked—at the forward position, where the essential traits required are physical rather than mental, and underrepresented at the guard and center positions, the most crucial positions for leadership and outcome control. Using data from a sample of 274 NCAA basketball teams from the 1970–71 season, they found that blacks were, in fact, substantially over-represented as forwards and under-represented at the guard and center positions. Whereas 32 percent of the total sample of players were black, 41 percent of forwards were black; only 26 percent of guards and 25 percent of centers were black. This pattern held regardless of whether the players were starters or second-stringers, for college or university division teams. Thus racial stacking is present in college basketball.

But in professional basketball in 1972, which was two-thirds black, this pattern was not present. It would be interesting to see whether such a pattern may have occurred earlier in the history of professional basketball, since during the 1974–75 collegiate season, the races were relatively evenly distributed by position. The pattern of stacking detected in 1970–71 had not persisted. Thus, although stacking has remained in football and baseball, the situation in basketball (most heavily black in racial composition of the three major sports) would appear to have undergone substantial change during the first half of the 1970's.

REWARDS AND AUTHORITY

Discrimination in professional sports is explicit in the discrepancy between the salaries of white and black players. At first glance such a charge appears to be unwarranted. Black players rank among the highest paid in professional baseball (seven of 10 superstars being paid more than $100,000 in 1970 were black), and the mean salaries of black outfielders, infielders, and pitchers exceed those of whites. However, it was reported that substantial salary discrimination against blacks exists when performance levels were held constant. Blacks earned less than whites for equivalent performance. In addition, the central positions in football are those where the salaries are the greatest.

An obvious case of monetary discrimination becomes apparent if one considers the total incomes of athletes (salary, endorsements, and off-season earnings). The Equal Employment Opportunity Commission report of 1968 revealed that in the fall of 1966 black athletes appeared in only 5 percent of the 351 commercials associated with New York sports events. Our own analysis of the advertising and media program slots featuring starting members of one professional football team in 1971 revealed that 8 in 11 whites had such opportunities, while only 2 of 13 blacks did.

Blacks do not have the same opportunities as whites when their playing careers are finished. This is reflected in radio and television sportscasting where no black person has had any job other than providing the "color."

Officiating is another area that is disproportionately white. Major league baseball has had only two black umpires in its history. Professional basketball has only recently broken the color line, and in football, blacks are typically head linesmen.

Although the percentage of black players in each of the three most prominent American professional sports greatly exceeds their percentage of the total population, there is ample evidence that few managerial opportunities are available to blacks. (Black ownership, of course, is nil). Data from 1976 sources (*The Baseball Register, Football Register,* and *National Basketball Association Guide*) show that of the 24 major league baseball managers and 26 National Football League head coaches, only one was black. Five of the 17 head coaches (29 percent) in the National Basketball Association (NBA) were black.

Assistant coaches and coaches or managers of minor league baseball teams also are conspicuously white. In 1973, there were but two black managers among more than 100 minor league teams. During the same year in the National Football League, which had a black player composition of 36 percent, there were only 12 blacks, or 6.7 percent, among the 180 assistant coaches.

Finally, despite the disproportionate representation of blacks in major league baseball, only three coaches (less than 3 percent) were black. Moreover, black coaches were relegated to the less responsible coaching jobs.

Baseball superstar, Frank Robinson, who was appointed the first black major league field general after the conclusion of the regular 1974 season, has pointed out that blacks are excluded from the most important roles. "You hardly see any black third-base or pitching coaches. And those are the most important coaching jobs. The only place you see blacks coaching is at first base, where most anybody can do the job."

Robinson's appointment, coming more than 27 years after the entrance of another Robinson—Jackie—into major league baseball, was the exception that proves the rule. So historic was the occasion that it drew news headlines throughout the Nation and a congratulatory telegram from President Ford.

The dearth of black coaches in professional sports is paralleled at the college and high school levels. Although many predominantly white colleges and universities have, in response to pressures from angry black athletes, recently made frantic efforts to hire black coaches, they have been hired almost exclusively as assistant coaches, and seldom has a coaching staff included more than one black. As of this writing (1976), not a single major college has a black head football coach, and only a handful of major colleges (Arizona, Georgetown, Harvard, Illinois State, E. Michigan, and Washington State) have head basketball or track coaches who are black.

Blacks, however, are increasingly found on the coaching staffs of college basketball teams. Researchers have reported that the number of black head coaches increased from two in 1970 to 21 in 1973. However, their data are misleading since they included both major (NCAA Division I) and smaller schools. Nevertheless, an appreciable change did occur between 1970 and 1975, when the percentage of black head basketball coaches at major colleges increased from 0.64 percent to 5.1 percent, while the percentage of major colleges with black members on their coaching staffs increased from 20 percent in 1971 to 45 percent in 1975.

The pattern of exclusion of blacks from integrated coaching situations also has characterized American high schools. Blacks, historically, have found coaching jobs only in predominantly black high schools. And, although the precise figures are unavailable, it would appear that the movement toward integration of schools in the South during the 1960s has had the effect of eliminating blacks from coaching positions, as it has eliminated black principals and black teachers in general. So anomalous is a black head coach at a predominantly white high school in the South, that when, in 1970, this barrier was broken, it was heralded by feature stories in the *New York Times* and *Sports Illustrated*. And the situation appears to be little different outside the South, where head coaches are almost exclusively white.

The paucity of black coaches and managers could be the result of two forms of discrimination. Overt discrimination occurs when owners ignore competent blacks because of their prejudices or because they fear the negative reaction of fans to blacks in leadership positions.

The other form of discrimination is more subtle, however. Blacks are not considered for coaching positions because they did not, during their playing days, occupy positions requiring leadership and decisionmaking. For example, in baseball, 68 percent of all the managers from 1871 to 1968 were former infielders. Since blacks have tended to be "stacked" in the outfield, they do not possess the requisite infield experience that traditionally has provided access to the position of manager.

Blacks are also excluded from executive positions in organizations that govern both amateur and professional sports. In 1976, only one major NCAA college had a black athletic director. On the professional level, there was no black representation in the principal ownership of a major league franchise. No black held a high executive capacity in any of baseball's 24 teams, although there was one black assistant to Baseball Commissioner Bowie Kuhn. Nor have there been any black general managers in pro football. Professional basketball's management structure is most progressive in this regard, although ownership remains white. Two of 17 NBA clubs had black general managers in 1973. However, it was a noteworthy event, when in 1970, former NBA star Wayne Embry was named general manager of the NBA Milwaukee Bucks, thereby becoming the first black to occupy such a position in professional sports.

ABILITY AND OPPORTUNITY

Another form of discrimination in sport is unequal opportunity for equal ability. This means that entrance requirements to the major leagues are more rigorous for blacks. Black players, therefore, must be better than white players to succeed in the sports world. Aaron Rosenblatt was one of the first to demonstrate this mode of discrimination. He found that in the period from 1953 to 1957 the mean batting average for blacks in the major leagues was 20.6 points above the average for whites. In the 1958-to-1961 time period the difference was 20.1 points, while from 1962 to 1965 it was 21.2 points. In 1967, he concluded that:

> . . . discriminatory hiring practices are still in effect in the major leagues. The superior Negro is not subject to discrimination because he is more likely to help win games than fair to poor players. Discrimination is aimed, whether by design or not, against the substar Negro ball player. The findings clearly indicate that the undistinguished Negro player is less likely to play regularly in the major leagues than the generally undistinguished white player.

Since Rosenblatt's analysis was through 1965, we extended it to include the years 1966-70. The main difference between blacks and whites persisted; for that 5-year period blacks batted an average of 20.8 points higher than whites. Updating this analysis, we found that in 1975 the gap between black and white averages was virtually identical (21 points) to what it had been previously.

The existence of racial entry barriers in major league baseball was further supported by Anthony H. Pascal and Leonard A. Rapping, who extended Rosenblatt's research by including additional years and by examining the performance of blacks and whites in each separate position, including pitchers. They found, for instance, that the 19 black pitchers in 1967 who appeared in at least 10 games won a mean number of 10.2 games, while white pitchers won an average of 7.5. This, coupled with the findings that blacks were superior to whites in all other playing positions, led to the conclusion that: ". . . on the average a black player must be better than a white player if he is to have an equal chance of transiting from the minor leagues to the major."

Moreover, Gerald Scully's elaborate analysis of baseball performance data has led him to conclude that, ". . . not only do blacks have to outperform whites to get into baseball, but they must consistently outperform them over their playing careers in order to stay in baseball." Similarly, another analysis of professional basketball in 1973 revealed that black marginal players are less likely to continue to play after 5 years than are marginal white players.

Jonathan Brower found that the situation in professional football paralleled that in baseball and basketball. First, the most dramatic increases in the numbers of black professional football players occurred during the middle sixties and early seventies. Table 2 shows the increasing percentages of blacks in professional football; basketball data are in Table 3.

Moreover, Brower found that, as in baseball and basketball, "Black . . . players must be superior in athletic performance to their white counterparts if they are to be accepted into professional football." His data revealed statistically significant differences in the percentages of black and white starters and nonstarters. Blacks were found disproportionately as starters, while second-string status was more readily accorded to whites. Whereas 63 percent of black players were starters in 1970, 51 percent of white players were. Conversely, 49 percent of white players, but only 37 percent of black players, were not starters in that year. These findings led Brower to conclude that "mediocrity is a white luxury."

INEQUALITY ON THE BENCH

Our earlier research investigated whether black athletes were disproportionately overrepresented in the "star" category and underrepresented in the average, or journeyman, category on college and professional basketball teams. Our investigation showed that the black predominance in basketball is a relatively recent phenomenon, and that basketball, like football and baseball, was largely segregated until the late 1950's and early 1960's.

Table 2   Percentage of Blacks
in Professional Football

Year	Percentage of Black Players
1950	0
1954	5
1958	9
1962	16
1966	26
1970	34
1975	42

Table 3   Racial Composition of College and Professional
Basketball Teams
1948–1975

	College			Professional
Year	% of teams with blacks	Black players as % of total	Average # of blacks on integrated squads	Black players as % of total
1948	9.8	1.4	1.4	none
1954	28.3	4.5	1.6	4.6
1958	44.3	9.1	2.0	11.8
1962	45.2	10.1	2.2	30.4
1966	58.3	16.2	2.8	50.9
1970	79.8	27.1	3.4	55.6
1975	92.3	33.4	5.0	63.3

There are records of black basketball players on teams from predominantly white colleges as far back as 1908, but such instances were rare during the first half of the century. In professional sports, the National Basketball Association remained an all-white institution until 1950, 3 years after Jackie Robinson had broken the color line in baseball and 4 years after blacks reentered major league football after having been totally excluded since the early 1930's.

Table 3 documents the striking changes in racial composition of basketball since 1954. From the immediate post-World War II situation (1948), when less than 10 percent of collegiate squads were integrated, to 1975, when over 90 percent contained members of both races, substantial and impressive progress was made toward integration. Not only were more schools recruiting blacks, but the number of black players being recruited at each school increased dramatically. The most substantial increase among collegiate teams was during the period between 1966 and 1975, which can be partly attributed to the breakdown in previously segregated teams throughout the South.

Although blacks comprise approximately one-tenth (11 percent) of the total U.S. population, by 1975 they accounted for more than one-third (33.4 percent) of the Nation's collegiate basketball players. The percentage of black players on college basketball teams is even more striking when one considers that in 1975 blacks comprised only 9 percent of undergraduate students, and nearly half (44 percent) attended predominantly black institutions.

The change in the professional game is even more marked, for blacks have clearly come to dominate the game—numerically and, as we shall note more fully below, statistically as well. As contrasted to the situation two decades ago, organized basketball—on both the collegiate and professional levels—has eliminated many of the barriers that once excluded blacks from participation. The changes in professional baseball and football, while not so dramatic, occurred primarily during the middle sixties.

Having determined that black players are disproportionately over-represented on collegiate and professional basketball teams relative to their distribution within the general population, we systematically examined the roles they played. Specifically, we wanted to determine whether blacks have been found disproportionately as starters and whether the average number of points they score has been higher than that of whites. In order to determine whether starting patterns had changed significantly in the years during which the percentage of black players had increased so dramatically, it was necessary to examine the distribution of blacks by scoring rank over time.

Defining the top players as those with high offensive productivity as measured by their scoring average, we discovered the same situation of unequal opportunity for equal ability in basketball that others found in professional baseball. Using data from 1958, 1962, 1966, and 1970 professional and collegiate records, we found that the higher the scoring rank, the greater the likelihood that it would be occupied by a black player.

Table 4   Percentage of Blacks
Among the Top Five Scorers

1958	69
1962	76
1966	72
1971	66
1975	61

While black players comprised no more than 29 percent of all the members of integrated teams during the years 1958-70, in each of these years nearly half—and in some years, more than half—of the leading scorers were black. Conversely, blacks were disproportionately underrepresented in the lowest scoring position. Moreover, our data revealed that between 1958 and 1970, no less than two-thirds—and in some years as high as three-fourths—of all black players were starters.

RECENT PROGRESS

Data from the 1975 season, however, indicates that although blacks continue to be overrepresented in starting positions, a steady and substantial decline has occurred between 1962, when 76 percent of all black college basketball players were starters, and 1975, when the percentage has dropped to 61.

These changes are shown above. In other words, black basketball recruits are no longer only those likely to be starters. Thus, unlike professional baseball and football, which show little change during the past two decades, college basketball appears increasingly to provide equal opportunity for equal ability. Moreover, these changes parallel the decline in positional stacking and the increase of black coaches in college basketball previously noted.

In professional basketball, where they have come to dominate the game, blacks were slightly over-represented in starting roles until 1970, when equal numbers of blacks were starters and nonstarters. Following Rosenblatt's approach in comparing white and black batting averages, we compared the scoring averages of black and white basketball players for 5 years (1957-58, 1961-62, 1965-66, 1969-70, 1974-75).

Although scoring averages were identical for both races in 1957-58, blacks outscored whites in the remaining years by an average of 5.2, 3.3, 2.9, and 1.5 points, respectively. While a slight gap remains between the scoring averages of whites and blacks, the magnitude of the difference has declined as the percentage of black players in the league has increased. This is in contrast to the situation in professional baseball, where the mean batting average for blacks has remained 20 points greater than the average for whites for nearly two decades.

BLACK PARTICIPATION

The data presented here suggest both continuity and change in traditional patterns of race relations. Perhaps the most striking fact is that black participation in intercollegiate and professional sports continues to increase—especially in football and basketball. Several possible explanations for this phenomenon—the genetic, the structural, and the cultural—have been advanced.

First, it has been suggested that blacks are naturally better athletes and their predominance in American professional sports can be attributed to their innate athletic and/or physical superiority. As sociologists, we are inclined to reject interpretations of black athletic superiority as genetically or physiologically based, especially since racial categories in any society, but particularly in the United States, are socially and not scientifically defined. At best, given the paucity of data to support such a position, our stance can be no better than an agnostic one.

Another explanation that has been advanced to explain the disproportionate number of blacks in professional and collegiate sports resides in the structural limitations to which black children and adults are subjected. Since opportunities for vertical mobility by blacks in American society are circumscribed, athletics may become perceived as one of the few means by which a black can succeed in a highly competitive American society; a black male's primary role models during childhood and adolescence are much more likely to be athletic heroes than are the role models of white males. And the determination and motivation devoted to the pursuit of an athletic career may therefore be more intense for blacks than for whites whose career options are greater.

Jack Olsen, in *The Black Athlete,* quotes a prominent coach:

People keep reminding me that there is a difference in physical ability between the races, but I think there isn't. The Negro boy practices longer and harder. The Negro has a keener desire to excel in sports because it is more mandatory for his future opportunities than it is for a white boy. There are nine thousand different jobs available to a person if he is white.

A final explanation of the disproportionate black prowess in major sports emphasizes the extent to which the cultural milieu of young blacks positively rewards athletic performance. James Green has questioned whether the lure of a professional career completely explains the strong emphasis on athletics among blacks. He argues that the explanation that a black manifests a "keener desire to excel . . . because it is mandatory for his future . . ." simply reflects the commentator's own future orientation.

An alternative explanation of strong black motivation, according to Green, is the positive emphasis in black subculture that is placed on the importance of physical (and verbal) skill and dexterity. Athletic prowess in men is highly valued by both women and men. The athletically capable male is in the comparable position of the hustler or the blues singer; he is something of a folk hero. He achieves a level of status and recognition among his peers whether he is a publicly applauded sports hero or not.

Nearly as dramatic as the proportion of blacks in player roles is the dearth of blacks in administrative, managerial, and officiating positions. Although significant advances have occurred for black athletes in the past quarter of a century, there has been no comparable access of blacks to decisionmaking positions. With the exception of professional basketball, the corporate and decisionmaking structure of professional sports is virtually as white as it was when Jackie Robinson entered major league baseball in 1947. The distribution of blacks in the sports world is therefore not unlike that in the larger society, where blacks are admitted to lower-level occupations but virtually excluded from positions of authority and power.

The fact that black participation in the three major professional team sports continues to increase has led many observers to conclude incorrectly that sports participation is free of racial discrimination. As our analysis has demonstrated, stacking in football and baseball remains pronounced. Blacks are disproportionately found in those positions requiring physical rather than cognitive or leadership abilities.

Moreover, the data indicate that although the patterns have been substantially altered in collegiate and professional basketball, black athletes in the two other major team sports have been and continue to be found disproportionately in starting roles and absent from journeymen positions. The three interpretations previously considered—the genetic, the structural, and the cultural—appear inadequate to explain these patterns.

A genetic interpretation cannot explain the prevalence of blacks in starting roles or their relegation to playing positions that do not require qualities of leadership or outcome control. Even if blacks possessed genetically based athletic superiority, they should not be systematically overrepresented in starting positions or "stacked" in "black" positions, but should still be randomly distributed throughout the entire team.

As Jim Bouton (a former major league baseball player who has challenged the racial composition of major league baseball teams) has written, "If 19 of the top 30 hitters are black, then almost two-thirds of all hitters should be black. Obviously it is not that way."

Similarly, explanations emphasizing the narrow range of opportunities available to blacks or the emphasis upon athletic skills in black subculture fail to explain adequately the distribution of blacks by position and performance.

SPORT AS EXAMPLE

Despite some indications of change, discrimination against black athletes continues in American team sports; sport is not a meritocratic realm where race is ignored. Equality of opportunity is not the rule where the race is a variable. These conclusions have implications that extend beyond the sports world. If discrimination occurs in so public an arena, one so generally acknowledged to be discrimination free, and one where a premium is placed on individual achievement rather than race, how much more subtly pervasive must discrimination be in other areas of American life, where personal interaction is crucial and where the actions of power wielders are not subjected to public scrutiny.

THE SEGREGATION BY PLAYING POSITION HYPOTHESIS IN SPORT: AN ALTERNATIVE EXPLANATION

Barry D. McPherson

In recent years social scientists and journalists have increasingly considered discrimination in sport to be a problem worthy of investigation.[2] As a result of this interest, unequal opportunity in the assignment to playing positions has been identified as one form of discrimination within the sport milieu. To date this discrimination has been attributed to subtle or overt discrimination by whites in decision-making roles, to stereotyping[3] or to the degree of relative outcome control or leadership responsibilities associated with the various sport roles.[4] That is, individuals are excluded from occupying specific roles on arbitrary grounds. This paper suggests that involvement in specific sport roles by members of minority groups may be self-induced, rather than due to overt or subtle discrimination by white leaders within the sport system.

SEGREGATION BY PLAYING POSITION

In addition to journalistic accounts which have documented the percentage of Afro-Americans occupying specific positions on sport teams, recent empirical studies have attempted to explain this phenomenon.

Rosenblatt[5] hypothesized that it is difficult for a black to be a pitcher because it is a decision-making position. He also suggested that by occupying the role of pitcher, a black is placed in a face-to-face confrontation (in which he has control) with whites, thus creating a situation wherein racial conflict could be initiated. Similarly, he stated that when a black occupies a position in the outfield he does not interact directly with white teammates or opponents. Rosenblatt concluded that blacks are forced to occupy follower rather than leadership roles within organized sport.

Loy and McElvogue,[6] drawing upon Grusky's[7] theory of the formal structure of organizations, generated the proposition that discrimination is positively related to centrality. In their investigation of baseball they classified outfield positions as non-central and found that blacks occupied these positions to a greater extent. Similar results were noted when the offensive and defensive positions in professional football were dichotomized into

Barry D. McPherson, "The Segregation by Playing Position Hypothesis in Sport: An Alternative Explanation," from *Social Science Quarterly*, Vol. 55, No. 4 (March, 1975), pp. 960–966. Reprinted by permission of the author and the University of Texas Press.

central and non-central roles.[8] Thus, they concluded that racial segregation in professional sport is positively related to centrality.

Based on a survey of the 1968 Baseball Register, Pascal and Rapping[9] found that a high percentage of blacks were outfielders (53 percent) and first basemen (40 percent), while a low percentage were pitchers (9 percent) and catchers (12 percent). They attributed this segregation by playing position to the fact that blacks are excluded from the key decision-making positions of pitcher and catcher because blacks cannot be trusted with this responsibility.[10] A second explanation argued that pitchers and catchers require more coaching and minor league experience, and therefore, if managers and coaches prefer not to interact with blacks, players attempting to play these positions are at a disadvantage. A final explanation by Pascal and Rapping recognized the importance of role models. They suggested that segregation by position is reinforced by black youths concentrate on positions in which black stars are most visible. More recently, Edwards[11] argued that blacks are excluded from positions where leadership and outcome control role responsibilities are attached to a specific sport position, while Brower[12] reported that blacks are found in specific positions because of stereotypes held by themselves and white decision-makers.

In summary, although it appears that Afro-Americans are underrepresented in certain sport positions, a definitive explanation for this phenomenon has yet to be derived. In the following section it is argued that involvement in sport by members of minority groups may be accounted for by differential socialization experiences in early life, and that the learning and subsequent occupation of specific sport roles may result from self-induced imitative learning, rather than from overt or subtle discrimination by members of the majority group in the sport system.

SOCIALIZATION OF THE BLACK INTO A SPORT ROLE

The socialization process for individuals in minority groups appears to have a differential pattern and outcome. That is, differences in socializing agents, social structure, and group-influenced personal traits and expectations exist and should be considered in any attempt to describe and explain black involvement in white social institutions such as sport. With their entrance into amateur and professional athletics, blacks were extremely successful in a wide variety of sports, especially baseball, basketball, boxing, football, and track and field. In attempting to account for this supremacy, it was frequently argued that the black had a superior genetic and physiological make-up which suited him for hard physical work, and therefore sport. Anthropologists, physical educators, and psychologists, who compared blacks and whites on anthropometric and motor performance measures, generally concluded that there are few, if any, physical differences which could account for this supremacy. Alternatively, investigators have suggested that the success of the black in athletic competition is related to either environmental forces,[13] cultural influences,[14] or sociological and psychological differences.[15] Therefore, in an attempt to explain how blacks become involved in specific sport roles, the following factors are utilized in a conceptual framework: the social situation, the personal attributes of the socializee, and the role of significant others.

Social Situation

The social environment in which the black is socialized exerts a profound influence on his life-style, including his recreational pursuits. Davis[16] suggested that the majority of blacks are forced to develop their athletic skill in a sports ghetto. Clift[17] reported that ghetto youth are being deprived of the opportunity to establish worthy leisure habits. In addition, he reported that limited economic resources prohibit certain types of leisure activities, that longer employment hours restrict their ability to engage in leisure-time pursuits because of physical fatigue, and that the ghetto schools are financially burdened to the extent that they are unable to provide for the formation of desirable leisure-time attitudes, interests, and behavioral patterns. Kraus[18] found that black neighborhoods possessed the oldest, most limited and least adequate facilities in the communities studied. He also reported that when blacks entered the school or park recreational programs, a substantial number of whites withdrew. Thus prejudice within the social situation appears to influence black involvement in sport. Despite being economically disadvantaged the black does learn to participate and attain success in a variety of sport roles. For example, Brown[19] drew a parallel between the elite Jewish basketball players of the 1920's and 1930's and the elite black basketball players of today—both came from a ghetto where basketball courts and nets were the most accessible sport facility. In summary, it appears that the availability of facilities, leadership, and organized programs in the social milieu influences the extent to which blacks become involved in sport.

Personal Attributes

The personal attributes of black youth also contribute to the learning of sport roles. Stoll, Inbar and Fennessey[20] investigated the role of play and games in the socialization process and found that sports are played by black students who hold attitudes conducive to achievement, yet who are uninterested in school; whereas white students who participate in sport are very interested in school. The investigators suggested that the frequent participation in sport and individual games exhibited by blacks is related to a feeling that one can learn and succeed in at least one domain. In an attempt to account for the differences between races, they suggested that there is a differential selection process into the same game by race. They found that blacks who frequently participated in sport had higher achievement scores than infrequent players. Similarly, Rosenblatt[21] found that compared to white adolescents, blacks assigned greater esteem to a sport career and thus a larger proportion had aspirations to become professional athletes. In addition, he suggested that the black considers success in sport more within his grasp than careers which require years of academic training.

Closely allied with achievement is the attainment of status. Henderson[22] stated that being an athlete gives black youth a status they might not otherwise attain. In a study of black involvement in voluntary associations, Babchuk and Thompson[23] noted that blacks were more active in voluntary associations because they were not permitted to be active in other facets of society. In summary, it appears that black youth may have different values and different achievement motivation with respect to involvement in sport. Thus, personal attributes may also account for differential socialization into sport involvement.

Significant Others

If a novice is to learn a sport role then significant others who enact these roles must be available. Thus, a socializee must have the opportunity to observe a member of the family, a peer, or a professional athlete enacting the role. For example, Loy[24] suggested that there is much identification or mimicry associated with sport by some economic or social classes, and that generally the lower economic groups tend to indulge in hero worship and ethnic identification with athletes from their own group. Similarly, Henderson[25] stated that blacks usually identify with entertainers and athletes. Frazier[26] reported that black athletes have become symbols of achievement and symbols of black participation in a white world. This has occurred to such an extent that black youths may be segregating themselves into specific sport roles because they concentrate on positions in which black stars are most notable.[27] Similarly, Davis[28] suggested that one reason, in addition to lack of facilities, that there have been few black golfers, tennis players or swimmers is that there has been no tradition of successful black role models.

Weinberg and Arond[29] also supported this view when they reported that successful amateur and professional boxers serve as highly visible role models for lower-class males, especially urban blacks. They found that most boxers seem to have been influenced by a boxer in the neighborhood or by a member of the family. On the other hand, Brown[30] suggested that teachers and coaches often discourage black youth from participating in such activities as golf, tennis and swimming in order to prevent later frustration and embarrassment. Finally, Boyle[31] reported that most major league teams have unofficial black leaders who socialize black rookies into the major leagues with respect to acceptable behavior on and off the field.

In summary, an individual's aspirations and behavior are greatly influenced by the achievements of visible role models. For the black male, the most visible black role models are successful professional athletes. Therefore, even though it is unrealistic to place such emphasis on the attainment of a professional sport role, the role attractiveness, plus the lack of black high-level achievers in other domains, leads to imitation of black professional athletes. More specifically, since success increases visibility, the greater the success achieved by an individual occupying a specific role (e.g., pitcher), the greater the exposure and the greater the imitation of this role by novices. Therefore, it is argued that black youth, who are in the early stages of sport socialization, will seek to enact the specific role played by blacks who currently have attained a high level of achievement. For example, it is hypothesized that the recent success of black pitchers and quarterbacks will result, within the next two decades, in an increasing number of blacks in these positions at all levels of competition.

The following system of propositions may be useful in explaining why blacks are over-represented in specific sport roles:

1. The lower the socioeconomic status, the greater the identification with athletes from their own ethnic or racial group.

2. The greater the success achieved by the occupant of a sport role, the greater the exposure in the mass media.

3. The greater the exposure, the greater the role attractiveness.

4. The greater the role attractiveness, the greater the imitation of the role by novices.

Although empirical support for these hypotheses is not available at the present time, by way of retrospect it is noted that the first black baseball players to enter the major leagues played first base and in the outfield. At the present time, blacks are over-represented at these positions. Similarly, in football the first positions to be occupied by blacks were offensive and defensive backs; today, blacks are over-represented in these positions. Finally, until empirical support indicating the number of blacks who receive negative sanctions for attempting to play a specific sport role in sandlot, high school, or college leagues is available, there is little evidence to support the segregation by playing position hypothesis.

SOCIALIZATION INTO THE ROLE OF OLYMPIC TRACK AND FIELD ATHLETE

In order to provide some support for the hypothesis that members of minority groups are differentially socialized into sport roles, interpretations based on an examination of the frequency distributions of data collected in 1968 are presented.[32] On August, 1968, questionnaires were completed by 96 white athletes and 17 black athletes who were competing in the Olympic Track and Field trials at Lake Tahoe.[33] The basic differences between the two groups with respect to the socialization process are presented below.

Significant Others

It was noted that compared to white athletes, the black athletes: (a) before high school, received more encouragement (positive sanctions) from the mother than the father, thereby suggesting that matriarchal domination is present; (b) before high school, considered their peers to be most influential as role models; (c) in high school, received the most encouragement to participate in sport from track coaches and peers; (d) more frequently reported that they had an idol in high school; and that the idol was a success-ful track and field athlete (100 percent of the blacks indicated that their idol was an athlete, whereas only 81 percent of the whites indicated that their idol was an athlete); and, (e) in college, received the most encouragements from peers, track coaches, and the father.[34]

Thus, different role models may serve as significant others for blacks, and there may be variations in the amount of influence the models exert at various stages in the athlete's career.

Social Situation

An examination of the frequency distributions for the variables related to the social situation suggested that compared to white athletes, the black athletes: (a) came from larger families (4.5 children compared to 2.4 children for whites); (b) were from a lower socio-economic background (none of the fathers had a college degree whereas 25 percent of the fathers of the white athletes did); (c) were raised in large cities to a greater extent (56 percent to 29 percent); (d) were more involved in other sports before specializing in track and field; (e) were involved in track events at an earlier age (75 percent of the blacks were competing by the end of elementary school whereas only 25 percent of the whites were competing at this time; and, (f) developed their first interest in track in the neighborhood and home, rather than in the school as the white athletes had.

Thus, it is suggested that a different opportunity structure and a different social milieu may account for an earlier involvement in sport, and for the learning of the specific role of track and field athlete.

Personal Attributes

An examination of the frequency distributions revealed only two major differences between the two groups. First, the black athletes experienced success at an earlier age and, second, they were less religious.

SUMMARY AND CONCLUSIONS

Although little empirical support is available at this time, it is argued that the opportunity set, the value orientations, and the type of role models present early in life may account for involvement in sport by members of a minority group. More specifically, it is hypothesized that members of a minority group may segregate themselves into specific sport positions due to imitation of members of the minority group who are highly successful in a specific sport role. Until further empirical evidence is presented which indicates that members of minority groups are required by whites to play specific positions in the youth, high school, college and minor professional leagues, the segregation by playing position hypothesis is open to alternative explanations.

NOTES

1. Based on a paper presented at the Third International Symposium on the Sociology of Sport, Waterloo, Ontario, Canada (Aug. 22–28, 1971).

2. See B. D. McPherson, "Minority Group Involvement In Sport: The Black Athlete," in J. H. Wilmore, ed., *Exercise and Sport Sciences Reviews* (New York: Academic Press, 1974), Vol. 2, pp. 71–101.

3. J. Brower, "The Racial Basis of the Division of Labor Among Players in The NFL as a Function of Stereotypes," Paper presented at the Pacific Sociological Association (April, 1972).

4. H. Edwards, *Sociology of Sport* (Homewood, Ill.: The Dorsey Press, 1973).

5. A. Rosenblatt, "Negroes in Baseball: The Failure of Success," *Transaction*, 5 (Sept., 1967), pp. 51–53.

6. J. W. Loy and J. F. McElvogue, "Racial Segregation in American Sport," *International Review of Sport Sociology*, 5 (1970), pp. 5–23.

7. O. Grusky, "The Effects of Formal Structure on Managerial Recruitment," *Sociometry*, 26 (Sept., 1963), pp. 345–353.

8. It should be noted that while there may be clusters of positions which are structurally central, these same positions may not be functionally central in terms of the purpose of the game, namely success. For example, some baseball managers would argue that the key to a team's success is the level of ability "down the middle"—that is, catcher, pitcher, second baseman, and centerfielder. Therefore, it might be worthwhile to re-analyze the data in terms of functionally central roles.

9. A. H. Pascal and L. A. Rapping, "The Economics of Racial Discrimination in Organized Baseball," in A. H. Pascal, ed., *Racial Discrimination in Economic Life* (Lexington, Mass.: D. C. Heath, 1972), pp. 119–156.

10. The validity of this argument is questionable in view of the many outstanding pitchers and catchers who have been highly instrumental in their team's success.

11. Edwards, *Sociology of Sport*.

12. Brower, "The Racial Basis."

13. J. R. Williams and R. B. Scott, "Growth and Development of Negro Infants: Motor Development and Its Relationship to Child Rearing Practices in Two Groups of Negro Infants," *Child Development*, 24 (June, 1953), pp. 103–121.

14. R. Malina, "An Anthropological Perspective of Man in Action," in R. C.

Brown and B. J. Cratty, eds., *New Perspectives of Man in Action* (Englewood Cliffs, N.J.: Prentice-Hall, 1969), pp. 147–162.

15. E. Jokl, *Medical Sociology and Cultural Anthropology of Sport and Physical Education* (Springfield: C. C. Thomas, 1964), pp. 65–71.

16. J. P. Davis, "The Negro in American Sports," J. P. Davis, Ed., *The American Negro Reference Book,* (Englewood Cliffs, N.J.: Prentice-Hall, 1966), pp. 775–825.

17. V. A. Clift, "Recreational and Leisure-Time Problems and Needs of Negro Children and Youth," *Journal of Negro Education,* **19** (1950), pp. 333–340.

18. R. Kraus, "Race and Sports: The Challenge To Recreation," *J.O.H.P.E.R.,* **40** (April, 1969), pp. 32–34.

19. R. C. Brown, "The Black Athlete in Perspective," Paper presented at the Annual Meeting of the American College of Sports Medicine, Atlanta, Georgia (May 1, 1969).

20. C. S. Stoll, M. Inbar, and J. S. Fennessey, "Socialization and Games: An Exploration Study of Race Differences," Report No. 31 (Baltimore: Center For The Study of Social Organization of Schools, John Hopkins University, 1968).

21. Rosenblatt, "Negroes in Baseball."

22. E. G. Henderson, *The Black Athlete–Emergence and Arrival* (New York: Publishers Company Inc., 1968).

23. N. Babchuk and R. V. Thompson, "The Voluntary Associations of Negroes," *American Sociological Review,* **27** (Oct., 1962), pp. 647–655.

24. J. W. Loy, "Game Forms, Social Structure, and Anomie," in Brown and Cratty, eds., *New Perspectives of Man in Action.*

25. Henderson, *The Black Athlete–Emergence and Arrival.*

26. E. F. Frazier, *Black Bourgeoisie* (Glencoe, Ill.: The Free Press, 1957).

27. Pascal and Rapping, "The Economics of Racial Discrimination."

28. Davis, "The Negro in American Sports."

29. S. K. Weinberg and H. Arond, "The Occupational Culture of the Boxer," *American Journal of Sociology,* **57** (March, 1952), pp. 460–469.

30. Brown, "The Black Athlete in Perspective."

31. R. H. Boyle, "A Minority Group–The Negro Baseball Player," in *Sport– Mirror of American Life* (Boston: Little, Brown and Company, 1963), pp. 100–134.

32. The author is indebted to G. S. Kenyon for permitting access to the data.

33. Forty-seven percent of the black athletes and 27 percent of the white athletes were ultimately selected for the Olympic team.

34. The reinforcement by the father late in the athlete's career may reflect a desire by the father to identify with a successful individual.

FOR FURTHER READING

1. Ashe, A., "Send Your Children to the Libraries," *The New York Times* February 6, 1977, Section 5, Page 2.

2. Axthelm, P., *The City Game,* New York: Simon and Schuster, 1971.

3. Frazier, W., "Talk About Doctors Instead of Athletes," *The New York Times.* May 1, 1977, Section 5, Page 2.

4. Leonard, W. M., "Stacking and Performance Differentials of Whites, Blacks, and Latins in Professional Baseball," *Review of Sport and Leisure* **2** (June): 77–106, 1977.

5. Lapchick, R. E., "Apartheid Sport: South Africa's Use of Sport in its Foreign Policy," *Journal of Sport and Social Issues* **1** (1): 52–79, 1976.

6. McPherson, B. D., "Minority Group Involvement in Sport: The Black Athlete," In *Exercise and Sport Science Reviews,* Vol. 2 edited by Jack H. Wilmore, New York: Academic Press, 1974, pp. 71–101.

7. Phillips, J. C., "Toward an Explanation of Racial Variations in Top-Level Sports Participation," *International Review of Sport Sociology* **11** (3): 39–55, 1976.

8. "The Black Dominance," *Time Magazine* May 9, 1977, pp. 57–60.

CHAPTER 8

SPORT AND SOCIAL CHANGE AND CONFLICT

Every society possesses stable and permanent structures and functions but they are always subject to change through time, indeed change seems to be universal among societies. In observing change within societies, there are some which seem hardly to change at all while others change rapidly and dramatically. Social change, then, might be viewed as a continuum from static to revolutionary. The contemporary world seems to have very few static societies, a few revolutionary societies, with the great bulk of societies between these two extremes. However, worldwide change seems to be occurring more rapidly than at any time in human history.

There are a number of factors which affect the acceptance of social change. Perceived need for change is one factor. Material inventions or innovations are more readily accepted than changes in basic values and beliefs because they typically reduce human labor or enhance lifestyles. Values and beliefs of various kinds are commonly based upon religious foundations about truth, good, salvation, etc., and are therefore less ammendable to modification. Another factor with regard to acceptance of change is the extent to which the proposed change is different from current practices or conditions. A small change is more readily accepted and assimilated into human actions than a dramatic change. The structure of a society is a third factor which affects the acceptance of change. Societies which vest authority in the older members and which adhere to immutable laws of a "supreme" being are likely to be highly resistant to change. Thus, we see the Amish sect in Pennsylvania practicing a way of life reminiscent of centuries ago.

Every society is characterized by forces which make for stability and forces that make for change. Resistance to change comes from various sources. Older members of a society tend to resist change. They often feel that their cultural heritage is being taken from them when change occurs.

The wealthy in a society tend to resist change; in most societies the wealthy are the most conservative group. These persons are threatened by change because they have the most to lose if the change fails or if it produces a new group of wealthy persons, since the new may weaken the economic status of the old. Where vested interests are involved, there is a tendency to resist change. Those who have vested interest in a certain area wish to maintain the advantage they have. Change tends to transform or redistribute resources and this is opposed by the vested interests. Those in authority positions, the powerful, tend to resist change, especially if it is initiated from subordinates. In some societies there is enormous respect for authority, persons who hold leadership positions are expected to be obeyed without question. Of course, social change is quite threatening to authority figures because they feel that change may bring about a reduction in their authority and indeed perhaps even their demise. Furthermore, those in powerful positions often feel that their authority has been conferred by some "higher being" or has been earned because of their special abilities and talents, therefore, for a subordinate to suggest change is blasphemous, or at least rude and insolent. Change, when and if it is to come, authority figures often believe, will be properly initiated and controlled by them.

Historically, sport has played a prominent role in social change in Western civilization. The extreme asceticism which was promoted by religious groups such as the early Catholic church and later by the Puritans was gradually modified as people insisted that they be allowed to participate in sports. Sports came into direct conflict with some religious mores and it was the religions which had to be modified, as people violated religious customs in order to engage in sports.

Sport has often been responsible for breaking down social class lines, racial and ethnic barriers, and sex role stereotypes. Sport often is the common denominator for members of different social classes—they may use sport as a focus for conversation or may band together to participate or support a sport team. Thus members of different social classes may unify in the cause of sport. Although sport has not been as equalitarian as some idealists believe, it nevertheless has played a prominent role in American life in assimilating different races and ethnic minorities into American culture. Racial and ethnic integration appeared in sport before it was accepted by the general society. The liberation of the female has its linkage in sport. The bicycle and tennis craze of the later 19th century broke the fad of long skirts and confining undergarments. Bare legs for women were first displayed in sports and then became acceptable in everyday life. The short tennis skirts appear to have been the prelude to the miniskirt. Sport seems to have brought about considerable changes in lifestyles within the past generation. With increasing affluence and leisure, people have come to build a large part of their waking hours around sports involvement. The American weekend has become a time for watching college and professional sports on television or, for the doer, a time to play tennis, golf, etc., go fishing, boating, skiing, or to participate in any number of sports that are now available. Finally, sport has played a role in bringing about a breakdown in national barriers. Sportsmen have been used as goodwill ambassadors and have brought about changed relations between countries, the "Ping Pong Diplomacy" between the United States and China being the most recent example.

Sport is a microcosm of any society and therefore reflects the mores, values, and general culture of a society. The similarities between the evolution of sport and the development of American society are evident to even a casual observer. The traditional American cultural values are pretty generally the values which have been prominent in sports. Indeed, educators and businessmen have agreed that sports participation is an excellent medium for socializing youth into the adult world of America. So the relationship between sport and the promotion of cultural values and behaviors have been mutually supportive.

Within the past decade, the United States has undergone a staggering attack upon its cultural heritage. Several factors have been responsible for this: the race issue, the Vietnam war, pollution and overcrowding in the cities, disillusionment of youth with traditional values and customs, among others. These conditions have spawned riots, assassinations, sit-ins, boycotts, and general social upheaval in recent years. The old culture, and the things for which it stood, have been attacked and a "counter-culture" has been proposed as a substitute.

The social change occurring throughout American society has invaded the sports world and produced considerable soul-searching, and even turmoil. Authority is being challenged in all spheres of sports life, and tyrannical control is particularly being attacked. Since athletic coaches have one of the most powerful positions in any social institution in American society, this authority is being challenged throughout sports—from the Little Leagues to the professional ranks. This challenge is coming from the athletes themselves because they believe some coaches are oppressive. They also believe that coaches tend to assume too much control over the functioning of the sports team. Criticism of coaches is also coming from social reformers who regard the coach as a symbol of the old cultural values which, they believe, need to be changed.

Although the initial reaction of coaches to these attacks has been resistance, and in some cases counterattacks, coaches are changing. Events in the past few years give evidence that coaches are capable of making significant changes because rules on grooming, training, and general social behavior have been relaxed and some coaches are giving greater responsibilities for the team's functioning to the players.

In the first reading George H. Sage describes humanistic trends that are occurring in the social sciences and then discusses the implications of these trends for the world of sport. In psychology the two major traditions of the

20th century, Freudism and Behaviorism, are being challenged by a psychological theory that is very different—Humanism. Whereas the older psychological theories viewed humans pessimistically and basically stimulus-bound, humanistic psychology views humans optimistically as having potential for remarkable behavior. In sociology this humanistic trend has spawned several new paradigms, whose focus is on the unique, interpersonal, and symbolic behavior of humans, and it has an emphathetic concern for humanity. In the field of business management humanistic tendencies are manifested in giving workers opportunities to participate in the organization's decision processes.

Sage suggests that traditional practices and value orientations in American sports were congruent with the older psychological and sociological theories but they are not resonant with humanistic theory. He then describes how humanism may be applied to sport.

In the second reading Wayne Wilson describes one of the trends in sport involvement that has accompanied the transformation of consciousness that is a part of the humanistic orientation discussed in the previous reading. The focus of Wilson's article is the emergence and widespread enthusiasm for outdoor sports, such as mountaineering, backpacking, skiing, and bicycle touring. Wilson contends that the growth of these sports is evidence of disillusionment with modern technological-industrial-urbanized life. He argues that this trend is an effort to get back to nature, to be a part of the "real," natural world that has been obliterated as modernization occurred. Wilson expresses fear that this movement may fall prey to commercialization, and, indeed his fears are well-founded because one of the major problems in wilderness areas is the encroachment of commercially-produced technologically sophisticated equipment such as campers, motorcycles, outboard motors, etc.

In the third reading Harry Edwards discusses the role of conflict and revolution in modern sport. He argues that while there have been some reforms within the world of sport over the past decade, revolutionary change in sport can only occur in conjuction with, or after, revolutionary changes in the entire society. Up to the present, according to Edwards, there have been no revolutions in sports, only minor reforms to give additional people a piece of the existing sports reward system.

Edwards discusses the implications of 20th century revolutions, the decline of colonialism, and technological advances for sport and suggests that sport may be incapable of meeting the dramatic social changes that are occurring throughout the world. If this is true, Edwards sees the collapse of sport as we know it.

The last reading is a wide-ranging essay on futurism by Vern Dickinson. Predictions about the future have come from many sources, but there is little consensus among them. The one thing that seems certain is that change will be ubiquitous, and whatever change does occur will certainly have its impact on sport. Several of the potential changes and conflicts in sport of the future are discussed by Dickinson.

HUMANISM AND SPORT

George H. Sage

To examine the relations between the concepts of humanism and sport, I have structured my observations around four topical areas:

1. Humanistic Developments in the Social Sciences
2. Basic Principles of Humanism
3. Traditional Practices and Value Orientations in American Sport
4. Humanism Applied to Sport

HUMANISTIC DEVELOPMENTS IN THE SOCIAL SCIENCES

There are some rather dramatic events going on in the social sciences, and these activities have already had an impact on the basic disciplines out of which they have evolved, and they are also having an enormous impact in applied fields such as education, business management, religion, and other "people oriented" professions. These events are related to new theories about humanity and methods of interpersonal relations which have emerged in the social sciences over the past couple of decades.

The essence of the new ideas is a more optimistic, democratic, humanistic conception of human beings. In psychology this movement has been called Third Force, or Humanistic, Psychology. In sociology the new wave has been given various names: Symbolic Interactionism, Ethnomethodology, Phenomenological Sociology, and Existential Sociology. In business management the more humane form of management leadership has become known as "Human Relations" management. I shall describe each of these developments briefly.

George H. Sage, "Humanism and Sport." From: Revision of a paper presented at the annual meeting of the Central Association for Physical Education for College Women, Lincoln, Nebraska, October, 1975.

A. Humanism in Psychology

In psychology, throughout most of the 20th century, psychologists have primarily traced their thinking to either Sigmund Freud or John B. Watson. Freudism and Behaviorism (Watson's contribution) are deeply embedded into much of the psychology which is taught in American universities and applied throughout much of American child rearing, formal education, and other activities in which there are frequent interpersonal relations. Thus, most of you as well as most coaches and other educators, have had a heavy indoctrination in these approaches to human personality and behavior.

An essential theme of both of these approaches is basically a pessimistic view of humanity—it permeates these theories. For Freud, man was an animal and only an animal. In his book, *Creativity and the Unconscious* (1958), Freud wrote:

> In the course of his development toward culture, man acquired a dominating position over his fellow creatures in the animal kingdom. Not content with this supremacy, however, he began to place a gulf between his nature and theirs. He denied the possession of reason to them, and to himself he attributed an immortal soul, and made claims to a divine descent which permitted him to annihilate the bond of community between him and the animal kingdom . . . [but] we all know that . . . the researches of Charles Darwin, [and] . . . his collaborators . . . put an end to this presumption on the part of man. Man is not a being different from animals or superior to them; he himself originates in the animal race and is related more closely to some of its members and more distantly to others.

From his animal origins, according to Freud, came basic human instincts, which Freud divided into two major categories: the life instinct and the death instinct—the first is exemplified in the sex drive and the second is the aggression drive. That humans are basically an aggressive, dominating animal is central to Freud's theory. In the *New Introductory Lectures on Psychoanalysis,* (1933) he describes this basic hostility of persons towards each other. He says: "Culture has to call up every possible reinforcement to erect barriers against the aggressive instincts . . . its ideal command to love one's neighbor as oneself is really a hoax since "nothing is so completely at variance with human nature as this." In another place he proclaims: "Hatred is at the bottom of all relations of affection and love between human beings. . . ." (Brown, 1963)

Behaviorism, the second force in psychology, had its origins with Ivan Pavlov and Edward Thorndike near the beginning of the 20th century and bloomed into a full theory of Behaviorism under John B. Watson. Behaviorists excluded the subjectivism of Freud and placed their emphasis on a dispassionate observation of behavior. "The Behaviorist," said Watson (1930) "dropped from his scientific vocabulary all subjective terms . . . even thinking and emotion as they were subjectively defined." With regard to morality, Watson declared: "The Behaviorist is not interested in [man's] . . . morals, except as a scientist; in fact, he doesn't care what kind of man he is." Humans, thus, are considered to be flexible, malleable, and passive victims of their environment, which determines their behavior. In his book, *The Broken Image,* Floyd Matson (1966) quotes Watson as saying: "In short, the cry of the Behaviorist is, 'Give me the baby and my world to bring it up in and I'll make it crawl and walk; I'll make it climb and use its hands in constructing buildings of stone or wood; I'll make it a thief, a gunman, or a dope fiend. The possibilities of shaping in any direction is almost endless!' "

Like Freud, and Darwin before him, the Behaviorist saw humans as merely another type of animal, with no essential differences from animals and with the same destructive, anti-social tendencies. Watson (1930) stated: "We believed then [1912] as we do now, that man is an animal, different from other animals only in the types of behavior he displays [and] . . . the extent to which most of us are shot through with a savage background is almost unbelievable." B. F. Skinner, the current spokesman for Behaviorism says: "The only difference I expect to see revealed between the behavior of rats and man (aside from the enormous differences in complexity) lie in the field of verbal behavior" (Matson, 1966).

Starting in the 1930's, but not gaining any real recognition or momentum until the past decade, a new theory in psychology is advancing which provides a viable alternative to the first two major forces. This approach has become known as humanistic, or Third Force, psychology and the generally acknowledged founder of this movement is Abraham Maslow. This approach is different in many ways to the previous psychological theories, but its most unique and central difference is an entirely different perspective of the nature of humanity. It views humans optimistically, and having the potential for truly remarkable behavior. Maslow (1970) says: "What is happening now is a change in the image of man. . . . In the case of the humanistic and Third Force image, which shows so clearly that we have been selling human nature short throughout the whole of recorded history, this is certainly . . . a revolution in terms of its consequences. It can and will change the world and everything in it."

B. Humanism in Sociology

As sociology emerged as a unique discipline in the first half of this century "structural-functionalism" took over the theory side of most sociology departments. This theoretical orientation is best personified by the work of Talcott Parsons at Harvard and Robert Merton at Columbia. Just as with psychology, most persons who have taken sociology classes have received the dominant perspective.

Structural-functionalism views society as a set of institutions serving its functional needs; it sees change and conflict as deviations rather than as inherent social processes. The dominant concern of structural-functionalism is with order in society—an order based on conformity to shared values, and one in which joy, freedom, and self-fulfillment, usually do not appear.

Structural-functionalism is basically an amoral, conservative approach to social behavior, with an emphasis on social order; social change is virtually neglected or treated as pathological or abnormal. Change agents are labeled deviants. Recent critics of structural-functionalism have argued that too often the effect of this perspective is to label all non-conformist behavior as aberrant, no matter what the person's intention.

This theory is both implicitly and explicitly conservative and justifies the status quo. It focuses on human adjustment to society, on conformity and adaptation, on an individual as a controlled product of society and culture rather than as a determiner of his own fate. The model of humanity, often not explicit in the theory, resembles the Freudian and Behavioristic models.

Although structural-functionalism has had the most visible position in sociology, several new perspectives have been gaining ground rapidly and show many indications of displacing structural-functionalism. The most prominant of these alternative groups is the Symbolic Interactionists. The Symbolic Interactionist views humans as living in a symbolicly meaningful world and he recognizes that the meanings that guide conduct are not inherent in the actions of institutions, but are created by persons through their choices and their definitions of their life situations. It is through our choices that we endow selected aspects of "reality" with significance (Staude, 1972). This perspective clearly takes an optimistic view of humanity because it affirms that humans are a thinking animal, rational, and essentially in control of their own situation; they can make their own future.

For the Symbolic Interactionist, human beings are neither creatures of impulse nor heedless victims of external stimulation. They are active organisms, guiding and constructing their lines of action while continuously coming to terms with the demands of an ever-changing world as they interpret it. This is a perspective that encourages sympathy for the non-conformist, the outcast, and the downtrodden.

Another of the new approaches in social theory is an approach called ethnomethodology. This is the study of the methods used by members of a group for understanding communication, making decisions, being rational, accounting for action, and so on. Ethnomethodologists study the routine grounds of everyday activities. The focus is on the individual, how he interacts with his environment—especially the meanings which he derives from interaction.

The Symbolic Interactionists and the Ethnomethodologists represent only two groups of several which are currently active within sociology that clearly reject a worship of science and have an empathetic concern for humanity.

C. Business Management and Humanism

Business management theory and practice has undergone some significant changes in the past generation too. The latter 19th century witnessed the enormous growth of large bureaucratic business and industrial enterprises with the merger of industrialization and technological know-how. At the turn of the 20th century, a bustling time of population growth and industrial expansion, managements were faced with the problem of bringing large numbers of workers, many of whom were unskilled and untrained, together into a cooperative enterprise. At this time, the core ideas for a system to increase productivity through better utilization of manpower took shape through the writings of Frederick Taylor. This management theory, often referred to as Scientific Management, was enthusiastically adopted by American business and industrial organizations and has over the past 60 years been used by various industrial as well as non-business organizations such as schools, the military, and sports.

The underlying notions about the nature of humans, from the Scientific Management perspective, have been enumerated by Douglas McGregor (1957):

1. The average person is by nature indolent—he works as little as possible.

2. He lacks ambition, dislikes responsibility, prefers to be led.

3. He is inherently self-centered, indifferent to organizational needs.

4. He is by nature resistent to change.

5. He is gullible, not very bright, the ready dupe of the charlatan and demagogue.

The overriding notion is that workers in the mass are economic creatures, each impelled by an irresistible force to seek the maximum wage at a minimum effort.

Beginning with the research of Elton Mayo at the Western Electric Hawthorne plant in the 1920's, which showed that when people are treated as important human beings they are more productive and happier, an entirely new approach to organizational leadership has been formulated and supported with experimental findings. It is called Human Relations management theory. There are several key elements to Human Relations theory:

1. People are not by nature passive or resistent to organizational needs. They have become so as a result of experience in organizations; the motivation, the capacity for assuming responsibility, and the readiness to direct behavior toward group goals are all present in people.

2. It is deeply concerned with attitudes, values, emotional reactions of individual group members.

The Human Relations approach differs from Scientific Management in that it emphasizes that external control will not motivate persons to apply all their talents in behalf of group goals. The emphasis is on non-authoritarian styles of leadership, member participation in group decision making, and the encouragement of organizational activities in the service of individual needs. In short, this approach promotes individual autonomy and intrinsic motivation.

Organizational research over the past 20 years has convincingly shown that when employees are given an opportunity to participate in the organization's decision structure, and when they are treated in such a way as to recognize their uniqueness and humanness, they achieve greater production and are more satisfied with themselves and with their jobs. There is growing evidence that strongly suggests that Human Relations values are not only resonate with an increasing number of people in today's world, but are also highly consistant with the effective functioning of organizations built on the new view of humanity.

BASIC PRINCIPLES OF HUMANISM

The basic foundations of the humanistic orientation that is now sweeping the social sciences is a fundamental concern for the human person as an entity having a measure of autonomy, choice, and self-determination. There is a fundamental conviction that "best" individuals are those who possess a positive self-concept and accept themselves in an appreciating way. There is a belief that one cannot function to his fullest capacity without believing in and accepting the totality of himself. There is a belief that individuals possess a dignity and integrity which should be respected; that they are basically able to make their own decisions and deal with events. As one humanistic psychologist says:

> An essentially positive view of the self permits adequate people to be effective without the worry about conformity or non-conformity. . . . It provides a kind of security that permits the owner a freedom he could not have otherwise. . . . This permits him to be creative, original, spontaneous. . . . Feeling he is much more, he has much more to give (Combs, 1962).

The acceptance of one's self is also expanded into feelings of oneness with one's group. Humanists confirm that this feeling is necessary to their conceptions of the adequate person. Combs (1962) states:

> Truly adequate people have a greatly expanded feeling of self. . . . It is a feeling of unity or oneness, a feeling of sharing a common fate, or striving for a common goal . . . most adequate men and women . . . seem to reach a point where they identify with great blocks of mankind, with 'all' mankind, without reference to creed, color, or nationality.

Humanism posits an expanded awareness, a willingness to accept all facets of reality and perception. Maslow (1970) notes: "Self-actualizing people have the wonderful capacity to appreciate . . . freshly and naively, the basic goods of life, with awe, pleasure, and wonder, and even ecstasy, however stale these experiences may have become to others. . . ." Finally, humanism views "life success" differently than has been traditional; it views success not so much with making a living as making a life.

Accompanying and supporting a great deal of the theoretical structure of the humanistic perspective is a strong disillusionment with values and interpersonal relations as manifested in corporate organization values and behaviors and traditional ethics. While corporate organization and the Protestant Ethic were central themes of an industrial society, humanism addresses itself to a post-industrial society. The emphasis on basic needs gives way to a focus upon what Maslow calls the growth of meta needs. The enhancement of human potential receives more of our attention as basic survival needs are satisfied more easily (Poseschi, 1974).

Although humanism recognizes the environmental demands upon individuals, it views human beings as having an intrinsic nature and it views them optimistically, concentrating on healthy, self-actualizing persons who are fulfilling their idiosyncratic as well as their universal human potential (Podeschi, 1974). In his essay "The Theoretical Foundations of Humanistic Sociology," John Staude (1973) notes that the humanistic orientations restores the individual person in his rightful place as the principal agent of action. The humanists see men and women as the creators of their own acts, with all the uncertainty, ambiguity, dread, anxiety, and responsibility that such freedom, choice, and decision imply.

This movement has already had an impact upon a broad spectrum of American life. Witness the influence it has had upon the educational system, religion, minority rights, women's rights, and the freedom of greater choice in individual life styles. There has also been an awakening among the masses of blue-collar workers, whose financial responsibilities tie them to meaningless jobs. The dissatisfaction with the endless rat race is surfacing more and more, and employers are going to have enormous problems if change does not occur.

TRADITIONAL PRACTICES AND VALUE ORIENTATIONS IN AMERICAN SPORT

Before discussing applications of humanism to American school sports, it is necessary to describe in some detail the traditional practices and value orientations of American sports. This will illuminate present conditions and then I shall contrast the humanistic approach as it applies to sports. Although most of what I will have to say applies to boys' and men's programs, the current direction of the women's sports movement suggests that it may soon model that of the men in every respect.

Inter-school sports began in the latter 19th century and were a creation of college students. Until the beginning of this century, intercollegiate sports were basically student affairs, with little faculty or administration intervention. However, by the early years of the 20th century, control of the programs was taken away from the students, for all intents and purposes, and became vested in the alumni, faculty, and administrators. Now colleges began using athletics to publicize the institution and what started as student recreation became public entertainment and big business for the colleges. True to the patterns of American education, high schools adopted the practices and procedures of colleges, and secondary school athletic programs mirrored, in many details, the collegiate programs.

Once the entertainment and public relations functions of school sports became dominant, the need for experienced coaches arose. Whereas previously the coaching functions were performed by older players or by adults in their spare time, now coaching became a serious business and teachers of athletics (coaches) were employed to direct the athletic teams. Thus, there developed a vocation out of what was, and indeed still is throughout most of the world, an avocation—teaching games. There were several consequences of employing full-time coaches and using school sports for entertainment and publicity.

Once coaching became an occupation, performance criteria became associated with competence. Although inter-school athletics have always been justified as an educational enterprise, objective, marketplace criteria have become virtually the only measure of coaching ability, and "win" has become synonymous with success and "lose" has become associated with failure. Prestige in coaching is based upon won-loss records. A coach, according to all accepted standards, must win in order to have coached well. One college coach recently proclaimed: "I'd give anything—my house, my bank account, anything but my wife and family—to get [an undefeated season]." I think that it is easy to see how this system may produce coaching behavior which emphasizes the treatment of players for what they can do for the coach—win —rather than the treatment of players based upon what coaches can do for the personal-social growth of athletes as individuals.

With the rise of increasingly institutional and codified school sports, the characteristics of the enterprise closely modeled the older psychological and traditional value perspectives. The emphasis on intensive competition and a "Winning is the only thing" ideology, which for many has become the norm, is grounded in the idea that we must struggle against others to get ahead. If one has to be ruthless and unscrupulous in accomplishing the objective, well tough, the important thing is beating out the opposition.

Leadership practices commonly employed by coaches in American sport are firmly based on the older psychology, sociology and business management theories. Corporate organization and traditional values have made sport an element for the promotion of these systems. There is an acceptance of the priority of institutions and organizations and a belief that the individual must subordinate his will to them. It is consistent with this orientation, but an example of its consequences, that almost unanimously the public rose up in righteous indignation against Bill Walton when he spoke out in defense of personal freedoms and individual rights while this same public has reacted to violations of NCAA policies and unethical coaching behavior with a shoulder shrug and a response that "after all one has to win to have a successful program, and besides everyone else is doing it." The organization must be served. The moral stance of basketball coach, Bill Musselman, who departed the University of Minnesota for the pros just as the NCAA was poised to charge him with numerous violations is symptomatic of this value orientation. When he was asked how he felt about the charges against Minnesota, Musselman replied, "I'm not a member of the university staff anymore, so my conscience is clear." Where is the public outrage against this behavior? Where is the public outrage against coaches who change transcripts?

The individual player is expected to do his best to fit himself into functions which are needed by the organization. This is vividly exemplified in the popular locker room slogan: "There is no 'I' in team." A system of incentives and rewards, i.e., letter awards, helmet decals, etc. are instituted to "motivate" athletes to perform. In this approach decisions are made by management (the coach), after a thorough cost efficiency analysis, and the players are expected to carry out the will of the coach for the accomplishment of organizational goals (Sage, 1973). This is precisely the kind of behavior that is sought after in an efficiency-conscious business society.

Instead of coaching from the expressive foundation of personal fulfillment, coaches often adopt a production profile in working with athletes. Victories, fame, or whatever become products designed to satisfy felt insufficiencies; and obviously, one's athletes then become a necessary cog in the chain of production. Under the banner of efficiency, personal relationships give way to distance and manipulation.

The most important foundation of both American sport and corporate organization is authority. In both activities rigid and bureaucratized hierarchy controls more and more aspects of the workers' and athletes' lives both on and off the job or, in the case of sports, the field of play. As Hoch (1972) says:

> In football, like business . . . every pattern of movement on the field is increasingly being brought under the control of a group of non-playing managerial technocrats who sit up in the stands . . . with their headphones and dictate offenses, defenses, special plays, substitutions, and so forth to the players below.

The relation between school sports and the business world can be seen very vividly when one realizes that coaches typically justify school sports programs on the basis that they help prepare youth for the highly competitive business-industrial ideology of American corporate capitalism in which they will live as adults—thus sports become a means for socializing youth for adulthood.

Paul (1974) says: "The much maligned 'old coach' often, if not always, felt that by developing in his players tenacity, aggressiveness, and a will to win, he was providing them with the psychological armor that would sustain them against the assaults of a competitive, hostile world." It makes one wonder if this is the kind of training which prepares persons for a Watergate. Or prepares persons for business positions that when their corporation is caught violating federal laws, as IBM recently was, the chairman of the board says: "We don't train losers" (IBM, 1973). Presumably they train executives to win at any cost, and the hell with federal laws—winning is everything, you know. But perhaps they didn't have to train them at all. They might have already possessed this ethical norm—learned from inter-school sports participation.

It is clear that the dominant approach in current institutionalized sport is an authoritarian, product-oriented enterprise. The basic concern is with athletes subjecting themselves to the will of the coach whose primary concern often becomes winning athletic contests. The rise of increasingly institutionalized and codified sports teams has caused many coaches to view team members as objects in a machine-like environment who need to be conditioned to perform prescribed, fragmented tasks as instrumental to team performance. Thus, the players become another person's (the coach's) instrument, and are used to reach the objectives and goals of the organizational collectivity; they are reduced to cogs in the organization's machinery.

HUMANISM APPLIED TO SPORT

What is a humanistic approach to sport? Well, I think you have probably already ascertained several clues to the applications of humanism to sport, but I wish to suggest more specific practices and procedures now. First, the humanist rejects the traditional sex-role stereotypes; and with regard to sport, sees it as a human province, not as either masculine or feminine. It is believed that sport has the same potential for personal growth and self-actualization for females as it does for males. I hasten to add, though that it also possesses the same dangers of exploitation and subjection of the individual. I hope female coaches will mark this well in their quest to model women's sports after men's programs.

The ideology of humanistic leadership gives emphasis to an empathetic identification with others, an openness to experience, acceptance of a wide and rich perceptual field for information from which to draw, and a commitment to enhancement of a positive self concept of those with whom the leader comes in contact. In this approach, leadership is perceived as one of freeing people to be more open to their experiences. The leader sees his/her task as one of releasing, facilitating, and assisting, not one of manipulating, coercing and appeasing in order to "shape" appropriate behavior. Leader behavior is flexible and open to revision in view of long term issues and consequences rather than focused on immediate goals and short term, current consequences. Finally, the leader perceives his/her task as beginning from a clear acceptance of other persons and their current ways of thinking, feeling, and behaving. He/she believes that his/her own acceptance and openness will in turn promote acceptance and openness in others. The importance of these viewpoints for sport are particularly related to coaching and management methods which most effectively facilitate these goals.

The traditional coaching model, with its emphasis on relatively rigid structure, imposition of conformity through requirements, direction and control exercised through a formal hierarchy of authority is proving dysfunctional to contemporary realities. No matter how much emphasis is placed on such other qualities in coaching as coaching technique, technology, equipment, facilities, the humanity of the coach is the vital ingredient if athletes are to learn self-identity, self-responsibility, self-direction, and self-fulfillment. Traditionally, many coaches have defined coaching as analogous to sculpturing—making the players what the coaches want them to become. Thus, we have two sport psychologists, Bruce Ogilvie and Thomas Tutko (1966), labeling athletes who will not be molded in the ways coaches wish as "problem athletes." The humanistic coach views the coaching experience as gardening—helping athletes grow and find what they want to be.

The goal of school sports, and all of education, for the humanist, is the production of increasing uniqueness and independence, and this cannot be achieved in an autocratic atmosphere in which the team is built around an omniscient authority figure where all decisions are made by the coach while players are relegated to passive followers of orders. A common sense principle of school sport, then, is that it should promote the fulfillment of the individuals engaged in and influenced by it; thus the real goal of sport, or any educational venture, is seen to encompass nothing less than the fulfillment of the student. In the sense I am using it here, fulfillment implies the actualization of the full potentialities for personal-social growth latent in the individual.

With regard to school sports programs, the humanistic coach starts with the basic premise that the sport is for the players, not the coaches. He/she believes that it is a serious mistake to adopt business-industrial practices and values in an area whose primary purpose is human expression. He/she believes that educational endeavors must measure efficiency not in terms of so many work hours per product but they must measure their efficiency in terms of increased humanism, increased power to do, and increased capacity to appreciate. The coach, then strives to be more a resource person than an authority figure. He/she strives to make his/her players free of his/her, able to make their own decisions, self-reliant, responsible for their actions (Laughlin, 1974).

Statements like the following one which was made by a former University of Wyoming football coach are completely rejected by the humanist for the hoax that they are. In talking about the development of self-discipline in sports, the coach said: ". . . establishing a pattern of discipline to the extent of telling a player when to go to breakfast, when to cut his hair, and how much hair he can have will help a player develop self-discipline." (Shurmer, 1973)

The humanist coach acknowledges that contemporary society requires self-directing, responsible adults who are capable of independent behavior but he/she believes that athletes learn to control themselves by being given opportunities to make their own decisions. Self-discipline comes from practice in disciplining oneself, not by being obedient to others' demands. If, as humanists argue, choice is a basic fact of human existence, then athletes should be given the opportunity to make choices. They cannot be expected to develop the ability to choose wisely if all choices are made for them (Laughlin, 1974).

The traditional pattern of training for self-discipline is exposed for the joke that it is by former All-Pro football player George Sauer (See Scott, 1971) who said:

> It's interesting to go back and listen to the people on the high school level talk about sport programs and how they develop a kid's self-discipline and responsibility. I think the giveaway, that most of this stuff being preached on the lower levels is a lie, is when you get to college and professional levels, the coaches still treat you as an adolescent. They know damn well that you were never given a chance to become responsible or self-disciplined. Even in the pros you are told when to go to bed, when to turn your lights off, when to wake up, when to eat, and what to eat.

It is ironic, but pitifully illustrative of how traditional sports practices, which claim to develop self-discipline, keep those who have been exposed to these methods the longest, the pros, in virtual bondage. Note that freedom for the players has been a key issue in the negotiations between the NFL players association and the owners. That is, professional athletes are asking for freedom from curfews, fines, and other silly rules. These are grown men asking for their individual freedom, not adolescents!

If sports helps kids build character, as coaches claim, then players need a chance to make their own choices. In a way, character is composed of the choices one makes. So if coaches make all the decisions they are stunting character development, not nurturing it. (Laughlin, 1974) Moreover, coaches are not military leaders, fashion designers, or judges and the preoccupation with rigid standards of personal appearance, political beliefs, interests, and private behavior is misplaced. Coaches should realize that clothes, hair cuts, personal likes and dislikes are not valid criteria for judging people and their worth to society. (Mosston and Mueller, 1974)

While humanism gives preference to cooperation over competition, it does not reject competition in a sport context. Competition, within limits of sport is accepted for its own pleasure. But, except when carried out as fun, there is a belief that intensive competition has the danger of generating conditional self-worth, role-specific relationships, excellence based on competitive merit, self as a means, and subjection of self to external control. (Schafer, 1971b) Perhaps George Leonard (1973) best summarizes the humanistic perspective with regard to competition. He says, "There is nothing wrong with competition in the proper perspective. Like a little salt, it adds zest to the game and to life itself. But when the seasoning is mistaken for the substance, only sickness can follow. Similarly, when winning becomes 'the only thing,' it can lead only to eventual emptiness and anomie." One does not have to search far for examples of the consequences of "win at any cost" mentality: Basketball scandals of 1950's and 1960's, recruiting violations in the past few years by Oklahoma, Southwest Louisiana, Long Beach State, Minnesota, and numerous others, and even Watergate.

Invariably, when anyone criticizes the "winning is the only thing" ethic traditionalists smugly counter with: "If winning is not important, why keep score?" For the humanist, it is not a question of whether a score is kept; of course a score is kept in sport competition, and it is important. It is important for measuring one's quality of performance; it is a means for ascertaining the skill which one displayed during competition. But it is not an end; it is a means! The end in sport is the joy, exhilaration, and self-fulfillment that one obtains from movement; it is the display of skill, the challenge of matching tactical wits with competitors, and the sensual feelings that arise in competition. Using victory as the only end, the goal of sport competition, is too limiting, confining, too shallow, too short-sighted for humanism. One reason winning is so overvalued is that we haven't been taught to enjoy the doing— the process—of whatever it is we are attempting.

Miller (1970) suggests that individuals who play games in order to win are actually not "playing" games, they are working at them. Thus, they do not win anything of value. In a program which is ends-oriented, the game is for winning; in the means-oriented program the game is the game; it is for playing. In the first program the player cannot be happy unless he/she is winning, is successful, whereas in the second, if one is satisfied and happy with the play he/she is successful. In this second program the expressive nature of sport is emphasized, and, as Ingham and Loy (1973) say: "Sport needs no other justification than that it provides a setting for sociability and fun." So it goes without saying that the "winning is the only thing" ethic is rejected by humanism since it so severely restricts the rich potential for human growth, development of a positive self concept, and opportunity for peak experiences through competition.

The humanistic coach places individual expression above group conformity, self-discipline above authority, independence above dependence. He/she makes concerted effort to give attention to every player on the team, not just the starters. He/she might even develop a system whereby every player plays a part of every game. He/she makes an effort to treat opponents as worthy competitors; he/she has empathy for the weak opponent and will not try to pour it on when he/she has this opponent out-classed. In short, the coach cares, really cares, about each and every sports participant, not just his/her own athletes, but *all* athletes. In a sense, opponents are viewed as extended teammates, for if they had decided not to compete there would be no contest; they, in effect, cooperate so that the contest can be enjoyed together.

By now you may be saying: "But the humanistic coach will have no authority, no control." It is true that as one becomes more concerned with individuality and the processes of living there may be an overreaction where impulsiveness and spontaneity runs in circles chasing itself. (Podeschi, 1974) However, there is no suggestion in the humanist perspective that directive and dynamic leadership is to be abandoned to complete equalitarianism. Of course the coach needs authority but it is to be exercised in a humane and supportive way. Maslow (1965) noted that the great leader is one who has just the right combination of humility and flexibility while at the same time possessing the strength of character to stand alone when an important principle is involved. He says: "The kind of person who must be loved by all probably will not make a good leader."

A critical factor with regard to the legitimate use of authority by the coach is the scope. In this regard, Schafer (1971a) says:

> Authority ought to be narrow rather than broad in scope in that it is exercised over behavior clearly and directly related to training and performance. Determination of the precise limits of authority in the end must depend upon the good judgment of the sensitive coach, although athletes can hardly be faulted for increasingly resisting the authority of the unnecessarily intruding and controlling coach and for demanding that he stay within his justifiable limits in controlling their lives.

Edwards (1972) has noted that ". . . America would gain far more than she would lose through initiation of . . . an alternative sport structure . . . in which the younger generation can be socialized with values stressing cooperation rather than antagonism, participation and self-actualization rather than confrontation and domination."

Perhaps John Stuart Mill, the 19th century philosopher, who certainly knew nothing about inter-school sports but a lot about human nature, best expresses what might be a guiding humanistic principle for sports programs. In his essay "On Liberty" he says:

> Human nature is not a machine to be built after a model, and set to do exactly the work prescribed for it, but a tree, which requires to grow and develop itself on all sides, according to the tendency of the inward forces which make it a living thing (In Commins and Linscott, 1974).

Will the humanistic movement be adopted in the field of sport as the dominant model? No one knows for sure. There are many reasons to expect it won't but there are encouraging signs that it might. Perhaps humanism is an idea whose time has come. Podeschi (1974) believes that the greatest effects of the humanistic perspective will produce their greatest effects in the coming century. Only time will tell.

REFERENCES

Brown, J. A. B., *Freud and the Post-Freudians,* New York: Cassell, 1963.

Combs, A. W., "A Perceptual View of the Adequate Personality," in A. W. Combs (ed.) *Perceiving, Behaving, Becoming,* ASCD Yearbook, Washington, D.C., 1962.

Commins, S. and Linscott, R. N., (eds.) *Man and the State: The Political Philosophers,* New York: Random House, 1974. ("On Liberty" by John Stuart Mill reproduced in its entirety, pp. 135–260).

Edwards, H., *Sociology of Sport,* Homewood, Ill.: Dorsey Press, 1973.

Freud, S., *New Introductory Lectures on Psychoanalysis,* New York: W. W. Norton, 1933.

Freud, S., *On Creativity and the Unconscious,* New York: Harper and Row, 1958.

Hoch, P., *Rip Off the Big Game,* Garden City, New York: Doubleday, 1972.

IBM: "Time to Think Small," *Newsweek,* October 1, 1973, pp. 80–84.

Laughlin, N. T., "Existentialism, Education, and Sport," in G. H. McGlynn (ed.) *Issues in Physical Education and Sport,* Palo Alto, California: National Press Books, 1974, pp. 169–180.

Leonard, G. B., "Winning Isn't Everything, It's Nothing," *Intellectual Digest,* **4** (October): 45–47, 1973.

McGregor, D., "The Human Side of Enterprise," *The Management Review,* **46**: 22–28, 88–89, 1957.

McGregor, D., *The Human Side of Enterprise,* New York: McGraw-Hill, 1960.

McGregor, D., *The Professional Manager,* New York: McGraw-Hill, 1967.

Maslow, A. H., *Eupsychian Management,* Homewood, Ill.: Dorsey Press, 1965.

Maslow, A., "Personal letter to Frank Goble, February 6, 1968, Published in F. Goble, *The Third Force,* New York: Grossman, 1970.

Maslow, A. H., *Motivation and Personality,* (2nd ed.) New York: Harper and Row, 1970.

Maslow, A. H., *The Farther Reaches of Human Nature,* New York: Viking, 1971.

Matson, F., *The Broken Image,* New York: Doubleday, 1966.

Miller, D. L., *Gods and Games: Toward a Theology of Play,* New York: World, 1970.

Mosston, M. and Mueller, R., "Mission, Omission, and Submission in Physical Education," In G. H. McGlynn, (ed.) *Issues in Physical Education and Sport,* Palo Alto, California: National Press Books, 1974, pp. 97–106.

Ogilvie, B. and Tutko, T. A., *Problem Athletes and How to Handle Them,* London: Pelham Books, 1966.

Paul, W., "Authoritarianism in Physical Education and Sports," In G. H. McGlynn (ed.) *Issues in Physical Education and Sports,* Palo Alto, California: National Press Books, 1974, pp. 194–205.

Podeschi, R., "The Farther Reaches of Physical Activity," *Quest* XXI (January): 12–18, 1974.

Sage, G. H., "The Coach as Management: Organizational Leadership in American Sport," *Quest* XIX (January): 35–40, 1973.

Schafer, W. E., "Sport, Socialization and the School: Toward Maturity or Enculturation?" Paper presented at the Third International Symposium on the Sociology of Sport, Waterloo, Ontario, Canada, August, 1971(a).

Schafer, W. E., "Sport and Youth Counter-Culture: Contrasting Socialization Themes," Paper presented at the Conference on Sport and Social Deviancy, SUNY, Brockport, December, 1971(b).

Scott, J., "The Souring of George Sauer," *Intellectual Digest,* 2 (December): 52–55, 1971.

Shurmer, F., Quoted in *Greeley Tribune,* September 12, 1973.

Staude, J. R., "The Theoretical Foundations of Humanistic Sociology," In J. F. Glass and J. R. Staude (eds.) *Humanistic Society,* Pacific Palisades, California: Goodyear, 1972, pp. 262–268.

Watson, J. B., *Behaviorism,* Chicago: University of Chicago Press, 1930.

SOCIAL DISCONTENT AND THE GROWTH OF WILDERNESS SPORT

Wayne Wilson

Charles Reich's *The Greening of America* (1970) was received with mixed reactions. Some acclaimed the book as a penetrating analysis of American society. Others assailed it as naive, simplistic, and superficial. As one who was a member of the college generation about which Reich wrote so glowingly, this writer found Reich's sycophantic descriptions of young people to be slightly embarrassing and often inaccurate. Nevertheless, I believe the book is valuable.

Its thesis contends that many Americans in the 1960's experienced a transformation of consciousness and that the trend would continue into the 1970's. The emerging consciousness was most prominent among young middle and upper-middle class whites, and it was characterized by a rejection of the "artificiality of work and culture (Reich, 1970, p. 8)," a search for a sense of self, and an increased appreciation of the natural environment. This changing system of values, according to Reich (1970), had developed in opposition to the "immense apparatus of technology and organization that American has built (p. 18)."

The emergence of widespread popular interest in such outdoor sports as backpacking, mountaineering, cross-country skiing, and bicycle touring, between 1965 and 1974, lends support to Reich's thesis. The growth of these sports offers evidence of a dissatisfaction with modern American life and suggests that the source of this discontent was excessive technology and urbanization.

Between the middle of the 1960's and the mid-1970's the number of Americans engaging in wilderness sport activities grew dramatically. The number of cross-country skiers increased from approximately 2,000 in 1964 to 500,000 in 1974 (Brady & Skjemstad, 1974, p. 206). A 1965 study by the Interior Department's Bureau of Outdoor Recreation estimated that there were 10 million American hikers (Streetman, 1972). By 1971, *The New York Times* estimated that the total had risen to 20 million (Sands, 1971). At Kings Canyon and Sequoia National Parks, backpacking increased 100 percent between 1968 and 1971 ("Backpackers," 1971). At Yosemite National Park the number of "visitor-days" spent on back trails increased from 77,654 in 1967 to 220,835 in 1972; in New Hampshire's White Mountain National

Wayne Wilson, "Social Discontent and the Growth of Wilderness Sport," *Quest*, Monograph **27** (Winter, 1977), pp. 54–60. Reprinted by permission of the publishers and author.

Forest the number of visitor days increased from 234,000 in 1968 to 482,000 in 1972 (Newman, 1973). Approximately 2,000 people climbed California's Mount Whitney in 1963. By 1970, the National Park and Forest Services were predicting that between 10 and 20,000 climbers would make the ascent that year ("Trash Plagues," 1970). The number of mountaineers in Grand Teton National Park doubled between 1965 and 1972 (Wilford, 1972). In 1965 bikepaths were virtually unknown in the United States. In 1974, however, there were more than 15,000 miles of bikepaths in the country and the Interior Department had proposed development of 100,000 more miles in national park and recreation areas (Sherman, 1974, p. 16).

Who were the new wilderness sport enthusiasts of the 1960's and 1970's and what motivated their involvement? According to a study conducted by Leisure Group, Inc., a camping goods company, most backpackers were between eighteen and thirty-four years old, were married, and had a family income of $7,000 or more (Sands, 1971). Adding further to this profile the National Park Service noted that almost all were from non-rural areas (Sands, 1971). On the basis of Leisure Group's study, the Park Service's profile of of backpackers, and numerous journalistic accounts of mountaineers, cross-country skiers, and bicycle tourists, it may be concluded that wilderness sport participants tended to be relatively affluent young white people from non-rural backgrounds.

The comments and writings of the new wilderness sport participants indicated that their involvement was motivated by two closely related desires. One quite simply was the wish to escape the technology and urbanization of modern living. The second was the desire to achieve a greater sense of self-awareness. These two related concerns surfaced again and again as mountaineers, backpackers, cross-country skiers, and bicyclists explained their sport participation. British mountaineer Showell Styles, for example, stated:

> (mountaineering is) an escapist occupation filling an increasing need by an increasing number of people. To these it gives a simplification of being that is like a revelation, stripping away the vast unnecessary load of cares and tensions forced upon them by the modern way of life (James, 1972, p. 1).

Backpackers offered similar comments: " 'It's an escape. You can get back to thinking about and for yourself. It's a very satisfying sport ("Lots of Bucks," 1972, p. 8).' " A seventeen year old explained to the *New York Times:* " 'It's just being in contact with nature. It's a whole different atmosphere, the whole way your mind works and changes ("Backpackers," 1971, p. 19).' " And another said, " 'Here you set your own goals and you know if you reach them ("Backpackers," 1971, p. 19).' " A cross-country skier (Tapeley, 1973) listed the virtues of his sport: "It doesn't involve . . . what we mean by 'plastic' things. It preserves the environment. It's beautiful (p. 14)." And, about bicycle touring one cyclist (Sherman, 1974) wrote:

> The sky is high and blue and the open road slants down the earth.
> The wind is at your back. The new rhythm swashes through your body.
> It's in your pumping insides. Simplicity. Fullness. Exhilaration. (p. 11)

Indeed, so well founded was the belief that outdoor pursuits were thera-
peutic that in 1969 a Los Angeles psychologist who believed that "being out
in the wilderness would add another dimension to the psychotherapy experience (Sands, 1971, p. III 7)," began sponsoring backpacking trips for his
patients. And, Cornell University, in 1972, initiated a "wilderness reflections
(Peterson, 1972, p. 43)" freshman orientation program consisting of backpacking, canoe, and bicycle trips designed to teach new students how to cope
with "loneliness, self-doubts and confusions (p. 43)." The growing popularity
of wilderness sports may thus be viewed as part of a wider search for emotional and spiritual contentment, a search which has spawned American interest
in and approval of such phenomena as Transcendental Meditation, yoga, Zen,
est, and a host of other "True Ways."

Cynics may contend that the growth of wilderness sports was not
a reaction to urban living, but rather was something engineered by enterpris-
ing businessmen who created a "back to nature" ethic in the minds of
consumers in order to sell more camping equipment. Such an assumption,
however, would be misleading. Businessmen were not blind to the growth
potential of the outdoor sports industry, but they consistently underesti-
mated that potential. For instance, the Coleman Company in the mid-1960's
set out to establish a sales volume of $100 million by 1970. By 1970, Cole-
man had gone well beyond its earlier projections achieving a volume of $144
million ("Merchandising," 1971). The reason for underestimating the magnitude of the potential market seems to have stemmed from a failure to com-
prehend the nature and extent of changing American values. Entrepreneurs
assumed that increased amounts of "expendable income and more leisure
time ('Merchandising,' 1971, p. 68)" would increase participation in wilderness sports. But, the realization that the growing dissatisfaction with technology and urbanization could accelerate that increase generally came only
after the fact.

Consumer demands for outdoor sporting goods expanded at a rate disproportionate to the relatively modest promotional efforts of the sporting
goods industry. In some cases development of new consumer interests
preceded the industry's recognition of these interests to such an extent that
manufacturers and retailers were unable to meet them. It is not surprising,
then, to note that a 1971 study by the National Sporting Goods Association
criticized the industry for not recognizing and taking advantage of opportunities in the marketing of outdoor sports equipment ("Out of Doors,"
1971). In short, the sporting goods industry did not initiate a boom in sales

by manipulating the consuming public.

It was not until the sudden emergence of the ecological movement in 1970 that the business community began to sense the actual potential of the wilderness sports market. As all segments of the population became increasingly cognizant of the ecological movement, business journals and periodicals began to take note of the implications for the sporting goods industry. Articles with titles such as "Coleman Aims $1,000,000 Push at Outdoor Folk (1970)" painted a rosy picture of sales, profits, and growth in the industry.

Yet, the trend toward wilderness sport activity had been well established before 1970. In 1965, for example, Camptrails of Phoenix, a camping goods company, began a period of growth that increased its sales volume at a rate of 25 percent in each year before 1970 ("Lots of Bucks," 1972). Leisure group' Inc. experienced an annual sales increase of 15 percent for " 'several years ("Backpackers," 1971, p. 19)' " prior to the early 1970's. Jim Whittaker's Recreation Equipment, Inc., which deals in backpacking and mountaineering equipment, doubled its sales volume every year between 1963 and 1970 (Hall, 1973). The Coleman Company more than doubled its sales between 1965 and 1970 ("Merchandising," 1971). And, a 1971 *New York Times* article reported that "every major manufacturer (Sands, 1971, p. III 1)" consulted had indicated that sales had at least doubled in the previous three to five years, which is to say that their sales increases had been established prior to 1970.

Even with the wide publicity surrounding the ecological movement, entrepreneurs were slow to fully recognize the implications inherent in expressions of discontent directed at environmental abuse. Granted, a number of companies and advertising agencies jumped on the ecology bandwagon by marketing "natural" clothes, bath products, and cosmetics, but the true nature and extent of the sentiments underlying the ecological movement were not perceived. Thus, while corporate energy was expended marketing such transparent hypocrises as "natural" hairspray, opportunities to promote and capitalize on genuinely natural sporting activities were initially overlooked.

The sport of cross-country skiing is a case in point; it is a sport tailormade to provide intimacy with nature. Its biggest spurt of growth began at about the same time that the ecological movement began to attract public attention, yet no major American sporting goods company anticipated the business opportunities to be gained through the promotion of cross-country skiing. Instead, manufacturers and retailers were caught by surprise as thousands of would-be skiers sought products. G. H. Bass and Co. of Maine, for instance, imported approximately 200 pairs of cross-country skis in the winter of 1969–70. By the following year, orders were in the "thousands (McLean, 1971, p. 1)" and Bass could not fill the orders. Nationally, imports increased from 80,000 in 1970 to 300,000 in 1972 (Tapeley, 1973 and "Business Bulletin," 1973). All told, 350,000 pairs of skis were sold in the United States in 1972 (Brady & Skjemstad, 1974, p. 206). Still there were complaints by retailers about shortages. As late as 1973, for example, Thak Inc. of Newbury, Massachusetts, a company which had increased its cross-country ski sales six-fold since 1970, informed the *Wall Street Journal* that it could not get enough skis to sell ("Business Bulletin," 1973).

An analogous situation occurred in the bicycle industry. Had the industry correctly understood changing American attitudes toward the environment, it would have sought from the beginning to promote the bicycle as the perfect instrument with which to "get back to nature." This did not happen.

A large jump in bicycle sales occurred in 1971 when 8.5 million were sold (Bender, 1971). This represented a sales increase of 20 percent over the previous year according to the Bicycle Manufacturers of America (Cardwell, 1971); an increase of 30 percent according to *Business Week* ("Deere Pedals," 1972). The sudden expansion of the market was caused by increased demands for adult bicycles. The percentage of sales to adults in 1970 was 15 percent. That percentage increased to over 30 percent in 1971 (Bender, 1971), and to 50 percent in 1972 (Sherman, 1974, pp. 11-12). Concurrent with sales increases were the creation of thousands of miles of bike-paths and the publication of a variety of new books about bicycle touring and bicycle maintenance (Gardener, 1972).

The sharp upswing in adult demand was not caused by promotional efforts in the industry. In fact, it was not until after the bicycle boom had established itself that manufacturers turned their attention to adult oriented advertising (Drew, 1971). As was the case with cross-country skiing, consumer demands caught manufacturers and retailers by surprise. Reporting on the increase of bicycle sales, the *New York Times* noted that one Schwinn executive spent "a considerable part of his time and energy . . . appeasing dealers' demands for his company's product (Bender, 1971, p. III 1)." The same executive was quoted as saying that even if production had been increased "50% or even 100% (Bender, 1971, p. III, 1)," Schwinn could not have filled all of its orders. While it is true, of course, that many of the bicycles sold during this period were never used for touring, the point nevertheless remains that the growth of interest in touring and the development of the bicycle boom in general were not engineered by the industry. Bicycle manufacturers could not have engineered the boom because they did not even anticipate it.

Thus, it is evident that the movement toward wilderness sport activities was a response to the conditions of modern American life; it was not primarily the result of manipulative entrepreneurial efforts by the sporting goods industry. People who engaged in sports such as backpacking, mountaineering, cross-country skiing, and bicycle touring were motivated by a desire to escape technological urban life and by a desire to attain a greater sense of self-awareness. The increasing participation in wilderness sports between 1965 and 1974 supports Reich's (1970) contention that a segment of American society was moving or had moved to a rejection of America's immense apparatus of technology and organization (p. 18)." Reich (1970) may have overstated the degree to which people had forsaken the arch-typical rat-race life, but by focusing his attention on the "artificiality of work and culture (p. 8)" resulting from rampant technology and urbanization, he correctly identified a source of discontent for a significant number of Americans.

Two additional points are worth noting. First, while wilderness sport enthusiasts sought an escape from modern life, it should be remembered that their efforts were considerably aided by technological advancements. Were it not for such innovations as freeze-dried food, synthetic water resistant tents and clothing, and light weight ten-speed bicycles, the back-to-nature movement would undoubtedly have been considerably limited. Thus, the growth of wilderness sport in the 1960's and 1970's closely resembled the rise of nineteenth-century American sport, which according to sport historian John Betts (1969), "was as much a product of industrialization as an antidote to it (p. 165)."

Finally, it should be noted that although the business community initially failed to take full advantage of changing American attitudes with regard to the environment, there is no reason to assume that entrepreneurs have not begun and will not continue to attempt to capitalize on these changing attitudes. It is therefore not surprising that some observers have expressed the concern that the joys of wilderness sport will diminish as these activities fall victim to the:

> . . . classic American spoiler: commercialization . . . with advertising preying upon us, manipulating us, creating stupid desires for more and more plastic in our boots, more and more status in our clothes. (Tapeley, 1973, p. 14.)

Indeed it remains to be seen, if what started out as an escapist activity can remain so.

REFERENCES

Backpackers Find Wilderness Trails Are Becoming Crowded, *New York Times,* August 10, 1971, 19.

Bender, M., Bicycle business is booming. *New York Times,* August 15, 1971, III 1, 4.

Betts, J., The technological revolution and the rise of sport: 1850–1900. In J. W. Loy & G. W. Kenyon (Eds.) *Sport, Culture and Society.* New York: MacMillan Publishing, 1969, 145–66.

Brady, M. & Skjemstad, L. *Ski cross-country.* New York: Dial Press, 1974.

Business Bulletin: Cross-Country Skis. *Wall Street Journal,* February 8, 1973, 1.

Coleman aims $1,000,000 push at outdoor folk. *Advertising Age,* March 2, 1970, 2.

Deere pedals into the bike market. *Business Week,* August 19, 1972, 68.

Drew, L., Bike marketers switch strategy as '71 sales to adults sprint. *Advertising Age,* September 6, 1971, 8.

Gardener, H., Tripping on bikes, *New York Times Book Review,* June 4, 1972, 8–10.

Hall, G., Business' high climbers, *Dun's,* August 1973, 52.

James, R., Mountaineering craze creates 3-hour jams; our man joins sport. *Wall Street Journal,* August 24, 1972, 1, 18.

Lots of bucks in backpacks. *Sales Management,* August 21, 1972, 8.

McLean, D., Nature walk on skis: "touring" enthusiasts spurn downhill racing. *Wall Street Journal,* April 1, 1971, 1.

Merchandising the outdoors. *Business Week,* May 22, 1971, 68.

Newman, B., The new hikers find backcountry is perilous as well as beautiful. *Wall Street Journal,* October 3, 1973, 1, 22.

Out of doors is out of sight. *Sales Management,* July 1, 1971, 21–24.

Peterson, I. 82 find road to college rocky but fun. *New York Times,* August 24, 1972, 43, 45.

Reich, C. *The greening of America.* New York: Random House, 1970.

Sands, S., Backpacking: I go to the wilderness to kick the man-world out of me. *New York Times,* May 9, 1971, III 1, 7, 9, 10.

Sherman, S. *Bike Hiking.* Garden City: Doubleday, 1974.

Streetman, C. Recreation trails—industry's answer to governmental acquisition. *Forest Industries,* June 1972, supplement 8–9.

Tapeley, L. *Ski touring in New England.* Lexington: Stone Wall Press, 1973.

Trash plagues Mount Whitney as climbers go into thousands. *New York Times,* August 30, 1970, 19.

Wilford, J. Mountain climbers litter trail. *New York Times,* September 5, 1972, 39.

CHANGE AND CRISIS IN MODERN SPORT

Harry Edwards

We live in an age of revolution. From the Eighteenth Century to the present, revolutions appear to have clustered together, to have become watermarks of a worldwide revolutionary tradition of spirit to which each upheaval has contributed. Thus the rush to define as "revolution" any more or less sustained, highly publicized or even loosely organized and minimally successful attack against an established order, institutionalized authority or belief system, is not a surprising tendency—particularly in the popular media. So in recent years in the United States we have experienced the "black revolution," the "women's revolution" and the "athletic revolution."

Of course, this raises the question of "what, exactly, is a revolution?" Unfortunately, the question cannot be answered with any high degree of conceptual precision. Indeed, it is unlikely that any one delineation would prove either universally applicable or completely acceptable to all who study revoltuions. This fact notwithstanding, it is quite likely that none of the above mentioned "revolutions" would be so characterized by very many serious students of the phenomena. For despite widespread disagreement on the question of what a revolution is, there exists considerable consensus on the view that, at a minimum, revolutions involve deepseated and substantial changes in institutional structures, authority relations and ideological defini- tions. Further, such changes are often accomplished through conflict em- ploying the threat or actual use of violence. On the basis of these criteria, it should be clear that developments over recent years in the realms of inter- racial relations, male-female relations, and in sport—even if taken cumula- tively—fall short of the boundaries of revolutionary tradition. Since the principal concern here is with sport, analysis of the so-called black and women's "revolutions" will be deferred as more appropriately warranting separate treatment.

THE DOMESTIC SPORT SCENE

Application of the label "revolution" to controversial or simply "new" developments in sport has achieved currency today. This is due less to conceptual accuracy than to the sometimes unanticipated, often dramatic and nearly always unsettling onset of events, that, in substance or by implica-

Harry Edwards, "Change and Crisis in Modern Sport," *The Black Scholar,* Vol. 8 (October-November, 1976), pp. 60–65. Reprinted by permission.

tion, appear alien to procrustean sports traditions. True enough, there have been rebellions among athletes, attempts to synthesizing "radical" ideological emphases relative to sports organization and participation, and on a minor scale some success in compelling sports authorities to implement some of the more superficial operational thrusts of these ideologies. But the continuing structural interrelatedness and ideological interpenetration extant between sport and society, and the goals, methods and orientations of the would-be revolutionaries have rendered such developments in sport—on both the domestic U.S. and international levels—a good deal less than revolutionary.

Any truly revolutionary change in sport can only occur concommitantly, or after revolutionary changes in the society as a whole. It is because of this synchronic relationship existing between sport and society that societies manifesting strong currents of racist or sexist ideology, for example, tend to exhibit patterned racism or sexism in the organization and operation of their sport institutions. Similarly, more militaristic societies are more likely to develop combative, collision-type sports than less militaristic societies. History shows that though there were many *reforms* and attempts at reforms in the organization and operation of sport in pre-revolutionary Russia, China and Cuba, more deep-seated and fundamental—which is to say *revolutionary*— changes in the structural organization, ideological thrust and operation of sport in each of these societies awaited the achievement of revolutionary change in society as a whole.

A second set of factors crucial in any evaluation of the "revolutionary" status of changes in domestic sport is the disposition of the expressed goals and the methods and orientations of those agitating for change. Even a casual reading of the works produced by the leading advocates of change reveals that their demands and methods as well as the moral and political foundations employed in their ideological justification are as American as cherry pie. They have sought equality of opportunity, provision for due process in disciplinary procedures, more equitable remuneration for services rendered, less autocracy and greater democracy in the operation of athletic organizations and an end to "dehumanizing" practices. On their part, women have simply demanded a larger share of the existing sports pie—roles, rewards and recognition.

Their tactical methods—organized protests, boycotts, disruptions, agitation and strikes—were established aspects of the American political scene long before the shadow of the British crown was vanquished from this land.

In part, then, there has been no revolution in domestic sport because there have been no revolutionaries.

THE INTERNATIONAL SPORT SCENE

The lack of a revolution in sport at the international level is due to the fact that revolution cannot be fomented in a situation that is structurally unamenable to revolution. Sport competition and organization at the international level exist at the very least at the sufferance of political authorities governing nations under whose flags athletes, athletic organizations and sports officials participate. The purely voluntary character of this association between representatives of sovereign nations makes revolutionary change, in any strict sense, impossible. Under the circumstances, the ultimate choices confronting parties in conflict within international sports relations are to accede, to compromise or, failing that, to dissolve the association—at least temporarily. In international sport, then, as in the United Nations organization, there exists neither sovereign power centers nor administrative apparatuses susceptible to change through revolutionary conquest.

The problems at the foundation of the various crises afflicting sport, both in the United States and at the international level, have been more directly *evolutionary* than revolutionary. There is a fundamental problem on both the national and international levels. This has been the failure of sport as a dynamic sphere of human interaction to develop and routinize mechanisms allowing for orderly and relatively rapid adaptation. There has been a failure to adapt to international political shifts indirectly affecting relations in sport. And there has been a failure to adapt to more long-range, but no less far-reaching, evolutionary social, political and technological developments impacting upon sport.

Over the greater part of the Twentieth Century, sport, by every measure, has been dominated by Western, developed nations. For the most part these societies have proffered the notion that sport is inherently *apolitical*. Based upon this definition of the situation, this myth of sport's insularity, the *raison d' etre* for sport has been laid generally to its presumed role as a vehicle of social integration, both within and between societies. Beyond the display of colors and the representational role of participants, any overt political demonstration has traditionally been abhorred as a betrayal of the ethics of sportsmanship and "good taste."

This concept of sport and its role in human affairs encountered no major contradictions so long as there existed:

1. functioning intra- and inter-societal mechanisms allowing for the effective management of potential or actual group conflicts; and/or

2. unity along ideological and political lines sufficient to preclude the development of interests and definitions so irreconcilable as to threaten the harmony of intergroup association through sport; or

3. power monopolies (political, economic, ideological or military) exercised in such a way as to forestall challenges to established definitions, processes and structures.

There is evidence, that tends to refute the theory that sport serves a safety-valve function. Therefore, radical alterations in structures that once did help sustain *general* intergroup cooperation may heighten the potential for discord in the *specific* area of sport. And under conditions of intensified cultural, national or racial identification—not to speak of chauvinism—it would appear *inevitable* that unmanaged conflicts in relations between groups (or societies) would extend to relations existing between them in the sports sphere.

CHAOS AND CRISIS: THE PRICE OF EVOLUTIONARY STAGNATION

In the past, the claimed insularity of sport (or its enforced isolation from the mundane business and politics of everyday human affairs) in combination with its solid grounding in ritual, ideological and organizational tradition have contributed toward both institutional continuity and the facilitation of inter-group cooperation in sport during times of rising, through not intense, intergroup antagonisms. Within the last three decades, however, there have occurred a number of developments external to sport which nonetheless appear to have effectively transmuted established sport's conservatism into a situation which may be dysfunctional and dangerous for western society. The shocks to sport have emanated from a number of sources:

1. revolutions that have established new governments, new ideological systems and/or new nations;

2. the demise of colonialism and the emergence of the "developing nations" as a world force;

3. advanced technological developments.

Let us look at some examples of how each of these developments have affected the vitality of modern sport as they have emerged simultaneously with, or have precipitated breakdowns in the mechanism for social stability.

REVOLUTIONS

Unquestionably the revolution that has most deeply affected the disposition of modern sport is the Russian Revolution of 1917. And if recent events are any indication, the Chinese Revolution, culminating in the founding of the Peoples' Republic of China in 1949, will have a similar impact.

Russia's decision to embark upon a course of international sport involve-ment was part of its general re-evaluation of the world situation. Having achieved primary economic and political consolidation, and having mastered nuclear technology by the late 1940's, the U.S.S.R. under Stalin developed the thesis that contradictions within and between capitalist states were becoming more intense than those between the Soviet Union and the West. This ideological pronouncement became the foundation of peaceful co-existence and later the policy of "detente."

Soviet athletes, like Soviet performers in the arts and humanities, be-came front line troops in a global cultural and ideological struggle. Mass communications technology, having rendered international sport truely *international,* enabled sport performances to be viewed or at least communicated to hundreds of millions of people. Thus, the Soviets saw sport as "war without employing the tools of war," as an extension of politics—politics being conceived as "war without bloodshed." The U.S.S.R. was most certainly not the first to see the potential of international sport as a propaganda vehicle. But what the Soviets did do was to *systematically* dismiss the "bourgeois Western illusion" of sport as *apolitical* and then set about forging a direct propaganda link between victory in sport on the one hand and the viability of a social system on the other. And since Russia was not only beyond the control of established mechanisms (diplomatic and otherwise) allowing for the effective management of potential conflicts among Western nations, and under any circumstances was unwilling to compromise on basic ideological principles, Western powers were in no way able to shield international sport from this new development. Indeed as a result of the Soviet challenge, other nations could only refuse to compete under such overtly politicized definitions, or they could compete, politics notwithstanding, and thereby *de facto* accede to Soviet definitions—definitions which destroyed for all time the established consensus that sport be regarded as apolitical.

Being the leading capitalist nation and the wealthiest and most populated country in the Western camp, the United States accepted the Soviet challenge. So in 1952, the attention of the world shifted from the performance of individual athletes competing for world recognition to a "cold war" drama being acted out in the international sports arena by two titans locked in ideological struggle.

The drama has always been at its height during the Olympic Games. Protest as it might, the International Olympic Committee could do nothing to either discourage or curtail this emergence of blatant politics in the Games.

By staking national prestige on outcomes in international sports competition, both the Soviets and the United States may have set a dangerous precedent that could backfire when other nations develop athletes of a world champion caliber. Reverses could occur also if the agreed-upon definition of the operative unit changes to include power blocs rather than simply individual nations—e.g. the developing or Third World nations viewed as the third party to a threeway struggle, including the Eastern and Western bloc nations, for sports supremacy—as has already occurred in the international political and economic realms.

Perhaps even more important has been the impact of the precedent upon the general perception of sport as a political tool. If it is legitimate for the Soviets and the U.S. to employ sport as a vehicle for political propaganda, then why cannot everyone play the game: Czechoslovakians, Afro-Americans, Cubans, black Africans, the Chinese, and so forth? The answer of course is that everyone can and many have. And quite likely the number who do so will increase as the People's Republic of China makes its bid for I.O.C. recognition, having already exerted political pressure upon Canada during the 1976 Games to exclude Taiwan from participation. With the Games scheduled for the Soviet Union in 1980 and Los Angeles in 1984, the political road ahead for international sports looks rough indeed.

THE DEMISE OF COLONIALISM

Perhaps the dual impact of the demise of colonialism upon traditional sport is epitomized by the involvement of the new black African nations in international competition. While squirming under the heel of British, French and Portuguese colonialism, the black African athletes frequently competed for these countries. The unyieldingly elitist perspectives on sport held by white colonizers led to the neglect of black African athletic development. Ineffective training, inadequate facilities and lax or nonexistent technical assistance reduced the African athlete to a laughing stock—lapped during races, often failing to meet even minimum qualifying standards in field events.

With the establishment of the Republic of Ghana in 1957, however, a new era in both African history and international sports competition was opened. In less than two decades black Africa has raised itself from the doldrums of both colonialism and athletic humiliation or simple obscurity to register undeniable accomplishments in the realms of both nationhood *and* international sport, and the future looks even *blacker*.

The new nations of black Africa have also had an impact in that they have learned to play the game of international "sport politics." In 1968, they threatened as a bloc to pull out of the Olympic Games if South Africa were allowed to participate. In 1976, thirty nations did pull out because of the I.O.C.'s refusal to ban New Zealand for its having allowed one of its rugby teams to tour South Africa during the time of the Soweto Township uprising, a tactic which undoubtedly contributed to South Africa's abandoning its aparthied rule in sport.

During colonial times, such action on the part of black Africans would have been as impossible as success in their on-the-field athletic achievements. The demise of colonialism led to improved individual performances on the one hand, and on the other to increased success by the former colonial nations singly and collectively in manipulating the political impact of the Games. Black Africans in their colonized status were totally without power to challenge Western political definitions which did and still do support racist South African and Southern Rhodesian regimes. In sport, the victories of dominated people are by political definition reputed to project, in the normal courses of events, the ideological sentiments of their oppressors. Only through rebellion (such as the protest by Afro-Americans at the 1968 Olympic Games) can any other sentiments be projected and only through the achievement of political independence can these be defended. With the demise of colonialism, black African nations were able to both project and defend, to the extent of their withdrawal from participation, their own definitions of the situation vis-a-vis the New Zealand controversy; and, again, there was absolutely nothing that any international sport body could do to compel compliance with established—which is to say traditional Western—definitions.

ADVANCED TECHNOLOGICAL DEVELOPMENTS

Advanced technological developments have had a tremendous impact upon modern sport, perhaps even greater than that of social and political changes on the world scene. Electronic mass communications technology for example has not only expanded sports spectatorship, but it has also expanded the volume and variety of information available about sport. This includes information such as the nature of sport's organization and role in various societies and its interconnectedness with other societal components and processes. In so doing, this technology has contributed toward the demise of traditionally parochial suppositions toward sport and its social significance.

A second element of communications technology—the speed of travel—has also affected sport. Fast and reasonably inexpensive travel has significantly shrunk the world, bringing more people from more nations into contact with one another more often than at any other time in human history. The effect upon sport has been the rapid dissemination of sport technology, training methods and increased participation.

But advanced technology has also had its more controversial influences. For instance, while mass communications technology has contributed to the demise of parochialism, it has also exposed the transient and arbitrary nature of values and perspectives that have been traditionally viewed as "truths." The jet travel that has allowed for increased international sports involvement has also placed the political forum provided by sport within easy reach of those whose business is more appropriately war than sport. And the sport technology which has generated advanced facilities, equipment and training methods has also spawned a burgeoning sport drug culture that threatens the very integrity of sports activities. And, of course, such problems, as the status of "transexual" athletes—created largely by "advances" in medical technology—have yet to even be considered at most levels in sport.

To date, there exists no apparatus within the sport world for effectively handling the recurrent crises created by the impact of such phenomena as revolutions, profound social and political changes within and between countries, and technological advancements. Of course it might be argued that administrative bodies in the sport world are not in the business of managing problems spawned by such developments. But the fact of course is that today sport is no longer insulary, if indeed it ever was. The social and political mechanisms guaranteeing stability in sport, such as ideological consensus and power monopolies which were extant over most of the last century of sport's evolutionary history, have been effectively challenged and neutralized by recent social, political and technological developments. The result of the failure of sport to involve routinized mechanisms to effectively handle these new and quite likely permanent "facts of life" in the sports world has been the generation of chaos.

It may be that sport, as a realm of human endeavor, is incapable of the profound changes necessary to successfully meet the challenges of modern life. It also may be too deeply imbedded in Nineteenth Century tradition to alter its character with the rapidity demanded by the situation. If this be the case, then the collapse of traditional sport appears inevitable—particularly on the international level—and perhaps a new sports order will then emerge.

MODERNIZATION AND SPORT

Vern Dickinson

Western civilized man is a stone age organism trying to exercise twenty-first century power in a world of eighteenth century institutions which are based on medieval humanistic principles. The general result is very much like that of imposing high powered chemicals on natural-life systems; eventually the older, natural structures begin to erode.

John S. Lambert,
The New Prometheans

The values of human beings in sport during the twenty-first century will reflect a modernized societal value system that interacts with sports as an institution, within the fluctuating social and technological change process. The term modernization, as utilized here, is broad in scope and refers to the process by which historically evolved institutions are adapted to the rapidly changing functions that reflect the unprecedented increase in man's knowledge, permitting control over his environment. Traditional and modern are, then, relative terms (Black, 1966). The term sport is used here in its broadest sense as defined by Loy (1968), particularly as a social system and as a social institution encompassing the sport order or all organizations in society which organize, facilitate, and regulate human action in sport situations.

Vern Dickinson, "Modernization and Sport," *Quest,* Monograph 24 (Summer 1975), pp. 48–58. Reprinted by permission of the author and publisher.

THE PRESENT

Golembiewski (1971) made an analogy to demonstrate the incompatibility between technological development and traditional organization structure. The development of an airplane that is gradually modified by installing larger and more powerful motors while, at the same time maintaining the original frame may result in a frame that will vibrate apart completely. Golembiewski saw the same problem in many modern organizations, including sport, and he predicted an increase in future technical-organizational incompatibility due to modernization. Toffler (1970) has already pointed out that seventy per cent of the world population now lives in the past—those who depend on agriculture and the very few who still live by hunting and food foraging. Twenty-five per cent of the earth's population lives in the industrial present and a very small per cent lives in the future by being in the mainstream of technological and cultural change.

Both Boyle (1963) and Kenyon (1972) conclude that sport tends to reflect society; however, Kenyon also alluded to the paradox evident as the traditional sport ideology continues to function in the midst of a modernized society. Sport may be the last bastion of discipline, morality, masculinity, amateurism, and competitive fervor, and at the same time reflect, in other ways, a transitional society that is less oriented toward all of these values. A paradox of this nature could be caused by cultural lag, by an orientation toward the sacred, or by opposing the coexisting human need dispositions. The prediction of an increase or decrease of the above from the effects of modernization becomes a complex phenomenon.

THE PREDICTION PROCESS

Many professionals and those involved with particular areas of concern have studied futurism, the assessment of probabilities, in order to predict the eventual changes in certain segments of society. A large body of literature is developing in this interdisciplinary antithesis of history, and analogies could certainly be made to such concerns as sport. However, the futurist has a precarious task and a task that has been known, in the past, for its innaccuracies. Page (1972) describes futurism as a probabilistic process involving a high level of uncertainty. This consideration may help to give the "blue skyer" a sense of proportion. The second factor that, hopefully, gives the futurist a sense of playfulness and humility, if the terms are appropriate, is the fact that those involved in the actual transition of a particular portion of society are usually too busy to write papers on its future. If, however, this particular transition takes place at the same time as the movement of society from one age to another, the complication may tend to increase exponentially for the involved individual as well as the writer.

Theobald (1973) describes four major futurist schools. The positive extrapolists, exemplified by works of the Commission on the Year 2000 and the writings of Herman Kahn, have approached the future as a continuation of existing industrial trends which would result in favorable ends.

The negative extrapolists, who again see the future as a continuation of existing trends, find disaster to be the result of their extrapolations. Malthusian discussion on population increase, the Club of Rome, and the "limits of growth" reflect this school of thought. Both the positive and negative extrapolists are highly academic in their scientific and statistical analyses of the future.

The "romantic" group of futurists sees the elimination of past and present evils through the somewhat automatic development of a utopian society. Charles Reich's *The Greening of America* (1970) and George Leonard's *Education and Ecstasy* (1968) portray this very desirable future.

The fourth approach is represented primarily by Robert Theobald, author of *An Alternative Future for America II* (1968), editor of the book *Futures Conditional* (1972), and editor of a journal by the same name. His position reflects a need for a definite change in trends if survival is to be accomplished. This change, he states, may take more imagination and perseverance than human beings have heretofore exhibited. The important element in this approach is value choice.

Technological developments tend to have second, third, and fourth order consequences that eventually may affect changes in individual values. Joseph F. Coates (1971) of the Exploratory Research and Assessment Office of the National Science Foundation, has made several consequence assessments. For example, the invention of the automobile had a first order consequence of a privately owned means of transportation that could go door to door. The second order consequence was that people could shop further away and the development of large shopping centers or department stores was possible. The third order consequence was that residents would not meet as often as before and, therefore, may not know each other as well. The fourth order consequence may be that community members found it difficult to unite in order to solve common problems, and increased isolation and alienation may result. A fifth order consequence is that family members may rely more on each other for satisfaction of psychological needs. The sixth order consequence may be frustration resulting from these increased psychological demands which, in turn, may result in a higher divorce rate.

Coates has given several such examples which may appear to be a little remote or at least may appear not to indicate a direct relationship. These techniques systematically suggest likely points of impact but do not indicate that an impact will, in fact, occur or that it will be significant; that is, assessment only points out possible alternative results. Looking at third, fourth, and fifth order consequences of technological advancements does, however, tend to explore the possible relations between technology and values, heretofore relatively unexplored. The same technological development may have possible opposing consequences. For example, the automobile, according to

Coates' assessment, has a sixth order consequence of possible divorce; however, the automobile may also provide more freedom during courtship so that couples have more opportunity to know each other before marriage, possibly lowering the divorce rate.

The invention of television could provide many technology assessments relative to sport. The first order consequence would be that people are provided with a new source of entertainment in the home. Second order consequences could be that people stay home more often instead of going out to participate in sports, and, at the same time, sports become top television entertainment. As a third consequence sport is conceptualized as entertainment more than as a form of participation. The fourth order consequence would be that there is less participation in sports except at the top entertainment level, but it is obvious that sport entertainment on television could also provide a stimulus for more participation.

The elder statesman representing a typical institution has, in the past, been able to speak with a certainty and confidence that may now, and in the future, be lacking. His experience could guide him to predict the future for human beings and his particular institution based upon precedents and a stable, traditional value system. The value differences of the younger generation relative to traditional ways are reflected in their criticism of present day institution and societal segments. The traditional values can be preserved as reference points; however, the generation of the post-industrial age may not be easily indoctrinated with traditional values. Those who would predict the future of any segment of our life will know of the "future shock" acceleration which interferes with calm and easy predictions. However, even with knowledge of "future shock" the future may be approached in several different ways.

Regardless of the school of futurism followed, in a pluralistic society alternative futures rather than one future may, of necessity, have to be considered. Change *process* prediction may be a viable alternative for goal setting, and the interaction between technical and social changes in different parts of society must be recognized by representatives of different professions and groups who attempt to make predictions for their own particular segment of society.

CHANGE PROCESS

Appelbaum (1970) gave several patterns for societal change based upon different theoretical viewpoints. Change is thought by some to be analogous to biological evolution of the living organism. Early attempts were made to follow the parallel evolution of entire societies from a less advanced to a more advanced state in terms of unilinear change. More recent attempts at evolutionary theory have been multilinear in nature by explaining social change as moving along several different lines at once and as influenced by an interaction of physical and cultural characteristics.

Equilibrium theory, borrowed originally from the homeostasis concept of mechanics and the biological sciences, explains social change as reduction in the amount of change by a mutual relationship where change in one of the elements of society is followed by change in another element. This can be modified as a moving equilibrium theory. This theory emphasizes boundary exchanges between social systems, subsystems, cultural systems, and personality systems. Territoriality and dominance act as biotic homeostatic mechanisms, and cultural lag is a basic aspect of these theories.

The conflict theory of change views society as in constant change resulting from changes in social structure as well as elements. Conflict is seen as an essential feature of every society and a systematic product of the culture. Society is an unstable system resulting from class conflict, forces of production, the state of technology, conflict of interest, and revolution.

Rise and fall theories of social change express the concept that societies may decline as well as evolve. They focus on the development, maturity, and fall of great civilizations in cyclical patterns.

With further analysis, strong points and weaknesses may be found in each of the above theories, and a somewhat eclectic approach may be taken; however, the moving equilibrium theory seems to apply best to a general analysis of the interaction of the institution of sport and the modernization process. The change process is complex and many faceted, however, and a survey of many causes of change in society is necessary.

Relative to value choice during the modernization process, the debate concerning the role of institutions as change agents or as reflectors of society is, perhaps, an oversimplification. An interaction between a cultural system, a social system, and a personality system is the primary component of study if acceptance is given to the basic assumptions of the systems approach as exemplified by the works of Sorokin (1947) and Parsons (1959a). Value patterns would, then, become the common sector of personalities and social systems, and these value patterns would reflect need dispositions of the personality and role expectations of the social system (Parsons, 1959b). Sport may be seen to function like other institutions in the preservation of some traditional cultural and societal values, and at the same time to reflect a transitional society. Sport aids in the socialization process and is also influenced by the value changes of individuals within the institution. According to Luschen (1967) sport may operate as an innovator relative to changes in the system of social classes and in the diffusion of technology, as for example the bicycle and the automobile as both sport and technological advances. The degree to which each institution carries out functions relative to modernization and tradition will, no doubt, vary from time to time and tend to be specific to the particular nature of that institution and the individuals involved. Some institutions, particularly in the realm of the sacred, that is, an idealistic and ritualistic social system, may place more emphasis on the preservation of traditional cultural values. It must be remembered, however, that an institution is only a human-made abstraction and that it is composed of and controlled by individuals for the purpose of meeting the needs of these individuals.

Ingham and Loy (1973) very succinctly describe the institutional justification for sport based upon socialization theory. They indicate that sport may impose itself upon the individual through this socialization process, and possibly the result of this process may be ideally stereotyped groups. They caution, however, against a deterministic, oversocialized conception of humanity; and they recognize that new institutional values may develop as individuals question the meaning of traditional values. Actual evidence of the socialization process is not available; however, results of several studies (Puretz, 1969; Kistler, 1957; Richardson, 1962) have indicated value differences between athletes and non-athletes. Fiske (1972) has compiled a list from several sources relative to personal qualities supposedly resulting from the socialization process of football and deemed valuable by a traditional society. Briefly these would include the following values: dedication to work, self-sacrifice, individuality within a pattern of conformity, quick thinking under pressure, leadership, socially acceptable expression of unacceptable drives, social competence, desire to win, and aggressiveness.

Many value differences between athletes and non-athletes might also be attributed to socialization by other social systems prior to the individual's entrance into sport. Ogilvie and Tutko (1971) see the personality of athletes resulting primarily from a selection process. Action upon alternatives from the diffusion of knowledge from one social system to another is one method by which change is initiated. The individual is usually involved in athletics, education, church, and family simultaneously and may have some contact with members of one or more subcultures. Luschen (1967) supports the idea that sport has potential for socialization; however, he also points out the dysfunctions relative to sport and social control with regard to certain values. Such values as spontaneity associated with play and the work orientation associated with athletics, cooperation and competition, achievement status and affiliation may not necessarily be related.

Changes in ways of thinking have accompanied the new ages in the form of Copernican-type revolutions. These changes, primarily in the last three centuries, have led man to consider that he might help to formulate his own future rather than become a victim of fate and custom. The scientific revolution led man to consider cause and effect. Developments in transportation and communication led the way to the realization that institutions functioned differently in other locations and these institutions could, perhaps, be altered. The resulting lack of value stability has led, in many cases, to the frustration caused by doubtful institutions—doubtful, at least, to those who no longer accept the custom and tradition of deeply rooted institutional values. These individuals find the frustration difficult to bear if the institutional values are no longer an ameliorative part of life's unalterable crises. The innovating individual is the person who may appear to be marginal or deviant in his behavior? however, he may, through cultural lead, merely be ahead of his time. Actually any change process must, in the final analysis, be directly concerned with the approach taken by individuals; and the study of the innovating individual is fascinating.

Value socialization through sport and individual values relative to sport may be subject to changes as a result of future differences in the mode of self-conception. Research studies by Zurcher (1972) at the University of Texas have indicated that individual modes of self-conception vary according to generation. Younger generations tend to view themselves in terms of characteristic ways of acting, feeling, or responding such as being worried, being religious, or being happy. The older generations tended to view themselves more in terms of roles played such as athlete, teacher, or housewife. Few responses from either generation were in the concrete category relative to bodily descriptions or in the rather nebulous category concerned with states of being or relations with the cosmos. Zurcher concluded that rapid sociocultural change tends to cause individuals to become more accommodating to role change, value shift, and value conflict; accordingly, they no longer seek the stability of social roles and unchallenged values.

PREDICTIONS

A recent Associated Press news release described the fourteen year old Phnom Penh sports stadium, once a monument to fitness and competition, as inhabited by nearly 300 starving wives and children of Cambodian soldiers missing in action—these refugees sleeping on straw mats placed on the rough concrete. The basketball field house is an emergency surgery station for war wounded, and thousands of other war victims are taking shelter in the rooms, corridors, and corners overlooking the playing field, the 60,000 seats, and Olympic size swimming pool. Tattered laundry hangs from the flagpoles while stench and flies cover the grand staircase, which has become the toilet for these dying inhabitants. If dynamic societal changes produce holocaust, the gymnasiums and sport arenas often turn to unplanned primary functions. According to Hopkins (1971), in his review of *Der Kampf um die Zukunft* by Ossip K. Flechtheim, there are three general alternatives for the future. The first would be the destruction of civilization and a retreat to barbarism. The second would be a complete technological society dominated by robots. Examples of this future abound in literature from *1984* (1948) to *Walden Two* (1948). The third possible future would be humanistic socialism.

The effects of change on sport may certainly appear mundane in comparison to effects of such crises as nuclear war, food shortage, biosphere deteriorization, or the energy shortage. Survival has been and will continue to be an essential part of planning; however, planning relative to change of social institutions cannot be separated from these survival crises.

The knowledge explosion that is already upon us will, most likely, expand to even greater heights in the future so that there will be an education-centered society. Marien (1972), however, speculates that our learning needs will outdistance our attainments and that we will become increasingly ignorant relative to coping with the complexity surrounding us unless restructuring of education takes place. With either the positive or negative approach to the knowledge explosion, the importance of education for the citizen of the 21st century seems apparent.

In 1969 the General Electric Company published a synthesis of several reports under the title *Our Future Business Environment: A Re-evaluation.* This report (Wilson, 1970) expressed doubt concerning original studies showing education to be a change agent, and indicated that without structural changes the universities, colleges, and high schools would become so involved in their own adaptation processes, such as curriculum and educational technology, that they would become less concerned with innovation and more concerned with information processing.

Affluence, as an alternative to scarcity, could, most likely, result in a new leisure ethic which will contrast to the work ethic value basis for many of our present institutions. Urbanization, centralization of control with reference to government, and definite changes in racial composition are all seen as speculations for the future. Society may be blacker and more feminine.

Shifts in the basic values of individuals may be the single most important element in speculating about the environment in which institutions and people will function in the future. Wilson (1970), in reference to reports made by the Business Environment Section of the General Electric Company, describes a synthesis of eighteen future value system changes. Their forecasts follow Maslow's basic hypothesis that when a level of needs has been satisfied, individuals will proceed up the hierarchy from physiological needs to the development of the fullest human potential.

The general interpretation of the future value system forecast by the group from the General Electric Company is, in addition to moving up Maslow's hierarchy of needs, that values are changing from those concerned with strength, vigor, competitiveness, and power to values concerned more with cooperation, empathy, process, and intuition. According to Theobald (1968) the former values have been somewhat defined by our culture as masculine and the latter as feminine. He also points out that as society changes from a production-transportation net to an information net, the major areas of work will be education, the care of human beings, and the creation of the good community. The values needed for these tasks are those that have previously been considered feminine.

From a very general analysis of contemporary sport, its modernized future, and the change process, predictions may be made relative to a new organizational structure, a new value system, and a new kind of individual in sport. However, any attempt to probe the uncertainty of speculation about the result of modernization leads to the view described by Ralph Lapp (1961). He sees most of society looking backwards from the caboose of a train that is gathering speed and racing down a track on which there are an unknown number of switches leading to unknown destinations. The engine cab may be manned by a few scientists or there may be demons at the switch.

The above predictions necessitate a future that is planned to a much greater degree than at the present time. In fact, with the exponential increase in rate of change and the increase of complexity, the survival of a modernized society depends upon its being a planned society. For the sport order this means more than planning game schedules ten years ahead of time. It means an attempt to avoid the incongruence between ideology and practice of sport in the future. Perhaps the warning signals have not been recognized or they have been forgotten too soon. The structure is crumbling financially in some cases; there is violence in international competition as well as police involvement in local contests; there are athletic revolutions, racial strife, hypocrisy in leadership; and entertainment has become a controlling factor. The interpretation of these warning signals as well as other changes takes widespread involvement for those related to sport.

The predictions definitely have a humanistic trend and those involved in the governing bodies of sport and in the management of sport at local levels may have to make a distinction between achievement and competition and between play and competition. These distinctions have been discussed by Hellison (1973) and by Keating (1972). Those in leadership positions may also find their roles changing in the direction of advisor rather than authority figure. The shift away from competition along with the emphasis on social action and social justice may lead to less exclusion and elimination—the basis now for much of sport and many present games even at the elementary school level.

There are several alternatives for the organizational structure of sport. Traditionally, many levels of sport have been tied to education; however, this tie has already been questioned and a move in the direction of private enterprise is a distinct possibility. One of the reasons mentioned for incongruence between ideology and practice in sport is the sacred and ritualistic factor. The intensification of this factor could easily make some forms of sport enclaves of the past where modernization could only penetrate with great difficulty. If pragmatism is a primary factor in society, as Kahn predicts, the idealistic and sacred dogma relative to behavior of athletes may decline.

The values inherent in the realm of sport have been primarily those of power, although cooperation both with and without cohesion has been a tool utilized for the attainment of that power. Some sport forms may, at the present time, be more oriented toward cooperation, empathy, and expression. If sport takes on the values that have been described as feminine it would possibly tend to lose function as a masculinity rite, and recent trends in women's sport toward those values considered to be masculine might be reversed. Realization of diversity may allow for parallel existence not only of the humanistic and the highly competitive for both sexes, but also of the sacred and the pragmatic, and private and educational elements.

According to Hage (1970) the following organizational characteristics are needed in order to expedite the change process within the organization: high complexity, low centralization, low formalization, low stratification, low production volume, low efficiency emphasis, and a high morale. Sport, although highly complex, has been viewed and made to appear somewhat simple. It tends toward high centralization, high formalization, and high stratification in its organizational structure. Particularly in highly organized sport, the production volume related to consumerism and the emphasis on efficiency of performance is quite high. However, as the sacred and ritualistic element of sport is considered, the morale appears to be high. Although the organizational structure of sport may be interpreted differently, it appears from the above analysis to be static rather than dynamic, which means that attempts to maximize the rate or degree of change would result in a high degree of conflict.

Traveling various paths to modernity and open, at the same time, to involvement in sport, the individual may experience dislocation with the past and a break with the symbols of historical tradition such as the rites of passage connected with sport. He may be a new kind of person psychologically as a result of the phenomenon of modernization. Although society may be increasingly planned, it may, at the same time, allow for individual variations of the protean man described by Lifton (1961), who is always in transition with continuous shift of identity, yet maintaining a new kind of stability heretofore unknown. Although he would not be classified as a sportsman or athlete, his choices would include sport as a part of the search for identity.

The basic question in discussing modernization and sport is the feasibility of the continued tolerance of conflicting sets of values. Technological advances and changing organizational structure may only increase value conflict. Humanistic trends place competition in a different perspective and sport may, through intensification of the sacred, become an enclave of the past. Regardless of the prediction, planning through widespread involvement is of the utmost importance. It should include the study of human potential, cybernetics, existential responsibility, relations with technology, and a thorough value-free analysis of competition. Certainly, the existence of a revolution or even evolution cannot be demonstrated experimentally; however, there is evidence of changes in equilibrium and emerging value changes within sport that may require farsighted and dedicated leadership.

REFERENCES

Appelbaum, R. P. *Theories of Social Change*. Chicago: Marcham Publishing Co., 1970.

Black, C. E. *Dynamics of Modernization,* New York: Harper and Row, 1966.

Boyle, R. H. *Sport: Mirror of American Life,* Boston: Little, Brown, 1963.

Coates, J. F. Technology assessment: The benefits, the costs, the consequences. *The Futurist,* 1971, **5**, 225-231.

Fiske, S. Pigskin review: An American initiation. In M. M. Hart (Ed.), *Sport in the Socio-cultural Process.* Dubuque, Iowa: William C. Brown Co., 1972.

Golembiewski, R. T. Organizational renewal. Guest Lecture at Oregon State University, Corvallis, July 14, 1971.

Hage, J., & Aiken, M. *Social Change in Complex Organizations.* New York: Random House, 1970.

Hellison, D. R. *Humanistic Physical Education,* Englewood Cliffs, N.J.: Prentice-Hall, 1973.

Hopkins, F. S. Humanism, robotism, or destruction. *The Futurist,* 1971, **5**, 23-24.

Ingham, A. G., & Loy, J. W. The social system of sport: A humanistic perspective, *Quest,* 1973, **19**, 3-23.

Kahn, H., & Weiner, A. *The year 2000: A framework for speculation on the next 33 years,* New York: Macmillan, 1967.

Keating, J. W. Paradoxes in American athletics. In A. Flath (Ed.), *Athletics in America.* Corvallis: Oregon State University Press, 1972.

Kenyon, J. S., Sport and society; At odds or in concert? In A. Flath (Ed.), *Athletics in America.* Corvallis: Oregon State University Press, 1972.

Kistler, J. W. Attitudes expressed about behavior demonstrated in certain specific situations occurring in sports. *Proceedings of the National College Physical Education Association for Men,* 1957, **60**, 55-58.

Lambert, J. S. *The New Prometheans,* New York: Harper and Row, 1973.

Lapp, R. E. *The New Priesthood.* New York: Harper and Row, 1961.

Leonard, G. B. *Education and Ecstasy.* New York: Delacorte Press, 1968.

Lifton, R. J. *History and Human Survival.* New York: Random House, 1961.

Loy, J. W. The nature of sport: A definitional effort. *Quest,* 1968, **10**, 1-15.

Luschen, G. The Interdependence of sport and culture. *International Review of Sport Sociology,* 1967, **2**, 27-41.

Marien, M. Higher learning in the ignorant society. *The Futurist,* 1972, **6**, 49-54.

Ogilvie, B. C., & Tutko, T. A. Sport: If you want to build character, try something else. *Psychology Today,* October 1971, *5,* 61-63.

Orwell, G. *1984.* New York: Harcourt, Brace, 1948.

Page, J. K. Past and future distribution of *homo sapiens* and his activities in Great Britain. In F. J. Ebling and G. W. Heath (Eds.), *The Future of Man.* London: Academic Press, 1972.

Parsons, T. The place of sociological theory among the analytical sciences of action. In R. Bierstedt (Ed.), *The Making of Society.* New York: Random House, 1959. (a)

Parsons, T. *The Social System.* Glencoe, Illinois: Free Press, 1959. (b)

Puretz, D. H. Athletics and the development of values. A paper presented at the American Association of Health, Physical Education and Recreation Convention, Boston, Mass., April 11, 1969.

Reich, C. *The Greening of America.* New York: Random House, 1970.

Richardson, D. Ethical conduct in sport situations, *Proceedings of the National College Physical Education Association for Men,* 1962, **66,** 98-103.

Skinner, B. F. *Walden Two.* New York: Macmillan, 1948.

Sorokin, P. A. *Society, Culture and Personality.* New York: Harper, 1947.

Theobald, R. *An Alternative Future for America II.* Chicago: Swallow Press, 1968.

Theobald, R. (Ed.) *Futures Conditional.* New York: Bobbs Merrill, 1972.

Theobald, R. How can we plan for the future? *Futures Conditional,* 1973, **1,** 1-2.

Toffler, A. *Future Shock.* New York: Random House, 1970.

Washburne, N. F. *Interpreting Social Change in America.* New York: Random House, 1954.

Wilson, I. H. How our values are changing. *The Futurist,* 1970, **4,** 5-9.

Zurcher, L. A. The mutable self. *The Futurist,* 1972, **5,** 181-185.

FOR FURTHER READING

1. Donnelly, P., "Vertigo in America: A Social Comment," *Quest* **27** (Winter): 106-113, 1977.

2. Gilbert, B., "Play As You Go," *Sports Illustrated* **44** (May 10): 50-55, 1976.

3. Gilbert, B., "Imagine Going to School to Learn to Play," *Sports Illustrated* **43** (October 13): 84-98, 1975.

4. Hellison, D. R., *Humanistic Physical Education.* Englewood Cliffs, N.J.: Prentice-Hall, 1973.

5. Heywood, L. A. and Warnick, R. B., "Campus Recreation: The Intramural Revolution," *Journal of Physical Education and Recreation* **47** (October): 52–54, 1976.

6. Johnson, W. O., "From Here to 2000," *Sports Illustrated* **41** (December 23) 73–83, 1974.

7. "Keeping Fit: American Tries to Shape Up," *Newsweek* May 23, 1977, pp. 78–86.

8. Leonard, G. B., *The Ultimate Athlete,* New York: Viking Press, 1975.

9. Orlick, T., "Cooperative Games," *Journal of Physical Education and Recreation* **48** (September): 33–35, 1977.

10. Deford, F. "Gridiron 2000," *Sports Illustrated* **51** (September 3): 42–49, 1979.